The Architecture of Open Source Applications

The Architecture of Open Source Applications
Volume II: Structure, Scale, and a Few More Fearless Hacks

Edited by Amy Brown & Greg Wilson

The Architecture of Open Source Applications, Volume 2
Edited by Amy Brown and Greg Wilson

This work is licensed under the Creative Commons Attribution 3.0 Unported license (CC BY 3.0). You are free:

- to Share—to copy, distribute and transmit the work
- to Remix—to adapt the work

under the following conditions:

- Attribution—you must attribute the work in the manner specified by the author or licensor (but not in any way that suggests that they endorse you or your use of the work).

with the understanding that:

- Waiver—Any of the above conditions can be waived if you get permission from the copyright holder.
- Public Domain—Where the work or any of its elements is in the public domain under applicable law, that status is in no way affected by the license.
- Other Rights—In no way are any of the following rights affected by the license:
  - Your fair dealing or fair use rights, or other applicable copyright exceptions and limitations;
  - The author's moral rights;
  - Rights other persons may have either in the work itself or in how the work is used, such as publicity or privacy rights.
- Notice—For any reuse or distribution, you must make clear to others the license terms of this work. The best way to do this is with a link to http://creativecommons.org/licenses/by/3.0/.

To view a copy of this license, visit http://creativecommons.org/licenses/by/3.0/ or send a letter to Creative Commons, 444 Castro Street, Suite 900, Mountain View, California, 94041, USA.

The full text of this book is available online at http://www.aosabook.org/.
All royalties from its sale will be donated to Amnesty International.

Product and company names mentioned herein may be the trademarks of their respective owners.

While every precaution has been taken in the preparation of this book, the editors and authors assume no responsibility for errors or omissions, or for damages resulting from the use of the information contained herein.

Front cover photo ©James Howe.

Revision Date: April 20, 2012

ISBN: 978-1-105-57181-7

In memory of Dennis Ritchie (1941-2011)
We hope he would have enjoyed reading
what we have written.

Contents

Introduction ... ix
    by Amy Brown and Greg Wilson

1 Scalable Web Architecture and Distributed Systems ... 1
    by Kate Matsudaira

2 Firefox Release Engineering ... 23
    by Chris AtLee, Lukas Blakk, John O'Duinn, and Armen Zambrano Gasparnian

3 FreeRTOS ... 39
    by Christopher Svec

4 GDB ... 53
    by Stan Shebs

5 The Glasgow Haskell Compiler ... 67
    by Simon Marlow and Simon Peyton Jones

6 Git ... 89
    by Susan Potter

7 GPSD ... 101
    by Eric Raymond

8 The Dynamic Language Runtime and the Iron Languages ... 113
    by Jeff Hardy

9 ITK ... 127
    by Luis Ibáñez and Brad King

10 GNU Mailman ... 149
    by Barry Warsaw

11 matplotlib ... 165
    by John Hunter and Michael Droettboom

12 MediaWiki ... 179
    by Sumana Harihareswara and Guillaume Paumier

13 Moodle *by Tim Hunt*	195
14 nginx *by Andrew Alexeev*	211
15 Open MPI *by Jeffrey M. Squyres*	225
16 OSCAR *by Jennifer Ruttan*	239
17 Processing.js *by Mike Kamermans*	251
18 Puppet *by Luke Kanies*	267
19 PyPy *by Benjamin Peterson*	279
20 SQLAlchemy *by Michael Bayer*	291
21 Twisted *by Jessica McKellar*	315
22 Yesod *by Michael Snoyman*	331
23 Yocto *by Elizabeth Flanagan*	347
24 ZeroMQ *by Martin Sústrik*	359

Introduction
Amy Brown and Greg Wilson

In the introduction to Volume 1 of this series, we wrote:

> Building architecture and software architecture have a lot in common, but there is one crucial difference. While architects study thousands of buildings in their training and during their careers, most software developers only ever get to know a handful of large programs well... As a result, they repeat one another's mistakes rather than building on one another's successes... This book is our attempt to change that.

In the year since that book appeared, over two dozen people have worked hard to create the sequel you have in your hands. They have done so because they believe, as we do, that software design can and should be taught by example—that the best way to learn how think like an expert is to study how experts think. From web servers and compilers through health record management systems to the infrastructure that Mozilla uses to get Firefox out the door, there are lessons all around us. We hope that by collecting some of them together in this book, we can help you become a better developer.

— Amy Brown and Greg Wilson

Contributors

Andrew Alexeev (nginx): Andrew is a co-founder of Nginx, Inc.—the company behind nginx. Prior to joining Nginx, Inc. at the beginning of 2011, Andrew worked in the Internet industry and in a variety of ICT divisions for enterprises. Andrew holds a diploma in Electronics from St. Petersburg Electrotechnical University and an executive MBA from Antwerp Management School.

Chris AtLee (Firefox Release Engineering): Chris is loving his job managing Release Engineers at Mozilla. He has a BMath in Computer Science from the University of Waterloo. His online ramblings can be found at http://atlee.ca.

Michael Bayer (SQLAlchemy): Michael Bayer has been working with open source software and databases since the mid-1990s. Today he's active in the Python community, working to spread good software practices to an ever wider audience. Follow Mike on Twitter at @zzzeek.

Lukas Blakk (Firefox Release Engineering): Lukas graduated from Toronto's Seneca College with a bachelor of Software Development in 2009, but started working with Mozilla's Release Engineering team while still a student thanks to Dave Humphrey's (http://vocamus.net/dave/) *Topics in Open Source* classes. Lukas Blakk's adventures with open source can be followed on her blog at http://lukasblakk.com.

Amy Brown (editorial): Amy worked in the software industry for ten years before quitting to create a freelance editing and book production business. She has an underused degree in Math from the University of Waterloo. She can be found online at http://www.amyrbrown.ca/.

Michael Droettboom (matplotlib): Michael Droettboom works for STScI developing science and calibration software for the Hubble and James Webb Space Telescopes. He has worked on the matplotlib project since 2007.

Elizabeth Flanagan (Yocto): Elizabeth Flanagan works for the Open Source Technologies Center at Intel Corp as the Yocto Project's Build and Release engineer. She is the maintainer of the Yocto Autobuilder and contributes to the Yocto Project and OE-Core. She lives in Portland, Oregon and can be found online at http://www.hacklikeagirl.com.

Jeff Hardy (Iron Languages): Jeff started programming in high school, which led to a bachelor's degree in Software Engineering from the University of Alberta and his current position writing Python code for Amazon.com in Seattle. He has also led IronPython's development since 2010. You can find more information about him at http://jdhardy.ca.

Sumana Harihareswara (MediaWiki): Sumana is the community manager for MediaWiki as the volunteer development coordinator for the Wikimedia Foundation. She previously worked with the GNOME, Empathy, Telepathy, Miro, and AltLaw projects. Sumana is an advisory board member for the Ada Initiative, which supports women in open technology and culture. She lives in New York City. Her personal site is at http://www.harihareswara.net/.

Tim Hunt (Moodle): Tim Hunt started out as a mathematician, getting as far as a PhD in non-linear dynamics from the University of Cambridge before deciding to do something a bit less esoteric with his life. He now works as a Leading Software Developer at the Open University in Milton Keynes, UK, working on their learning and teaching systems which are based on Moodle. Since 2006 he has been the maintainer of the Moodle quiz module and the question bank code, a role he still enjoys. From 2008 to 2009, Tim spent a year in Australia working at the Moodle HQ offices. He blogs at http://tjhunt.blogspot.com and can be found @tim_hunt on Twitter.

John Hunter (matplotlib): John Hunter is a Quantitative Analyst at TradeLink Securities. He received his doctorate in neurobiology at the University of Chicago for experimental and numerical modeling work on synchronization, and continued his work on synchronization processes as a postdoc in Neurology working on epilepsy. He left academia for quantitative finance in 2005. An avid Python programmer and lecturer in scientific computing in Python, he is original author and lead developer of the scientific visualization package matplotlib.

Luis Ibáñez (ITK): Luis has worked for 12 years on the development of the Insight Toolkit (ITK), an open source library for medical imaging analysis. Luis is a strong supporter of open access and the revival of reproducibility verification in scientific publishing. Luis has been teaching a course on Open Source Software Practices at Rensselaer Polytechnic Institute since 2007.

Mike Kamermans (Processing.js): Mike started his career in computer science by failing technical Computer Science and promptly moved on to getting a master's degree in Artificial Intelligence, instead. He's been programming in order not to have to program since 1998, with a focus on getting people the tools they need to get the jobs they need done, done. He has focussed on many other things as well, including writing a book on Japanese grammar, and writing a detailed explanation of the math behind Bézier curves. His under-used home page is at http://pomax.nihongoresources.com.

Luke Kanies (Puppet): Luke founded Puppet and Puppet Labs in 2005 out of fear and desperation, with the goal of producing better operations tools and changing how we manage systems. He has been publishing and speaking on his work in Unix administration since 1997, focusing on development since 2001. He has developed and published multiple simple sysadmin tools and contributed to established products like Cfengine, and has presented on Puppet and other tools around the world, including at OSCON, LISA, Linux.Conf.au, and FOSS.in. His work with Puppet has been an important part of DevOps and delivering on the promise of cloud computing.

Brad King (ITK): Brad King joined Kitware as a founding member of the Software Process group. He earned a PhD in Computer Science from Rensselaer Polytechnic Institute. He is one of the original developers of the Insight Toolkit (ITK), an open source library for medical imaging analysis. At Kitware Dr. King's work focuses on methods and tools for open source software development. He is a core developer of CMake and has made contributions to many open source projects including VTK and ParaView.

Simon Marlow (The Glasgow Haskell Compiler): Simon Marlow is a developer at Microsoft Research's Cambridge lab, and for the last 14 years has been doing research and development using Haskell. He is one of the lead developers of the Glasgow Haskell Compiler, and amongst other things is responsible for its runtime system. Recently, Simon's main focus has been on providing great support for concurrent and parallel programming with Haskell. Simon can be reached via @simonmar on Twitter, or +Simon Marlow on Google+.

Kate Matsudaira (Scalable Web Architecture and Distributed Systems): Kate Matsudaira has worked as the VP Engineering/CTO at several technology startups, including currently at Decide, and formerly at SEOmoz and Delve Networks (acquired by Limelight). Prior to joining the startup world she spent time as a software engineer and technical lead/manager at Amazon and Microsoft. Kate has hands-on knowledge and experience with building large scale distributed web systems, big data, cloud computing and technical leadership. Kate has a BS in Computer Science from Harvey Mudd College, and has completed graduate work at the University of Washington in both Business and Computer Science (MS). You can read more on her blog and website http://katemats.com.

Jessica McKellar (Twisted): Jessica is a software engineer from Boston, MA. She is a Twisted maintainer, Python Software Foundation member, and an organizer for the Boston Python user group. She can be found online at http://jesstess.com.

John O'Duinn (Firefox Release Engineering): John has led Mozilla's Release Engineering group since May 2007. In that time, he's led work to streamline Mozilla's release mechanics, improve developer productivity—and do it all while also making the lives of Release Engineers better. John got involved in Release Engineering 19 years ago when he shipped software that reintroduced a bug that had been fixed in a previous release. John's blog is at http://oduinn.com/.

Guillaume Paumier (MediaWiki): Guillaume is Technical Communications Manager at the Wikimedia Foundation, the nonprofit behind Wikipedia and MediaWiki. A Wikipedia photographer and editor since 2005, Guillaume is the author of a Wikipedia handbook in French. He also holds an engineering degree in Physics and a PhD in microsystems for life sciences. His home online is at http://guillaumepaumier.com.

Benjamin Peterson (PyPy): Benjamin contributes to CPython and PyPy as well as several Python libraries. In general, he is interested in compilers and interpreters, particularly for dynamic languages. Outside of programming, he enjoys music (clarinet, piano, and composition), pure math, German literature, and great food. His website is http://benjamin-peterson.org.

Simon Peyton Jones (The Glasgow Haskell Compiler): Simon Peyton Jones is a researcher at Microsoft Research Cambridge, before which he was a professor of computer science at Glasgow University. Inspired by the elegance of purely-functional programming when he was a student, Simon has focused nearly thirty years of research on pursuing that idea to see where it leads. Haskell is his first baby, and still forms the platform for much of his research. http://research.microsoft.com/~simonpj

Susan Potter (Git): Susan is a polyglot software developer with a penchant for skepticism. She has been designing, developing and deploying distributed trading services and applications since

1996, recently switching to building multi-tenant systems for software firms. Susan is a passionate power user of Git, Linux, and Vim. You can find her tweeting random thoughts on Erlang, Haskell, Scala, and (of course) Git @SusanPotter.

Eric Raymond (GPSD): Eric S. Raymond is a wandering anthropologist and trouble-making philosopher. He's written some code, too. If you're not laughing by now, why are you reading this book?

Jennifer Ruttan (OSCAR): Jennifer Ruttan lives in Toronto. Since graduating from the University of Toronto with a degree in Computer Science, she has worked as a software engineer for Indivica, a company devoted to improving patient health care through the use of new technology. Follow her on Twitter @jenruttan.

Stan Shebs (GDB): Stan has had open source as his day job since 1989, when a colleague at Apple needed a compiler to generate code for an experimental VM and GCC 1.31 was conveniently at hand. After following up with the oft-disbelieved Mac System 7 port of GCC (it was the experiment's control case), Stan went to Cygnus Support, where he maintained GDB for the FSF and helped on many embedded tools projects. Returning to Apple in 2000, he worked on GCC and GDB for Mac OS X. A short time at Mozilla preceded a jump to CodeSourcery, now part of Mentor Graphics, where he continues to develop new features for GDB. Stan's professorial tone is explained by his PhD in Computer Science from the University of Utah.

Michael Snoyman (Yesod): Michael Snoyman received his BS in Mathematics from UCLA. After working as an actuary in the US, he moved to Israel and began a career in web development. In order to produce high-performance, robust sites quickly, he created the Yesod Web Framework and its associated libraries.

Jeffrey M. Squyres (Open MPI): Jeff works in the rack server division at Cisco; he is Cisco's representative to the MPI Forum standards body and is a chapter author of the MPI-2 standard. Jeff is Cisco's core software developer in the open source Open MPI project. He has worked in the High Performance Computing (HPC) field since his early graduate-student days in the mid-1990s. After some active duty tours in the military, Jeff received his doctorate in Computer Science and Engineering from the University of Notre Dame in 2004.

Martin Sústrik (ZeroMQ): Martin Sústrik is an expert in the field of messaging middleware, and participated in the creation and reference implementation of the AMQP standard. He has been involved in various messaging projects in the financial industry. He is a founder of the ØMQ project, and currently is working on integration of messaging technology with operating systems and the Internet stack. He can be reached at sustrik@250bpm.com, http://www.250bpm.com and on Twitter as @sustrik.

Christopher Svec (FreeRTOS): Chris is an embedded software engineer who currently develops firmware for low-power wireless chips. In a previous life he designed x86 processors, which comes in handy more often than you'd think when working on non-x86 processors. Chris has bachelor's and master's degrees in Electrical and Computer Engineering, both from Purdue University. He lives in Boston with his wife and golden retriever. You can find him on the web at http://saidsvec.com.

Barry Warsaw (Mailman): Barry Warsaw is the project leader for GNU Mailman. He has been a core Python developer since 1995, and release manager for several Python versions. He currently works for Canonical as a software engineer on the Ubuntu Platform Foundations team. He can be reached at barry@python.org or @pumpichank on Twitter. His home page is http://barry.warsaw.us.

Greg Wilson (editorial): Greg has worked over the past 25 years in high-performance scientific computing, data visualization, and computer security, and is the author or editor of several computing books (including the 2008 Jolt Award winner *Beautiful Code*) and two books for children. Greg received a PhD in Computer Science from the University of Edinburgh in 1993.

Armen Zambrano Gasparnian (Firefox Release Engineering): Armen has been working for Mozilla since 2008 as a Release Engineer. He has worked on releases, developers' infrastructure optimization and localization. Armen works with youth at the Church on the Rock, Toronto, and has worked with international Christian non-profits for years. Armen has a bachelor in Software Development from Seneca College and has taken a few years of Computer Science at the University of Malaga. He blogs at http://armenzg.blogspot.com.

Acknowledgments

We would like to thank Google for their support of Amy Brown's work on this project, and Cat Allman for arranging it. We would also like to thank all of our technical reviewers:

Johan Harjono	Josh McCarthy	Victor Ng
Justin Sheehy	Andrew Petersen	Blake Winton
Nikita Pchelin	Pascal Rapicault	Kim Moir
Laurie McDougall Sookraj	Eric Aderhold	Simon Stewart
Tom Plaskon	Jonathan Deber	Jonathan Dursi
Greg Lapouchnian	Trevor Bekolay	Richard Barry
Will Schroeder	Taavi Burns	Ric Holt
Bill Hoffman	Tina Yee	Maria Khomenko
Audrey Tang	Colin Morris	Erick Dransch
James Crook	Christian Muise	Ian Bull
Todd Ritchie	David Scannell	Ellen Hsiang

especially Tavish Armstrong and Trevor Bekolay, without whose above-and-beyond assistance this book would have taken a lot longer to produce. Thanks also to everyone who offered to review but was unable to for various reasons, and to everyone else who helped and supported the production of this book.

Thank you also to James Howe[1], who kindly let us use his picture of New York's Equitable Building for the cover.

Contributing

Dozens of volunteers worked hard to create this book, but there is still a lot to do. You can help by reporting errors, helping to translate the content into other languages, or describing the architecture of other open source projects. Please contact us at aosa@aosabook.org if you would like to get involved.

---

[1] http://jameshowephotography.com/

[chapter 1]

Scalable Web Architecture and Distributed Systems
Kate Matsudaira

Open source software has become a fundamental building block for some of the biggest websites. And as those websites have grown, best practices and guiding principles around their architectures have emerged. This chapter seeks to cover some of the key issues to consider when designing large websites, as well as some of the building blocks used to achieve these goals.

This chapter is largely focused on web systems, although some of the material is applicable to other distributed systems as well.

1.1 Principles of Web Distributed Systems Design

What exactly does it mean to build and operate a scalable web site or application? At a primitive level it's just connecting users with remote resources via the Internet—the part that makes it scalable is that the resources, or access to those resources, are distributed across multiple servers.

Like most things in life, taking the time to plan ahead when building a web service can help in the long run; understanding some of the considerations and tradeoffs behind big websites can result in smarter decisions at the creation of smaller web sites. Below are some of the key principles that influence the design of large-scale web systems:

- Availability: The uptime of a website is absolutely critical to the reputation and functional of many companies. For some of the larger online retail sites, being unavailable for even minutes can result in thousands or millions of dollars in lost revenue, so designing their systems to be constantly available and resilient to failure is both a fundamental business and a technology requirement. High availability in distributed systems requires the careful consideration of redundancy for key components, rapid recovery in the event of partial system failures, and graceful degradation when problems occur.
- Performance: Website performance has become an important consideration for most sites. The speed of a website affects usage and user satisfaction, as well as search engine rankings, a factor that directly correlates to revenue and retention. As a result, creating a system that is optimized for fast responses and low latency is key.
- Reliability: A system needs to be reliable, such that a request for data will consistently return the same data. In the event the data changes or is updated, then that same request should return

the new data. Users need to know that if something is written to the system, or stored, it will persist and can be relied on to be in place for future retrieval.

Scalability: When it comes to any large distributed system, size is just one aspect of scale that needs to be considered. Just as important is the effort required to increase capacity to handle greater amounts of load, commonly referred to as the scalability of the system. Scalability can refer to many different parameters of the system: how much additional traffic can it handle, how easy is it to add more storage capacity, or even how many more transactions can be processed.

Manageability: Designing a system that is easy to operate is another important consideration. The manageability of the system equates to the scalability of operations: maintenance and updates. Things to consider for manageability are the ease of diagnosing and understanding problems when they occur, ease of making updates or modifications, and how simple the system is to operate. (I.e., does it routinely operate without failure or exceptions?)

Cost: Cost is an important factor. This obviously can include hardware and software costs, but it is also important to consider other facets needed to deploy and maintain the system. The amount of developer time the system takes to build, the amount of operational effort required to run the system, and even the amount of training required should all be considered. Cost is the total cost of ownership.

Each of these principles provides the basis for decisions in designing a distributed web architecture. However, they also can be at odds with one another, such that achieving one objective comes at the cost of another. A basic example: choosing to address capacity by simply adding more servers (scalability) can come at the price of manageability (you have to operate an additional server) and cost (the price of the servers).

When designing any sort of web application it is important to consider these key principles, even if it is to acknowledge that a design may sacrifice one or more of them.

1.2 The Basics

When it comes to system architecture there are a few things to consider: what are the right pieces, how these pieces fit together, and what are the right tradeoffs. Investing in scaling before it is needed is generally not a smart business proposition; however, some forethought into the design can save substantial time and resources in the future.

This section is focused on some of the core factors that are central to almost all large web applications: *services*, *redundancy*, *partitions*, and *handling failure*. Each of these factors involves choices and compromises, particularly in the context of the principles described in the previous section. In order to explain these in detail it is best to start with an example.

Example: Image Hosting Application

At some point you have probably posted an image online. For big sites that host and deliver lots of images, there are challenges in building an architecture that is cost-effective, highly available, and has low latency (fast retrieval).

Imagine a system where users are able to upload their images to a central server, and the images can be requested via a web link or API, just like Flickr or Picasa. For the sake of simplicity, let's assume that this application has two key parts: the ability to upload (write) an image to the server, and the ability to query for an image. While we certainly want the upload to be efficient, we care most about having very fast delivery when someone requests an image (for example, images could be requested for a web page or other application). This is very similar functionality to what a web server or Content Delivery Network (CDN) edge server (a server CDN uses to store content in many locations so content is geographically/physically closer to users, resulting in faster performance) might provide.

Other important aspects of the system are:

- There is no limit to the number of images that will be stored, so storage scalability, in terms of image count needs to be considered.
- There needs to be low latency for image downloads/requests.
- If a user uploads an image, the image should always be there (data reliability for images).
- The system should be easy to maintain (manageability).
- Since image hosting doesn't have high profit margins, the system needs to be cost-effective.

Figure 1.1 is a simplified diagram of the functionality.

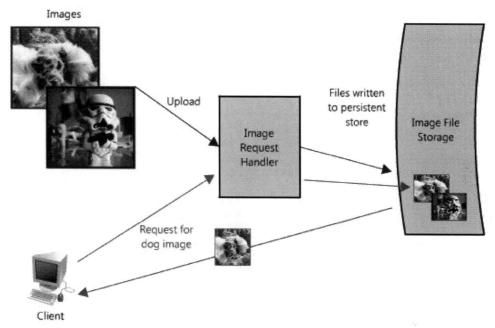

Figure 1.1: Simplified architecture diagram for image hosting application

In this image hosting example, the system must be perceivably fast, its data stored reliably and all of these attributes highly scalable. Building a small version of this application would be trivial and easily hosted on a single server; however, that would not be interesting for this chapter. Let's assume that we want to build something that could grow as big as Flickr.

Services

When considering scalable system design, it helps to decouple functionality and think about each part of the system as its own service with a clearly defined interface. In practice, systems designed in this way are said to have a Service-Oriented Architecture (SOA). For these types of systems, each service has its own distinct functional context, and interaction with anything outside of that context takes place through an abstract interface, typically the public-facing API of another service.

Deconstructing a system into a set of complementary services decouples the operation of those pieces from one another. This abstraction helps establish clear relationships between the service, its underlying environment, and the consumers of that service. Creating these clear delineations can help isolate problems, but also allows each piece to scale independently of one another. This sort of service-oriented design for systems is very similar to object-oriented design for programming.

In our example, all requests to upload and retrieve images are processed by the same server; however, as the system needs to scale it makes sense to break out these two functions into their own services.

Fast-forward and assume that the service is in heavy use; such a scenario makes it easy to see how longer writes will impact the time it takes to read the images (since they two functions will be competing for shared resources). Depending on the architecture this effect can be substantial. Even if the upload and download speeds are the same (which is not true of most IP networks, since most are designed for at least a 3:1 download-speed:upload-speed ratio), read files will typically be read from cache, and writes will have to go to disk eventually (and perhaps be written several times in eventually consistent situations). Even if everything is in memory or read from disks (like SSDs), database writes will almost always be slower than reads[1].

Another potential problem with this design is that a web server like Apache or lighttpd typically has an upper limit on the number of simultaneous connections it can maintain (defaults are around 500, but can go much higher) and in high traffic, writes can quickly consume all of those. Since reads can be asynchronous, or take advantage of other performance optimizations like gzip compression or chunked transfer encoding, the web server can switch serve reads faster and switch between clients quickly serving many more requests per second than the max number of connections (with Apache and max connections set to 500, it is not uncommon to serve several thousand read requests per second). Writes, on the other hand, tend to maintain an open connection for the duration for the upload, so uploading a 1MB file could take more than 1 second on most home networks, so that web server could only handle 500 such simultaneous writes.

Planning for this sort of bottleneck makes a good case to split out reads and writes of images into their own services, shown in Figure 1.2. This allows us to scale each of them independently (since it is likely we will always do more reading than writing), but also helps clarify what is going on at each point. Finally, this separates future concerns, which would make it easier to troubleshoot and scale a problem like slow reads.

The advantage of this approach is that we are able to solve problems independently of one another—we don't have to worry about writing and retrieving new images in the same context. Both of these services still leverage the global corpus of images, but they are free to optimize their own performance with service-appropriate methods (for example, queuing up requests, or caching popular images—more on this below). And from a maintenance and cost perspective each service can scale independently as needed, which is great because if they were combined and intermingled, one could inadvertently impact the performance of the other as in the scenario discussed above.

Of course, the above example can work well when you have two different endpoints (in fact this is very similar to several cloud storage providers' implementations and Content Delivery Networks). There are lots of ways to address these types of bottlenecks though, and each has different tradeoffs.

For example, Flickr solves this read/write issue by distributing users across different shards such that each shard can only handle a set number of users, and as users increase more shards are added to

---

[1] Pole Position, an open source tool for DB benchmarking, http://polepos.org/ and results http://polepos.sourceforge.net/results/PolePositionClientServer.pdf.

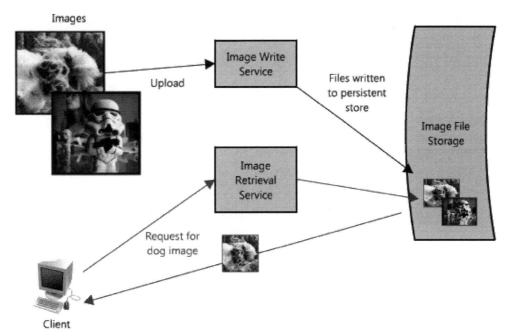

Figure 1.2: Splitting out reads and writes

the cluster[2]. In the first example it is easier to scale hardware based on actual usage (the number of reads and writes across the whole system), whereas Flickr scales with their user base (but forces the assumption of equal usage across users so there can be extra capacity). In the former an outage or issue with one of the services brings down functionality across the whole system (no-one can write files, for example), whereas an outage with one of Flickr's shards will only affect those users. In the first example it is easier to perform operations across the whole dataset—for example, updating the write service to include new metadata or searching across all image metadata—whereas with the Flickr architecture each shard would need to be updated or searched (or a search service would need to be created to collate that metadata—which is in fact what they do).

When it comes to these systems there is no right answer, but it helps to go back to the principles at the start of this chapter, determine the system needs (heavy reads or writes or both, level of concurrency, queries across the data set, ranges, sorts, etc.), benchmark different alternatives, understand how the system will fail, and have a solid plan for when failure happens.

Redundancy

In order to handle failure gracefully a web architecture must have redundancy of its services and data. For example, if there is only one copy of a file stored on a single server, then losing that server means losing that file. Losing data is seldom a good thing, and a common way of handling it is to create multiple, or redundant, copies.

This same principle also applies to services. If there is a core piece of functionality for an application, ensuring that multiple copies or versions are running simultaneously can secure against the failure of a single node.

---

[2]Presentation on Flickr's scaling: http://mysqldba.blogspot.com/2008/04/mysql-uc-2007-presentation-file.html

Creating redundancy in a system can remove single points of failure and provide a backup or spare functionality if needed in a crisis. For example, if there are two instances of the same service running in production, and one fails or degrades, the system can *failover* to the healthy copy. Failover can happen automatically or require manual intervention.

Another key part of service redundancy is creating a *shared-nothing architecture*. With this architecture, each node is able to operate independently of one another and there is no central "brain" managing state or coordinating activities for the other nodes. This helps a lot with scalability since new nodes can be added without special conditions or knowledge. However, and most importantly, there is no single point of failure in these systems, so they are much more resilient to failure.

For example, in our image server application, all images would have redundant copies on another piece of hardware somewhere (ideally in a different geographic location in the event of a catastrophe like an earthquake or fire in the data center), and the services to access the images would be redundant, all potentially servicing requests. (See Figure 1.3.) (Load balancers are a great way to make this possible, but there is more on that below).

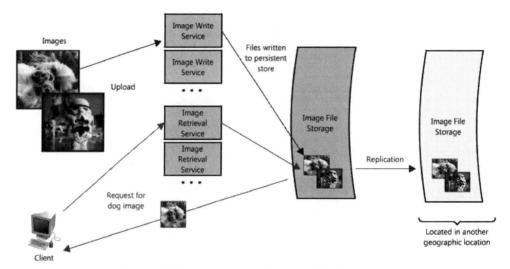

Figure 1.3: Image hosting application with redundancy

Partitions

There may be very large data sets that are unable to fit on a single server. It may also be the case that an operation requires too many computing resources, diminishing performance and making it necessary to add capacity. In either case you have two choices: scale vertically or horizontally.

Scaling vertically means adding more resources to an individual server. So for a very large data set, this might mean adding more (or bigger) hard drives so a single server can contain the entire data set. In the case of the compute operation, this could mean moving the computation to a bigger server with a faster CPU or more memory. In each case, vertical scaling is accomplished by making the individual resource capable of handling more on its own.

To scale horizontally, on the other hand, is to add more nodes. In the case of the large data set, this might be a second server to store parts of the data set, and for the computing resource it would mean splitting the operation or load across some additional nodes. To take full advantage of horizontal scaling, it should be included as an intrinsic design principle of the system architecture, otherwise it can be quite cumbersome to modify and separate out the context to make this possible.

When it comes to horizontal scaling, one of the more common techniques is to break up your services into partitions, or shards. The partitions can be distributed such that each logical set of functionality is separate; this could be done by geographic boundaries, or by another criteria like non-paying versus paying users. The advantage of these schemes is that they provide a service or data store with added capacity.

In our image server example, it is possible that the single file server used to store images could be replaced by multiple file servers, each containing its own unique set of images. (See Figure 1.4.) Such an architecture would allow the system to fill each file server with images, adding additional servers as the disks become full. The design would require a naming scheme that tied an image's filename to the server containing it. An image's name could be formed from a consistent hashing scheme mapped across the servers. Or alternatively, each image could be assigned an incremental ID, so that when a client makes a request for an image, the image retrieval service only needs to maintain the range of IDs that are mapped to each of the servers (like an index).

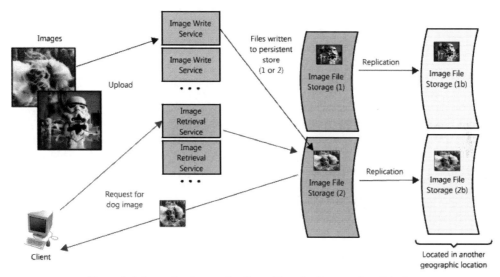

Figure 1.4: Image hosting application with redundancy and partitioning

Of course there are challenges distributing data or functionality across multiple servers. One of the key issues is *data locality*; in distributed systems the closer the data to the operation or point of computation, the better the performance of the system. Therefore it is potentially problematic to have data spread across multiple servers, as any time it is needed it may not be local, forcing the servers to perform a costly fetch of the required information across the network.

Another potential issue comes in the form of *inconsistency*. When there are different services reading and writing from a shared resource, potentially another service or data store, there is the chance for race conditions—where some data is supposed to be updated, but the read happens prior to the update—and in those cases the data is inconsistent. For example, in the image hosting scenario, a race condition could occur if one client sent a request to update the dog image with a new title, changing it from "Dog" to "Gizmo", but at the same time another client was reading the image. In that circumstance it is unclear which title, "Dog" or "Gizmo", would be the one received by the second client.

There are certainly some obstacles associated with partitioning data, but partitioning allows each problem to be split—by data, load, usage patterns, etc.—into manageable chunks. This can help with scalability and manageability, but is not without risk. There are lots of ways to mitigate risk and handle failures; however, in the interest of brevity they are not covered in this chapter. If you are interested in reading more, you can check out my blog post on fault tolerance and monitoring[3].

1.3 The Building Blocks of Fast and Scalable Data Access

Having covered some of the core considerations in designing distributed systems, let's now talk about the hard part: scaling access to the data.

Most simple web applications, for example, LAMP stack applications, look something like Figure 1.5.

Figure 1.5: Simple web applications

As they grow, there are two main challenges: scaling access to the app server and to the database. In a highly scalable application design, the app (or web) server is typically minimized and often embodies a shared-nothing architecture. This makes the app server layer of the system horizontally scalable. As a result of this design, the heavy lifting is pushed down the stack to the database server and supporting services; it's at this layer where the real scaling and performance challenges come into play.

The rest of this chapter is devoted to some of the more common strategies and methods for making these types of services fast and scalable by providing fast access to data.

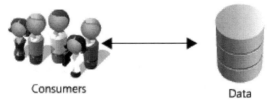

Figure 1.6: Oversimplified web application

Most systems can be oversimplified to Figure 1.6. This is a great place to start. If you have a lot of data, you want fast and easy access, like keeping a stash of candy in the top drawer of your desk. Though overly simplified, the previous statement hints at two hard problems: scalability of storage and fast access of data.

For the sake of this section, let's assume you have many terabytes (TB) of data and you want to allow users to access small portions of that data at random. (See Figure 1.7.) This is similar to locating an image file somewhere on the file server in the image application example.

---

[3] http://katemats.com/2011/11/13/distributed-systems-basics-handling-failure-fault-tolerance-and-monitoring/

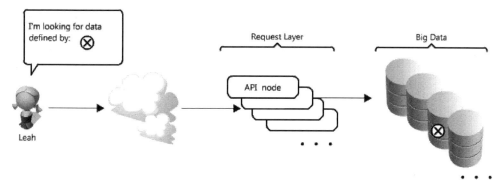

Figure 1.7: Accessing specific data

This is particularly challenging because it can be very costly to load TBs of data into memory; this directly translates to disk IO. Reading from disk is many times slower than from memory—memory access is as fast as Chuck Norris, whereas disk access is slower than the line at the DMV. This speed difference really adds up for large data sets; in real numbers memory access is as little as 6 times faster for sequential reads, or 100,000 times faster for random reads[4], than reading from disk. Moreover, even with unique IDs, solving the problem of knowing where to find that little bit of data can be an arduous task. It's like trying to get that last Jolly Rancher from your candy stash without looking.

Thankfully there are many options that you can employ to make this easier; four of the more important ones are caches, proxies, indexes and load balancers. The rest of this section discusses how each of these concepts can be used to make data access a lot faster.

Caches

Caches take advantage of the locality of reference principle: recently requested data is likely to be requested again. They are used in almost every layer of computing: hardware, operating systems, web browsers, web applications and more. A cache is like short-term memory: it has a limited amount of space, but is typically faster than the original data source and contains the most recently accessed items. Caches can exist at all levels in architecture, but are often found at the level nearest to the front end, where they are implemented to return data quickly without taxing downstream levels.

How can a cache be used to make your data access faster in our API example? In this case, there are a couple of places you can insert a cache. One option is to insert a cache on your request layer node, as in Figure 1.8.

Placing a cache directly on a request layer node enables the local storage of response data. Each time a request is made to the service, the node will quickly return local, cached data if it exists. If it is not in the cache, the request node will query the data from disk. The cache on one request layer node could also be located both in memory (which is very fast) and on the node's local disk (faster than going to network storage).

What happens when you expand this to many nodes? As you can see in Figure 1.9, if the request layer is expanded to multiple nodes, it's still quite possible to have each node host its own cache. However, if your load balancer randomly distributes requests across the nodes, the same request

---
[4]The Pathologies of Big Data, http://queue.acm.org/detail.cfm?id=1563874.

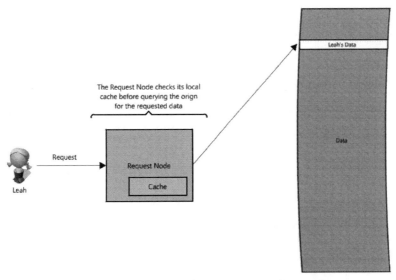

Figure 1.8: Inserting a cache on your request layer node

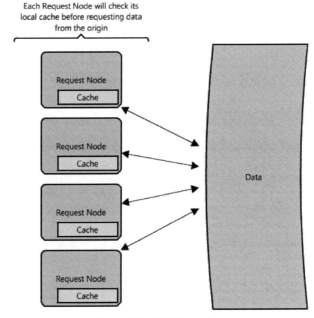

Figure 1.9: Multiple caches

will go to different nodes, thus increasing cache misses. Two choices for overcoming this hurdle are global caches and distributed caches.

Global Cache

A global cache is just as it sounds: all the nodes use the same single cache space. This involves adding a server, or file store of some sort, faster than your original store and accessible by all the request layer nodes. Each of the request nodes queries the cache in the same way it would a local one. This kind of caching scheme can get a bit complicated because it is very easy to overwhelm a single cache as the number of clients and requests increase, but is very effective in some architectures (particularly ones with specialized hardware that make this global cache very fast, or that have a fixed dataset that needs to be cached).

There are two common forms of global caches depicted in the diagrams. In Figure 1.10, when a cached response is not found in the cache, the cache itself becomes responsible for retrieving the missing piece of data from the underlying store. In Figure 1.11 it is the responsibility of request nodes to retrieve any data that is not found in the cache.

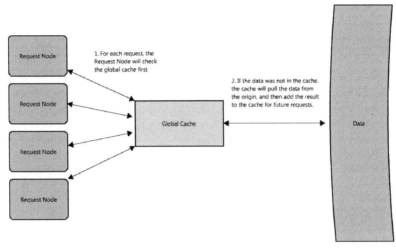

Figure 1.10: Global cache where cache is responsible for retrieval

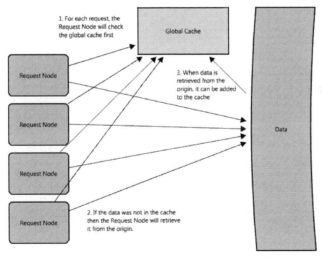

Figure 1.11: Global cache where request nodes are responsible for retrieval

The majority of applications leveraging global caches tend to use the first type, where the cache itself manages eviction and fetching data to prevent a flood of requests for the same data from the clients. However, there are some cases where the second implementation makes more sense. For example, if the cache is being used for very large files, a low cache hit percentage would cause the cache buffer to become overwhelmed with cache misses; in this situation it helps to have a large percentage of the total data set (or hot data set) in the cache. Another example is an architecture where the files stored in the cache are static and shouldn't be evicted. (This could be because of application requirements around that data latency—certain pieces of data might need to be very fast for large data sets—where the application logic understands the eviction strategy or hot spots better than the cache.)

Distributed Cache

In a distributed cache (Figure 1.12), each of its nodes own part of the cached data, so if a refrigerator acts as a cache to the grocery store, a distributed cache is like putting your food in several locations—your fridge, cupboards, *and* lunch box—convenient locations for retrieving snacks from, without a trip to the store. Typically the cache is divided up using a consistent hashing function, such that if a request node is looking for a certain piece of data it can quickly know where to look within the distributed cache to determine if that data is available. In this case, each node has a small piece of the cache, and will then send a request to another node for the data before going to the origin. Therefore, one of the advantages of a distributed cache is the increased cache space that can be had just by adding nodes to the request pool.

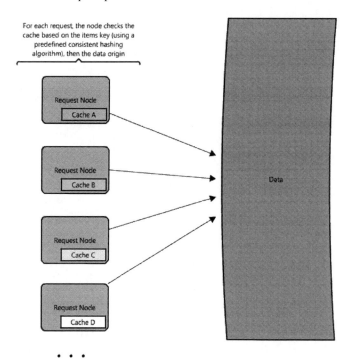

Figure 1.12: Distributed cache

A disadvantage of distributed caching is remedying a missing node. Some distributed caches get around this by storing multiple copies of the data on different nodes; however, you can imagine how this logic can get complicated quickly, especially when you add or remove nodes from the request layer. Although even if a node disappears and part of the cache is lost, the requests will just pull from the origin—so it isn't necessarily catastrophic!

The great thing about caches is that they usually make things much faster (implemented correctly, of course!) The methodology you choose just allows you to make it faster for even more requests. However, all this caching comes at the cost of having to maintain additional storage space, typically in the form of expensive memory; nothing is free. Caches are wonderful for making things generally faster, and moreover provide system functionality under high load conditions when otherwise there would be complete service degradation.

One example of a popular open source cache is Memcached[5] (which can work both as a local cache and distributed cache); however, there are many other options (including many language- or framework-specific options).

Memcached is used in many large web sites, and even though it can be very powerful, it is simply an in-memory key value store, optimized for arbitrary data storage and fast lookups ($O(1)$).

Facebook uses several different types of caching to obtain their site performance[6]. They use $GLOBALS and APC caching at the language level (provided in PHP at the cost of a function call) which helps make intermediate function calls and results much faster. (Most languages have these types of libraries to improve web page performance and they should almost always be used.) Facebook then use a global cache that is distributed across many servers[7], such that one function call accessing the cache could make many requests in parallel for data stored on different Memcached servers. This allows them to get much higher performance and throughput for their user profile data, and have one central place to update data (which is important, since cache invalidation and maintaining consistency can be challenging when you are running thousands of servers).

Now let's talk about what to do when the data isn't in the cache...

Proxies

At a basic level, a proxy server is an intermediate piece of hardware/software that receives requests from clients and relays them to the backend origin servers. Typically, proxies are used to filter requests, log requests, or sometimes transform requests (by adding/removing headers, encrypting/decrypting, or compression).

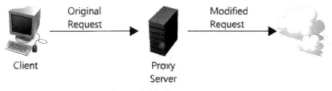

Figure 1.13: Proxy server

Proxies are also immensely helpful when coordinating requests from multiple servers, providing opportunities to optimize request traffic from a system-wide perspective. One way to use a proxy to speed up data access is to collapse the same (or similar) requests together into one request, and then return the single result to the requesting clients. This is known as collapsed forwarding.

Imagine there is a request for the same data (let's call it littleB) across several nodes, and that piece of data is not in the cache. If that request is routed thought the proxy, then all of those requests

---

[5] http://memcached.org/
[6] Facebook caching and performance, http://sizzo.org/talks/.
[7] Scaling memcached at Facebook, http://www.facebook.com/note.php?note_id=39391378919.

can be collapsed into one, which means we only have to read littleB off disk once. (See Figure 1.14.) There is some cost associated with this design, since each request can have slightly higher latency, and some requests may be slightly delayed to be grouped with similar ones. But it will improve performance in high load situations, particularly when that same data is requested over and over. This is similar to a cache, but instead of storing the data/document like a cache, it is optimizing the requests or calls for those documents and acting as a proxy for those clients.

In a LAN proxy, for example, the clients do not need their own IPs to connect to the Internet, and the LAN will collapse calls from the clients for the same content. It is easy to get confused here though, since many proxies are also caches (as it is a very logical place to put a cache), but not all caches act as proxies.

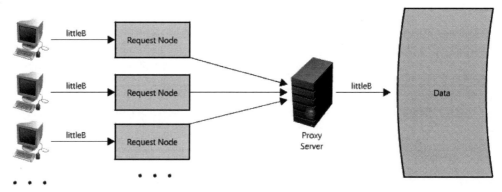

Figure 1.14: Using a proxy server to collapse requests

Another great way to use the proxy is to not just collapse requests for the same data, but also to collapse requests for data that is spatially close together in the origin store (consecutively on disk). Employing such a strategy maximizes data locality for the requests, which can result in decreased request latency. For example, let's say a bunch of nodes request parts of B: partB1, partB2, etc. We can set up our proxy to recognize the spatial locality of the individual requests, collapsing them into a single request and returning only bigB, greatly minimizing the reads from the data origin. (See Figure 1.15.) This can make a really big difference in request time when you are randomly accessing across TBs of data! Proxies are especially helpful under high load situations, or when you have limited caching, since they can essentially batch several requests into one.

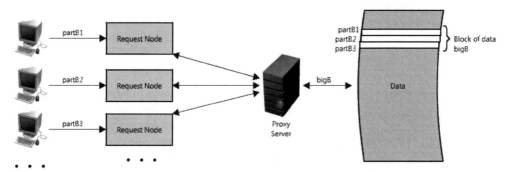

Figure 1.15: Using a proxy to collapse requests for data that is spatially close together

It is worth noting that you can use proxies and caches together, but generally it is best to put the cache in front of the proxy, for the same reason that it is best to let the faster runners start first in a crowded marathon race. This is because the cache is serving data from memory, it is very fast, and it doesn't mind multiple requests for the same result. But if the cache was located on the other side of the proxy server, then there would be additional latency with every request before the cache, and this could hinder performance.

If you are looking at adding a proxy to your systems, there are many options to consider; Squid[8] and Varnish[9] have both been road tested and are widely used in many production web sites. These proxy solutions offer many optimizations to make the most of client-server communication. Installing one of these as a reverse proxy (explained in the load balancer section below) at the web server layer can improve web server performance considerably, reducing the amount of work required to handle incoming client requests.

Indexes

Using an index to access your data quickly is a well-known strategy for optimizing data access performance; probably the most well known when it comes to databases. An index makes the trade-offs of increased storage overhead and slower writes (since you must both write the data and update the index) for the benefit of faster reads.

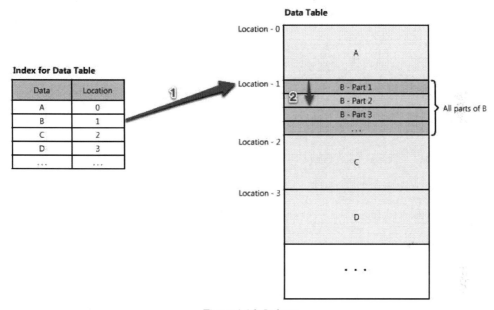

Figure 1.16: Indexes

Just as to a traditional relational data store, you can also apply this concept to larger data sets. The trick with indexes is you must carefully consider how users will access your data. In the case of data sets that are many TBs in size, but with very small payloads (e.g., 1 KB), indexes are a necessity for optimizing data access. Finding a small payload in such a large data set can be a real challenge since you can't possibly iterate over that much data in any reasonable time. Furthermore, it is very likely that such a large data set is spread over several (or many!) physical devices—this means you

---

[8] http://www.squid-cache.org/
[9] https://www.varnish-cache.org/

need some way to find the correct physical location of the desired data. Indexes are the best way to do this.

An index can be used like a table of contents that directs you to the location where your data lives. For example, let's say you are looking for a piece of data, part 2 of B—how will you know where to find it? If you have an index that is sorted by data type—say data A, B, C—it would tell you the location of data B at the origin. Then you just have to seek to that location and read the part of B you want. (See Figure 1.16.)

These indexes are often stored in memory, or somewhere very local to the incoming client request. Berkeley DBs (BDBs) and tree-like data structures are commonly used to store data in ordered lists, ideal for access with an index.

Often there are many layers of indexes that serve as a map, moving you from one location to the next, and so forth, until you get the specific piece of data you want. (See Figure 1.17.)

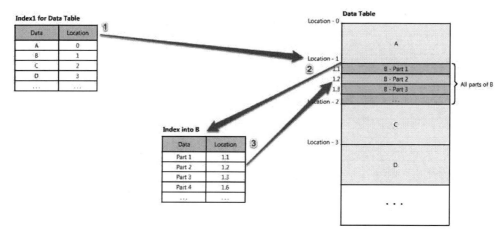

Figure 1.17: Many layers of indexes

Indexes can also be used to create several different views of the same data. For large data sets, this is a great way to define different filters and sorts without resorting to creating many additional copies of the data.

For example, imagine that the image hosting system from earlier is actually hosting images of book pages, and the service allows client queries across the text in those images, searching all the book content about a topic, in the same way search engines allow you to search HTML content. In this case, all those book images take many, many servers to store the files, and finding one page to render to the user can be a bit involved. First, inverse indexes to query for arbitrary words and word tuples need to be easily accessible; then there is the challenge of navigating to the exact page and location within that book, and retrieving the right image for the results. So in this case the inverted index would map to a location (such as book B), and then B may contain an index with all the words, locations and number of occurrences in each part.

An inverted index, which could represent Index1 in the diagram above, might look something like the following—each word or tuple of words provide an index of what books contain them.

Word(s)	Book(s)
being awesome	Book B, Book C, Book D
always	Book C, Book F
believe	Book B

16 Scalable Web Architecture and Distributed Systems

The intermediate index would look similar but would contain just the words, location, and information for book B. This nested index architecture allows each of these indexes to take up less space than if all of that info had to be stored into one big inverted index.

And this is key in large-scale systems because even compressed, these indexes can get quite big and expensive to store. In this system if we assume we have a lot of the books in the world— 100,000,000[10]—and that each book is only 10 pages long (to make the math easier), with 250 words per page, that means there are 250 billion words. If we assume an average of 5 characters per word, and each character takes 8 bits (or 1 byte, even though some characters are 2 bytes), so 5 bytes per word, then an index containing only each word once is over a terabyte of storage. So you can see creating indexes that have a lot of other information like tuples of words, locations for the data, and counts of occurrences, can add up very quickly.

Creating these intermediate indexes and representing the data in smaller sections makes big data problems tractable. Data can be spread across many servers and still accessed quickly. Indexes are a cornerstone of information retrieval, and the basis for today's modern search engines. Of course, this section only scratched the surface, and there is a lot of research being done on how to make indexes smaller, faster, contain more information (like relevancy), and update seamlessly. (There are some manageability challenges with race conditions, and with the sheer number of updates required to add new data or change existing data, particularly in the event where relevancy or scoring is involved).

Being able to find your data quickly and easily is important; indexes are an effective and simple tool to achieve this.

Load Balancers

Finally, another critical piece of any distributed system is a load balancer. Load balancers are a principal part of any architecture, as their role is to distribute load across a set of nodes responsible for servicing requests. This allows multiple nodes to transparently service the same function in a system. (See Figure 1.18.) Their main purpose is to handle a lot of simultaneous connections and route those connections to one of the request nodes, allowing the system to scale to service more requests by just adding nodes.

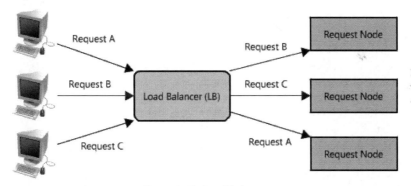

Figure 1.18: Load balancer

There are many different algorithms that can be used to service requests, including picking a random node, round robin, or even selecting the node based on certain criteria, such as memory or

---
[10] Inside Google Books blog post, http://booksearch.blogspot.com/2010/08/books-of-world-stand-up-and-be-counted.html.

CPU utilization. Load balancers can be implemented as software or hardware appliances. One open source software load balancer that has received wide adoption is HAProxy[11].

In a distributed system, load balancers are often found at the very front of the system, such that all incoming requests are routed accordingly. In a complex distributed system, it is not uncommon for a request to be routed to multiple load balancers as shown in Figure 1.19.

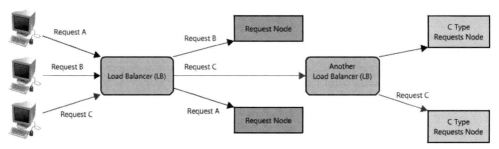

Figure 1.19: Multiple load balancers

Like proxies, some load balancers can also route a request differently depending on the type of request it is. (Technically these are also known as reverse proxies.)

One of the challenges with load balancers is managing user-session-specific data. In an e-commerce site, when you only have one client it is very easy to allow users to put things in their shopping cart and persist those contents between visits (which is important, because it is much more likely you will sell the product if it is still in the user's cart when they return). However, if a user is routed to one node for a session, and then a different node on their next visit, there can be inconsistencies since the new node may be missing that user's cart contents. (Wouldn't you be upset if you put a 6 pack of Mountain Dew in your cart and then came back and it was empty?) One way around this can be to make sessions sticky so that the user is always routed to the same node, but then it is very hard to take advantage of some reliability features like automatic failover. In this case, the user's shopping cart would always have the contents, but if their sticky node became unavailable there would need to be a special case and the assumption of the contents being there would no longer be valid (although hopefully this assumption wouldn't be built into the application). Of course, this problem can be solved using other strategies and tools in this chapter, like services, and many not covered (like browser caches, cookies, and URL rewriting).

If a system only has a couple of a nodes, systems like round robin DNS may make more sense since load balancers can be expensive and add an unneeded layer of complexity. Of course in larger systems there are all sorts of different scheduling and load-balancing algorithms, including simple ones like random choice or round robin, and more sophisticated mechanisms that take things like utilization and capacity into consideration. All of these algorithms allow traffic and requests to be distributed, and can provide helpful reliability tools like automatic failover, or automatic removal of a bad node (such as when it becomes unresponsive). However, these advanced features can make problem diagnosis cumbersome. For example, when it comes to high load situations, load balancers will remove nodes that may be slow or timing out (because of too many requests), but that only exacerbates the situation for the other nodes. In these cases extensive monitoring is important, because overall system traffic and throughput may look like it is decreasing (since the nodes are serving less requests) but the individual nodes are becoming maxed out.

Load balancers are an easy way to allow you to expand system capacity, and like the other techniques in this article, play an essential role in distributed system architecture. Load balancers

---

[11] http://haproxy.1wt.eu/

also provide the critical function of being able to test the health of a node, such that if a node is unresponsive or over-loaded, it can be removed from the pool handling requests, taking advantage of the redundancy of different nodes in your system.

Queues

So far we have covered a lot of ways to read data quickly, but another important part of scaling the data layer is effective management of writes. When systems are simple, with minimal processing loads and small databases, writes can be predictably fast; however, in more complex systems writes can take an almost non-deterministically long time. For example, data may have to be written several places on different servers or indexes, or the system could just be under high load. In the cases where writes, or any task for that matter, may take a long time, achieving performance and availability requires building asynchrony into the system; a common way to do that is with queues.

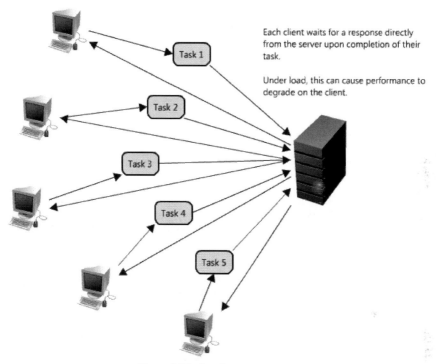

Figure 1.20: Synchronous request

Imagine a system where each client is requesting a task to be remotely serviced. Each of these clients sends their request to the server, where the server completes the tasks as quickly as possible and returns the results to their respective clients. In small systems where one server (or logical service) can service incoming clients just as fast as they come, this sort of situation should work just fine. However, when the server receives more requests than it can handle, then each client is forced to wait for the other clients' requests to complete before a response can be generated. This is an example of a synchronous request, depicted in Figure 1.20.

This kind of synchronous behavior can severely degrade client performance; the client is forced to wait, effectively performing zero work, until its request can be answered. Adding additional servers to address system load does not solve the problem either; even with effective load balancing in place it is extremely difficult to ensure the even and fair distribution of work required to maximize client performance. Further, if the server handling requests is unavailable, or fails, then the clients upstream will also fail. Solving this problem effectively requires abstraction between the client's request and the actual work performed to service it.

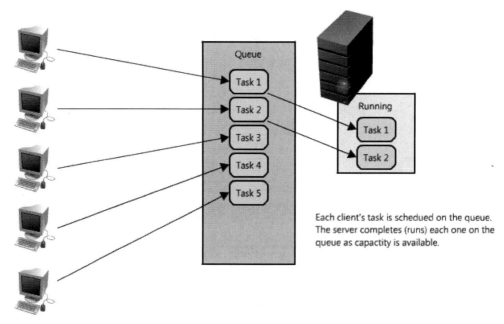

Figure 1.21: Using queues to manage requests

Enter queues. A queue is as simple as it sounds: a task comes in, is added to the queue and then workers pick up the next task as they have the capacity to process it. (See Figure 1.21.) These tasks could represent simple writes to a database, or something as complex as generating a thumbnail preview image for a document. When a client submits task requests to a queue they are no longer forced to wait for the results; instead they need only acknowledgement that the request was properly received. This acknowledgement can later serve as a reference for the results of the work when the client requires it.

Queues enable clients to work in an asynchronous manner, providing a strategic abstraction of a client's request and its response. On the other hand, in a synchronous system, there is no differentiation between request and reply, and they therefore cannot be managed separately. In an asynchronous system the client requests a task, the service responds with a message acknowledging the task was received, and then the client can periodically check the status of the task, only requesting the result once it has completed. While the client is waiting for an asynchronous request to be completed it is free to perform other work, even making asynchronous requests of other services. The latter is an example of how queues and messages are leveraged in distributed systems.

Queues also provide some protection from service outages and failures. For instance, it is quite easy to create a highly robust queue that can retry service requests that have failed due to transient server failures. It is more preferable to use a queue to enforce quality-of-service guarantees than to expose clients directly to intermittent service outages, requiring complicated and often-inconsistent client-side error handling.

Queues are fundamental in managing distributed communication between different parts of any large-scale distributed system, and there are lots of ways to implement them. There are quite a few open source queues like RabbitMQ[12], ActiveMQ[13], BeanstalkD[14], but some also use services like Zookeeper[15], or even data stores like Redis[16].

1.4 Conclusion

Designing efficient systems with fast access to lots of data is exciting, and there are lots of great tools that enable all kinds of new applications. This chapter covered just a few examples, barely scratching the surface, but there are many more—and there will only continue to be more innovation in the space.

---

[12] http://www.rabbitmq.com/
[13] http://activemq.apache.org/
[14] http://kr.github.com/beanstalkd/
[15] http://zookeeper.apache.org/
[16] http://redis.io/

[chapter 2]

Firefox Release Engineering

Chris AtLee, Lukas Blakk, John O'Duinn, and Armen Zambrano Gasparnian

Recently, the Mozilla Release Engineering team has made numerous advances in release automation for Firefox. We have reduced the requirements for human involvement during signing and sending notices to stakeholders, and have automated many other small manual steps, because each manual step in the process is an opportunity for human error. While what we have now isn't perfect, we're always striving to streamline and automate our release process. Our final goal is to be able to push a button and walk away; minimal human intervention will eliminate many of the headaches and do-overs we experienced with our older part-manual, part-automated release processes. In this chapter, we will explore and explain the scripts and infrastructure decisions that comprise the complete Firefox rapid release system, as of Firefox 10.

You'll follow the system from the perspective of a release-worthy Mercurial changeset as it is turned into a release candidate—and then a public release—available to over 450 million daily users worldwide. We'll start with builds and code signing, then customized partner and localization repacks, the QA process, and how we generate updates for every supported version, platform and localization. Each of these steps must be completed before the release can be pushed out to Mozilla Community's network of mirrors which provide the downloads to our users.

We'll look at some of the decisions that have been made to improve this process; for example, our sanity-checking script that helps eliminate much of what used to be vulnerable to human error; our automated signing script; our integration of mobile releases into the desktop release process; patcher, where updates are created; and AUS (Application Update Service), where updates are served to our users across multiple versions of the software.

This chapter describes the mechanics of how we generate release builds for Firefox. Most of this chapter details the significant steps that occur in a release process once the builds start, but there is also plenty of complex cross-group communication to deal with before Release Engineering even starts to generate release builds, so let's start there.

2.1 Look N Ways Before You Start a Release

When we started on the project to improve Mozilla's release process, we began with the premise that the more popular Firefox became, the more users we would have, and the more attractive a target Firefox would become to blackhat hackers looking for security vulnerabilities to exploit. Also, the more popular Firefox became, the more users we would have to protect from a newly discovered

Figure 2.1: Getting from code to "Go to build"

security vulnerability, so the more important it would be to be able to deliver a security fix as quickly as possible. We even have a term for this: a "chemspill" release[1]. Instead of being surprised by the occasional need for a chemspill release in between our regularly scheduled releases, we decided to plan as if every release could be a chemspill release, and designed our release automation accordingly.

This mindset has three important consequences:

1. We do a postmortem after *every* release, and look to see where things could be made smoother, easier, and faster next time. If at all possible, we find and fix at least one thing, no matter how small, immediately—before the next release. This constant polishing of our release automation means we're always looking for new ways to rely on less human involvement while also improving robustness and turnaround time. A lot of effort is spent making our tools and processes bulletproof so that "rare" events like network hiccups, disk space issues or typos made by real live humans are caught and handled as early as possible. Even though we're already fast enough for regular, non-chemspill releases, we want to reduce the risk of any human error in a future release. This is especially true in a chemspill release.

2. When we do have a chemspill release, the more robust the release automation, the less stressed the humans in Release Engineering are. We're used to the idea of going as fast as possible with calm precision, and we've built tools to do this as safely and robustly as we know how. Less stress means more calm and precise work within a well-rehearsed process, which in turn helps chemspill releases go smoothly.

---

[1] Short for "chemical spill".

3. We created a Mozilla-wide "go to build" process. When doing a regular (non-chemspill) release, it's possible to have everyone look through the same bug triage queries, see clearly when the last fix was landed and tested successfully, and reach consensus on when to start builds. However, in a chemspill release—where minutes matter—keeping track of all the details of the issue as well as following up bug confirmations and fixes gets very tricky very quickly. To reduce complexity and the risk of mistakes, Mozilla now has a full-time person to track the readiness of the code for a "go to build" decision. Changing processes during a chemspill is risky, so in order to make sure everyone is familiar with the process when minutes matter, we use this same process for chemspill and regular releases.

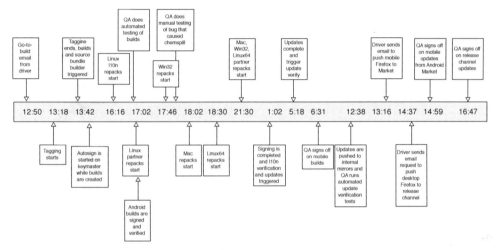

Figure 2.2: Complete release timeline, using a chemspill as example

2.2 "Go to Build"

Who Can Send the "Go to Build"?

Before the start of the release, one person is designated to assume responsibility for coordinating the entire release. This person needs to attend triage meetings, understand the background context on all the work being landed, referee bug severity disputes fairly, approve landing of late-breaking changes, and make tough back-out decisions. Additionally, on the actual release day this person is on point for all communications with the different groups (developers, QA, Release Engineering, website developers, PR, marketing, etc.).

Different companies use different titles for this role. Some titles we've heard include Release Manager, Release Engineer, Program Manager, Project Manager, Product Manager, Product Czar, Release Driver. In this chapter, we will use the term "Release Coordinator" as we feel it most clearly defines the role in our process as described above. The important point here is that the role, and the final authority of the role, is clearly understood by everyone before the release starts, regardless of their background or previous work experiences elsewhere. In the heat of a release day, it is important that everyone knows to abide by, and trust, the coordination decisions that this person makes.

The Release Coordinator is the only person outside of Release Engineering who is authorized to send "stop builds" emails if a show-stopper problem is discovered. Any reports of suspected show-stopper problems are redirected to the Release Coordinator, who will evaluate, make the final go/no-go decision and communicate that decision to everyone in a timely manner. In the heat of the moment of a release day, we all have to abide by, and trust, the coordination decisions that this person makes.

How to Send the "Go to Build"?

Early experiments with sending "go to build" in IRC channels or verbally over the phone led to misunderstandings, occasionally causing problems for the release in progress. Therefore, we now require that the "go to build" signal for every release is done by email, to a mailing list that includes everyone across all groups involved in release processes. The subject of the email includes "go to build" and the explicit product name and version number; for example:

```
go to build Firefox 6.0.1
```

Similarly, if a problem is found in the release, the Release Coordinator will send a new "all stop" email to the same mailing list, with a new subject line. We found that it was not sufficient to just hit reply on the most recent email about the release; email threading in some email clients caused some people to not notice the "all stop" email if it was way down a long and unrelated thread.

What Is In the "Go to Build" Email?

1. The exact code to be used in the build; ideally, the URL to the specific change in the source code repository that the release builds are to be created from.
    (a) Instructions like "use the latest code" are never acceptable; in one release, after the "go to build" email was sent and before builds started, a well-intentioned developer landed a change, without approval, in the wrong branch. The release included that unwanted change in the builds. Thankfully the mistake was caught before we shipped, but we did have to delay the release while we did a full stop and rebuilt everything.
    (b) In a time-based version control system like CVS, be fully explicit about the exact time to use; give the time down to seconds, and specify timezone. In one release, when Firefox was still based on CVS, the Release Coordinator specified the cutoff time to be used for the builds but did not give the timezone. By the time Release Engineering noticed the missing timezone info, the Release Coordinator was asleep. Release Engineering correctly guessed that the intent was local time (in California), but in a late-night mixup over PDT instead of PST we ended up missing the last critical bug fix. This was caught by QA before we shipped, but we had to stop builds and start the build over using the correct cutoff time.
2. A clear sense of the urgency for this particular release. While it sounds obvious, it is important when handling some important edge cases, so here is a quick summary:
    (a) Some releases are "routine", and can be worked on in normal working hours. They are a pre-scheduled release, they are on schedule, and there is no emergency. Of course, all release builds need to be created in a timely manner, but there is no need for release engineers to pull all-nighters and burn out for a routine release. Instead, we schedule them properly in advance so everything stays on schedule with people working normal hours. This keeps people fresh and better able to handle unscheduled urgent work if the need arises.

(b) Some releases are "chemspills", and are urgent, where minutes matter. These are typically to fix a published security exploit, or to fix a newly introduced top-crash problem impacting a large percentage of our user base. Chemspills need to be created as quickly as possible and are typically not pre-scheduled releases.

(c) Some releases change from routine to chemspill or from chemspill to routine. For example, if a security fix in a routine release was accidentally leaked, it is now a chemspill release. If a business requirement like a "special sneak preview" release for an upcoming conference announcement was delayed for business reasons, the release now changes from chemspill to routine.

(d) Some releases have different people holding different opinions on whether the release is normal or urgent, depending on their perspective on the fixes being shipped in the release.

It is the role of the Release Coordinator to balance all the facts and opinions, reach a decision, and then communicate that decision about urgency consistently across all groups. If new information arrives, the Release Coordinator reassesses, and then communicates the new urgency to all the same groups. Having some groups believe a release is a chemspill, while other groups believe the same release is routine can be destructive to cross-group cohesion.

Finally, these emails also became very useful to measure where time was spent during a release. While they are only accurate to wall-clock time resolution, this accuracy is really helpful when figuring out where next to focus our efforts on making things faster. As the old adage goes, before you can improve something, you have to be able to measure it.

Throughout the beta cycle for Firefox we also do weekly releases from our `mozilla-beta` repository[2]. Each one of these beta releases goes through our usual full release automation, and is treated almost identically to our regular final releases. To minimize surprises during a release, our intent is to have no new untested changes to release automation or infrastructure by the time we start the final release builds.

2.3 Tagging, Building, and Source Tarballs

In preparation for starting automation, we recently started to use a script, `release_sanity.py`[3], that was originally written by a Release Engineering summer intern. This Python script assists a release engineer with double-checking that all configurations for a release match what is checked into our tools and configuration repositories. It also checks what is in the specified release code revisions for `mozilla-release` and all the (human) languages for this release, which will be what the builds and language repacks are generated from.

The script accepts the buildbot config files for any release configurations that will be used (such as desktop or mobile), the branch to look at (e.g., `mozilla-release`), the build and version number, and the names of the products that are to be built (such as "fennec" or "firefox"). It will fail if the release repositories do not match what's in the configurations, if locale repository changesets don't match our shipping locales and localization changeset files, or if the release version and build number don't match what has been given to our build tools with the tag generated using the product, version, and build number. If all the tests in the script pass, it will reconfigure the buildbot master where the script is being run and where release builders will be triggered, and then generate the "send change" that starts the automated release process.

---

[2] http://hg.mozilla.org/releases/mozilla-beta/
[3] http://mxr.mozilla.org/build/source/tools/buildbot-helpers/release_sanity.py

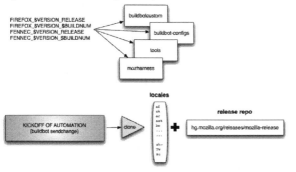

Figure 2.3: Automated tagging

After a release engineer kicks off builders, the first automated step in the Firefox release process is tagging all the related source code repositories to record which revision of the source, language repositories, and related tools are being used for this version and build number of a release candidate. These tags allow us to keep a history of Firefox and Fennec (mobile Firefox) releases' version and build numbers in our release repositories. For Firefox releases, one example tag set is FIREFOX_10_0_RELEASE FIREFOX_10_0_BUILD1 FENNEC_10_0_RELEASE FENNEC_10_0_BUILD1.

A single Firefox release uses code from about 85 version control repositories that host things such as the product code, localization strings, release automation code, and helper utilities. Tagging all these repositories is critical to ensure that future steps of the release automation are all executed using the same set of revisions. It also has a number of other benefits: Linux distributions and other contributors can reproduce builds with exactly the same code and tools that go into the official builds, and it also records the revisions of source and tools used on a per-release basis for future comparison of what changed between releases.

Once all the repositories are branched and tagged, a series of dependent builders automatically start up: one builder for each release platform plus a source bundle that includes all source used in the release. The source bundle and built installers are all uploaded to the release directory as they become available. This allows anyone to see exactly what code is in a release, and gives a snapshot that would allow us to re-create the builds if we ever needed to (for example, if our VCS failed somehow).

For the Firefox build's source, sometimes we need to import code from an earlier repository. For example, with a beta release this means pulling in the signed-off revision from Mozilla-Aurora (our more-stable-than-Nightly repository) for Firefox 10.0b1. For a release it means pulling in the approved changes from Mozilla-Beta (typically the same code used for 10.0b6) to the Mozilla-Release repository. This release branch is then created as a named branch whose parent changeset is the signed-off revision from the 'go to build' provided by the Release Coordinator. The release branch can be used to make release-specific modifications to the source code, such as bumping version numbers or finalizing the set of locales that will be built. If a critical security vulnerability is discovered in the future that requires an immediate fix—a chemspill—a minimal set of changes to address the vulnerability will be landed on this relbranch and a new version of Firefox generated and released from it. When we have to do another round of builds for a particular release, buildN, we use these relbranches to grab the same code that was signed off on for 'go to build', which is where any changes to that release code will have been landed. The automation starts again and bumps the tagging to the new changeset on that relbranch.

Our tagging process does a *lot* of operations with local and remote Mercurial repositories. To streamline some of the most common operations we've written a few tools to assist us: retry.py[4] and hgtool.py[5]. retry.py is a simple wrapper that can take a given command and run it, retrying several times if it fails. It can also watch for exceptional output conditions and retry or report failure in those cases. We've found it useful to wrap retry.py around most of the commands which can fail due to external dependencies. For tagging, the Mercurial operations could fail due to temporary network outages, web server issues, or the backend Mercurial server being temporarily overloaded. Being able to automatically retry these operations and continue saves a lot of our time, since we don't have to manually recover, clean up any fallout and then get the release automation running again.

hgtool.py is a utility that encapsulates several common Mercurial operations, like cloning, pulling, and updating with a single invocation. It also adds support for Mercurial's share extension, which we use extensively to avoid having several full clones of repositories in different directories on the same machine. Adding support for shared local repositories significantly sped up our tagging process, since most full clones of the product and locale repositories could be avoided.

An important motivation for developing tools like these is making our automation as testable as possible. Because tools like hgtool.py are small, single-purpose utilities built on top of reusable libraries, they're much easier to test in isolation.

Today our tagging is done in two parallel jobs: one for desktop Firefox which takes around 20 minutes to complete as it includes tagging 80+ locale repositories, and another for mobile Firefox which takes around 10 minutes to complete since we have fewer locales currently available for our mobile releases. In the future we would like to streamline our release automation process so that we tag *all* the various repositories in parallel. The initial builds can be started as soon as the product code and tools requirement repository is tagged, without having to wait for all the locale repositories to be tagged. By the time these builds are finished, the rest of the repositories will have been tagged so that localization repackages and future steps can be completed. We estimate this can reduce the total time to have builds ready by 15 minutes.

2.4 Localization Repacks and Partner Repacks

Once the desktop builds are generated and uploaded to ftp.mozilla.org, our automation triggers the localization repackaging jobs. A "localization repack" takes the original build (which contains the en-US locale), unpacks it, replaces the en-US strings with the strings for another locale that we are shipping in this release, then repackages all the files back up again (this is why we call them repacks). We repeat this for each locale shipping in the release. Originally, we did all repacks serially. However, as we added more locales, this took a long time to complete, and we had to restart from the beginning if anything failed out mid-way through.

---

[4] http://hg.mozilla.org/build/tools/file/7adc08bd1386/lib/python/util/retry.py
[5] http://hg.mozilla.org/build/mozharness/file/a0fce0162fd5/scripts/hgtool.py

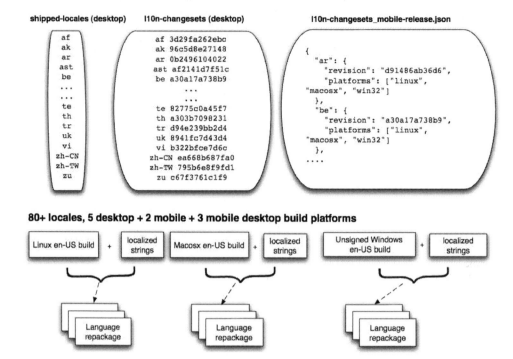

Figure 2.4: Repacking Firefox for each localization

Now, we instead split the entire set of repacks into six jobs, each processed concurrently on six different machines. This approach completes the work in approximately a sixth of the time. This also allows us to redo a subset of repacks if an individual repack fails, without having to redo all repacks. (We could split the repacks into even more, smaller, concurrent jobs, but we found it took away too many machines from the pool, which affected other unrelated jobs triggered by developers on our continuous integration system.)

The process for mobile (on Android) is slightly different, as we produce only two installers: an English version and a multi-locale version with over a dozen languages built into the installer instead of a separate build per locale. The size of this multi-locale version is an issue, especially with slow download speeds onto small mobile devices. One proposal for the future is to have other languages be requested on demand as add-ons from addons.mozilla.org.

In Figure 2.4, you can see that we currently rely on three different sources for our locale information: shipped_locales, l10_changesets and l10n-changesets_mobile-release.json. (There is a plan to move all three into a unified JSON file.) These files contain information about the different localizations we have, and certain platform exceptions. Specifically, for a given localization we need to know which revision of the repository to use for a given release and we need to know if the localization can build on all of our supported platforms (e.g., Japanese for Mac comes from a different repository all together). Two of these files are used for the Desktop releases and one for the Mobile release (this JSON file contains both the list of platforms and the changesets).

Who decides which languages we ship? First of all, localizers themselves nominate their specific changeset for a given release. The nominated changeset gets reviewed by Mozilla's localization team and shows up in a web dashboard that lists the changesets needed for each language. The Release Coordinator reviews this before sending the "go to build" email. On the day of a release, we retrieve this list of changesets and we repackage them accordingly.

Besides localization repackages we also generate partner repackages. These are customized builds for various partners we have who want to customize the experience for their customers. The main type of changes are custom bookmarks, custom homepage and custom search engines but many other things can be changed. These customized builds are generated for the latest Firefox release and not for betas.

2.5 Signing

In order for users to be sure that the copy of Firefox they have downloaded is indeed the unmodified build from Mozilla, we apply a few different types of digital signatures to the builds.

The first type of signing is for our Windows builds. We use a Microsoft Authenticode (signcode) signing key to sign all our `.exe` and `.dll` files. Windows can use these signatures to verify that the application comes from a trusted source. We also sign the Firefox installer executable with the Authenticode key.

Next we use GPG to generate a set of MD5 and SHA1 checksums for all the builds on all platforms, and generate detached GPG signatures for the checksum files as well as all the builds and installers. These signatures are used by mirrors and other community members to validate their downloads.

For security purposes, we sign on a dedicated signing machine that is blocked off via firewall and VPN from outside connections. Our keyphrases, passwords, and keystores are passed among release engineers only in secure channels, often in person, to minimize the risk of exposure as much as possible.

Until recently this signing process involved a release engineer working on a dedicated server (the "signing master") for almost an hour manually downloading builds, signing them, and uploading them back to `ftp.mozilla.org` before the automation could continue. Once signing on the master was completed and all files were uploaded, a log file of all the signing activities was uploaded to the release candidates directory on `ftp.mozilla.org`. The appearance of this log file on `ftp.mozilla.org` signified the end of human signing work and from that point, dependent builders watching for that log file could resume automation. Recently we've added an additional wrapper of automation around the signing steps. Now the release engineer opens a Cygwin shell on the signing master and sets up a few environment variables pertaining to the release, like VERSION, BUILD, TAG, and RELEASE_CONFIG, that help the script find the right directories on `ftp.mozilla.org` and know when all the deliverables for a release have been downloaded so that the signing can start. After checking out the most recent production version of our signing tools, the release engineer simply runs make autosign. The release engineer then enters two passphrases, one for gpg and one for signcode. Once these passphrases are automatically verified by the make scripts, the automation starts a download loop that watches for uploaded builds and repacks from the release automation and downloads them as they become available. Once all items have been downloaded, the automation begins signing immediately, without human intervention.

Not needing a human to sign is important for two reasons. Firstly, it reduces the risk of human error. Secondly, it allows signing to proceed during non-work hours, without needing a release engineer awake at a computer at the time.

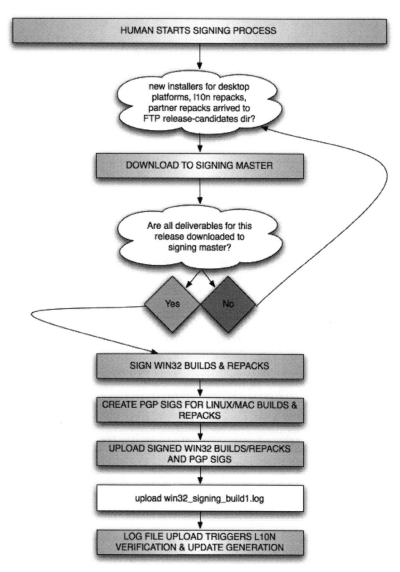

Figure 2.5: Signing Firefox installers

All deliverables have an MD5SUM and SHA1SUM generated for them, and those hash values are written to files of the same name. These files will be uploaded back to the release-candidates directory as well as synced into the final location of the release on ftp.mozilla.org once it is live, so that anyone who downloads a Firefox installer from one of our mirrors can ensure they got the correct object. When all signed bits are available and verified they are uploaded back to ftp.mozilla.org along with the signing log file, which the automation is waiting for to proceed.

Our next planned round of improvements to the signing process will create a tool that allows us to sign bits at the time of build/repack. This work requires creating a signing server application that can receive requests to sign files from the release build machines. It will also require a signing client tool which would contact the signing server, authenticate itself as a machine trusted to request signing, upload the files to be signed, wait for the build to be signed, download the signed bits, and then include them as part of the packaged build. Once these enhancements are in production, we can discontinue our current all-at-once signing process, as well as our all-at-once generate-updates process (more on this below). We expect this work to trim a few hours off our current end-to-end times for a release.

2.6 Updates

Updates are created so users can update to the latest version of Firefox quickly and easily using our built-in updater, without having to download and run a standalone installer. From the user's perspective, the downloading of the update package happens quietly in the background. Only after the update files are downloaded, and ready to be applied, will Firefox prompt the user with the option to apply the update and restart.

The catch is, we generate a *lot* of updates. For a series of releases on a product line, we generate updates from all supported previous releases in the series to the new latest release for that product line. For Firefox LATEST, that means generating updates for every platform, every locale, and every installer from Firefox LATEST-1, LATEST-2, LATEST-3, ... in both complete and partial forms. We do all this for several different product lines at a time.

Our update generation automation modifies the update configuration files of each release's build off a branch to maintain our canonical list of what version numbers, platforms, and localizations need to have updates created to offer users this newest release. We offer updates as "snippets". As you can see in the example below, this snippet is simply an XML pointer file hosted on our AUS (Application Update Service) that informs the user's Firefox browser where the complete and/or partial .mar (Mozilla Archive) files are hosted.

Major Updates vs. Minor Updates

As you can see in Figure 2.6, update snippets have a type attribute which can be either major or minor. Minor updates keep people updated to the latest version available in their release train; for example, it would update all 3.6.* release users to the latest 3.6 release, all rapid-release beta users to the latest beta, all Nightly users to the latest Nightly build, etc. Most of the time, updates are minor and don't require any user interaction other than a confirmation to apply the update and restart the browser.

Major updates are used when we need to advertise to our users that the latest and greatest release is available, prompting them that "A new version of Firefox is available, would you like to update?" and displaying a billboard showcasing the leading features in the new release. Our new rapid-release system means we no longer need to do as many major updates; we'll be able to stop generating major updates once the 3.6.* release train is no longer supported.

Complete Updates vs. Partial Updates

At build time we generate "complete update" .mar files which contain all the files for the new release, compressed with bz2 and then archived into a .mar file. Both complete and partial updates are downloaded automatically through the update channel to which a user's Firefox is registered. We have different update channels (that is, release users look for updates on release channel, beta users

```xml
<updates>
  <update type="minor" version="7.0.1" extensionVersion="7.0.1"
          buildID="20110928134238"
          detailsURL="https://www.mozilla.com/en-US/firefox/7.0.1/releasenotes/">
    <patch type="complete"
           URL="http://download.mozilla.org/?product=firefox-7.0.1-complete& os=osx&\
                lang=en-US&force=1"
           hashFunction="SHA512"
           hashValue="7ecdbc110468b9b4627299794d793874436353dc36c80151550b08830f9d8c\
                      5afd7940c51df9270d54e11fd99806f41368c0f88721fa17e01ea959144f47\
                      3f9d"
           size="28680122"/>
    <patch type="partial"
           URL="http://download.mozilla.org/?product=firefox-7.0.1-partial-6.0.2&\
                os=osx&lang=en-US&force=1"
           hashFunction="SHA512"
           hashValue="e9bb49bee862c7a8000de6508d006edf29778b5dbede4deaf3cfa05c22521f\
                      c775da126f5057621960d327615b5186b27d75a378b00981394716e93fc5cc\
                      a11a"
           size="10469801"/>
  </update>
</updates>
```

Figure 2.6: Sample update snippet

look on beta channel, etc.) so that we can serve updates to, for example, release users at a different time than we serve updates to beta users.

Partial update .mar files are created by comparing the complete .mar for the old release with the complete .mar for the new release to create a "partial-update" .mar file containing the binary diff of any changed files, and a manifest file. As you can see in the sample snippet in Figure 2.6, this results in a much smaller file size for partial updates. This is very important for users with slower or dial-up Internet connections.

In older versions of our update automation the generation of partial updates for all locales and platforms could take six to seven hours for one release, as the complete .mar files were downloaded, diffed, and packaged into a partial-update .mar file. Eventually it was discovered that even across platforms, many component changes were identical, therefore many diffs could be re-used. With a script that cached the hash for each part of the diff, our partial update creation time was brought down to approximately 40 minutes.

After the snippets are uploaded and are hosted on AUS, an update verification step is run to a) test downloading the snippets and b) run the updater with the downloaded .mar file to confirm that the updates apply correctly.

Generation of partial-update .mar files, as well as all the update snippets, is currently done after signing is complete. We do this because generation of the partial updates must be done between signed files of the two releases, and therefore generation of the snippets must wait until the signed builds are available. Once we're able to integrate signing into the build process, we can generate partial updates immediately after completing a build or repack. Together with improvements to our AUS software, this means that once we're finished builds and repacks we would be able to push immediately to mirrors. This effectively parallelizes the creation of all the updates, trimming several hours from our total time.

2.7 Pushing to Internal Mirrors and QA

Verifying that the release process is producing the expected deliverables is key. This is accomplished by QA's verification and sign offs process.

Once the signed builds are available, QA starts manual and automated testing. QA relies on a mix of community members, contractors and employees in different timezones to speed up this verification process. Meanwhile, our release automation generates updates for all languages and all platforms, for all supported releases. These update snippets are typically ready before QA has finished verifying the signed builds. QA then verifies that users can safely update from various previous releases to the newest release using these updates.

Mechanically, our automation pushes the binaries to our "internal mirrors" (Mozilla-hosted servers) in order for QA to verify updates. Only after QA has finished verification of the builds and the updates will we push them to our community mirrors. These community mirrors are essential to handle the global load of users, by allowing them to request their updates from local mirror nodes instead of from `ftp.mozilla.org` directly. It's worth noting that we do not make builds and updates available on the community mirrors until after QA signoff, because of complications that arise if QA finds a last-minute showstopper and the candidate build needs to be withdrawn.

The validation process after builds and updates are generated is:

- QA, along with community and contractors in other timezones, does manual testing.
- QA triggers the automation systems to do functional testing.
- QA independently verifies that fixed problems and new features for that release are indeed fixed and of good enough quality to ship to users.
- Meanwhile, release automation generates the updates.
- QA signs off the builds.
- QA signs off the updates.

Note that users don't get updates until QA has signed off and the Release Coordinator has sent the email asking to push the builds and updates live.

2.8 Pushing to Public Mirrors and AUS

Once the Release Coordinator gets signoff from QA and various other groups at Mozilla, they give Release Engineering the go-ahead to push the files to our community mirror network. We rely on our community mirrors to be able to handle a few hundred million users downloading updates over the next few days. All the installers, as well as the complete and partial updates for all platforms and locales, are already on our internal mirror network at this point. Publishing the files to our external mirrors involves making a change to an rsync exclude file for the public mirrors module. Once this change is made, the mirrors will start to synchronize the new release files. Each mirror has a score or weighting associated with it; we monitor which mirrors have synchronized the files and sum their individual scores to compute a total "uptake" score. Once a certain uptake threshold is reached, we notify the Release Coordinator that the mirrors have enough uptake to handle the release.

This is the point at which the release becomes "official". After the Release Coordinator sends the final "go live" email, Release Engineering will update the symlinks on the web server so that visitors to our web and ftp sites can find the latest new version of Firefox. We also publish all the update snippets for users on past versions of Firefox to AUS.

Firefox installed on users' machines regularly checks our AUS servers to see if there's an updated version of Firefox available for them. Once we publish these update snippets, users are able to automatically update Firefox to the latest version.

2.9 Lessons Learned

As software engineers, our temptation is to jump to solve what we see as the immediate and obvious technical problem. However, Release Engineering spans across different fields—both technical and non-technical—so being aware of technical and non-technical issues is important.

The Importance of Buy-in from Other Stakeholders

It was important to make sure that all stakeholders understood that our slow, fragile release engineering exposed the organization, and our users, to risks. This involved all levels of the organization acknowledging the lost business opportunities, and market risks, caused by slow fragile automation. Further, Mozilla's ability to protect our users with super-fast turnaround on releases became more important as we grew to have more users, which in turn made us more attractive as a target.

Interestingly, some people had only ever experienced fragile release automation in their careers, so came to Mozilla with low, "oh, it's always this bad" expectations. Explaining the business gains expected with a robust, scalable release automation process helped everyone understand the importance of the "invisible" Release Engineering improvement work we were about to undertake.

Involving Other Groups

To make the release process more efficient and more reliable required work, by Release Engineering and other groups across Mozilla. However, it was interesting to see how often "it takes a long time to ship a release" was mistranslated as "it takes Release Engineering a long time to ship a release". This misconception ignored the release work done by groups outside of Release Engineering, and was demotivating to the Release Engineers. Fixing this misconception required educating people across Mozilla on where time was actually spent by different groups during a release. We did this with low-tech "wall-clock" timestamps on emails of clear handoffs across groups, and a series of "wall-clock" blog posts detailing where time was spent.

- These helped raise awareness of which different groups were actually involved in a release.
- These helped people appreciate whenever RelEng got processes to run faster, which in turn helped motivate Release Engineers to make further improvements.
- These helped other groups think about how they too could help improve the overall release process—a big mindset shift for the entire organization.
- Finally, these also eliminated all the unclear handoff communications across groups, which had historically cost us many respins, false-starts, and other costly disruptions to the release process.

Establishing Clear Handoffs

Many of our "release engineering" problems were actually people problems: miscommunication between teams; lack of clear leadership; and the resulting stress, fatigue and anxiety during chemspill releases. By having clear handoffs to eliminate these human miscommunications, our releases immediately started to go more smoothly, and cross-group human interactions quickly improved.

Managing Turnover

When we started this project, we were losing team members too often. In itself, this is bad. However, the lack of accurate up-to-date documentation meant that most of the technical understanding of the release process was documented by folklore and oral histories, which we lost whenever a person left. We needed to turn this situation around, urgently.

We felt the best way to improve morale and show that things were getting better was to make sure people could see that we had a plan to make things better, and that people had some control over their own destiny. We did this by making sure that we set aside time to fix at least one thing—anything!—after each release. We implemented this by negotiating for a day or two of "do not disturb" time immediately after we shipped a release. Solving immediate small problems, while they were still fresh in people's minds, helped clear distractions, so people could focus on larger term problems in subsequent releases. More importantly, this gave people the feeling that we had regained some control over our own fate, and that things were truly getting better.

Managing Change

Because of market pressures, Mozilla's business and product needs from the release process changed while we were working on improving it. This is not unusual and should be expected.

We knew we had to continue shipping releases using the current release process, while we were building the new process. We decided against attempting to build a separate "greenfield project" while also supporting the existing systems; we felt the current systems were so fragile that we literally would not have the time to do anything new.

We also assumed from the outset that we didn't fully understand what was broken. Each incremental improvement allowed us to step back and check for new surprises, before starting work on the next improvement. Phrases like "draining the swamp", "peeling the onion", and "how did this ever work?" were heard frequently whenever we discovered new surprises throughout this project.

Given all this, we decided to make lots of small, continuous improvements to the existing process. Each iterative improvement made the next release a little bit better. More importantly, each improvement freed up just a little bit more time during the next release, which allowed a release engineer a little more time to make the next improvement. These improvements snowballed until we found ourselves past the tipping point, and able to make time to work on significant major improvements. At that point, the gains from release optimizations really kicked in.

2.10 For More Information

We're really proud of the work done so far, and the abilities that it has brought to Mozilla in a newly heated-up global browser market.

Four years ago, doing two chemspill releases in a month would be a talking point within Mozilla. By contrast, last week a published exploit in a third-party library caused Mozilla to ship eight chemspills releases in two low-fuss days.

As with everything, our release automation still has plenty of room for improvement, and our needs and demands continue to change. For a look at our ongoing work, please see:

- Chris AtLee's blog: http://atlee.ca/blog.
- Lukas Blakk's blog: http://lukasblakk.com.
- John O'Duinn's blog: http://oduinn.com.
- Armen Zambrano Gasparnian's blog: http://armenzg.blogspot.com.

- Documentation on the design and flow of our Mercurial-based release process: `https://wiki.mozilla.org/Release:Release_Automation_on_Mercurial:Documentation`.
- Release Engineering's build repositories: `http://hg.mozilla.org/build`. In particular, the buildbotcustom, buildbot-configs, and tools repositories are used heavily for releases.
- The Firefox 7.0 Beta 4 Build Notes: `https://wiki.mozilla.org/Releases/Firefox_7.0b4/BuildNotes`. In addition to code, we document every aspect of a release. This link is to our 7.0b4 release notes, but you can find all our release notes if you edit the URL appropriately.

[chapter 3]

FreeRTOS
Christopher Svec

FreeRTOS (pronounced "free-arr-toss") is an open source real-time operating system (RTOS) for embedded systems. FreeRTOS supports many different architectures and compiler toolchains, and is designed to be "small, simple, and easy to use"[1].

FreeRTOS is under active development, and has been since Richard Barry started work on it in 2002. As for me, I'm not a developer of or contributor to FreeRTOS, I'm merely a user and a fan. As a result, this chapter will favor the "what" and "how" of FreeRTOS's architecture, with less of the "why" than other chapters in this book.

Like all operating systems, FreeRTOS's main job is to run tasks. Most of FreeRTOS's code involves prioritizing, scheduling, and running user-defined tasks. Unlike all operating systems, FreeRTOS is a real-time operating system which runs on embedded systems.

By the end of this chapter I hope that you'll understand the basic architecture of FreeRTOS. Most of FreeRTOS is dedicated to running tasks, so you'll get a good look at exactly how FreeRTOS does that.

If this is your first look under the hood of an operating system, I also hope that you'll learn the basics about how any OS works. FreeRTOS is relatively simple, especially when compared to Windows, Linux, or OS X, but all operating systems share the same basic concepts and goals, so looking at any OS can be instructive and interesting.

3.1   What is "Embedded" and "Real-Time"?

"Embedded" and "real-time" can mean different things to different people, so let's define them as FreeRTOS uses them.

An embedded system is a computer system that is designed to do only a few things, like the system in a TV remote control, in-car GPS, digital watch, or pacemaker. Embedded systems are typically smaller and slower than general purpose computer systems, and are also usually less expensive. A typical low-end embedded system may have an 8-bit CPU running at 25MHz, a few KB of RAM, and maybe 32KB of flash memory. A higher-end embedded system may have a 32-bit CPU running at 750MHz, a GB of RAM, and multiple GB of flash memory.

Real-time systems are designed to do something within a certain amount of time; they guarantee that stuff happens when it's supposed to.

---
[1]http://www.freertos.org/index.html?http://www.freertos.org/FreeRTOS_Features.html

A pacemaker is an excellent example of a real-time embedded system. A pacemaker must contract the heart muscle at the right time to keep you alive; it can't be too busy to respond in time. Pacemakers and other real-time embedded systems are carefully designed to run their tasks on time, every time.

3.2 Architecture Overview

FreeRTOS is a relatively small application. The minimum core of FreeRTOS is only three source (.c) files and a handful of header files, totalling just under 9000 lines of code, including comments and blank lines. A typical binary code image is less than 10KB.

FreeRTOS's code breaks down into three main areas: tasks, communication, and hardware interfacing.

- Tasks: Almost half of FreeRTOS's core code deals with the central concern in many operating systems: tasks. A task is a user-defined C function with a given priority. tasks.c and task.h do all the heavy lifting for creating, scheduling, and maintaining tasks.
- Communication: Tasks are good, but tasks that can communicate with each other are even better! Which brings us to the second FreeRTOS job: communication. About 40% of FreeRTOS's core code deals with communication. queue.c and queue.h handle FreeRTOS communication. Tasks and interrupts use queues to send data to each other and to signal the use of critical resources using semaphores and mutexes.
- The Hardware Whisperer: The approximately 9000 lines of code that make up the base of FreeRTOS are hardware-independent; the same code runs whether FreeRTOS is running on the humble 8051 or the newest, shiniest ARM core. About 6% of FreeRTOS's core code acts a shim between the hardware-independent FreeRTOS core and the hardware-dependent code. We'll discuss the hardware-dependent code in the next section.

Hardware Considerations

The hardware-independent FreeRTOS layer sits on top of a hardware-dependent layer. This hardware-dependent layer knows how to talk to whatever chip architecture you choose. Figure 3.1 shows FreeRTOS's layers.

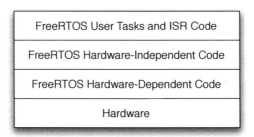

Figure 3.1: FreeRTOS software layers

FreeRTOS ships with all the hardware-independent as well as hardware-dependent code you'll need to get a system up and running. It supports many compilers (CodeWarrior, GCC, IAR, etc.) as well as many processor architectures (ARM7, ARM Cortex-M3, various PICs, Silicon Labs 8051, x86, etc.). See the FreeRTOS website for a list of supported architectures and compilers.

FreeRTOS is highly configurable by design. FreeRTOS can be built as a single CPU, bare-bones RTOS, supporting only a few tasks, or it can be built as a highly functional multicore beast with TCP/IP, a file system, and USB.

Configuration options are selected in `FreeRTOSConfig.h` by setting various `#define`s. Clock speed, heap size, mutexes, and API subsets are all configurable in this file, along with many other options. Here are a few examples that set the maximum number of task priority levels, the CPU frequency, the system tick frequency, the minimal stack size and the total heap size:

```
#define configMAX_PRIORITIES       ( ( unsigned portBASE_TYPE ) 5 )
#define configCPU_CLOCK_HZ         ( 12000000UL )
#define configTICK_RATE_HZ         ( ( portTickType ) 1000 )
#define configMINIMAL_STACK_SIZE   ( ( unsigned short ) 100 )
#define configTOTAL_HEAP_SIZE      ( ( size_t ) ( 4 * 1024 ) )
```

Hardware-dependent code lives in separate files for each compiler toolchain and CPU architecture. For example, if you're working with the IAR compiler on an ARM Cortex-M3 chip, the hardware-dependent code lives in the `FreeRTOS/Source/portable/IAR/ARM_CM3/` directory. `portmacro.h` declares all of the hardware-specific functions, while `port.c` and `portasm.s` contain all of the actual hardware-dependent code. The hardware-independent header file `portable.h` `#include`'s the correct `portmacro.h` file at compile time. FreeRTOS calls the hardware-specific functions using `#define`'d functions declared in `portmacro.h`.

Let's look at an example of how FreeRTOS calls a hardware-dependent function. The hardware-independent file `tasks.c` frequently needs to enter a critical section of code to prevent preemption. Entering a critical section happens differently on different architectures, and the hardware-independent `tasks.c` does not want to have to understand the hardware-dependent details. So `tasks.c` calls the global macro `portENTER_CRITICAL()`, glad to be ignorant of how it actually works. Assuming we're using the IAR compiler on an ARM Cortex-M3 chip, FreeRTOS is built with the file `FreeRTOS/Source/portable/IAR/ARM_CM3/portmacro.h` which defines `portENTER_CRITICAL()` like this:

```
#define portENTER_CRITICAL()    vPortEnterCritical()
```

`vPortEnterCritical()` is actually defined in `FreeRTOS/Source/portable/IAR/ARM_CM3/port.c`. The `port.c` file is hardware-dependent, and contains code that understands the IAR compiler and the Cortex-M3 chip. `vPortEnterCritical()` enters the critical section using this hardware-specific knowledge and returns to the hardware-independent `tasks.c`.

The `portmacro.h` file also defines an architecture's basic data types. Data types for basic integer variables, pointers, and the system timer tick data type are defined like this for the IAR compiler on ARM Cortex-M3 chips:

```
#define portBASE_TYPE  long                 // Basic integer variable type
#define portSTACK_TYPE unsigned long        // Pointers to memory locations
typedef unsigned portLONG portTickType;     // The system timer tick type
```

This method of using data types and functions through thin layers of `#define`s may seem a bit complicated, but it allows FreeRTOS to be recompiled for a completely different system architecture by changing only the hardware-dependent files. And if you want to run FreeRTOS on an architecture it doesn't currently support, you only have to implement the hardware-dependent functionality which is much smaller than the hardware-independent part of FreeRTOS.

As we've seen, FreeRTOS implements hardware-dependent functionality with C preprocessor #define macros. FreeRTOS also uses #define for plenty of hardware-independent code. For non-embedded applications this frequent use of #define is a cardinal sin, but in many smaller embedded systems the overhead for calling a function is not worth the advantages that "real" functions offer.

3.3 Scheduling Tasks: A Quick Overview

Task Priorities and the Ready List

Each task has a user-assigned priority between 0 (the lowest priority) and the compile-time value of configMAX_PRIORITIES-1 (the highest priority). For instance, if configMAX_PRIORITIES is set to 5, then FreeRTOS will use 5 priority levels: 0 (lowest priority), 1, 2, 3, and 4 (highest priority).

FreeRTOS uses a "ready list" to keep track of all tasks that are currently ready to run. It implements the ready list as an array of task lists like this:

```
static xList pxReadyTasksLists[ configMAX_PRIORITIES ];  /* Prioritised ready tasks. */
```

pxReadyTasksLists[0] is a list of all ready priority 0 tasks, pxReadyTasksLists[1] is a list of all ready priority 1 tasks, and so on, all the way up to pxReadyTasksLists[configMAX_PRIORITIES-1].

The System Tick

The heartbeat of a FreeRTOS system is called the system tick. FreeRTOS configures the system to generate a periodic tick interrupt. The user can configure the tick interrupt frequency, which is typically in the millisecond range. Every time the tick interrupt fires, the vTaskSwitchContext() function is called. vTaskSwitchContext() selects the highest-priority ready task and puts it in the pxCurrentTCB variable like this:

```
/* Find the highest-priority queue that contains ready tasks. */
while( listLIST_IS_EMPTY( &( pxReadyTasksLists[ uxTopReadyPriority ] ) ) )
{
    configASSERT( uxTopReadyPriority );
    --uxTopReadyPriority;
}

/* listGET_OWNER_OF_NEXT_ENTRY walks through the list, so the tasks of the same
priority get an equal share of the processor time. */
listGET_OWNER_OF_NEXT_ENTRY( pxCurrentTCB, &( pxReadyTasksLists[ uxTopReadyPriority ] ) );
```

Before the while loop starts, uxTopReadyPriority is guaranteed to be greater than or equal to the priority of the highest-priority ready task. The while() loop starts at priority level uxTopReadyPriority and walks down through the pxReadyTasksLists[] array to find the highest-priority level with ready tasks. listGET_OWNER_OF_NEXT_ENTRY() then grabs the next ready task from that priority level's ready list.

Now pxCurrentTCB points to the highest-priority task, and when vTaskSwitchContext() returns the hardware-dependent code starts running that task.

Those nine lines of code are the absolute heart of FreeRTOS. The other 8900+ lines of FreeRTOS are there to make sure those nine lines are all that's needed to keep the highest-priority task running.

Figure 3.2 is a high-level picture of what a ready list looks like. This example has three priority levels, with one priority 0 task, no priority 1 tasks, and three priority 2 tasks. This picture is accurate but not complete; it's missing a few details which we'll fill in later.

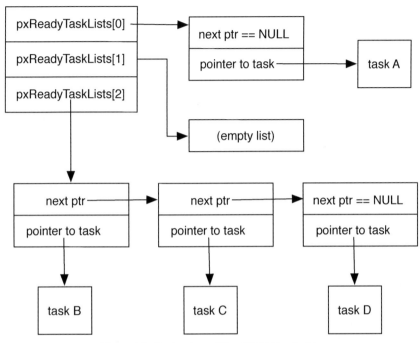

Figure 3.2: Basic view of FreeRTOS Ready List

Now that we have the high-level overview out of the way, let's dive in to the details. We'll look at the three main FreeRTOS data structures: tasks, lists, and queues.

3.4 Tasks

The main job of all operating systems is to run and coordinate user tasks. Like many operating systems, the basic unit of work in FreeRTOS is the task. FreeRTOS uses a Task Control Block (TCB) to represent each task.

Task Control Block (TCB)

The TCB is defined in `tasks.c` like this:

```
typedef struct tskTaskControlBlock
{
    volatile portSTACK_TYPE *pxTopOfStack;       /* Points to the location of
                                                    the last item placed on
                                                    the tasks stack. THIS
                                                    MUST BE THE FIRST MEMBER
```

```
                                                            OF THE STRUCT. */

    xListItem     xGenericListItem;                   /* List item used to place
                                                         the TCB in ready and
                                                         blocked queues. */

    xListItem     xEventListItem;                     /* List item used to place
                                                         the TCB in event lists.*/

    unsigned portBASE_TYPE uxPriority;                /* The priority of the task
                                                         priority. */

    portSTACK_TYPE *pxStack;                          /* Points to the start of
                                                         the stack. */

    signed char   pcTaskName[ configMAX_TASK_NAME_LEN ];  /* Descriptive name given
                                                         to the task when created.
                                                         Facilitates debugging
                                                         only. */

    #if ( portSTACK_GROWTH > 0 )
      portSTACK_TYPE *pxEndOfStack;                   /* Used for stack overflow
                                                         checking on architectures
                                                         where the stack grows up
                                                         from low memory. */
    #endif

    #if ( configUSE_MUTEXES == 1 )
      unsigned portBASE_TYPE uxBasePriority;          /* The priority last
                                                         assigned to the task -
                                                         used by the priority
                                                         inheritance mechanism. */
    #endif

} tskTCB;
```

The TCB stores the address of the stack start address in pxStack and the current top of stack in pxTopOfStack. It also stores a pointer to the end of the stack in pxEndOfStack to check for stack overflow if the stack grows "up" to higher addresses. If the stack grows "down" to lower addresses then stack overflow is checked by comparing the current top of stack against the start of stack memory in pxStack.

The TCB stores the initial priority of the task in uxPriority and uxBasePriority. A task is given a priority when it is created, and a task's priority can be changed. If FreeRTOS implements priority inheritance then it uses uxBasePriority to remember the original priority while the task is temporarily elevated to the "inherited" priority. (See the discussion about mutexes below for more on priority inheritance.)

Each task has two list items for use in FreeRTOS's various scheduling lists. When a task is inserted into a list FreeRTOS doesn't insert a pointer directly to the TCB. Instead, it inserts a pointer to either the TCB's xGenericListItem or xEventListItem. These xListItem variables let the FreeRTOS lists be smarter than if they merely held a pointer to the TCB. We'll see an example of this when we discuss lists later.

A task can be in one of four states: running, ready to run, suspended, or blocked. You might expect each task to have a variable that tells FreeRTOS what state it's in, but it doesn't. Instead, FreeRTOS tracks task state implicitly by putting tasks in the appropriate list: ready list, suspended list, etc. The presence of a task in a particular list indicates the task's state. As a task changes from one state to another, FreeRTOS simply moves it from one list to another.

Task Setup

We've already touched on how a task is selected and scheduled with the `pxReadyTasksLists` array; now let's look at how a task is initially created. A task is created when the `xTaskCreate()` function is called. FreeRTOS uses a newly allocated TCB object to store the name, priority, and other details for a task, then allocates the amount of stack the user requests (assuming there's enough memory available) and remembers the start of the stack memory in TCB's `pxStack` member.

The stack is initialized to look as if the new task is already running and was interrupted by a context switch. This way the scheduler can treat newly created tasks exactly the same way as it treats tasks that have been running for a while; the scheduler doesn't need any special case code for handling new tasks.

The way that a task's stack is made to look like it was interrupted by a context switch depends on the architecture FreeRTOS is running on, but this ARM Cortex-M3 processor's implementation is a good example:

```
unsigned int *pxPortInitialiseStack( unsigned int *pxTopOfStack,
                                     pdTASK_CODE pxCode,
                                     void *pvParameters )
{
  /* Simulate the stack frame as it would be created by a context switch interrupt. */
  pxTopOfStack--; /* Offset added to account for the way the MCU uses the stack on
                     entry/exit of interrupts. */
  *pxTopOfStack = portINITIAL_XPSR; /* xPSR */
  pxTopOfStack--;
  *pxTopOfStack = ( portSTACK_TYPE ) pxCode;  /* PC */
  pxTopOfStack--;
  *pxTopOfStack = 0;  /* LR */
  pxTopOfStack -= 5;  /* R12, R3, R2 and R1. */
  *pxTopOfStack = ( portSTACK_TYPE ) pvParameters;  /* R0 */
  pxTopOfStack -= 8;  /* R11, R10, R9, R8, R7, R6, R5 and R4. */

  return pxTopOfStack;
}
```

The ARM Cortex-M3 processor pushes registers on the stack when a task is interrupted. `pxPortInitialiseStack()` modifies the stack to look like the registers were pushed even though the task hasn't actually started running yet. Known values are stored to the stack for the ARM registers xPSR, PC, LR, and R0. The remaining registers R1 – R12 get stack space allocated for them by decrementing the top of stack pointer, but no specific data is stored in the stack for those registers. The ARM architecture says that those registers are undefined at reset, so a (non-buggy) program will not rely on a known value.

After the stack is prepared, the task is almost ready to run. First though, FreeRTOS disables interrupts: We're about to start mucking with the ready lists and other scheduler structures and we don't want anyone else changing them underneath us.

If this is the first task to ever be created, FreeRTOS initializes the scheduler's task lists. Free-RTOS's scheduler has an array of ready lists, `pxReadyTasksLists[]`, which has one ready list for each possible priority level. FreeRTOS also has a few other lists for tracking tasks that have been suspended, killed, and delayed. These are all initialized now as well.

After any first-time initialization is done, the new task is added to the ready list at its specified priority level. Interrupts are re-enabled and new task creation is complete.

3.5 Lists

After tasks, the most used FreeRTOS data structure is the list. FreeRTOS uses its list structure to keep track of tasks for scheduling, and also to implement queues.

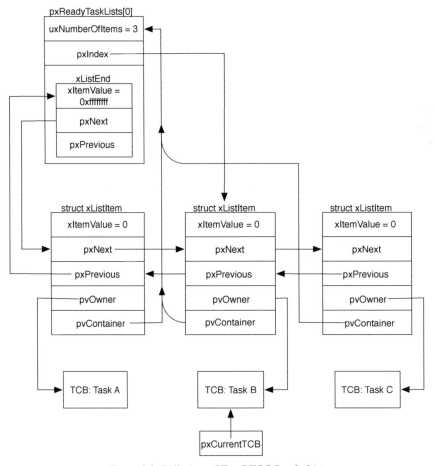

Figure 3.3: Full view of FreeRTOS Ready List

The FreeRTOS list is a standard circular doubly linked list with a couple of interesting additions. Here's a list element:

```
struct xLIST_ITEM
{
    portTickType xItemValue;            /* The value being listed.  In most cases
                                           this is used to sort the list in
```

46 FreeRTOS

```
                                                       descending order. */
    volatile struct xLIST_ITEM * pxNext;               /* Pointer to the next xListItem in the
                                                          list. */
    volatile struct xLIST_ITEM * pxPrevious;           /* Pointer to the previous xListItem in
                                                          the list. */
    void * pvOwner;                                    /* Pointer to the object (normally a TCB)
                                                          that contains the list item.  There is
                                                          therefore a two-way link between the
                                                          object containing the list item and
                                                          the list item itself. */
    void * pvContainer;                                /* Pointer to the list in which this list
                                                          item is placed (if any). */
};
```

Each list element holds a number, xItemValue, that is the usually the priority of the task being tracked or a timer value for event scheduling. Lists are kept in high-to-low priority order, meaning that the highest-priority xItemValue (the largest number) is at the front of the list and the lowest priority xItemValue (the smallest number) is at the end of the list.

The pxNext and pxPrevious pointers are standard linked list pointers. pvOwner is a pointer to the owner of the list element. This is usually a pointer to a task's TCB object. pvOwner is used to make task switching fast in vTaskSwitchContext(): once the highest-priority task's list element is found in pxReadyTasksLists[], that list element's pvOwner pointer leads us directly to the TCB needed to schedule the task.

pvContainer points to the list that this item is in. It is used to quickly determine if a list item is in a particular list. Each list element can be put in a list, which is defined as:

```
typedef struct xLIST
{
    volatile unsigned portBASE_TYPE uxNumberOfItems;
    volatile xListItem * pxIndex;                      /* Used to walk through the list.  Points to
                                                          the last item returned by a call to
                                                          pvListGetOwnerOfNextEntry (). */
    volatile xMiniListItem xListEnd;                   /* List item that contains the maximum
                                                          possible item value, meaning it is always
                                                          at the end of the list and is therefore
                                                          used as a marker. */
} xList;
```

The size of a list at any time is stored in uxNumberOfItems, for fast list-size operations. All new lists are initialized to contain a single element: the xListEnd element. xListEnd.xItemValue is a sentinel value which is equal to the largest value for the xItemValue variable: 0xffff when portTickType is a 16-bit value and 0xffffffff when portTickType is a 32-bit value. Other list elements may also have the same value; the insertion algorithm ensures that xListEnd is always the last item in the list.

Since lists are sorted high-to-low, the xListEnd element is used as a marker for the start of the list. And since the list is circular, this xListEnd element is also a marker for the end of the list.

Most "traditional" list accesses you've used probably do all of their work within a single for() loop or function call like this:

```
for (listPtr = listStart; listPtr != NULL; listPtr = listPtr->next) {
  // Do something with listPtr here...
}
```

FreeRTOS frequently needs to access a list across multiple for() and while() loops as well as function calls, and so it uses list functions that manipulate the pxIndex pointer to walk the list. The list function listGET_OWNER_OF_NEXT_ENTRY() does pxIndex = pxIndex->pxNext; and returns pxIndex. (Of course it does the proper end-of-list-wraparound detection too.) This way the list itself is responsible for keeping track of "where you are" while walking it using pxIndex, allowing the rest of FreeRTOS to not worry about it.

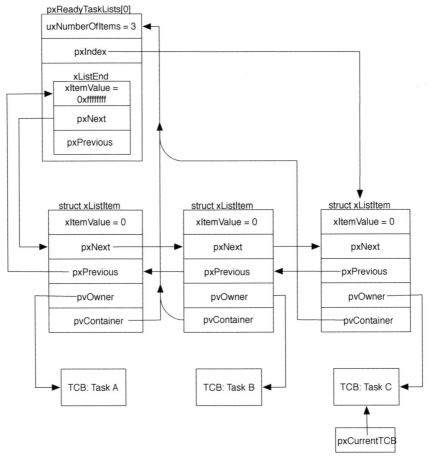

Figure 3.4: Full view of FreeRTOS Ready List after a system timer tick

The pxReadyTasksLists[] list manipulation done in vTaskSwitchContext() is a good example of how pxIndex is used. Let's assume we have only one priority level, priority 0, and there are three tasks at that priority level. This is similar to the basic ready list picture we looked at earlier, but this time we'll include all of the data structures and fields.

As you can see in Figure 3.3, pxCurrentTCB indicates that we're currently running Task B. The next time vTaskSwitchContext() runs, it calls listGET_OWNER_OF_NEXT_ENTRY() to get the next task to run. This function uses pxIndex->pxNext to figure out the next task is Task C, and now pxIndex points to Task C's list element and pxCurrentTCB points to Task C's TCB, as shown in Figure 3.4.

Note that each struct xListItem object is actually the xGenericListItem object from the associated TCB.

3.6 Queues

FreeRTOS allows tasks to communicate and synchronize with each other using queues. Interrupt service routines (ISRs) also use queues for communication and synchronization.

The basic queue data structure is:

```
typedef struct QueueDefinition
{
  signed char *pcHead;                  /* Points to the beginning of the queue
                                           storage area. */
  signed char *pcTail;                  /* Points to the byte at the end of the
                                           queue storage area. One more byte is
                                           allocated than necessary to store the
                                           queue items; this is used as a marker. */
  signed char *pcWriteTo;               /* Points to the free next place in the
                                           storage area. */
  signed char *pcReadFrom;              /* Points to the last place that a queued
                                           item was read from. */

  xList xTasksWaitingToSend;            /* List of tasks that are blocked waiting
                                           to post onto this queue.  Stored in
                                           priority order. */
  xList xTasksWaitingToReceive;         /* List of tasks that are blocked waiting
                                           to read from this queue. Stored in
                                           priority order. */

  volatile unsigned portBASE_TYPE uxMessagesWaiting; /* The number of items currently
                                           in the queue. */
  unsigned portBASE_TYPE uxLength;      /* The length of the queue
                                           defined as the number of
                                           items it will hold, not the
                                           number of bytes. */
  unsigned portBASE_TYPE uxItemSize;    /* The size of each items that
                                           the queue will hold. */
} xQUEUE;
```

This is a fairly standard queue with head and tail pointers, as well as pointers to keep track of where we've just read from and written to.

When creating a queue, the user specifies the length of the queue and the size of each item to be tracked by the queue. pcHead and pcTail are used to keep track of the queue's internal storage. Adding an item into a queue does a deep copy of the item into the queue's internal storage.

FreeRTOS makes a deep copy instead of storing a pointer to the item because the lifetime of the item inserted may be much shorter than the lifetime of the queue. For instance, consider a queue of simple integers inserted and removed using local variables across several function calls. If the queue stored pointers to the integers' local variables, the pointers would be invalid as soon as the integers' local variables went out of scope and the local variables' memory was used for some new value.

The user chooses what to queue. The user can queue copies of items if the items are small, like in the simple integer example in the previous paragraph, or the user can queue pointers to the items if the items are large. Note that in both cases FreeRTOS does a deep copy: if the user chooses to queue copies of items then the queue stores a deep copy of each item; if the user chooses to queue pointers then the queue stores a deep copy of the pointer. Of course, if the user stores pointers in the queue then the user is responsible for managing the memory associated with the pointers. The queue doesn't care what data you're storing in it, it just needs to know the data's size.

FreeRTOS supports blocking and non-blocking queue insertions and removals. Non-blocking operations return immediately with a "Did the queue insertion work?" or "Did the queue removal work?" status. Blocking operations are specified with a timeout. A task can block indefinitely or for a limited amount of time.

A blocked task—call it Task A—will remain blocked as long as its insert/remove operation cannot complete and its timeout (if any) has not expired. If an interrupt or another task modifies the queue so that Task A's operation could complete, Task A will be unblocked. If Task A's queue operation is still possible by the time it actually runs then Task A will complete its queue operation and return "success". However, by the time Task A actually runs, it is possible that a higher-priority task or interrupt has performed yet another operation on the queue that prevents Task A from performing its operation. In this case Task A will check its timeout and either resume blocking if the timeout hasn't expired, or return with a queue operation "failed" status.

It's important to note that the rest of the system keeps going while a task is blocking on a queue; other tasks and interrupts continue to run. This way the blocked task doesn't waste CPU cycles that could be used productively by other tasks and interrupts.

FreeRTOS uses the xTasksWaitingToSend list to keep track of tasks that are blocking on inserting into a queue. Each time an element is removed from a queue the xTasksWaitingToSend list is checked. If a task is waiting in that list the task is unblocked.

Similarly, xTasksWaitingToReceive keeps track of tasks that are blocking on removing from a queue. Each time a new element is inserted into a queue the xTasksWaitingToReceive list is checked. If a task is waiting in that list the task is unblocked.

Semaphores and Mutexes

FreeRTOS uses its queues for communication between and within tasks. FreeRTOS also uses its queues to implement semaphores and mutexes.

What's The Difference?

Semaphores and mutexes may sound like the same thing, but they're not. FreeRTOS implements them similarly, but they're intended to be used in different ways. How should they be used differently? Embedded systems guru Michael Barr says it best in his article, "Mutexes and Semaphores Demystified"[2]:

---

[2] http://www.barrgroup.com/Embedded-Systems/How-To/RTOS-Mutex-Semaphore

The correct use of a semaphore is for signaling from one task to another. A mutex is meant to be taken and released, always in that order, by each task that uses the shared resource it protects. By contrast, tasks that use semaphores either signal ["send" in FreeRTOS terms] or wait ["receive" in FreeRTOS terms] - not both.

A mutex is used to protect a shared resource. A task acquires a mutex, uses the shared resource, then releases the mutex. No task can acquire a mutex while the mutex is being held by another task. This guarantees that only one task is allowed to use a shared resource at a time.

Semaphores are used by one task to signal another task. To quote Barr's article:

> For example, Task 1 may contain code to post (i.e., signal or increment) a particular semaphore when the "power" button is pressed and Task 2, which wakes the display, pends on that same semaphore. In this scenario, one task is the producer of the event signal; the other the consumer.

If you're at all in doubt about semaphores and mutexes, please check out Michael's article.

Implementation

FreeRTOS implements an N-element semaphore as a queue that can hold N items. It doesn't store any actual data for the queue items; the semaphore just cares how many queue entries are currently occupied, which is tracked in the queue's uxMessagesWaiting field. It's doing "pure synchronization", as the FreeRTOS header file semphr.h calls it. Therefore the queue has a item size of zero bytes (uxItemSize == 0). Each semaphore access increments or decrements the uxMessagesWaiting field; no item or data copying is needed.

Like a semaphore, a mutex is also implemented as a queue, but several of the xQUEUE struct fields are overloaded using #defines:

```
/* Effectively make a union out of the xQUEUE structure. */
#define uxQueueType        pcHead
#define pxMutexHolder      pcTail
```

Since a mutex doesn't store any data in the queue, it doesn't need any internal storage, and so the pcHead and pcTail fields aren't needed. FreeRTOS sets the uxQueueType field (really the pcHead field) to 0 to note that this queue is being used for a mutex. FreeRTOS uses the overloaded pcTail fields to implement priority inheritance for mutexes.

In case you're not familiar with priority inheritance, I'll quote Michael Barr again to define it, this time from his article, "Introduction to Priority Inversion"[3]:

> [Priority inheritance] mandates that a lower-priority task inherit the priority of any higher-priority task pending on a resource they share. This priority change should take place as soon as the high-priority task begins to pend; it should end when the resource is released.

FreeRTOS implements priority inheritance using the pxMutexHolder field (which is really just the overloaded-by-#define pcTail field). FreeRTOS records the task that holds a mutex in the pxMutexHolder field. When a higher-priority task is found to be waiting on a mutex currently taken by a lower-priority task, FreeRTOS "upgrades" the lower-priority task to the priority of the higher-priority task until the mutex is available again.

---

[3] http://www.eetimes.com/discussion/beginner-s-corner/4023947/Introduction-to-Priority-Inversion

3.7 Conclusion

We've completed our look at the FreeRTOS architecture. Hopefully you now have a good feel for how FreeRTOS's tasks run and communicate. And if you've never looked at any OS's internals before, I hope you now have a basic idea of how they work.

Obviously this chapter did not cover all of FreeRTOS's architecture. Notably, I didn't mention memory allocation, ISRs, debugging, or MPU support. This chapter also did not discuss how to set up or use FreeRTOS. Richard Barry has written an excellent book[4], *Using the FreeRTOS Real Time Kernel: A Practical Guide*, which discusses exactly that; I highly recommend it if you're going to use FreeRTOS.

3.8 Acknowledgements

I would like to thank Richard Barry for creating and maintaining FreeRTOS, and for choosing to make it open source. Richard was very helpful in writing this chapter, providing some FreeRTOS history as well as a very valuable technical review.

Thanks also to Amy Brown and Greg Wilson for pulling this whole AOSA thing together.

Last and most (the opposite of "not least"), thanks to my wife Sarah for sharing me with the research and writing for this chapter. Luckily she knew I was a geek when she married me!

---

[4]http://www.freertos.org/Documentation/FreeRTOS-documentation-and-book.html

[chapter 4]

GDB
Stan Shebs

GDB, the GNU Debugger, was among the first programs to be written for the Free Software Foundation, and it has been a staple of free and open source software systems ever since. Originally designed as a plain Unix source-level debugger, it has since been expanded to a wide range of uses, including use with many embedded systems, and has grown from a few thousand lines of C to over half a million.

This chapter will delve into the overall internal structure of GDB, showing how it has gradually developed as new user needs and new features have come in over time.

4.1 The Goal

GDB is designed to be a symbolic debugger for programs written in compiled imperative languages such as C, C++, Ada, and Fortran. Using its original command-line interface, a typical usage looks something like this:

```
% gdb myprog
[...]
(gdb) break buggy_function
Breakpoint 1 at 0x12345678: file myprog.c, line 232.
(gdb) run 45 92
Starting program: myprog
Breakpoint 1, buggy_function (arg1=45, arg2=92) at myprog.c:232
232     result = positive_variable * arg1 + arg2;
(gdb) print positive_variable
$$1 = -34
(gdb)
```

GDB shows something that is not right, the developer says "aha" or "hmmm", and then has to decide both what the mistake is and how to fix it.

The important point for design is that a tool like GDB is basically an interactive toolbox for poking around in a program, and as such it needs to be responsive to an unpredictable series of requests. In addition, it will be used with programs that have been optimized by the compiler, and programs that exploit every hardware option for performance, so it needs to have detailed knowledge down to the lowest levels of a system.

GDB also needs to be able to debug programs compiled by different compilers (not just the GNU C compiler), to debug programs compiled years earlier by long-obsolete versions of compilers, and to debug programs whose symbolic info is missing, out of date, or simply incorrect; so, another design consideration is that GDB should continue to work and be useful even if data about the program is missing, or corrupted, or simply incomprehensible.

The following sections assume a passing familiarity with using GDB from the command line. If you're new to GDB, give it a try and peruse the manual.[SPS+00]

4.2 Origins of GDB

GDB is an old program. It came into existence around 1985, written by Richard Stallman along with GCC, GNU Emacs, and other early components of GNU. (In those days, there were no public source control repositories, and much of the detailed development history is now lost.)

The earliest readily available releases are from 1988, and comparison with present-day sources shows that only a handful of lines bear much resemblance; nearly all of GDB has been rewritten at least once. Another striking thing about early versions of GDB is that the original goals were rather modest, and much of the work since then has been extension of GDB into environments and usages that were not part of the original plan.

4.3 Block Diagram

At the largest scale, GDB can be said to have two sides to it:

1. The "symbol side" is concerned with symbolic information about the program. Symbolic information includes function and variable names and types, line numbers, machine register usage, and so on. The symbol side extracts symbolic information from the program's executable file, parses expressions, finds the memory address of a given line number, lists source code, and in general works with the program as the programmer wrote it.
2. The "target side" is concerned with the manipulation of the target system. It has facilities to start and stop the program, to read memory and registers, to modify them, to catch signals, and so on. The specifics of how this is done can vary drastically between systems; most Unix-type systems provide a special system call named `ptrace` that gives one process the ability to read and write the state of a different process. Thus, GDB's target side is mostly about making `ptrace` calls and interpreting the results. For cross-debugging an embedded system, however, the target side constructs message packets to send over a wire, and waits for response packets in return.

The two sides are somewhat independent of each other; you can look around your program's code, display variable types, etc., without actually running the program. Conversely, it is possible to do pure machine-language debugging even if no symbols are available.

In the middle, tying the two sides together, is the command interpreter and the main execution control loop.

4.4 Examples of Operation

To take a simple case of how it all ties together, consider the `print` command from above. The command interpreter finds the `print` command function, which parses the expression into a simple tree structure and then evaluates it by walking the tree. At some point the evaluator will consult the

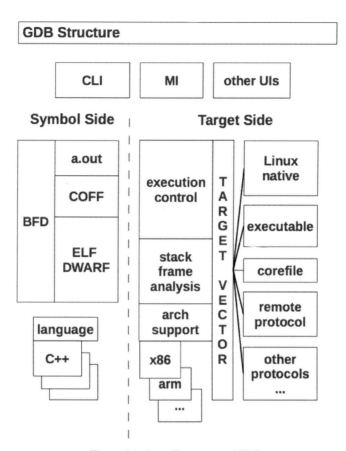

Figure 4.1: Overall structure of GDB

symbol table to find out that positive_variable is an integer global variable that is stored at, say, memory address 0x601028. It then calls a target-side function to read the four bytes of memory at that address, and hands the bytes to a formatting function that displays them as a decimal number.

To display source code and its compiled version, GDB does a combination of reads from the source file and the target system, then uses compiler-generated line number information to connect the two. In the example here, line 232 has the address 0x4004be, line 233 is at 0x4004ce, and so on.

```
[...]
232    result = positive_variable * arg1 + arg2;
0x4004be <+10>:   mov    0x200b64(%rip),%eax    # 0x601028 <positive_variable>
0x4004c4 <+16>:   imul   -0x14(%rbp),%eax
0x4004c8 <+20>:   add    -0x18(%rbp),%eax
0x4004cb <+23>:   mov    %eax,-0x4(%rbp)

233    return result;
0x4004ce <+26>:   mov    -0x4(%rbp),%eax
[...]
```

The single-stepping command `step` conceals a complicated dance going on behind the scenes. When the user asks to step to the next line in the program, the target side is asked to execute only a single instruction of the program and then stop it again (this is one of the things that `ptrace` can do). Upon being informed that the program has stopped, GDB asks for the program counter (PC) register (another target side operation) and then compares it with the range of addresses that the symbol side says is associated with the current line. If the PC is outside that range, then GDB leaves the program stopped, figures out the new source line, and reports that to the user. If the PC is still in the range of the current line, then GDB steps by another instruction and checks again, repeating until the PC gets to a different line. This basic algorithm has the advantage that it always does the right thing, whether the line has jumps, subroutine calls, etc., and does not require GDB to interpret all the details of the machine's instruction set. A disadvantage is that there are many interactions with the target for each single-step which, for some embedded targets, results in noticeably slow stepping.

4.5 Portability

As a program needing extensive access all the way down to the physical registers on a chip, GDB was designed from the beginning to be portable across a variety of systems. However, its portability strategy has changed considerably over the years.

Originally, GDB started out similar to the other GNU programs of the time; coded in a minimal common subset of C, and using a combination of preprocessor macros and Makefile fragments to adapt to a specific architecture and operating system. Although the stated goal of the GNU project was a self-contained "GNU operating system", bootstrapping would have to be done on a variety of existing systems; the Linux kernel was still years in the future. The `configure` shell script is the first key step of the process. It can do a variety of things, such as making a symbolic link from a system-specific file to a generic header name, or constructing files from pieces, more importantly the Makefile used to build the program.

Programs like GCC and GDB have additional portability needs over something like `cat` or `diff`, and over time, GDB's portability bits came to be separated into three classes, each with its own Makefile fragment and header file.

- "Host" definitions are for the machine that GDB itself runs on, and might include things like the sizes of the host's integer types. Originally done as human-written header files, it eventually occurred to people that they could be calculated by having `configure` run little test programs, using the same compiler that was going to be used to build the tool. This is what autoconf[aut12] is all about, and today nearly all GNU tools and many (if not most) Unix programs use `autoconf`-generated configure scripts.
- "Target" definitions are specific to the machine running the program being debugged. If the target is the same as the host, then we are doing "native" debugging, otherwise it is "cross" debugging, using some kind of wire connecting the two systems. Target definitions fall in turn into two main classes:
  - "Architecture" definitions: These define how to disassemble machine code, how to walk through the call stack, and which trap instruction to insert at breakpoints. Originally done with macros, they were migrated to regular C accessed by via "gdbarch" objects, described in more depth below.
  - "Native" definitions: These define the specifics of arguments to `ptrace` (which vary considerably between flavors of Unix), how to find shared libraries that have been loaded,

and so forth, which only apply to the native debugging case. Native definitions are a last holdout of 1980s-style macros, although most are now figured out using `autoconf`.

4.6 Data Structures

Before drilling down into the parts of GDB, let's take a look at the major data structures that GDB works with. As GDB is a C program, these are implemented as `structs` rather than as C++-style objects, but in most cases they are treated as objects, and here we follow GDBers' frequent practice in calling them objects.

Breakpoints

A breakpoint is the main kind of object that is directly accessible to the user. The user creates a breakpoint with the `break` command, whose argument specifies a *location*, which can be a function name, a source line number, or a machine address. GDB assigns a small positive integer to the breakpoint object, which the user subsequently uses to operate on the breakpoint. Within GDB, the breakpoint is a C `struct` with a number of fields. The location gets translated to a machine address, but is also saved in its original form, since the address may change and need recomputation, for instance if the program is recompiled and reloaded into a session.

Several kinds of breakpoint-like objects actually share the breakpoint `struct`, including watchpoints, catchpoints, and tracepoints. This helps ensure that creation, manipulation, and deletion facilities are consistently available.

The term "location" also refers to the memory addresses at which the breakpoint is to be installed. In the cases of inline functions and C++ templates, it may be that a single user-specified breakpoint may correspond to several addresses; for instance, each inlined copy of a function entails a separate location for a breakpoint that is set on a source line in the function's body.

Symbols and Symbol Tables

Symbol tables are a key data structure to GDB, and can be quite large, sometimes growing to occupy multiple gigabytes of RAM. To some extent, this is unavoidable; a large application in C++ can have millions of symbols in its own right, and it pulls in system header files which can have millions more symbols. Each local variable, each named type, each value of an enum—all of these are separate symbols.

GDB uses a number of tricks to reduce symbol table space, such as partial symbol tables (more about those later), bit fields in `structs`, etc.

In addition to symbol tables that basically map character strings to address and type information, GDB builds line tables that support lookup in two directions; from source lines to addresses, and then from addresses back to source lines. (For instance, the single-stepping algorithm described earlier crucially depends on the address-to-source mapping.)

Stack Frames

The procedural languages for which GDB was designed share a common runtime architecture, in that function calls cause the program counter to be pushed on a stack, along with some combination of function arguments and local arguments. The assemblage is called a *stack frame*, or "frame" for short, and at any moment in a program's execution, the stack consists of a sequence of frames chained together. The details of a stack frame vary radically from one chip architecture to the next, and is also dependent on the operating system, compiler, and optimization options.

A port of GDB to a new chip may need a considerable volume of code to analyze the stack, as programs (especially buggy ones, which are the ones debugger users are mostly interested in) can stop anywhere, with frames possibly incomplete, or partly overwritten by the program. Worse, constructing a stack frame for each function call slows down the application, and a good optimizing compiler will take every opportunity to simplify stack frames, or even eliminate them altogether, such as for tail calls.

The result of GDB's chip-specific stack analysis is recorded in a series of frame objects. Originally GDB kept track of frames by using the literal value of a fixed-frame pointer register. This approach breaks down for inlined function calls and other kinds of compiler optimizations, and starting in 2002, GDBers introduced explicit frame objects that recorded what had been figured out about each frame, and were linked together, mirroring the program's stack frames.

Expressions

As with stack frames, GDB assumes a degree of commonality among the expressions of the various languages it supports, and represents them all as a tree structure built out of node objects. The set of node types is effectively a union of all the types of expressions possible in all the different languages; unlike in the compiler, there is no reason to prevent the user from trying to subtract a Fortran variable from a C variable—perhaps the difference of the two is an obvious power of two, and that gives us the "aha" moment.

Values

The result of evaluation may itself be more complex than an integer or memory address, and GDB also retains evaluation results in a numbered history list, which can then be referred to in later expressions. To make all this work, GDB has a data structure for values. Value structs have a number of fields recording various properties; important ones include an indication of whether the value is an r-value or l-value (l-values can be assigned to, as in C), and whether the value is to be constructed lazily.

4.7 The Symbol Side

The symbol side of GDB is mainly responsible for reading the executable file, extracting any symbolic information it finds, and building it into a symbol table.

The reading process starts with the BFD library. BFD is a sort of universal library for handling binary and object files; running on any host, it can read and write the original Unix a.out format, COFF (used on System V Unix and MS Windows), ELF (modern Unix, GNU/Linux, and most embedded systems), and some other file formats. Internally, the library has a complicated structure of C macros that expand into code incorporating the arcane details of object file formats for dozens of different systems. Introduced in 1990, BFD is also used by the GNU assembler and linker, and its ability to produce object files for any target is key to cross-development using GNU tools. (Porting BFD is also a key first step in porting the tools to a new target.)

GDB only uses BFD to read files, using it to pull blocks of data from the executable file into GDB's memory. GDB then has two levels of reader functions of its own. The first level is for basic symbols, or "minimal symbols", which are just the names that the linker needs to do its work. These are strings with addresses and not much else; we assume that addresses in text sections are functions, addresses in data sections are data, and so forth.

The second level is detailed symbolic information, which typically has its own format different from the basic executable file format; for instance, information in the DWARF debug format is contained in specially named sections of an ELF file. By contrast, the old stabs debug format of Berkeley Unix used specially flagged symbols stored in the general symbol table.

The code for reading symbolic information is somewhat tedious, as the different symbolic formats encode every kind of type information that could be in a source program, but each goes about it in its own idiosyncratic way. A GDB reader just walks through the format, constructing GDB symbols that we think correspond to what the symbolic format intends.

Partial Symbol Tables

For a program of significant size (such as Emacs or Firefox), construction of the symbol table can take quite a while, maybe even several minutes. Measurements consistently show that the time is *not* in file reading as one might expect, but in the in-memory construction of GDB symbols. There are literally millions of small interconnected objects involved, and the time adds up.

Most of the symbolic information will never be looked at in a session, since it is local to functions that the user may never examine. So, when GDB first pulls in a program's symbols, it does a cursory scan through the symbolic information, looking for just the globally visible symbols and recording only them in the symbol table. Complete symbolic info for a function or method is filled in only if the user stops inside it.

Partial symbol tables allow GDB to start up in only a few seconds, even for large programs. (Shared library symbols are also dynamically loaded, but the process is rather different. Typically GDB uses a system-specific technique to be notified when the library is loaded, then builds a symbol table with functions at the addresses that were decided on by the dynamic linker.)

Language Support

Source language support mainly consists of expression parsing and value printing. The details of expression parsing are left up to each language, but in the general the parser is based on a Yacc grammar fed by a hand-crafted lexical analyzer. In keeping with GDB's goal of providing more flexibility to the interactive user, the parser is not expected to be especially stringent; for instance, if it can guess at a reasonable type for an expression, it will simply assume that type, rather than require the user to add a cast or type conversion.

Since the parser need not handle statements or type declarations, it is much simpler than the full language parser. Similarly, for printing, there are just a handful of types of values that need to be displayed, and oftentimes the language-specific print function can call out to generic code to finish the job.

4.8 Target Side

The target side is all about manipulation of program execution and raw data. In a sense, the target side is a complete low-level debugger; if you are content to step by instructions and dump raw memory, you can use GDB without needing any symbols at all. (You may end up operating in this mode anyway, if the program happens to stop in a library whose symbols have been stripped out.)

Target Vectors and the Target Stack

Originally the target side of GDB was composed of a handful of platform-specific files that handled the details of calling `ptrace`, launching executables, and so on. This is not sufficiently flexible for long-running debugging sessions, in which the user might switch from local to remote debugging, switch from files to core dumps to live programs, attach and detach, etc., so in 1990 John Gilmore redesigned the target side of GDB to send all target-specific operations through the *target vector*, which is basically a class of objects, each of which defines the the specifics of a type of target system. Each target vector is implemented as a structure of several dozen function pointers (often called "methods"), whose purposes range from the reading and writing of memory and registers, to resuming program execution, to setting parameters for the handling of shared libraries. There are about 40 target vectors in GDB, ranging from the well-used target vector for Linux to obscure vectors such as the one that operates a Xilinx MicroBlaze. Core dump support uses a target vector that gets data by reading a corefile, and there is another target vector that reads data from the executable.

It is often useful to blend methods from several target vectors. Consider the printing of an initialized global variable on Unix; before the program starts running, printing the variable should work, but at that point there is no process to read, and bytes need to come from the executable's `.data` section. So, GDB uses the target vector for executables and reads from the binary file. But while the program is running, the bytes should instead come from the process's address space. So, GDB has a "target stack" where the target vector for live processes is pushed on top of the executable's target vector when the process starts running, and is popped when it exits.

In reality, the target stack turns out not to be quite as stack-like as one might think. Target vectors are not really orthogonal to each other; if you have both an executable and a live process in the session, while it makes sense to have the live process's methods override the executable's methods, it almost never makes sense to do the reverse. So GDB has ended up with a notion of a *stratum* in which "process-like" target vectors are all at one stratum, while "file-like" target vectors get assigned to a lower stratum, and target vectors can get inserted as well as pushed and popped.

(Although GDB maintainers don't like the target stack much, no one has proposed—or prototyped— any better alternative.)

Gdbarch

As a program that works directly with the instructions of a CPU, GDB needs in-depth knowledge about the details of the chip. It needs to know about all the registers, the sizes of the different kinds of data, the size and shape of the address space, how the calling convention works, what instruction will cause a trap exception, and so on. GDB's code for all this typically ranges from 1,000 to over 10,000 lines of C, depending on the architecture's complexity.

Originally this was handled using target-specific preprocessor macros, but as the debugger became more sophisticated, these got larger and larger, and over time long macro definitions were made into regular C functions called from the macros. While this helped, it did not help much with architectural variants (ARM vs. Thumb, 32-bit vs. 64-bit versions of MIPS or x86, etc.), and worse, multiple-architecture designs were on the horizon, for which macros would not work at all. In 1995,

I proposed solving this with an object-based design, and starting in 1998 Cygnus Solutions[1] funded Andrew Cagney to start the changeover. It took several years and contributions from dozens of hackers to finish the job, affecting perhaps 80,000 lines of code in all.

The introduced constructs are called gdbarch objects, and at this point may contain as many as 130 methods and variables defining a target architecture, although a simple target might only need a dozen or so of these.

To get a sense of how the old and new ways compare, see the declaration that x86 long doubles are 96 bits in size from gdb/config/i386/tm-i386.h, circa 2002:

```
#define TARGET_LONG_DOUBLE_BIT 96
```

and from gdb/i386-tdep.c, in 2012:

```
i386_gdbarch_init( [...] )
{
  [...]

  set_gdbarch_long_double_bit (gdbarch, 96);

  [...]
}
```

Execution Control

The heart of GDB is its execution control loop. We touched on it earlier when describing single-stepping over a line; the algorithm entailed looping over multiple instructions until finding one associated with a different source line. The loop is called wait_for_inferior, or "wfi" for short.

Conceptually it is inside the main command loop, and is only entered for commands that cause the program to resume execution. When the user types continue or step and then waits while nothing seems to be happening, GDB may in fact be quite busy. In addition to the single-stepping loop mentioned above, the program may be hitting trap instructions and reporting the exception to GDB. If the exception is due to the trap being a breakpoint inserted by GDB, it then tests the breakpoint's condition, and if false, it removes the trap, single-steps the original instruction, re-inserts the trap, and then lets the program resume. Similarly, if a signal is raised, GDB may choose to ignore it, or handle it one of several ways specified in advance.

All of this activity is managed by wait_for_inferior. Originally this was a simple loop, waiting for the target to stop and then deciding what to do about it, but as ports to various systems needed special handling, it grew to a thousand lines, with goto statements criss-crossing it for poorly understood reasons. For instance, with the proliferation of Unix variants, there was no one person who understood all their fine points, nor did we have access to all of them for regression testing, so there was a strong incentive to modify the code in a way that exactly preserved behavior for existing ports—and a goto skipping over part of the loop was an all-too-easy tactic.

The single big loop was also a problem for any kind of asynchronous handling or debugging of threaded programs, in which the user wants to start and stop a single thread while allowing the rest of the program to continue running.

The conversion to an event-oriented model took several years. I broke up wait_for_inferior in 1999, introducing an execution control state structure to replace the pile of local and global variables,

---

[1]Cygnus Solutions was a company founded in 1989 to provide commercial support for free software. It was acquired in 2000 by Red Hat.

and converting the tangle of jumps into smaller independent functions. At the same time Elena Zannoni and others introduced event queues that included both input from the user and notifications from the inferior.

The Remote Protocol

Although GDB's target vector architecture allows for a broad variety of ways to control a program running on a different computer, we have a single preferred protocol. It does not have a distinguishing name, and is typically called just the "remote protocol", "GDB remote protocol", "remote serial protocol" (abbreviating to "RSP"), "remote.c protocol" (after the source file that implements it), or sometimes the "stub protocol", referring to the target's implementation of the protocol.

The basic protocol is simple, reflecting the desire to have it work on small embedded systems of the 1980s, whose memories were measured in kilobytes. For instance, the protocol packet $g requests all registers, and expects a reply consisting of all the bytes of all the registers, all run together—the assumption being that their number, size, and order will match what GDB knows about.

The protocol expects a single reply to each packet sent, and assumes the connection is reliable, adding only a checksum to packets sent (so $g is really sent as $g#67 over the wire).

Although there are only a handful of required packet types (corresponding to the half-dozen target vector methods that are most important), scores of additional optional packets have been added over the years, to support everything from hardware breakpoints, to tracepoints, to shared libraries.

On the target itself, the implementation of the remote protocol can take a wide variety of forms. The protocol is fully documented in the GDB manual, which means that it is possible to write an implementation that is not encumbered with a GNU license, and indeed many equipment manufacturers have incorporated code that speaks the GDB remote protocol, both in the lab and in the field. Cisco's IOS, which runs much of their networking equipment, is one well-known example.

A target's implementation of the protocol is often referred to as a "debugging stub", or just "stub", connoting that it is not expected to do very much work on its own. The GDB sources include a few example stubs, which are typically about 1,000 lines of low-level C. On a totally bare board with no OS, the stub must install its own handlers for hardware exceptions, most importantly to catch trap instructions. It will also need serial driver code if the hardware link is a serial line. The actual protocol handling is simple, since all the required packets are single characters that can be decoded with a switch statement.

Another approach to remote protocol is to build a "sprite" that interfaces between GDB and dedicated debugging hardware, including JTAG devices, "wigglers", etc. Oftentimes these devices have a library that must run on the computer that is physically connected to a target board, and often the library API is not architecturally compatible with GDB's internals. So, while configurations of GDB have called hardware control libraries directly, it has proven simpler to run the sprite as an independent program that understands remote protocol and translates the packets into device library calls.

GDBserver

The GDB sources do include one complete and working implementation of the target side of the remote protocol: GDBserver. GDBserver is a *native* program that runs under the target's operating system, and controls other programs on the target OS using its native debugging support, in response to packets received via remote protocol. In other words, it acts as a sort of proxy for native debugging.

GDBserver doesn't do anything that native GDB can't do; if your target system can run GDBserver, then theoretically it can run GDB. However, GDBserver is 10 times smaller and doesn't need to manage symbol tables, so it is very convenient for embedded GNU/Linux usages and the like.

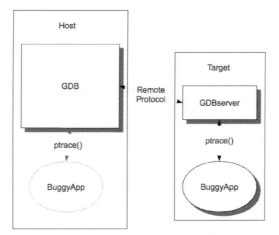

Figure 4.2: GDBserver

GDB and GDBserver share some code, but while it is an obvious idea to encapsulate OS-specific process control, there are practical difficulties with separating out tacit dependencies in native GDB, and the transition has gone slowly.

4.9 Interfaces to GDB

GDB is fundamentally a command-line debugger. Over time people have tried various schemes to make it into a graphical windowed debugger but, despite all the time and effort, none of these are universally accepted.

Command-Line Interface

The command-line interface uses the standard GNU library `readline` to handle the character-by-character interaction with the user. Readline takes care of things like line editing and command completion; the user can do things like use cursor keys to go back in a line and fix a character.

GDB then takes the command returned by `readline` and looks it up using a cascaded structure of command tables, where each successive word of the command selects an additional table. For instance `set print elements 80` involves three tables; the first is the table of all commands, the second is a table of options that can be `set`, and the third is a table of value printing options, of which `elements` is the one that limits the number of objects printed from an aggregate like a string or array. Once the cascaded tables have called an actual command-handling function, it takes control, and argument parsing is completely up to the function. Some commands, such as `run`, handle their arguments similarly to traditional C argc/argv standards, while others, such as `print`, assume that the remainder of the line is a single programming language expression, and give the entire line over to a language-specific parser.

Machine Interface

One way to provide a debugging GUI is to use GDB as a sort of "backend" to a graphical interface program, translating mouse clicks into commands and formatting print results into windows. This has been made to work several times, including KDbg and DDD (Data Display Debugger), but it's not the ideal approach because sometimes results are formatted for human readability, omitting details and relying on human ability to supply context.

To solve this problem, GDB has an alternate "user" interface, known as the Machine Interface or MI for short. It is still fundamentally a command-line interface, but both commands and results have additional syntax that makes everything explicit—each argument is bounded by quotes, and complex output has delimiters for subgroups and parameter names for component pieces. In addition, MI commands can be prefixed with sequence identifiers that are echoed back in results, ensuring reported results are matched up with the right commands.

To see how the two forms compare, here is a normal step command and GDB's response:

```
(gdb) step

buggy_function (arg1=45, arg2=92) at ex.c:232
232     result = positive_variable * arg1 + arg2;
```

With the MI, the input and output are more verbose, but easier for other software to parse accurately:

```
4321-exec-step

4321^done,reason="end-stepping-range",
     frame={addr="0x00000000004004be",
            func="buggy_function",
            args=[{name="arg1",value="45"},
                  {name="arg2",value="92"}],
            file="ex.c",
            fullname="/home/sshebs/ex.c",
            line="232"}
```

The Eclipse[ecl12] development environment is the most notable client of the MI.

Other User Interfaces

Additional frontends include a tcl/tk-based version called GDBtk or Insight, and a curses-based interface called the TUI, originally contributed by Hewlett-Packard. GDBtk is a conventional multi-paned graphical interface built using the tk library, while the TUI is a split-screen interface.

4.10 Development Process

Maintainers

As an original GNU program, GDB development started out following the "cathedral" model of development. Originally written by Stallman, GDB then went through a succession of "maintainers", each of whom was a combination of architect, patch reviewer, and release manager, with access to the source repository limited to a handful of Cygnus employees.

In 1999, GDB migrated to a public source repository and expanded to a team of several dozen maintainers, aided by scores of individuals with commit privileges. This has accelerated development considerably, with the 10-odd commits each week growing to 100 or more.

Testing Testing

As GDB is highly system-specific, has a great many ports to systems ranging from the smallest to the largest in computerdom, and has hundreds of commands, options, and usage styles, it is difficult for even an experienced GDB hacker to anticipate all the effects of a change.

This is where the test suite comes in. The test suite consists of a number of test programs combined with expect scripts, using a tcl-based testing framework called DejaGNU. The basic model is that each script drives GDB as it debugs a test program, sending commands and then pattern-matching the output against regular expressions.

The test suite also has the ability to run cross-debugging to both live hardware and simulators, and to have tests that are specific to a single architecture or configuration.

At the end of 2011, the test suite includes some 18,000 test cases, which include tests of basic functionality, language-specific tests, architecture-specific tests, and MI tests. Most of these are generic and are run for any configuration. GDB contributors are expected to run the test suite on patched sources and observe no regressions, and new tests are expected to accompany each new feature. However, as no one has access to all platforms that might be affected by a change, it is rare to get all the way to zero failures; 10–20 failures is usually reasonable for a trunk snapshot configured for native debugging, and some embedded targets will have more failures.

4.11 Lessons Learned

Open Development Wins

GDB started out as an exemplar of the "cathedral" development process, in which the maintainer keeps close control of the sources, with the outside world only seeing progress via periodic snapshots. This was rationalized by the relative infrequence of patch submissions, but the closed process was actually discouraging patches. Since the open process has been adopted, the number of patches is much larger than ever before, and quality is just as good or better.

Make a Plan, but Expect It to Change

The open source development process is intrinsically somewhat chaotic, as different individuals work on the code for a while, then fall away, leaving others to continue on.

However, it still makes sense to make a development plan and publish it. It helps guide developers as they work on related tasks, it can be shown to potential funders, and it lets volunteers think about what they can do to advance it.

But don't try to force dates or time frames; even if everyone is enthusiastic about a direction, it is unlikely that people can guarantee full-time effort for long enough to finish by a chosen date.

For that matter, don't cling to the plan itself if it has become outdated. For a long time, GDB had a plan to restructure as a library, libgdb, with a well-defined API, that could be linked into other programs (in particular ones with GUIs); the build process was even changed to build a libgdb.a as an intermediate step. Although the idea has come up periodically since then, the primacy of Eclipse and MI meant that the library's main rationale has been sidestepped, and as of January 2012 we have abandoned the library concept and are expunging the now-pointless bits of code.

Things Would Be Great If We Were Infinitely Intelligent

After seeing some of the changes we made, you might be thinking: Why didn't we do things right in the first place? Well, we just weren't smart enough.

Certainly we could have anticipated that GDB was going to be tremendously popular, and was going to be ported to dozens and dozens of architectures, both native and cross. If we had known that, we could have started with the gdbarch objects, instead of spending years upgrading old macros and global variables; ditto for the target vector.

Certainly we could have anticipated GDB was going to be used with GUIs. After all in 1986 both the Mac and the X Window System had already been out for two years! Instead of designing a traditional command interface, we could have set it up to handle events asynchronously.

The real lesson though is that not that GDBers were dumb, but that we couldn't possibly have been smart enough to anticipate how GDB would need to evolve. In 1986 it was not at all clear that the windows-and-mouse interface was going to become ubiquitous; if the first version of GDB was perfectly adapted for GUI use, we'd have looked like geniuses, but it would have been sheer luck. Instead, by making GDB useful in a more limited scope, we built a user base that enabled more extensive development and re-engineering later.

Learn to Live with Incomplete Transitions

Try to complete transitions, but they may take a while; expect to live with them being incomplete.

At the GCC Summit in 2003, Zack Weinberg lamented the "incomplete transitions" in GCC, where new infrastructure had been introduced, but the old infrastructure could not be removed. GDB has these also, but we can point to a number of transitions that have been completed, such as the target vector and gdbarch. Even so, they can take a number of years to complete, and in the meantime one has to keep the debugger running.

Don't Get Too Attached to the Code

When you spend a long time with a single body of code, and it's an important program that also pays the bills, it's easy to get attached to it, and even to mold your thinking to fit the code, rather than the other way around.

Don't.

Everything in the code originated with a series of conscious decisions: some inspired, some less so. The clever space-saving trick of 1991 is a pointless complexity with the multi-gigabyte RAMs of 2011.

GDB once supported the Gould supercomputer. When they turned off the last machine, around 2000, there really wasn't any point in keeping those bits around. That episode was the genesis of an obsoletion process for GDB, and most releases now include the retirement of some piece or another.

In fact, there are a number of radical changes on the table or already underway, ranging from the adoption of Python for scripting, to support for debugging of highly parallel multicore systems, to recoding into C++. The changes may take years to complete; all the more reason to get started on them now.

[chapter 5]

The Glasgow Haskell Compiler
Simon Marlow and Simon Peyton Jones

The Glasgow Haskell Compiler (GHC) started as part of an academic research project funded by the UK government at the beginning of the 1990s, with several goals in mind:
- To make freely available a robust and portable compiler for Haskell that generates high performance code;
- To provide a modular foundation that other researchers can extend and develop;
- To learn how real programs behave, so that we can design and build better compilers.

GHC is now over 20 years old, and has been under continuous active development since its inception. Today, GHC releases are downloaded by hundreds of thousands of people, the online repository of Haskell libraries has over 3,000 packages, GHC is used to teach Haskell in many undergraduate courses, and there are a growing number of instances of Haskell being depended upon commercially.

Over its lifetime GHC has generally had around two or three active developers, although the number of people who have contributed some code to GHC is in the hundreds. While the ultimate goal for us, the main developers of GHC, is to produce research rather than code, we consider developing GHC to be an essential prerequisite: the artifacts of research are fed back into GHC, so that GHC can then be used as the basis for further research that builds on these previous ideas. Moreover, it is important that GHC is an industrial-strength product, since this gives greater credence to research results produced with it. So while GHC is stuffed full of cutting-edge research ideas, a great deal of effort is put into ensuring that it can be relied on for production use. There has often been some tension between these two seemingly contradictory goals, but by and large we have found a path that is satisfactory both from the research and the production-use angles.

In this chapter we want to give an overview of the architecture of GHC, and focus on a handful of the key ideas that have been successful in GHC (and a few that haven't). Hopefully throughout the following pages you will gain some insight into how we managed to keep a large software project active for over 20 years without it collapsing under its own weight, with what is generally considered to be a very small development team.

5.1 What is Haskell?

Haskell is a functional programming language, defined by a document known as the "Haskell Report" of which the latest revision is Haskell 2010 [Mar10]. Haskell was created in 1990 by several members of the academic research community interested in functional languages, to address the lack of a common language that could be used as a focus for their research.

Two features of Haskell stand out amongst the programming languages crowd:

- It is *purely functional*. That is, functions cannot have side effects or mutate data; for a given set of inputs (arguments) a function always gives the same result. The benefits of this model for reasoning about code (and, we believe, writing code) are clear, but integrating input/output into the purely functional setting proved to be a significant challenge. Fortunately an elegant solution in the form of *monads* was discovered, which not only allowed input/output to be neatly integrated with purely functional code, but introduced a powerful new abstraction that revolutionised coding in Haskell (and subsequently had an impact on other languages too).
- It is *lazy*. This refers to the evaluation strategy of the language: most languages use *strict* evaluation in which the arguments to a function are evaluated before the function is called, whereas in Haskell the arguments to a function are passed *unevaluated*, and only evaluated on demand. This aspect of Haskell also has benefits for reasoning about programs, but more than anything else serves as a barrier to prevent the leakage of impure non-functional features into the language: such features fundamentally cannot work in conjunction with lazy semantics.

Haskell is also *strongly-typed*, while supporting *type inference* which means that type annotations are rarely necessary.

Those interested in a complete history of Haskell should read [HHPW07].

5.2 High-Level Structure

At the highest level, GHC can be divided into three distinct chunks:

- The compiler itself. This is essentially a Haskell program whose job is to convert Haskell source code into executable machine code.
- The Boot Libraries. GHC comes with a set of libraries that we call the boot libraries, because they constitute the libraries that the compiler itself depends on. Having these libraries in the source tree means that GHC can bootstrap itself. Some of these libraries are very tightly coupled to GHC, because they implement low-level functionality such as the Int type in terms of primitives defined by the compiler and runtime system. Other libraries are more high-level and compiler-independent, such as the Data.Map library.
- The Runtime System (RTS). This is a large library of C code that handles all the tasks associated with *running* the compiled Haskell code, including garbage collection, thread scheduling, profiling, exception handling and so on. The RTS is linked into every compiled Haskell program. The RTS represents a significant chunk of the development effort put into GHC, and the design decisions made there are responsible for some of Haskell's key strengths, such as its efficient support for concurrency and parallelism. We'll describe the RTS in more detail in Section 5.5.

In fact, these three divisions correspond exactly to three subdirectories of a GHC source tree: compiler, libraries, and rts respectively.

We won't spend much time here discussing the boot libraries, as they are largely uninteresting from an architecture standpoint. All the key design decisions are embodied in the compiler and runtime system, so we will devote the rest of this chapter to discussing these two components.

Code Metrics

The last time we measured the number of lines in GHC was in 1992[1], so it is interesting to look at how things have changed since then. Figure 5.1 gives a breakdown of the number of lines of code in GHC divided up into the major components, comparing the current tallies with those from 1992.

Module	Lines (1992)	Lines (2011)	Increase
Compiler			
Main	997	11,150	11.2
Parser	1,055	4,098	3.9
Renamer	2,828	4,630	1.6
Type checking	3,352	24,097	7.2
Desugaring	1,381	7,091	5.1
Core transformations	1,631	9,480	5.8
STG transformations	814	840	1
Data-Parallel Haskell	—	3,718	—
Code generation	2913	11,003	3.8
Native code generation	—	14,138	—
LLVM code generation	—	2,266	—
GHCi	—	7,474	—
Haskell abstract syntax	2,546	3,700	1.5
Core language	1,075	4,798	4.5
STG language	517	693	1.3
C-- (was Abstract C)	1,416	7,591	5.4
Identifier representations	1,831	3,120	1.7
Type representations	1,628	3,808	2.3
Prelude definitions	3,111	2,692	0.9
Utilities	1,989	7,878	3.96
Profiling	191	367	1.92
Compiler Total	28,275	139,955	4.9
Runtime System			
All C and C-- code	43,865	48,450	1.10

Figure 5.1: Lines of code in GHC, past and present

There are some notable aspects of these figures:

- Despite nearly 20 years of non-stop development the compiler has only increased in size by a factor of 5, from around 28,000 to around 140,000 lines of Haskell code. We obsessively refactor while adding new code, keeping the code base as fresh as possible.
- There are several new components, although these only account for about 28,000 new lines. Much of the new components are concerned with code generation: native code generators for various processors, and an LLVM[2] code generator. The infrastructure for the interactive interpreter GHCi also added over 7,000 lines.

---

[1] "The Glasgow Haskell compiler: a technical overview", JFIT technical conference digest, 1992

[2] Formerly the "Low Level Virtual Machine", the LLVM project includes a generic code-generator with targets for many different processors. For more information see http://llvm.org/, and the chapter on LLVM in Volume 1 of *The Architecture of Open Source Applications*.

- The biggest increase in a single component is the type checker, where over 20,000 lines were added. This is unsurprising given that much of the recent research using GHC has been into new type system extensions (for example GADTs [PVWW06] and Type Families [CKP05]).
- A lot of code has been added to the `Main` component; this is partly because there was previously a 3,000-line Perl script called the "driver" that was rewritten in Haskell and moved into GHC proper, and also because support for compiling multiple modules was added.
- The runtime system has barely grown: it is only 10% larger, despite having accumulated a lot of new functionality and being ported to more platforms. We rewrote it completely around 1997.
- GHC has a complex build system, which today comprises about 6,000 lines of GNU make code. It is on its fourth complete rewrite, the latest being about two years ago, and each successive iteration has reduced the amount of code.

The Compiler

We can divide the compiler into three:

- The *compilation manager*, which is responsible for the compilation of multiple Haskell source files. The job of the compilation manager is to figure out in which order to compile the different files, and to decide which modules do not need to be recompiled because none of their dependencies have changed since the last time they were compiled.
- The *Haskell compiler* (we abbreviate this as `Hsc` inside GHC), which handles the compilation of a single Haskell source file. As you might imagine, most of the action happens in here. The output of `Hsc` depends on what backend is selected: assembly, LLVM code, or bytecode.
- The *pipeline*, which is responsible for composing together any necessary external programs with `Hsc` to compile a Haskell source file to object code. For example, a Haskell source file may need preprocessing with the C preprocessor before feeding to `Hsc`, and the output of `Hsc` is usually an assembly file that must be fed into the assembler to create an object file.

The compiler is not simply an executable that performs these functions; it is itself a *library* with a large API that can be used to build other tools that work with Haskell source code, such as IDEs and analysis tools. More about this later in Section 5.4.

Compiling Haskell Code

As with most compilers, compiling a Haskell source file proceeds in a sequence of phases, with the output of each phase becoming the input of the subsequent phase. The overall structure of the different phases is illustrated in Figure 5.2.

Parsing

We start in the traditional way with parsing, which takes as input a Haskell source file and produces as output abstract syntax. In GHC the abstract syntax datatype `HsSyn` is parameterised by the types of the identifiers it contains, so an abstract syntax tree has type `HsSyn t` for some type of identifiers `t`. This enables us to add more information to identifiers as the program passes through the various stages of the compiler, while reusing the same type of abstract syntax trees.

The output of the parser is an abstract syntax tree in which the identifiers are simple strings, which we call `RdrName`. Hence, the abstract syntax produced by the parser has type `HsSyn RdrName`.

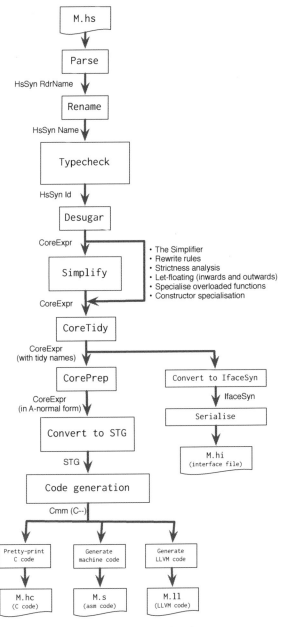

Figure 5.2: The compiler phases

GHC uses the tools Alex and Happy to generate its lexical analysis and parsing code respectively, which are analogous to the tools lex and yacc for C.

GHC's parser is purely functional. In fact, the API of the GHC library provides a pure function called parser that takes a String (and a few other things) and returns either the parsed abstract syntax or an error message.

Renaming

Renaming is the process of resolving all of the identifiers in the Haskell source code into fully qualified names, at the same time identifying any out-of-scope identifiers and flagging errors appropriately.

In Haskell it is possible for a module to re-export an identifier that it imported from another module. For example, suppose module A defines a function called f, and module B imports module A and re-exports f. Now, if a module C imports module B, it can refer to f by the name B.f—even though f is originally defined in module A. This is a useful form of namespace manipulation; it means that a library can use whatever module structure it likes internally, but expose a nice clean API via a few interface modules that re-export identifiers from the internal modules.

The compiler however has to resolve all this, so that it knows what each name in the source code corresponds to. We make a clean distinction between the *entities*, the "things themselves" (in our example, A.f), and the names by which the entities can be referred to (e.g., B.f). At any given point in the source code, there are a set of entities in scope, and each may be known by one or more different names. The job of the renamer is to replace each of the names in the compiler's internal representation of the code by a reference to a particular entity. Sometimes a name can refer to several different entities; by itself that is not an error, but if the name is actually used, then the renamer will flag an ambiguity error and reject the program.

Renaming takes Haskell abstract syntax (HsSyn RdrName) as input, and also produces abstract syntax as output (HsSyn Name). Here a Name is a reference to a particular entity.

Resolving names is the main job of the renamer, but it performs a plethora of other tasks too: collecting the equations of a function together and flagging an error if they have differing numbers of arguments; rearranging infix expressions according to the fixity of the operators; spotting duplicate declarations; generating warnings for unused identifiers, and so on.

Type Checking

Type checking, as one might imagine, is the process of checking that the Haskell program is type-correct. If the program passes the type checker, then it is guaranteed to not crash at runtime.[3]

The input to the type checker is HsSyn Name (Haskell source with qualified names), and the output is HsSyn Id. An Id is a Name with extra information: notably a *type*. In fact, the Haskell syntax produced by the type checker is fully decorated with type information: every identifier has its type attached, and there is enough information to reconstruct the type of any subexpression (which might be useful for an IDE, for example).

In practice, type checking and renaming may be interleaved, because the Template Haskell feature generates code at runtime that itself needs to be renamed and type checked.

Desugaring, and the Core language

Haskell is a rather large language, containing many different syntactic forms. It is intended to be easy for humans to read and write—there is a wide range of syntactic constructs which gives the programmer plenty of flexibility in choosing the most appropriate construct for the situation at hand. However, this flexibility means that there are often several ways to write the same code; for example, an if expression is identical in meaning to a case expression with True and False branches, and list-comprehension notation can be translated into calls to map, filter, and concat.

---

[3] The term "crash" here has a formal definition that includes hard crashes like "segmentation fault", but not things like pattern-matching failure. The non-crash guarantee can be subverted by using certain unsafe language features, such as the Foreign Function Interface.

In fact, the definition of the Haskell language defines all these constructs by their translation into simpler constructs; the constructs that can be translated away like this are called "syntactic sugar".

It is much simpler for the compiler if all the syntactic sugar is removed, because the subsequent optimisation passes that need to work with the Haskell program have a smaller language to deal with. The process of desugaring therefore removes all the syntactic sugar, translating the full Haskell syntax into a much smaller language that we call Core. We'll talk about Core in detail in Section 5.3.

Optimisation

Now that the program is in Core, the process of optimisation begins. One of GHC's great strengths is in optimising away layers of abstraction, and all of this work happens at the Core level. Core is a tiny functional language, but it is a tremendously flexible medium for expressing optimisations, ranging from the very high-level, such as strictness analysis, to the very low-level, such as strength reduction.

Each of the optimisation passes takes Core and produces Core. The main pass here is called the *Simplifier*, whose job it is to perform a large collection of correctness-preserving transformations, with the goal of producing a more efficient program. Some of these transformations are simple and obvious, such as eliminating dead code or reducing a case expression when the value being scrutinised is known, and some are more involved, such as function inlining and applying rewrite rules (Section 5.4).

The simplifier is normally run between the other optimisation passes, of which there are about six; which passes are actually run and in which order depends on the optimisation level selected by the user.

Code Generation

Once the Core program has been optimised, the process of code generation begins. After a couple of administrative passes, the code takes one of two routes: either it is turned into *byte code* for execution by the interactive interpreter, or it is passed to the *code generator* for eventual translation to machine code.

The code generator first converts the Core into a language called STG, which is essentially just Core annotated with more information required by the code generator. Then, STG is translated to Cmm, a low-level imperative language with an explicit stack. From here, the code takes one of three routes:

- **Native code generation**: GHC contains simple native code generators for a few processor architectures. This route is fast, and generates reasonable code in most cases.
- **LLVM code generation**: The Cmm is converted to LLVM code and passed to the LLVM compiler. This route can produce significantly better code in some cases, although it takes longer than the native code generator.
- **C code generation**: GHC can produce ordinary C code. This route produces significantly slower code than the other two routes, but can be useful for porting GHC to new platforms.

5.3 Key Design Choices

In this section we focus on a handful of the design choices that have been particularly effective in GHC.

The Intermediate Language

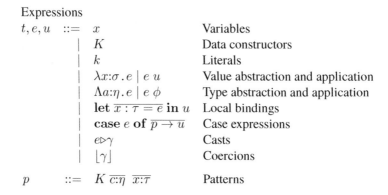

Figure 5.3: The syntax of Core

A typical structure for a compiler for a statically-typed language is this: the program is type checked, and transformed to some *untyped* intermediate language, before being optimised. GHC is different: it has a *statically-typed intermediate language*. As it turns out, this design choice has had a pervasive effect on the design and development of GHC.

GHC's intermediate language is called Core (when thinking of the implementation) or System FC (when thinking about the theory). Its syntax is given in Figure 5.3. The exact details are not important here; the interested reader can consult [SCPD07] for more details. For our present purposes, however, the following points are the key ones:

- Haskell is a very large source language. The data type representing its syntax tree has literally hundreds of constructors.

  In contrast Core is a tiny, principled, lambda calculus. It has extremely few syntactic forms, yet we can translate all of Haskell into Core.

- Haskell is an *implicitly-typed* source language. A program may have few or no type annotations; instead it is up to the type inference algorithm to figure out the type of every binder and sub-expressions. This type inference algorithm is complex, and occasionally somewhat ad hoc, reflecting the design compromises that every real programming language embodies.

  In contrast Core is an *explicitly-typed* language. Every binder has an explicit type, and terms include explicit type abstractions and applications. Core enjoys a very simple, fast type checking algorithm that checks that the program is type correct. The algorithm is entirely straightforward; there are no ad hoc compromises.

All of GHC's analysis and optimisation passes work on Core. This is great: because Core is such a tiny language an optimisation has only a few cases to deal with. Although Core is small, it is extremely expressive—System F was, after all, originally developed as a foundational calculus for typed computation. When new language features are added to the source language (and that happens all the time) the changes are usually restricted to the front end; Core stays unchanged, and hence so does most of the compiler.

But why is Core typed? After all, if the type inference engine accepts the source program, that program is presumably well typed, and each optimisation pass presumably maintains that type-correctness. Core may enjoy a fast type checking algorithm, but why would you ever want to run it? Moreover, making Core typed carries significant costs, because every transformation or optimisation pass must produce a well-typed program, and generating all those type annotations is often non-trivial.

Nevertheless, it has been a huge win to have an explicitly-typed intermediate language, for several reasons:

- Running the Core type checker (we call it Lint) is a very powerful consistency check on the compiler itself. Imagine that you write an "optimisation" that accidentally generates code that treats an integer value as a function, and tries to call it. The chances are that the program will segmentation fault, or fail at runtime in a bizarre way. Tracing a seg-fault back to the particular optimisation pass that broke the program is a long road.

  Now imagine instead that we run Lint after every optimisation pass (and we do, if you use the flag -dcore-lint): it will report a precisely located error immediately after the offending optimisation. What a blessing.

  Of course, type soundness is not the same as correctness: Lint will not signal an error if you "optimise" $(x * 1)$ to 1 instead of to x. But if the program passes Lint, it will guarantee to run without seg-faults; and moreover in practice we have found that it is surprisingly hard to accidentally write optimisations that are type-correct but not semantically correct.

- The type inference algorithm for Haskell is very large and very complex: a glance at Figure 5.1 confirms that the type checker is by far the largest single component of GHC. Large and complex means error-prone. But Lint serves as an 100% independent check on the type inference engine; if the type inference engine accepts a program that is not, in fact, type-correct, Lint will reject it. So Lint serves as a powerful auditor of the type inference engine.

- The existence of Core has also proved to be a tremendous sanity check on the *design* of the source language. Our users constantly suggest new features that they would like in the language. Sometimes these features are manifestly "syntactic sugar", convenient new syntax for something you can do already. But sometimes they are deeper, and it can be hard to tell how far-reaching the feature is.

  Core gives us a precise way to evaluate such features. If the feature can readily be translated into Core, that reassures us that nothing fundamentally new is going on: the new feature is syntactic-sugar-like. On the other hand, if it would require an extension to Core, then we think much, much more carefully.

In practice Core has been incredibly stable: over a 20-year time period we have added exactly one new major feature to Core (namely coercions and their associated casts). Over the same period, the source language has evolved enormously. We attribute this stability not to our own brilliance, but rather to the fact that Core is based directly on foundational mathematics: bravo Girard!

Type Checking the Source Language

One interesting design decision is whether type checking should be done before or after desugaring. The trade-offs are these:

- Type checking before desugaring means that the type checker must deal directly with Haskell's very large syntax, so the type checker has many cases to consider. If we desugared into (an untyped variant of) Core first, one might hope that the type checker would become much smaller.

- On the other hand, type checking after desugaring would impose a significant new obligation: that desugaring does not affect which programs are type-correct. After all, desugaring implies a deliberate loss of information. It is probably the case that in 95% of the cases there is no problem, but *any* problem here would force some compromise in the design of Core to preserve some extra information.
- Most seriously of all, type checking a desugared program would make it much harder to report errors that relate to the original program text, and not to its (sometimes elaborate) desugared version.

Most compilers type check after desugaring, but for GHC we made the opposite choice: we type check the full original Haskell syntax, and then desugar the result. It sounds as if adding a new syntactic construct might be complicated, but (following the French school) we have structured the type inference engine in a way that makes it easy. Type inference is split into two parts:

1. Constraint generation: walk over the source syntax tree, generating a collection of type constraints. This step deals with the full syntax of Haskell, but it is very straightforward code, and it is easy to add new cases.
2. Constraint solving: solve the gathered constraints. This is where the subtlety of the type inference engine lies, but it is independent of the source language syntax, and would be the same for a much smaller or much larger language.

On the whole, the type-check-before-desugar design choice has turned out to be a big win. Yes, it adds lines of code to the type checker, but they are *simple* lines. It avoids giving two conflicting roles to the same data type, and makes the type inference engine less complex, and easier to modify. Moreover, GHC's type error messages are pretty good.

No Symbol Table

Compilers usually have one or more data structures known as *symbol tables*, which are mappings from symbols (e.g., variables) to some information about the variable, such as its type, or where in the source code it was defined.

In GHC we use symbol tables quite sparingly; mainly in the renamer and type checker. As far as possible, we use an alternative strategy: a variable is a data structure that *contains* all the information about itself. Indeed, a large amount of information is reachable by traversing the data structure of a variable: from a variable we can see its type, which contains type constructors, which contain their data constructors, which themselves contain types, and so on. For example, here are some data types from GHC (heavily abbreviated and simplified):

```
data Id     = MkId Name Type
data Type   = TyConApp TyCon [Type]
            | ....
data TyCon  = AlgTyCon Name [DataCon]
            | ...
data DataCon = MkDataCon Name Type ...
```

An Id contains its Type. A Type might be an application of a type constructor to some arguments (e.g., Maybe Int), in which case it contains the TyCon. A TyCon can be an algebraic data type, in which case it includes a list of its data constructors. Each DataCon includes its Type, which of course mentions the TyCon. And so on. The whole structure is highly interconnected. Indeed it is cyclic; for example, a TyCon may contain a DataCon which contains a Type, which contains the very TyCon we started with.

This approach has some advantages and disadvantages:
- Many queries that would require a lookup in a symbol table are reduced to a simple field access, which is great for efficiency and code clarity.
- There is no need to carry around extra symbol tables, the abstract syntax tree already contains all the information.
- The space overheads are better: all instances of the same variable share the same data structure, and there is no space needed for the table.
- The only difficulties arise when we need to *change* any of the information associated with a variable. This is where a symbol table has the advantage: we would just change the entry in the symbol table. In GHC we have to traverse the abstract syntax tree and replace all the instances of the old variable with the new one; indeed the simplifier does this regularly, as it needs to update certain optimisation-related information about each variable.

It is hard to know whether it would be better or worse overall to use symbol tables, because this aspect of the design is so fundamental that it is almost impossible to change. Still, avoiding symbol tables is a natural choice in the purely functional setting, so it seems likely that this approach is a good choice for Haskell.

Inter-Module Optimisation

Functional languages encourage the programmer to write small definitions. For example, here is the definition of && from the standard library:

```
(&&) :: Bool -> Bool -> Bool
True && True = True
_    && _    = False
```

If every use of such a function really required a function call, efficiency would be terrible. One solution is to make the compiler treat certain functions specially; another is to use a pre-processor to replace a "call" with the desired inline code. All of these solutions are unsatisfactory in one way or another, especially as another solution is so obvious: simply inline the function. To "inline a function" means to replace the call by a copy of the function body, suitably instantiating its parameters.

In GHC we have systematically adopted this approach [PM02]. Virtually nothing is built into the compiler. Instead, we define as much as possible in libraries, and use aggressive inlining to eliminate the overheads. This means that *programmers can define their own libraries that will be inlined and optimised as well as the ones that come with GHC.*

A consequence is that GHC must be able to do cross-module, and indeed cross-package, inlining. The idea is simple:
- When compiling a Haskell module Lib.hs, GHC produces object code in Lib.o and an "interface file" in Lib.hi. This interface file contains information about all the functions that Lib exports, including both their types and, for sufficiently small functions, their definitions.
- When compiling a module Client.hs that imports Lib, GHC reads the interface Lib.hi. So if Client calls a function Lib.f defined in Lib, GHC can use the information in Lib.hi to inline Lib.f.

By default GHC will expose the definition of a function in the interface file only if the function is "small" (there are flags to control this size threshold). But we also support an INLINE pragma, to instruct GHC to inline the definition aggressively at call sites, regardless of size, thus:

```
foo :: Int -> Int
{-# INLINE foo #-}
foo x = <some big expression>
```

Cross-module inlining is absolutely essential for defining super-efficient libraries, but it does come with a cost. If the author upgrades his library, it is not enough to re-link Client.o with the new Lib.o, because Client.o contains inlined fragments of the old Lib.hs, and they may well not be compatible with the new one. Another way to say this is that the ABI (Application Binary Interface) of Lib.o has changed in a way that requires recompilation of its clients.

In fact, the only way for compilation to generate code with a fixed, predictable ABI is to disable cross-module optimisation, and this is typically too high a price to pay for ABI compatibility. Users working with GHC will usually have the source code to their entire stack available, so recompiling is not normally an issue (and, as we will describe later, the package system is designed around this mode of working). However, there are situations where recompiling is not practical: distributing bug fixes to libraries in a binary OS distribution, for example. In the future we hope it may be possible to find a compromise solution that allows retaining ABI compatibility while still allowing some cross-module optimisation to take place.

5.4 Extensibility

It is often the case that a project lives or dies according to how extensible it is. A monolithic piece of software that is not extensible has to do everything and do it right, whereas an extensible piece of software can be a useful base even if it doesn't provide all the required functionality out of the box.

Open source projects are of course extensible by definition, in that anyone can take the code and add their own features. But modifying the original source code of a project maintained by someone else is not only a high-overhead approach, it is also not conducive to sharing your extension with others. Therefore successful projects tend to offer forms of extensibility that do not involve modifying the core code, and GHC is no exception in this respect.

User-Defined Rewrite Rules

The core of GHC is a long sequence of optimisation passes, each of which performs some semantics-preserving transformation, Core into Core. But the author of a library defines functions that often have some non-trivial, domain-specific transformations of their own, ones that cannot possibly be predicted by GHC. So GHC allows library authors to define *rewrite rules* that are used to rewrite the program during optimisation [PTH01]. In this way, programmers can, in effect, extend GHC with domain-specific optimisations.

One example is the foldr/build rule, which is expressed like this:

```
{-# RULES "fold/build"
    forall k z (g::forall b. (a->b->b) -> b -> b) .
      foldr k z (build g) = g k z
 #-}
```

The entire rule is a pragma, introduced by {-# RULES. The rule says that whenever GHC sees the expression (foldr k z (build g)) it should rewrite it to (g k z). This transformation is semantics-preserving, but it takes a research paper to argue that it is [GLP93], so there is no chance of GHC performing it automatically. Together with a handful of other rules, and some INLINE pragmas, GHC is able to fuse together list-transforming functions. For example, the two loops in (map f (map g xs)) are fused into one.

Although rewrite rules are simple and easy to use, they have proved to be a very powerful extension mechanism. When we first introduced the feature into GHC ten years ago we expected it to be an occasionally useful facility. But in practice it has turned out to be useful in very many libraries, whose efficiency often depends crucially on rewrite rules. For example, GHC's own base library contains upward of 100 rules, while the popular vector library uses several dozen.

Compiler Plugins

One way in which a compiler can offer extensibility is to allow programmers to write a pass that is inserted directly into the compiler's pipeline. Such passes are often called "plugins". GHC supports plugins in the following way:

- The programmer writes a Core to Core pass, as an ordinary Haskell function in a module P.hs, say, and compiles it to object code.
- When compiling some module, the programmer uses the command-line flag -plugin P. (Alternatively, he can give the flag in a pragma at the start of the module.)
- GHC searches for P.o, dynamically links it into the running GHC binary, and calls it at the appropriate point in the pipeline.

But what is "the appropriate point in the pipeline"? GHC does not know, and so it allows the plugin to make that decision. As a result of this and other matters, the API that the plugin must offer is a bit more complicated than a single Core to Core function—but not much.

Plugins sometimes require, or produce, auxiliary plugin-specific data. For example, a plugin might perform some analysis on the functions in the module being compiled (M.hs, say), and might want to put that information in the interface file M.hi, so that the plugin has access to that information when compiling modules that import M. GHC offers an annotation mechanism to support this.

Plugins and annotations are relatively new to GHC. They have a higher barrier to entry than rewrite rules, because the plugin is manipulating GHC's internal data structures, but of course they can do much more. It remains to be seen how widely they will be used.

GHC as a Library: The GHC API

One of GHC's original goals was to be a *modular* foundation that others could build on. We wanted the code of GHC to be as transparent and well-documented as possible, so that it could be used as the basis for research projects by others; we imagined that people would want to make their own modifications to GHC to add new experimental features or optimisations. Indeed, there have been some examples of this: for example, there exists a version of GHC with a Lisp front-end, and a version of GHC that generates Java code, both developed entirely separately by individuals with little or no contact with the GHC team.

However, producing modified versions of GHC represents only a small subset of the ways in which the code of GHC can be re-used. As the popularity of the Haskell language has grown, there has been an increasing need for tools and infrastructure that understand Haskell source code, and GHC of course contains a lot of the functionality necessary for building these tools: a Haskell parser, abstract syntax, type checker and so on.

With this in mind, we made a simple change to GHC: rather than building GHC as a monolithic program, we build GHC as a *library*, that is then linked with a small *Main* module to make the GHC executable itself, but also shipped in library form so that users can call it from their own programs.

At the same time we built an API to expose GHC's functionality to clients. The API provides enough functionality to implement the GHC batch compiler and the GHCi interactive environment, but it also provides access to individual passes such as the parser and type checker, and allows the data structures produced by these passes to be inspected. This change has given rise to a wide range of tools built using the GHC API, including:

- A documentation tool, *Haddock*[4], which reads Haskell source code and produces HTML documentation.
- New versions of the GHCi front end with additional features; e.g., *ghci-haskeline*[5] which was subsequently merged back into GHC.
- IDEs that offer advanced navigation of Haskell source code; e.g., *Leksah*[6].
- *hint*[7], a simpler API for on-the-fly evaluation of Haskell source code.

The Package System

The package system has been a key factor in the growth in use of the Haskell language in recent years. Its main purpose is to enable Haskell programmers to share code with each other, and as such it is an important aspect of extensibility: the package system extends the shared codebase beyond GHC itself.

The package system embodies various pieces of infrastructure that together make sharing code easy. With the package system as the enabler, the community has built a large body of shared code; rather than relying on libraries from a single source, Haskell programmers draw on libraries developed by the whole community. This model has worked well for other languages; CPAN for Perl, for example, although Haskell being a predominantly compiled rather than interpreted language presents a somewhat different set of challenges.

Basically, the package system lets a user manage libraries of Haskell code written by other people, and use them in their own programs and libraries. Installing a Haskell library is as simple as uttering a single command, for example:

```
$ cabal install zlib
```

downloads the code for the `zlib` package from `http://hackage.haskell.org`, compiles it using GHC, installs the compiled code somewhere on your system (e.g., in your home directory on a Unix system), and registers the installation with GHC. Furthermore, if `zlib` depends on any other packages that are not yet installed, those will also be downloaded, compiled and installed automatically before `zlib` itself is compiled. It is a tremendously smooth way to work with libraries of Haskell code shared by others.

The package system is made of four components, only the first of which is strictly part of the GHC project:

- Tools for managing the *package database*, which is simply a repository for information about the packages installed on your system. GHC reads the package database when it starts up, so that it knows which packages are available and where to find them.
- A library called `Cabal` (Common Architecture for Building Applications and Libraries), which implements functionality for building, installing and registering individual packages.

---

[4]`http://www.haskell.org/haddock/`
[5]`http://hackage.haskell.org/package/ghci-haskeline`
[6]`http://hackage.haskell.org/package/leksah`
[7]`http://hackage.haskell.org/package/hint`

- A website at http://hackage.haskell.org which hosts packages written and uploaded by users. The website automatically builds documentation for the packages which can be browsed online. At the time of writing, Hackage is hosting over 3,000 packages covering functionality including database libraries, web frameworks, GUI toolkits, data structures, and networking.
- The cabal tool which ties together the Hackage website and the Cabal library: it downloads packages from Hackage, resolves dependencies, and builds and installs packages in the right order. New packages can also be uploaded to Hackage using cabal from the command line.

These components have been developed over several years by members of the Haskell community and the GHC team, and together they make a system that fits perfectly with the open source development model. There are no barriers to sharing code or using code that others have shared (provided you respect the relevant licenses, of course). You can be using a package that someone else has written literally within seconds of finding it on Hackage.

Hackage has been so successful that the remaining problems it has are now those of scale: users find it difficult to choose amongst the four different database frameworks, for example. Ongoing developments are aimed at solving these problems in ways that leverage the community. For example, allowing users to comment and vote on packages will make it easier to find the best and most popular packages, and collecting data on build success or failures from users and reporting the results will help users avoid packages that are unmaintained or have problems.

5.5 The Runtime System

The Runtime System is a library of mostly C code that is linked into every Haskell program. It provides the support infrastructure needed for running the compiled Haskell code, including the following main components:

- Memory management, including a parallel, generational, garbage collector;
- Thread management and scheduling;
- The primitive operations provided by GHC;
- A bytecode interpreter and dynamic linker for GHCi.

The rest of this section is divided into two: first we focus on a couple of the aspects of the design of the RTS that we consider to have been successful and instrumental in making it work so well, and secondly we talk about the coding practices and infrastructure we have built in the RTS for coping with what is a rather hostile programming environment.

Key Design Decisions

In this section we describe two of the design decisions in the RTS that we consider to have been particularly successful.

The Block Layer

The garbage collector is built on top of a *block layer* that manages memory in units of blocks, where a block is a multiple of 4 KB in size. The block layer has a very simple API:

```
typedef struct bdescr_ {
    void *              start;
    struct bdescr_ *    link;
```

```
    struct generation_ * gen;    // generation
    // .. various other fields
} bdescr;

bdescr * allocGroup (int n);
void     freeGroup  (bdescr *p);
bdescr * Bdescr     (void *p);    // a macro
```

This is the only API used by the garbage collector for allocating and deallocating memory. Blocks of memory are allocated with `allocGroup` and freed with `freeGroup`. Every block has a small structure associated with it called a *block descriptor* (`bdescr`). The operation `Bdescr(p)` returns the block descriptor associated with an arbitrary address p; this is purely an address calculation based on the value of p and compiles to a handful of arithmetic and bit-manipulation instructions.

Blocks may be linked together into chains using the `link` field of the `bdescr`, and this is the real power of the technique. The garbage collector needs to manage several distinct areas of memory such as *generations*, and each of these areas may need to grow or shrink over time. By representing memory areas as linked lists of blocks, the GC is freed from the difficulties of fitting multiple resizable memory areas into a flat address space.

The implementation of the block layer uses techniques that are well-known from C's `malloc()`/`free()` API; it maintains lists of free blocks of various sizes, and coalesces free areas. The operations `freeGroup()` and `allocGroup()` are carefully designed to be $O(1)$.

One major advantage of this design is that it needs very little support from the OS, and hence is great for portability. The block layer needs to allocate memory in units of 1 MB, aligned to a 1 MB boundary. While none of the common OSs provide this functionality directly, it is implementable without much difficulty in terms of the facilities they do provide. The payoff is that GHC has no dependence on the particular details of the address-space layout used by the OS, and it coexists peacefully with other users of the address space, such as shared libraries and operating system threads.

There is a small up-front complexity cost for the block layer, in terms of managing chains of blocks rather than contiguous memory. However, we have found that this cost is more than repaid in flexibility and portability; for example, the block layer enabled a particularly simple algorithm for parallel GC to be implemented [MHJP08].

Lightweight Threads and Parallelism

We consider concurrency to be a vitally important programming abstraction, particularly for building applications like web servers that need to interact with large numbers of external agents simultaneously. If concurrency is an important abstraction, then it should not be so expensive that programmers are forced to avoid it, or build elaborate infrastructure to amortise its cost (e.g., thread pools). We believe that concurrency should just work, and be cheap enough that you don't worry about forking threads for small tasks.

All operating systems provide threads that work perfectly well, the problem is that they are far too expensive. Typical OSs struggle to handle thousands of threads, whereas we want to manage threads by the million.

Green threads, otherwise known as lightweight threads or user-space threads, are a well-known technique for avoiding the overhead of operating system threads. The idea is that threads are managed by the program itself, or a library (in our case, the RTS), rather than by the operating system.

Managing threads in user space should be cheaper, because fewer traps into the operating system are required.

In the GHC RTS we take full advantage of this idea. A context switch only occurs when the thread is at a *safe point*, where very little additional state needs to be saved. Because we use accurate GC, the stack of the thread can be moved and expanded or shrunk on demand. Contrast these with OS threads, where every context switch must save the entire processor state, and where stacks are immovable so a large chunk of address space has to be reserved up front for each thread.

Green threads can be vastly more efficient than OS threads, so why would anyone want to use OS threads? It comes down to three main problems:

- Blocking and foreign calls. A thread should be able to make a call to an OS API or a foreign library that blocks, without blocking all the other threads in the system.
- Parallelism. Threads should automatically run in parallel if there are multiple processor cores on the system.
- Some external libraries (notably OpenGL and some GUI libraries) have APIs that must be called from the same OS thread each time, because they use thread-local state.

It turns out that all of these are difficult to arrange with green threads. Nevertheless, we persevered with green threads in GHC and found solutions to all three:

- When a Haskell thread makes a foreign call, another OS thread takes over the execution of the remaining Haskell threads [MPT04]. A small pool of OS threads are maintained for this purpose, and new ones are created on demand.
- GHC's scheduler multiplexes many lightweight Haskell threads onto a few heavyweight OS threads; it implements a transparent M:N threading model. Typically N is chosen to be the same as the number of processor cores in the machine, allowing real parallelism to take place but without the overhead of having a full OS thread for each lightweight Haskell thread.

In order to run Haskell code, an OS thread must hold a *Capability*[8]: a data structure that holds the resources required to execute Haskell code, such as the nursery (memory where new objects are created). Only one OS thread may hold a given Capability at a time.

- We provide an API for creating a *bound thread*: a Haskell thread that is tied to one specific OS thread, such that any foreign calls made by this Haskell thread are guaranteed to be made by that OS thread.

So in the vast majority of cases, Haskell's threads behave exactly like OS threads: they can make blocking OS calls without affecting other threads, and they run in parallel on a multicore machine. But they are orders of magnitude more efficient, in terms of both time and space.

Having said that, the implementation does have one problem that users occasionally run into, especially when running benchmarks. We mentioned above that lightweight threads derive some of their efficiency by only context-switching at "safe points", points in the code that the compiler designates as safe, where the internal state of the virtual machine (stack, heap, registers, etc.) is in a tidy state and garbage collection could take place. In GHC, a safe point is whenever memory is allocated, which in almost all Haskell programs happens regularly enough that the program never executes more than a few tens of instructions without hitting a safe point. However, it is possible in highly optimised code to find loops that run for many iterations without allocating memory. This tends to happen often in benchmarks (e.g., functions like factorial and Fibonacci). It occurs less often in real code, although it does happen. The lack of safe points prevents the scheduler from running, which can have detrimental effects. It is possible to solve this problem, but not without

---

[8]We have also called it a "Haskell Execution Context", but the code currently uses the Capability terminology.

impacting the performance of these loops, and often people care about saving every cycle in their inner loops. This may just be a compromise we have to live with.

5.6 Developing GHC

GHC is a single project with a twenty-year life span, and is still in a ferment of innovation and development. For the most part our infrastructure and tooling has been conventional. For example, we use a bug tracker (Trac), a wiki (also Trac), and Git for revision control. (This revision-control mechanism evolved from purely manual, then CVS, then Darcs, before finally moving to Git in 2010.) There are a few points that may be less universal, and we offer them here.

Comments and Notes

One of the most serious difficulties in a large, long-lived project is keeping technical documentation up to date. We have no silver bullet, but we offer one low-tech mechanism that has served us particularly well: Notes.

When writing code, there is often a moment when a careful programmer will mentally say something like "This data type has an important invariant". She is faced with two choices, both unsatisfactory. She can add the invariant as a comment, but that can make the data type declaration too long, so that it is hard to see what the constructors are. Alternatively, she can document the invariant elsewhere, and risk it going out of date. Over twenty years, *everything* goes out of date!

Thus motivated, we developed the following very simple convention:

- Comments of any significant size are not interleaved with code, but instead set off by themselves, with a heading in standard form, thus:

  ```
  Note [Equality-constrained types]
  ~~~~~~~~~~~~~~~~~~~~~~~~~~~~~~~~~
  The type   forall ab. (a ~ [b]) => blah
  is encoded like this:

      ForAllTy (a:*) $ ForAllTy (b:*) $
      FunTy (TyConApp (~) [a, [b]]) $
      blah
  ```

- A the point where the comment is relevant, we add a short comment referring to the Note:

  ```
  data Type
    = FunTy Type Type   -- See Note [Equality-constrained types]

    | ...
  ```

  The comment highlights that something interesting is going on, and gives a precise reference to the comment that explains. It sounds trivial, but the precision is vastly better than our previous habit of saying "see the comment above", because it often was not clear *which* of the many comments above was intended, and after a few years the comment was not even above (it was below, or gone altogether).

Not only is it possible to go from the code that refers to the Note to the Note itself, but the reverse is also possible, and that is often useful. Moreover, the same Note may be referred to from multiple points in the code.

This simple, ASCII-only technique, with no automated support, has transformed our lives: GHC has around 800 Notes, and the number grows daily.

How to Keep On Refactoring

The code of GHC is churning just as quickly as it was ten years ago, if not more so. There is no doubt that the complexity of the system has increased manyfold over that same time period; we saw measures of the amount of code in GHC earlier. Yet, the system remains manageable. We attribute this to three main factors:

- There's no substitute for good software engineering. Modularity always pays off: making the APIs between components as small as possible makes the individual components more flexible because they have fewer interdependencies. For example, GHC's Core{} datatype being small reduces the coupling between Core-to-Core passes, to the extent that they are almost completely independent and can be run in arbitrary order.
- Developing in a strongly-typed language makes refactoring a breeze. Whenever we need to change a data type, or change the number of arguments or type of a function, the compiler immediately tells us what other places in the code need to be fixed. Simply having an absolute guarantee that a large class of errors have been statically ruled out saves a huge amount of time, especially when refactoring. It is scary to imagine how many hand-written test cases we would need to provide the same level of coverage that the type system provides.
- When programming in a purely functional language, it is hard to introduce accidental dependencies via state. If you decide that you suddenly need access to a piece of state deep in an algorithm, in an imperative language you might be tempted to just make the state globally visible rather than explicitly pass it down to the place that needs it. This way eventually leads to a tangle of invisible dependencies, and *brittle code*: code that breaks easily when modified. Pure functional programming forces you to make all the dependencies explicit, which exerts some negative pressure on adding new dependencies, and fewer dependencies means greater modularity. Certainly when it is *necessary* to add a new dependency then purity makes you write more code to express the dependency, but in our view it is a worthwhile price to pay for the long-term health of the code base.

  As an added benefit, purely functional code is thread-safe by construction and tends to be easier to parallelise.

Crime Doesn't Pay

Looking back over the changes we've had to make to GHC as it has grown, a common lesson emerges: being less than purely functional, whether for the purposes of efficiency or convenience, tends to have negative consequences down the road. We have a couple of great examples of this:

- GHC uses a few data structures that rely on mutation internally. One is the FastString type, which uses a single global hash table; another is a global NameCache that ensures all external names are assigned a unique number. When we tried to parallelise GHC (that is, make GHC compile multiple modules in parallel on a multicore processor), these data structures based on mutation were the *only* sticking points. Had we not resorted to mutation in these places, GHC would have been almost trivial to parallelise.

In fact, although we did build a prototype parallel version of GHC, GHC does not currently contain support for parallel compilation, but that is largely because we have not yet invested the effort required to make these mutable data structures thread-safe.

- GHC's behaviour is governed to a large extent by command-line flags. These command-line flags are by definition constant over a given run of GHC, so in early versions of GHC we made the values of these flags available as top-level constants. For example, there was a top-level value opt_GlasgowExts of type Bool, that governed whether certain language extensions should be enabled or not. Top-level constants are highly convenient, because their values don't have to be explicitly passed as arguments to all the code that needs access to them.

Of course these options are not really *constants*, because they change from run to run, and the definition of opt_GlasgowExts involves calling unsafePerformIO because it hides a side effect. Nevertheless, this trick is normally considered "safe enough" because the value is constant within any given run; it doesn't invalidate compiler optimisations, for example.

However, GHC was later extended from a single-module compiler to a multi-module compiler. At this point the trick of using top-level constants for flags broke, because the flags may have different values when compiling different modules. So we had to refactor large amounts of code to pass around the flags explicitly.

Perhaps you might argue that treating the flags as *state* in the first place, as would be natural in an imperative language, would have sidestepped the problem. To some extent this is true, although purely functional code has a number of other benefits, not least of which is that representing the flags by an immutable data structure means that the resulting code is already thread-safe and will run in parallel without modification.

Developing the RTS

GHC's runtime system presents a stark contrast to the compiler in many ways. There is the obvious difference that the runtime system is written in C rather than Haskell, but there are also considerations unique to the RTS that give rise to a different design philosophy:

1. Every Haskell program spends a lot of time executing code in the RTS: 20–30% is typical, but characteristics of Haskell programs vary a lot and so figures greater or less than this range are also common. Every cycle saved by optimising the RTS is multiplied many times over, so it is worth spending a lot of time and effort to save those cycles.
2. The runtime system is statically linked into every Haskell program[9], so there is an incentive to keep it small.
3. Bugs in the runtime system are often inscrutable to the user (e.g., "segmentation fault") and are hard to work around. For example, bugs in the garbage collector tend not to be tied to the use of a particular language feature, but arise when some complex combination of factors emerges at runtime. Furthermore, bugs of this kind tend to be non-deterministic (only occurring in some runs), and highly sensitive (tiny changes to the program make the bug disappear). Bugs in the multithreaded version of the runtime system present even greater challenges. It is therefore worth going to extra lengths to prevent these bugs, and also to build infrastructure to make identifying them easier.

---

[9]That is, unless dynamic linking is being used.

The symptoms of an RTS bug are often indistinguishable from two other kinds of failure: hardware failure, which is more common than you might think, and misuse of unsafe Haskell features like the FFI (Foreign Function Interface). The first job in diagnosing a runtime crash is to rule out these two other causes.

4. The RTS is low-level code that runs on several different architectures and operating systems, and is regularly ported to new ones. Portability is important.

Every cycle and every byte is important, but correctness is even more so. Moreover, the tasks performed by the runtime system are inherently complex, so correctness is hard to begin with. Reconciling these has lead us to some interesting defensive techniques, which we describe in the following sections.

Coping With Complexity

The RTS is a complex and hostile programming environment. In contrast to the compiler, the RTS has almost no type safety. In fact, it has even less type safety than most other C programs, because it is managing data structures whose types live at the Haskell level and not at the C level. For example, the RTS has no idea that the object pointed to by the tail of a cons cell is either [] or another cons: this information is simply not present at the C level. Moreover, the process of compiling Haskell code erases types, so even if we told the RTS that the tail of a cons cell is a list, it would still have no information about the pointer in the head of the cons cell. So the RTS code has to do a lot of casting of C pointer types, and it gets very little help in terms of type safety from the C compiler.

So our first weapon in this battle is to *avoid putting code in the RTS*. Wherever possible, we put the minimum amount of functionality into the RTS and write the rest in a Haskell library. This has rarely turned out badly; Haskell code is far more robust and concise than C, and performance is usually perfectly acceptable. Deciding where to draw the line is not an exact science, although in many cases it is reasonably clear. For example, while it might be theoretically possible to implement the garbage collector in Haskell, in practice it is extremely difficult because Haskell does not allow the programmer precise control of memory allocation, and so dropping down to C for this kind of low-level task makes practical sense.

There is plenty of functionality that can't be (easily) implemented in Haskell, and writing code in the RTS is not pleasant. In the next section we focus on one aspect of managing complexity and correctness in the RTS: maintaining invariants.

Invariants, and Checking Them

The RTS is full of invariants. Many of them are trivial and easy to check: for example, if the pointer to the head of a queue is NULL, then the pointer to the tail should also be NULL. The code of the RTS is littered with assertions to check these kinds of things. Assertions are our go-to tool for finding bugs before they manifest; in fact, when a new invariant is added, we often add the assertion before writing the code that implements the invariant.

Some of the invariants in the runtime are far more difficult to satisfy, and to check. One invariant of this kind that pervades more of the RTS than any other is the following: *the heap has no dangling pointers*.

Dangling pointers are easy to introduce, and there are many places both in the compiler and the RTS itself that can violate this invariant. The code generator could generate code that creates invalid heap objects; the garbage collector might forget to update the pointers of some object when it scans the heap. Tracking down these kinds of bugs can be extremely time-consuming[10] because by the time the program eventually crashes, execution might have progressed a long way from where the dangling pointer was originally introduced. There are good debugging tools available, but they tend not to be good at executing the program in reverse.[11]

The general principle is: *if a program is going to crash, it should crash as soon, as noisily, and as often as possible.*[12]

The problem is, the no-dangling-pointer invariant is not something that can be checked with a constant-time assertion. The assertion that checks it must do a full traversal of the heap! Clearly we cannot run this assertion after every heap allocation, or every time the GC scans an object (indeed, this would not even be enough, as dangling pointers don't appear until the end of GC, when memory is freed).

So, the debug RTS has an optional mode that we call *sanity checking*. Sanity checking enables all kinds of expensive assertions, and can make the program run many times more slowly. In particular, sanity checking runs a full scan of the heap to check for dangling pointers (amongst other things), before *and* after every GC. The first job when investigating a runtime crash is to run the program with sanity checking turned on; sometimes this will catch the invariant violation well before the program actually crashes.

5.7 Conclusion

GHC has consumed a significant portion of the authors' lives over the last 20 years, and we are rather proud of how far it has come. It is not the only Haskell implementation, but it is the only one in regular use by hundreds of thousands of people to get real work done. We are constantly surprised when Haskell turns up being used in unusual places; one recent example is Haskell being used to control the systems in a garbage truck[13].

For many, Haskell and GHC are synonymous: it was never intended to be so, and indeed in many ways it is counterproductive to have just one implementation of a standard, but the fact is that maintaining a good implementation of a programming language is a lot of work. We hope that our efforts in GHC, to support the standard and to clearly delimit each separate language extension, will make it feasible for more implementations to emerge and to integrate with the the package system and other infrastructure. Competition is good for everyone!

We are deeply indebted to Microsoft in particular for giving us the opportunity to develop GHC as part of our research and to distribute it as open source.

---

[10] It is, however, one of the author's favourite activities!

[11] Recent versions of GDB and the Microsoft Visual Studio debugger do have some support for reverse execution, however.

[12] This quote comes from the GHC coding style guidelines, and was originally written by Alastair Reid, who worked on an early version of the RTS.

[13] http://www.haskell.org/pipermail/haskell-cafe/2010-April/075647.html

Git
Susan Potter

6.1 Git in a Nutshell

Git enables the maintenance of a digital body of work (often, but not limited to, code) by many collaborators using a peer-to-peer network of repositories. It supports distributed workflows, allowing a body of work to either eventually converge or temporarily diverge.

This chapter will show how various aspects of Git work under the covers to enable this, and how it differs from other version control systems (VCSs).

6.2 Git's Origin

To understand Git's design philosophy better it is helpful to understand the circumstances in which the Git project was started in the Linux Kernel Community.

The Linux kernel was unusual, compared to most commercial software projects at that time, because of the large number of committers and the high variance of contributor involvement and knowledge of the existing codebase. The kernel had been maintained via tarballs and patches for years, and the core development community struggled to find a VCS that satisfied most of their needs.

Git is an open source project that was born out of those needs and frustrations in 2005. At that time the Linux kernel codebase was managed across two VCSs, BitKeeper and CVS, by different core developers. BitKeeper offered a different view of VCS history lineage than that offered by the popular open source VCSs at this time.

Days after BitMover, the maker of BitKeeper, announced it would revoke the licenses of some core Linux kernel developers, Linus Torvalds began development, in haste, of what was to become Git. He began by writing a collection of scripts to help him manage email patches to apply one after the other. The aim of this initial collection of scripts was to be able to abort merges quickly so the maintainer could modify the codebase mid-patch-stream to manually merge, then continue merging subsequent patches.

From the outset, Torvalds had one philosophical goal for Git—to be the anti-CVS—plus three usability design goals:

- Support distributed workflows similar to those enabled by BitKeeper
- Offer safeguards against content corruption
- Offer high performance

These design goals have been accomplished and maintained, to a degree, as I will attempt to show by dissecting Git's use of directed acyclic graphs (DAGs) for content storage, reference pointers for heads, object model representation, and remote protocol; and finally how Git tracks the merging of trees.

Despite BitKeeper influencing the original design of Git, it is implemented in fundamentally different ways and allows even more distributed plus local-only workflows, which were not possible with BitKeeper. Monotone[1], an open source distributed VCS started in 2003, was likely another inspiration during Git's early development.

Distributed version control systems offer great workflow flexibility, often at the expense of simplicity. Specific benefits of a distributed model include:

- Providing the ability for collaborators to work offline and commit incrementally.
- Allowing a collaborator to determine when his/her work is ready to share.
- Offering the collaborator access to the repository history when offline.
- Allowing the managed work to be published to multiple repositories, potentially with different branches or granularity of changes visible.

Around the time the Git project started, three other open source distributed VCS projects were initiated. (One of them, Mercurial, is discussed in Volume 1 of *The Architecture of Open Source Applications*.) All of these dVCS tools offer slightly different ways to enable highly flexible workflows, which centralized VCSs before them were not capable of handling directly. Note: Subversion has an extension named SVK maintained by different developers to support server-to-server synchronization.

Today popular and actively maintained open source dVCS projects include Bazaar, Darcs, Fossil, Git, Mercurial, and Veracity.

6.3 Version Control System Design

Now is a good time to take a step back and look at the alternative VCS solutions to Git. Understanding their differences will allow us to explore the architectural choices faced while developing Git.

A version control system usually has three core functional requirements, namely:

- Storing content
- Tracking changes to the content (history including merge metadata)
- Distributing the content and history with collaborators

Note: The third requirement above is not a functional requirement for all VCSs.

Content Storage

The most common design choices for storing content in the VCS world are with a delta-based changeset, or with directed acyclic graph (DAG) content representation.

Delta-based changesets encapsulate the differences between two versions of the flattened content, plus some metadata. Representing content as a directed acyclic graph involves objects forming a hierarchy which mirrors the content's filesystem tree as a snapshot of the commit (reusing the unchanged objects inside the tree where possible). Git stores content as a directed acyclic graph using different types of objects. The "Object Database" section later in this chapter describes the different types of objects that can form DAGs inside the Git repository.

---

[1] http://www.monotone.ca/

Commit and Merge Histories

On the history and change-tracking front most VCS software uses one of the following approaches:
- Linear history
- Directed acyclic graph for history

Again Git uses a DAG, this time to store its history. Each commit contains metadata about its ancestors; a commit in Git can have zero or many (theoretically unlimited) parent commits. For example, the first commit in a Git repository would have zero parents, while the result of a three-way merge would have three parents.

Another primary difference between Git and Subversion and its linear history ancestors is its ability to directly support branching that will record most merge history cases.

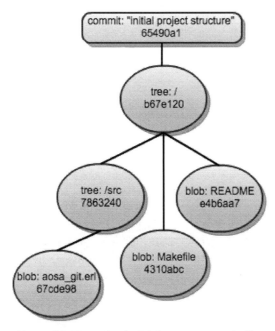

Figure 6.1: Example of a DAG representation in Git

Git enables full branching capability using directed acyclic graphs to store content. The history of a file is linked all the way up its directory structure (via nodes representing directories) to the root directory, which is then linked to a commit node. This commit node, in turn, can have one or more parents. This affords Git two properties that allow us to reason about history and content in more definite ways than the family of VCSs derived from RCS do, namely:

- When a content (i.e., file or directory) node in the graph has the same reference identity (the SHA in Git) as that in a different commit, the two nodes are guaranteed to contain the same content, allowing Git to short-circuit content diffing efficiently.
- When merging two branches we are merging the content of two nodes in a DAG. The DAG allows Git to "efficiently" (as compared to the RCS family of VCS) determine common ancestors.

Distribution

VCS solutions have handled content distribution of a working copy to collaborators on a project in one of three ways:
- Local-only: for VCS solutions that do not have the third functional requirement above.
- Central server: where all changes to the repository must transact via one specific repository for it to be recorded in history at all.
- Distributed model: where there will often be publicly accessible repositories for collaborators to "push" to, but commits can be made locally and pushed to these public nodes later, allowing offline work.

To demonstrate the benefits and limitations of each major design choice, we will consider a Subversion repository and a Git repository (on a server), with equivalent content (i.e., the HEAD of the default branch in the Git repository has the same content as the Subversion repository's latest revision on trunk). A developer, named Alex, has a local checkout of the Subversion repository and a local clone of the Git repository.

Let us say Alex makes a change to a 1 MB file in the local Subversion checkout, then commits the change. Locally, the checkout of the file mimics the latest change and local metadata is updated. During Alex's commit in the centralized Subversion repository, a diff is generated between the previous snapshot of the files and the new changes, and this diff is stored in the repository.

Contrast this with the way Git works. When Alex makes the same modification to the equivalent file in the local Git clone, the change will be recorded locally first, then Alex can "push" the local pending commits to a public repository so the work can be shared with other collaborators on the project. The content changes are stored identically for each Git repository that the commit exists in. Upon the local commit (the simplest case), the local Git repository will create a new object representing a file for the changed file (with all its content inside). For each directory above the changed file (plus the repository root directory), a new tree object is created with a new identifier. A DAG is created starting from the newly created root tree object pointing to blobs (reusing existing blob references where the files content has not changed in this commit) and referencing the newly created blob in place of that file's previous blob object in the previous tree hierarchy. (A *blob* represents a file stored in the repository.)

At this point the commit is still local to the current Git clone on Alex's local device. When Alex "pushes" the commit to a publicly accessible Git repository this commit gets sent to that repository. After the public repository verifies that the commit can apply to the branch, the same objects are stored in the public repository as were originally created in the local Git repository.

There are a lot more moving parts in the Git scenario, both under the covers and for the user, requiring them to explicitly express intent to share changes with the remote repository separately from tracking the change as a commit locally. However, both levels of added complexity offer the team greater flexibility in terms of their workflow and publishing capabilities, as described in the "Git's Origin" section above.

In the Subversion scenario, the collaborator did not have to remember to push to the public remote repository when ready for others to view the changes made. When a small modification to a larger file is sent to the central Subversion repository the delta stored is much more efficient than storing the complete file contents for each version. However, as we will see later, there is a workaround for this that Git takes advantage of in certain scenarios.

6.4 The Toolkit

Today the Git ecosystem includes many command-line and UI tools on a number of operating systems (including Windows, which was originally barely supported). Most of these tools are mostly built on top of the Git core toolkit.

Due to the way Git was originally written by Linus, and its inception within the Linux community, it was written with a toolkit design philosophy very much in the Unix tradition of command line tools.

The Git toolkit is divided into two parts: the plumbing and the porcelain. The plumbing consists of low-level commands that enable basic content tracking and the manipulation of directed acyclic graphs (DAG). The porcelain is the smaller subset of `git` commands that most Git end users are likely to need to use for maintaining repositories and communicating between repositories for collaboration.

While the toolkit design has provided enough commands to offer fine-grained access to functionality for many scripters, application developers complained about the lack of a linkable library for Git. Since the Git binary calls `die()`, it is not reentrant and GUIs, web interfaces or longer running services would have to fork/exec a call to the Git binary, which can be slow.

Work is being done to improve the situation for application developers; see the "Current And Future Work" section for more information.

6.5 The Repository, Index and Working Areas

Let's get our hands dirty and dive into using Git locally, if only to understand a few fundamental concepts.

First to create a new initialized Git repository on our local filesystem (using a Unix inspired operating system) we can do:

```
$ mkdir testgit
$ cd testgit
$ git init
```

Now we have an empty, but initialized, Git repository sitting in our testgit directory. We can branch, commit, tag and even communicate with other local and remote Git repositories. Even communication with other types of VCS repositories is possible with just a handful of `git` commands.

The `git init` command creates a .git subdirectory inside of testgit. Let's have a peek inside it:

```
tree .git/
.git/
|-- HEAD
|-- config
|-- description
|-- hooks
|   |-- applypatch-msg.sample
|   |-- commit-msg.sample
|   |-- post-commit.sample
|   |-- post-receive.sample
|   |-- post-update.sample
|   |-- pre-applypatch.sample
|   |-- pre-commit.sample
|   |-- pre-rebase.sample
```

```
|   |-- prepare-commit-msg.sample
|   |-- update.sample
|-- info
|   |-- exclude
|-- objects
|   |-- info
|   |-- pack
|-- refs
    |-- heads
    |-- tags
```

The .git directory above is, by default, a subdirectory of the root working directory, testgit. It contains a few different types of files and directories:

- *Configuration*: the .git/config, .git/description and .git/info/exclude files essentially help configure the local repository.
- *Hooks*: the .git/hooks directory contains scripts that can be run on certain lifecycle events of the repository.
- *Staging Area*: the .git/index file (which is not yet present in our tree listing above) will provide a staging area for our working directory.
- *Object Database*: the .git/objects directory is the default Git object database, which contains all content or pointers to local content. All objects are immutable once created.
- *References*: the .git/refs directory is the default location for storing reference pointers for both local and remote branches, tags and heads. A reference is a pointer to an object, usually of type tag or commit. References are managed outside of the Object Database to allow the references to change where they point to as the repository evolves. Special cases of references may point to other references, e.g. HEAD.

The .git directory is the actual repository. The directory that contains the working set of files is the *working directory*, which is typically the parent of the .git directory (or *repository*). If you were creating a Git remote repository that would not have a working directory, you could initialize it using the git init --bare command. This would create just the pared-down repository files at the root, instead of creating the repository as a subdirectory under the working tree.

Another file of great importance is the *Git index*: .git/index. It provides the staging area between the local working directory and the local repository. The index is used to stage specific changes within one file (or more), to be committed all together. Even if you make changes related to various types of features, the commits can be made with like changes together, to more logically describe them in the commit message. To selectively stage specific changes in a file or set of files you can using git add -p.

The Git index, by default, is stored as a single file inside the repository directory. The paths to these three areas can be customized using environment variables.

It is helpful to understand the interactions that take place between these three areas (the repository, index and working areas) during the execution of a few core Git commands:

- git checkout [branch]

    This will move the HEAD reference of the local repository to branch reference path (e.g. refs/heads/master), populate the index with this head data and refresh the working directory to represent the tree at that head.

- git add [files]

This will cross reference the checksums of the *files* specified with the corresponding entries in the Git index to see if the index for staged files needs updating with the working directory's version. Nothing changes in the Git directory (or repository).

Let us explore what this means more concretely by inspecting the contents of files under the .git directory (or repository).

```
$ GIT_DIR=$PWD/.git
$ cat $GIT_DIR/HEAD

ref: refs/heads/master

$ MY_CURRENT_BRANCH=$(cat .git/HEAD | sed 's/ref: //g')
$ cat $GIT_DIR/$MY_CURRENT_BRANCH

cat: .git/refs/heads/master: No such file or directory
```

We get an error because, before making any commits to a Git repository at all, no branches exist except the default branch in Git which is `master`, whether it exists yet or not.

Now if we make a new commit, the master branch is created by default for this commit. Let us do this (continuing in the same shell, retaining history and context):

```
$ git commit -m "Initial empty commit" --allow-empty
$ git branch

* master

$ cat $GIT_DIR/$MY_CURRENT_BRANCH

3bce5b130b17b7ce2f98d17b2998e32b1bc29d68

$ git cat-file -p $(cat $GIT_DIR/$MY_CURRENT_BRANCH)
```

What we are starting to see here is the content representation inside Git's object database.

6.6 The Object Database

Git has four basic primitive objects that every type of content in the local repository is built around. Each object type has the following attributes: *type*, *size* and *content*. The primitive object types are:
- *Tree*: an element in a tree can be another tree or a blob, when representing a content directory.
- *Blob*: a blob represents a file stored in the repository.
- *Commit*: a commit points to a tree representing the top-level directory for that commit as well as parent commits and standard attributes.
- *Tag*: a tag has a name and points to a commit at the point in the repository history that the tag represents.

All object primitives are referenced by a SHA, a 40-digit object identity, which has the following properties:
- If two objects are identical they will have the same SHA.
- if two objects are different they will have different SHAs.

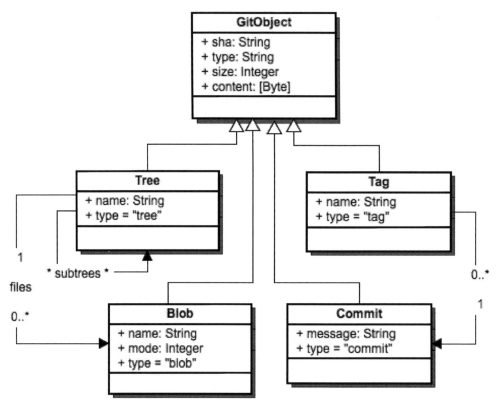

Figure 6.2: Git objects

- If an object was only copied partially or another form of data corruption occurred, recalculating the SHA of the current object will identify such corruption.

The first two properties of the SHA, relating to identity of the objects, is most useful in enabling Git's distributed model (the second goal of Git). The latter property enables some safeguards against corruption (the third goal of Git).

Despite the desirable results of using DAG-based storage for content storage and merge histories, for many repositories delta storage will be more space-efficient than using *loose* DAG objects.

6.7 Storage and Compression Techniques

Git tackles the storage space problem by packing objects in a compressed format, using an index file which points to offsets to locate specific objects in the corresponding *packed* file.

We can count the number of loose (or unpacked) objects in the local Git repository using `git count-objects`. Now we can have Git pack loose objects in the object database, remove loose objects already packed, and find redundant pack files with Git plumbing commands if desired.

The pack file format in Git has evolved, with the initial format storing CRC checksums for the pack file and index file in the index file itself. However, this meant there was the possibility of undetectable corruption in the compressed data since the repacking phase did not involve any further checks. Version 2 of the pack file format overcomes this problem by including the CRC checksums

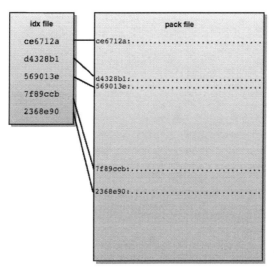

Figure 6.3: Diagram of a pack file with corresponding index file

of each compressed object in the pack index file. Version 2 also allows packfiles larger than 4 GB, which the initial format did not support. As a way to quickly detect pack file corruption the end of the pack file contains a 20-byte SHA1 sum of the ordered list of all the SHAs in that file. The emphasis of the newer pack file format is on helping fulfill Git's second usability design goal of safeguarding against data corruption.

For remote communication Git calculates the commits and content that need to be sent over the wire to synchronize repositories (or just a branch), and generates the pack file format on the fly to send back using the desired protocol of the client.

6.8   Merge Histories

As mentioned previously, Git differs fundamentally in merge history approach than the RCS family of VCSs. Subversion, for example, represents file or tree history in a linear progression; whatever has a higher revision number will supercede anything before it. Branching is not supported directly, only through an unenforced directory structure within the repository.

Let us first use an example to show how this can be problematic when maintaining multiple branches of a work. Then we will look at a scenario to show its limitations.

When working on a "branch" in Subversion at the typical root branches/branch-name, we are working on directory subtree adjacent to the trunk (typically where the live or *master* equivalent code resides within). Let us say this branch is to represent parallel development of the trunk tree.

For example, we might be rewriting a codebase to use a different database. Part of the way through our rewrite we wish to merge in upstream changes from another branch subtree (not trunk). We merge in these changes, manually if necessary, and proceed with our rewrite. Later that day we finish our database vendor migration code changes on our branches/branch-name branch and merge our changes into trunk. The problem with the way linear-history VCSs like Subversion handle this is that there is no way to know that the changesets from the other branch are now contained within the trunk.

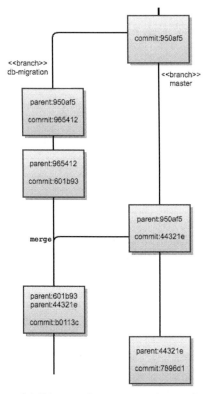

Figure 6.4: Diagram showing merge history lineage

DAG-based merge history VCSs, like Git, handle this case reasonably well. Assuming the other branch does not contain commits that have not been merged into our database vendor migration branch (say, db-migration in our Git repository), we can determine—from the commit object parent relationships—that a commit on the db-migration branch contained the *tip* (or HEAD) of the other upstream branch. Note that a commit object can have zero or more (bounded by only the abilities of the merger) parents. Therefore the merge commit on the db-migration branch *knows* it merged in the current HEAD of the current branch and the HEAD of the other upstream branch through the SHA hashes of the parents. The same is true of the merge commit in the master (the trunk equivalent in Git).

A question that is hard to answer definitively using DAG-based (and linear-based) merge histories is which commits are contained within each branch. For example, in the above scenario we assumed we merged into each branch all the changes from both branches. This may not be the case.

For simpler cases Git has the ability to cherry pick commits from other branches in to the current branch, assuming the commit can cleanly be applied to the branch.

6.9 What's Next?

As mentioned previously, Git core as we know it today is based on a toolkit design philosophy from the Unix world, which is very handy for scripting but less useful for embedding inside or linking with longer running applications or services. While there is Git support in many popular

Integrated Development Environments today, adding this support and maintaining it has been more challenging than integrating support for VCSs that provide an easy-to-link-and-share library for multiple platforms.

To combat this, Shawn Pearce (of Google's Open Source Programs Office) spearheaded an effort to create a linkable Git library with more permissive licensing that did not inhibit use of the library. This was called libgit2[2]. It did not find much traction until a student named Vincent Marti chose it for his Google Summer of Code project last year. Since then Vincent and Github engineers have continued contributing to the libgit2 project, and created bindings for numerous other popular languages such as Ruby, Python, PHP, .NET languages, Lua, and Objective-C.

Shawn Pearce also started a BSD-licensed pure Java library called JGit that supports many common operations on Git repositories[3]. It is now maintained by the Eclipse Foundation for use in the Eclipse IDE Git integration.

Other interesting and experimental open source endeavours outside of the Git core project are a number of implementations using alternative datastores as backends for the Git object database such as:

- jgit_cassandra[4], which offers Git object persistence using Apache Cassandra, a hybrid datastore using Dynamo-style distribution with BigTable column family data model semantics.
- jgit_hbase[5], which enables read and write operations to Git objects stored in HBase, a distributed key-value datastore.
- libgit2-backends[6], which emerged from the libgit2 effort to create Git object database backends for multiple popular datastores such as Memcached, Redis, SQLite, and MySQL.

All of these open source projects are maintained independently of the Git core project.

As you can see, today there are a large number of ways to use the Git format. The face of Git is no longer just the toolkit command line interface of the Git Core project; rather it is the repository format and protocol to share between repositories.

As of this writing, most of these projects, according to their developers, have not reached a stable release, so work in the area still needs to be done but the future of Git appears bright.

6.10 Lessons Learned

In software, every design decision is ultimately a trade-off. As a power user of Git for version control and as someone who has developed software around the Git object database model, I have a deep fondness for Git in its present form. Therefore, these lessons learned are more of a reflection of common recurring complaints about Git that are due to design decisions and focus of the Git core developers.

One of the most common complaints by developers and managers who evaluate Git has been the lack of IDE integration on par with other VCS tools. The toolkit design of Git has made this more challenging than integrating other modern VCS tools into IDEs and related tools.

Earlier in Git's history some of the commands were implemented as shell scripts. These shell script command implementations made Git less portable, especially to Windows. I am sure the Git core developers did not lose sleep over this fact, but it has negatively impacted adoption of

---

[2] https://github.com/libgit2/libgit2
[3] https://github.com/eclipse/jgit
[4] https://github.com/spearce/jgit_cassandra
[5] https://github.com/spearce/jgit_hbase
[6] https://github.com/libgit2/libgit2-backends

Git in larger organizations due to portability issues that were prevalent in the early days of Git's development. Today a project named Git for Windows has been started by volunteers to ensure new versions of Git are ported to Windows in a timely manner.

An indirect consequence of designing Git around a toolkit design with a lot of plumbing commands is that new users get lost quickly; from confusion about all the available subcommands to not being able to understand error messages because a low level plumbing task failed, there are many places for new users to go astray. This has made adopting Git harder for some developer teams.

Even with these complaints about Git, I am excited about the possibilities of future development on the Git Core project, plus all the related open source projects that have been launched from it.

[chapter 7]

GPSD
Eric Raymond

GPSD is a suite of tools for managing collections of GPS devices and other sensors related to navigation and precision timekeeping, including marine AIS (Automatic Identification System) radios and digital compasses. The main program, a service daemon named gpsd, manages a collection of sensors and makes reports from all of them available as a JSON object stream on a well-known TCP/IP port. Other programs in the suite include demonstration clients usable as code models and various diagnostic tools.

GPSD is widely deployed on laptops, smartphones, and autonomous vehicles including self-driving automobiles and robot submarines. It features in embedded systems used for navigation, precision agriculture, location-sensitive scientific telemetry, and network time service. It's even used in the Identification-Friend-or-Foe system of armored fighting vehicles including the M1 "Abrams" main battle tank.

GPSD is a mid-sized project—about 43 KLOC, mainly in C and Python—with a history under its current lead going back to 2005 and a prehistory going back to 1997. The core team has been stable at about three developers, with semi-regular contributions from about two dozen more and the usual one-off patches from hundreds of others.

GPSD has historically had an exceptionally low defect rate, as measured both by auditing tools such as `splint`, `valgrind`, and Coverity and by the incidence of bug reports on its tracker and elsewhere. This did not come about by accident; the project has been very aggressive about incorporating technology for automated testing, and that effort has paid off handsomely.

GPSD is sufficiently good at what it does that it has coopted or effectively wiped out all of its approximate predecessors and at least one direct attempt to compete with it. In 2010, GPSD won the first Good Code Grant from the Alliance for Code Excellence. By the time you finish this chapter you should understand why.

7.1 Why GPSD Exists

GPSD exists because the application protocols shipped with GPSs and other navigation-related sensors are badly designed, poorly documented, and highly variable by sensor type and model. See [Ray] for a detailed discussion; in particular, you'll learn there about the vagaries of NMEA 0183 (the sort-of standard for GPS reporting packets) and the messy pile of poorly documented vendor protocols that compete with it.

If applications had to handle all this complexity themselves the result would be huge amounts of brittle and duplicative code, leading to high rates of user-visible defects and constant problems as hardware gradually mutated out from under the applications.

GPSD isolates location-aware applications from hardware interface details by knowing about all the protocols itself (at time of writing we support about 20 different ones), managing serial and USB devices so the applications don't have to, and reporting sensor payload information in a simple device-independent JSON format. GPSD further simplifies life by providing client libraries so client applications need not even know about that reporting format. Instead, getting sensor information becomes a simple procedure call.

GPSD also supports precision timekeeping; it can act as a time source for ntpd (the Network Time Protocol Daemon) if any of its attached sensors have PPS (pulse-per-second) capability. The GPSD developers cooperate closely with the ntpd project in improving the network time service.

We are presently (mid-2011) working on completing support for the AIS network of marine navigational receivers. In the future, we expect to support new kinds of location-aware sensors—such as receivers for second-generation aircraft transponders—as protocol documentation and test devices become available.

To sum up, the single most important theme in GPSD's design is hiding all the device-dependent ugliness behind a simple client interface talking to a zero-configuration service.

7.2 The External View

The main program in the GPSD suite is the gpsd service daemon. It can collect the take from a set of attached sensor devices over RS232, USB, Bluetooth, TCP/IP, and UDP links. Reports are normally shipped to TCP/IP port 2947, but can also go out via a shared-memory or D-BUS interface.

The GPSD distribution ships with client libraries for C, C++, and Python. It includes sample clients in C, C++, Python, and PHP. A Perl client binding is available via CPAN. These client libraries are not merely a convenience for application developers; they save GPSD's developers headaches too, by isolating applications from the details of GPSD's JSON reporting protocol. Thus, the API exposed to clients can remain the same even as the protocol grows new features for new sensor types.

Other programs in the suite include a utility for low-level device monitoring (gpsmon), a profiler that produces reports on error statistics and device timing (gpsprof), a utility for tweaking device settings (gpsctl), and a program for batch-converting sensor logs into readable JSON (gpsdecode). Together, they help technically savvy users look as deeply into the operation of the attached sensors as they care to.

Of course, these tools also help GPSD's own developers verify the correct operation of gpsd. The single most important test tool is gpsfake, a test harness for gpsd which can connect it to any number of sensor logs as though they were live devices. With gpsfake, we can re-run a sensor log shipped with a bug report to reproduce specific problems. gpsfake is also the engine of our extensive regression-test suite, which lowers the cost of modifying the software by making it easy to spot changes that break things.

One of the most important lessons we think we have for future projects is that it is not enough for a software suite to be correct, it should also be able to *demonstrate its own correctness*. We have found that when this goal is pursued properly it is not a hair shirt but rather a pair of wings—the time we've take to write test harnesses and regression tests has paid for itself many times over in the freedom it gives us to modify code without fearing that we are wreaking subtle havoc on existing functionality.

7.3 The Software Layers

There is a lot more going on inside GPSD than the "plug a sensor in and it just works" experience might lead people to assume. gpsd's internals break naturally into four pieces: the *drivers*, the *packet sniffer*, the *core library* and the *multiplexer*. We'll describe these from the bottom up.

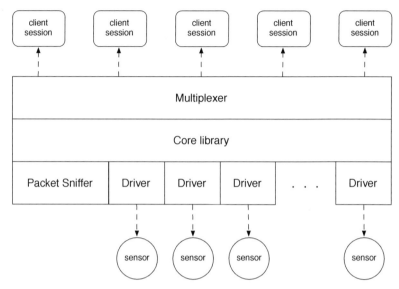

Figure 7.1: Software layers

The *drivers* are essentially user-space device drivers for each kind of sensor chipset we support. The key entry points are methods to parse a data packet into time-position-velocity or status information, change its mode or baud rate, probe for device subtype, etc. Auxiliary methods may support driver control operations, such as changing the serial speed of the device. The entire interface to a driver is a C structure full of data and method pointers, deliberately modeled on a Unix device driver structure.

The *packet sniffer* is responsible for mining data packets out of serial input streams. It's basically a state machine that watches for anything that looks like one of our 20 or so known packet types (most of which are checksummed, so we can have high confidence when we think we have identified one). Because devices can hotplug or change modes, the type of packet that will come up the wire from a serial or USB port isn't necessarily fixed forever by the first one recognized.

The *core library* manages a session with a sensor device. The key entry points are:

- starting a session by opening the device and reading data from it, hunting through baud rates and parity/stopbit combinations until the packet sniffer achieves synchronization lock with a known packet type;
- polling the device for a packet; and
- closing the device and wrapping up the session.

A key feature of the core library is that it is responsible for switching each GPS connection to using the correct device driver depending on the packet type that the sniffer returns. This is *not configured in advance* and may change over time, notably if the device switches between different reporting protocols. (Most GPS chipsets support NMEA and one or more vendor binary protocols, and devices like AIS receivers may report packets in two different protocols on the same wire.)

Finally, the *multiplexer* is the part of the daemon that handles client sessions and device assignment. It is responsible for passing reports up to clients, accepting client commands, and responding to hotplug notifications. It is essentially all contained in one source file, gpsd.c, and never talks to the device drivers directly.

The first three components (other than the multiplexer) are linked together in a library called libgpsd and can be used separately from the multiplexer. Our other tools that talk to sensors directly, such as gpsmon and gpsctl, do it by calling into the core library and driver layer directly.

The most complex single component is the packet sniffer at about two thousand lines of code. This is irreducible; a state machine that can recognize as many different protocols as it does is bound to be large and gnarly. Fortunately, the packet sniffer is also easy to isolate and test; problems in it do not tend to be coupled to other parts of the code.

The multiplexer layer is about same size, but somewhat less gnarly. The device drivers make up the bulk of the daemon code at around 15 KLOC. All the rest of the code—all the support tools and libraries and test clients together—adds up to about the size of the daemon (some code, notably the JSON parser, is shared between the daemon and the client libraries).

The success of this layering approach is demonstrated in a couple of different ways. One is that new device drivers are so easy to write that several have been contributed by people not on the core team: the driver API is documented, and the individual drivers are coupled to the core library only via pointers in a master device types table.

Another benefit is that system integrators can drastically reduce GPSD's footprint for embedded deployment simply by electing not to compile in unused drivers. The daemon is not large to begin with, and a suitably stripped-down build runs quite happily on low-power, low-speed, small-memory ARM devices[1].

A third benefit of the layering is that the daemon multiplexer can be detached from atop the core library and replaced with simpler logic, such as the straight batch conversion of sensor logfiles to JSON reports that the gpsdecode utility does.

There is nothing novel about this part of the GPSD architecture. Its lesson is that conscious and rigorous application of the design pattern of Unix device handling is beneficial not just in OS kernels but also in userspace programs that are similarly required to deal with varied hardware and protocols.

7.4 The Dataflow View

Now we'll consider GPSD's architecture from a dataflow view. In normal operation, gpsd spins in a loop waiting for input from one of these sources:

1. A set of clients making requests over a TCP/IP port.
2. A set of navigation sensors connected via serial or USB devices.
3. The special control socket used by hotplug scripts and some configuration tools.
4. A set of servers issuing periodic differential-GPS correction updates (DGPS and NTRIP). These are handled as though they are navigation sensors.

When a USB port goes active with a device that might be a navigation sensor, a hotplug script (shipped with GPSD) sends a notification to the control socket. This is the cue for the multiplexer layer to put the device on its internal list of sensors. Conversely, a device-removal event can remove a device from that list.

---

[1] ARM is a 32-bit RISC instruction set architecture used in mobile and embedded electronics. See http://en.wikipedia.org/wiki/ARM_architecture.

When a client issues a watch request, the multiplexer layer opens the navigation sensors in its list and begins accepting data from them (by adding their file descriptors to the set in the main select call). Otherwise all GPS devices are closed (but remain in the list) and the daemon is quiescent. Devices that stop sending data get timed out of the device list.

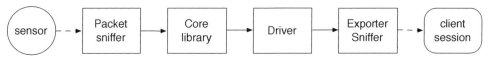

Figure 7.2: Dataflow

When data comes in from a navigation sensor, it's fed to the packet sniffer, a finite-state machine that works like the lexical analyzer in a compiler. The packet sniffer's job is to accumulate data from each port (separately), recognizing when it has accumulated a packet of a known type.

A packet may contain a position fix from a GPS, a marine AIS datagram, a sensor reading from a magnetic compass, a DGPS (Differential GPS) broadcast packet, or any of several other things. The packet sniffer doesn't care about the content of the packet; all it does is tell the core library when it has accumulated one and pass back the payload and the packet type.

The core library then hands the packet to the driver associated with its type. The driver's job is to mine data out of the packet payload into a per-device session structure and set some status bits telling the multiplexer layer what kind data it got.

One of those bits is an indication that the daemon has accumulated enough data to ship a report to its clients. When this bit is raised after a data read from a sensor device, it means we've seen the end of a packet, the end of a packet group (which may be one or more packets), and the data in the device's session structure should be passed to one of the exporters.

The main exporter is the "socket" one; it generates a report object in JSON and ships it to all the clients watching the device. There's a shared-memory exporter that copies the data to a shared-memory segment instead. In either of these cases, it is expected that a client library will unmarshal the data into a structure in the client program's memory space. A third exporter, which ships position updates via DBUS, is also available.

The GPSD code is as carefully partitioned horizontally as it vertically. The packet sniffer neither knows nor needs to know anything about packet payloads, and doesn't care whether its input source is a USB port, an RS232 device, a Bluetooth radio link, a pseudo-tty, a TCP socket connection, or a UDP packet stream. The drivers know how to analyze packet payloads, but know nothing about either the packet-sniffer internals nor the exporters. The exporters look only at the session data structure updated by the drivers.

This separation of function has served GPSD very well. For example, when we got a request in early 2010 to adapt the code to accept sensor data coming in as UDP packets for the on-board navigation system of a robot submarine, it was easy to implement that in a handful of lines of code without disturbing later stages in the data pipeline.

More generally, careful layering and modularization has made it relatively easy to add new sensor types. We incorporate new drivers every six months or so; some have been written by people who are not core developers.

7.5 Defending the Architecture

As an open source program like gpsd evolves, one of the recurring themes is that each contributor will do things to solve his or her particular problem case which gradually leak more information between layers or stages that were originally designed with clean separation.

One that we're concerned about at the time of writing is that some information about input source type (USB, RS232, pty, Bluetooth, TCP, UDP) seems to need to be passed up to the multiplexer layer, to tell it, for example, whether probe strings should be sent to an unidentified device. Such probes are sometimes required to wake up RS232C sensors, but there are good reasons not to ship them to any more devices than we have to. Many GPSs and other sensor devices are designed on low budgets and in a hurry; some can be confused to the point of catatonia by unexpected control strings.

For a similar reason, the daemon has a -b option that prevents it from attempting baud-rate changes during the packet-sniffer hunt loop. Some poorly made Bluetooth devices handle these so poorly that they have to be power-cycled to function again; in one extreme case a user actually had to unsolder the backup battery to unwedge his!

Both these cases are necessary exceptions to the project's design rules. Much more usually, though, such exceptions are a bad thing. For example, we've had some patches contributed to make PPS time service work better that messed up the vertical layering, making it impossible for PPS to work properly with more than the one driver they were intended to help. We rejected these in favor of working harder at device-type-independent improvement.

On one occasion some years ago, we had a request to support a GPS with the odd property that the checksums in its NMEA packets may be invalid when the device doesn't have a location fix. To support this device, we would have had to either (a) give up on validating the checksum on *any* incoming data that looked like an NMEA packet, risking that the packet-sniffer would hand garbage to the NMEA driver, or (b) add a command-line option to force the sensor type.

The project lead (the author of this chapter) refused to do either. Giving up on NMEA packet validation was an obvious bad idea. But a switch to force the sensor type would have been an invitation to get lazy about proper autoconfiguration, which would cause problems all the way up to GPSD's client applications and their users. The next step down that road paved with good intentions would surely have been a baud-rate switch. Instead, we declined to support this broken device.

One of the most important duties of a project's lead architect is to defend the architecture against expedient "fixes" that would break it and cause functional problems or severe maintenance headaches down the road. Arguments over this can get quite heated, especially when defending architecture conflicts against something that a developer or user considers a must-have feature. But these arguments are necessary, because the easiest choice is often the wrong one for the longer term.

7.6 Zero Configuration, Zero Hassles

An extremely important feature of gpsd is that it is a zero-configuration service[2]. It has no dotfile! The daemon deduces the sensor types it's talking to by sniffing the incoming data. For RS232 and USB devices gpsd even autobauds (that is, automatically detects the serial line speed), so it is not necessary for the daemon to know in advance the speed/parity/stopbits at which the sensor is shipping information.

When the host operating system has a hotplug capability, hotplug scripts can ship device-activation and deactivation messages to a control socket to notify the daemon of the change in its environment.

---

[2]With one minor exception for Bluetooth devices with broken firmware.

The GPSD distribution supplies these scripts for Linux. The result is that end users can plug a USB GPS into their laptop and expect it to immediately begin supplying reports that location-aware applications can read—no muss, no fuss, and no editing a dotfile or preferences registry.

The benefits of this ripple all the way up the application stack. Among other things, it means that location-aware applications don't have to have a configuration panel dedicated to tweaking the GPS and port settings until the whole mess works. This saves a lot of effort for application writers as well as users: they get to treat location as a service that is nearly as simple as the system clock.

One consequence of the zero-configuration philosophy is that we do not look favorably on proposals to add a config file or additional command-line options. The trouble with this is that configuration which can be edited, *must* be edited. This implies adding setup hassle for end users, which is precisely what a well-designed service daemon should avoid.

The GPSD developers are Unix hackers working from deep inside the Unix tradition, in which configurability and having lots of knobs is close to being a religion. Nevertheless, we think open source projects could be trying a lot harder to throw away their dotfiles and autoconfigure to what the running environment is actually doing.

7.7 Embedded Constraints Considered Helpful

Designing for embedded deployment has been a major goal of GPSD since 2005. This was originally because we got a lot of interest from system integrators working with single-board computers, but it has since paid off in an unexpected way: deployment on GPS-enabled smartphones. (Our very favorite embedded-deployment reports are still the ones from the robot submarines, though.)

Designing for embedded deployment has influenced GPSD in important ways. We think a lot about ways to keep memory footprint and CPU usage low so the code will run well on low-speed, small-memory, power-constrained systems.

One important attack on this issue, as previously mentioned, is to ensure that gpsd builds don't have to carry any deadweight over the specific set of sensor protocols that a system integrator needs to support. In June 2011 a minimum static build of gpsd on an x86 system has a memory footprint of about 69K (that is *with* all required standard C libraries linked in) on 64-bit x86. For comparison, the static build with all drivers is about 418K.

Another is that we profile for CPU hotspots with a slightly different emphasis than most projects. Because location sensors tend to report only small amounts of data at intervals on the order of 1 second, performance in the normal sense isn't a GPSD issue—even grossly inefficient code would be unlikely to introduce enough latency to be visible at the application level. Instead, our focus is on decreasing processor usage and power consumption. We've been quite successful at this: even on low-power ARM systems without an FPU, gpsd's fraction of CPU is down around the level of profiler noise.

While designing the core code for low footprint and good power efficiency is at this point largely a solved problem, there is one respect in which targeting embedded deployments still produces tension in the GPSD architecture: use of scripting languages. On the one hand, we want to minimize defects due to low-level resource management by moving as much code as possible out of C. On the other hand, Python (our preferred scripting language) is simply too heavyweight and slow for most embedded deployments.

We've split the difference in the obvious way: the gpsd service daemon is C, while the test framework and several of the support utilities are written in Python. Over time, we hope to migrate more of the auxiliary code out of C and into Python, but embedded deployment makes those choices a continuing source of controversy and discomfort.

Still, on the whole we find the pressures from embedded deployment quite bracing. It feels good to write code that is lean, tight, and sparing of processor resources. It has been said that art comes from creativity under constraints; to the extent that's true, GPSD is better art for the pressure.

That feeling doesn't translate directly into advice for other projects, but something else definitely does: don't guess, measure! There is nothing like regular profiling and footprint measurements to warn you when you're straying into committing bloat—and to reassure you that you're not.

7.8 JSON and the Architecturenauts

One of the most significant transitions in the history of the project was when we switched over from the original reporting protocol to using JSON as a metaprotocol and passing reports up to clients as JSON objects. The original protocol had used one-letter keys for commands and responses, and we literally ran out of keyspace as the daemon's capabilities gradually increased.

Switching to JSON was a big, big win. JSON combines the traditional Unix virtues of a purely textual format—easy to examine with a Mark 1 Eyeball, easy to edit with standard tools, easy to generate programmatically—with the ability to pass structured information in rich and flexible ways.

By mapping report types to JSON objects, we ensured that any report could contain mixes of string, numeric, and Boolean data with structure (a capability the old protocol lacked). By identifying report types with a `"class"` attribute, we guaranteed that we would always be able to add new report types without stepping on old ones.

This decision was not without cost. A JSON parser is a bit more computationally expensive than the very simple and limited parser it replaced, and certainly requires more lines of code (implying more places for defects to occur). Also, conventional JSON parsers require dynamic storage allocation in order to cope with the variable-length arrays and dictionaries that JSON describes, and dynamic storage allocation is a notorious defect attractor.

We coped with these problems in several ways. The first step was to write a C parser for a (sufficiently) large subset of JSON that uses entirely static storage. This required accepting some minor restrictions; for example, objects in our dialect cannot contain the JSON `null` value, and arrays always have a fixed maximum length. Accepting these restrictions allowed us to fit the parser into 600 lines of C.

We then built a comprehensive set of unit tests for the parser in order to verify error-free operation. Finally, for very tight embedded deployments where the overhead of JSON might be too high, we wrote a shared-memory exporter that bypasses the need to ship and parse JSON entirely if the daemon and its client have access to common memory.

JSON isn't just for web applications anymore. We think anyone designing an application protocol should consider an approach like GPSD's. Of course the idea of building your protocol on top of a standard metaprotocol is not new; XML fans have been pushing it for many years, and that makes sense for protocols with a document-like structure. JSON has the advantages of being lower-overhead than XML and better fitted to passing around array and record structures.

7.9 Designing for Zero Defects

Because of its use in navigational systems, any software that lives between the user and a GPS or other location sensor is potentially life-critical, especially at sea or when airborne. Open source navigation software has a tendency to try to evade this problem by shipping with disclaimers that say, "Don't rely on this if doing so might put lives at risk."

We think such disclaimers are futile and dangerous: futile because system integrators are quite likely to treat them as pro-forma and ignore them, and dangerous because they encourage developers to fool themselves that code defects won't have serious consequences, and that cutting corners in quality assurance is acceptable.

The GPSD project developers believe that the only acceptable policy is to design for zero defects. Software complexity being what it is, we have not quite achieved this—but for a project GPSD's size and age and complexity we come very close.

Our strategy for doing this is a combination of architecture and coding policies that aim to *exclude the possibility of defects in shipped code*.

One important policy is this: the gpsd daemon never uses dynamic storage allocation—no malloc or calloc, and no calls to any functions or libraries that require it. At a stroke this banishes the single most notorious defect attractor in C coding. We have no memory leaks and no double-malloc or double-free bugs, and we never will.

We get away with this because all of the sensors we handle emit packets with relatively small fixed maximum lengths, and the daemon's job is to digest them and ship them to clients with minimal buffering. Still, banishing malloc requires coding discipline and some design compromises, a few of which we previously noted in discussing the JSON parser. We pay these costs willingly to reduce our defect rate.

A useful side effect of this policy is that it increases the effectiveness of static code checkers such as splint, cppcheck, and Coverity. This feeds into another major policy choice; we make extremely heavy use of both these code-auditing tools and a custom framework for regression testing. (We do not know of any program suite larger than GPSD that is fully splint-annotated, and strongly suspect that none such yet exist.)

The highly modular architecture of GPSD aids us here as well. The module boundaries serve as cut points where we can rig test harnesses, and we have very systematically done so. Our normal regression test checks everything from the floating-point behavior of the host hardware up through JSON parsing to correct reporting behavior on over seventy different sensor logs.

Admittedly, we have a slightly easier time being rigorous than many applications would because the daemon has no user-facing interfaces; the environment around it is just a bunch of serial data streams and is relatively easy to simulate. Still, as with banishing malloc, actually exploiting that advantage requires the right attitude, which very specifically means being willing to spend as much design and coding time on test tools and harnesses as we do on the production code. This is a policy we think other open-source projects can and should emulate.

As I write (July 2011), GPSD's project bug tracker is empty. It has been empty for weeks, and based on past rates of bug submissions we can expect it to stay that way for a good many more. We haven't shipped code with a crash bug in six years. When we do have bugs, they tend to be the sort of minor missing feature or mismatch with specification that is readily fixed in a few minutes of work.

This is not to say that the project has been an uninterrupted idyll. Next, we'll review some of our mistakes...

7.10 Lessons Learned

Software design is difficult; mistakes and blind alleys are all too normal a part of it, and GPSD has been no exception to that rule. The largest mistake in this project's history was the design of the original pre-JSON protocol for requesting and reporting GPS information. Recovering from it took years of effort, and there are lessons in both the original mis-design and the recovery.

There were two serious problems with the original protocol:

1. Poor extensibility. It used requests and response tags consisting of a single letter each, case-insensitive. Thus, for example, the request to report longitude and latitude was "P" and a response looked like "P -75.32 40.05". Furthermore, the parser interpreted a request like "PA" as a "P" request followed by an "A" (altitude) request. As the daemon's capabilities gradually broadened, we literally ran out of command space.
2. A mismatch between the protocol's implicit model of sensor behavior and how they actually behave. The old protocol was request/response: send a request for position (or altitude, or whatever) get back a report sometime later. In reality, it is usually not possible to request a report from a GPS or other navigation-related sensors; they stream out reports, and the best a request can do is query a cache. This mismatch encouraged sloppy data-handling from applications; too often, they would ask for location data without also requesting a timestamp or any check information about the fix quality, a practice which could easily result in stale or invalid data getting presented to the user.

It became clear as early as 2006 that the old protocol design was inadequate, but it took nearly three years of design sketches and false starts to design a new one. The transition took two years after that, and caused some pain for developers of client applications. It would have cost a lot more if the project had not shipped client-side libraries that insulated users from most of the protocol details—but we didn't get the API of those libraries quite right either at first.

If we had known then what we know now, the JSON-based protocol would have been introduced five years sooner, and the API design of the client libraries would have required many fewer revisions. But there are some kinds of lessons only experience and experiment can teach.

There are at least two design guidelines that future service daemons could bear in mind to avoid replicating our mistakes:

1. Design for extensibility. If your daemon's application protocol can run out of namespace the way our old one did, you're doing it wrong. Overestimating the short-term costs and underestimating the long-term benefits of metaprotocols like XML and JSON is an error that's all too common.
2. Client-side libraries are a better idea than exposing the application protocol details. A library may be able to adapt its internals to multiple versions of the application protocol, substantially reducing both interface complexity and defect rates compared to the alternative, in which each application writer needs to develop an ad hoc binding. This difference will translate directly into fewer bug reports on your project's tracker.

One possible reply to our emphasis on extensibility, not just in GPSD's application protocol but in other aspects of the project architecture like the packet-driver interface, is to dismiss it as an over-elaboration brought about by mission creep. Unix programmers schooled in the tradition of "do one thing well" may ask whether gpsd's command set really needs to be larger in 2011 than it was in 2006, why gpsd now handles non-GPS sensors like magnetic compasses and Marine AIS receivers, and why we contemplate possibilities like ADS-B aircraft tracking.

These are fair questions. We can approach an answer by looking at the actual complexity cost of adding a new device type. For very good reasons, including relatively low data volumes and the high electrical-noise levels historically associated with serial wires to sensors, almost all reporting protocols for GPSs and other navigation-related sensors look broadly similar: small packets with a validation checksum of some sort. Such protocols are fiddly to handle but not really difficult to distinguish from each other and parse, and the incremental cost of adding a new one tends to be less than a KLOC each. Even the most complex of our supported protocols with their own report generators attached, such as Marine AIS, only cost on the order of 3 KLOC each. In aggregate, the drivers plus the packet-sniffer and their associated JSON report generators are about 18 KLOC total.

Comparing this with 43 KLOC for the project as a whole, we see that most of the complexity cost of GPSD is actually in the framework code around the drivers—and (importantly) in the test tools and framework for verifying the daemon's correctness. Duplicating these would be a much larger project than writing any individual packet parser. So writing a GPSD-equivalent for a packet protocol that GPSD doesn't handle would be a great deal more work than adding another driver and test set to GPSD itself. Conversely, the most economical outcome (and the one with the lowest expected cumulative rate of defects) is for GPSD to grow packet drivers for many different sensor types.

The "one thing" that GPSD has evolved to do well is handle any collection of sensors that ship distinguishable checksummed packets. What looks like mission creep is actually preventing many different and duplicative handler daemons from having to be written. Instead, application developers get one relatively simple API and the benefit of our hard-won expertise at design and testing across an increasing range of sensor types.

What distinguishes GPSD from a mere mission-creepy pile of features is not luck or black magic but careful application of known best practices in software engineering. The payoff from these begins with a low defect rate in the present, and continues with the ability to support new features with little effort or expected impact on defect rates in the future.

Perhaps the most important lesson we have for other open-source projects is this: reducing defect rates asymptotically close to zero is difficult, but it's not impossible—not even for a project as widely and variously deployed as GPSD is. Sound architecture, good coding practice, and a really determined focus on testing can achieve it—and the most important prerequisite is the discipline to pursue all three.

[chapter 8]

The Dynamic Language Runtime and the Iron Languages
Jeff Hardy

The Iron languages are an informal group of language implementations with "Iron" in their names, in honour of the first one, IronPython. All of these languages have at least one thing in common—they are dynamic languages that target the Common Language Runtime (CLR), which is more commonly known as the .NET Framework[1], and they are built on top of the Dynamic Language Runtime (DLR). The DLR is a set of libraries for the CLR that provide much better support for dynamic languages on the CLR. IronPython and IronRuby are both used in a few dozen closed and open source projects, and are both under active development; the DLR, which started as an open-source project, is included as part of the .NET Framework and Mono.

Architecturally, IronPython, IronRuby, and the DLR are both simple and devilishly complex. From a high level, the designs are similar to many other language implementations, with parsers and compilers and code generators; however, look a little closer and the interesting details begin to emerge: call sites, binders, adaptive compilation, and other techniques are used to make dynamic languages perform nearly as fast as static languages on a platform that was designed for static languages.

8.1 History

The history of the Iron languages begins in 2003. Jim Hugunin had already written an implementation of Python, called Jython, for the Java Virtual Machine (JVM). At the time, the then-new .NET Framework Common Language Runtime (CLR) was considered by some (exactly who, I'm not sure) to be poorly suited for implementing dynamic languages such as Python. Having already implemented Python on the JVM, Jim was curious as to how Microsoft could have made .NET so much worse than Java. In a September 2006 blog post[2], he wrote:

> I wanted to understand how Microsoft could have screwed up so badly that the CLR was a worse platform for dynamic languages than the JVM. My plan was to take a couple of weeks to build a prototype implementation of Python on the CLR and then to use that work to write a short pithy article called, "Why the CLR is a terrible platform for dynamic languages". My plans quickly changed as I worked on the prototype, because I

---
[1] "CLR" is the generic term; the .NET Framework is Microsoft's implementation, and there is also the open-source Mono implementation.
[2] http://blogs.msdn.com/b/hugunin/archive/2006/09/05/741605.aspx

found that Python could run extremely well on the CLR—in many cases noticeably faster than the C-based implementation. For the standard pystone[3] benchmark, IronPython on the CLR was about 1.7x faster than the C-based implementation.

(The "Iron" part of the name was a play on the name of Jim's company at the time, Want of a Nail Software.)

Shortly afterwards, Jim was hired by Microsoft to make .NET an even better platform for dynamic languages. Jim (and several others) developed the DLR by factoring the language-neutral parts out of the original IronPython code. The DLR was designed to provide a common core for implementing dynamic languages for .NET, and was a major new feature of .NET 4.

At the same time as the DLR was announced (April 2007), Microsoft also announced that, in addition to a new version of IronPython built on top of the DLR (IronPython 2.0), they would be developing IronRuby on top of the DLR to demonstrate the DLR's adaptability to multiple languages[4]. Integration with dynamic languages using the DLR would also be a major part of C# and Visual Basic, with a new keyword (dynamic) that allowed those languages to easily call into any language implemented on the DLR, or any other dynamic data source. The CLR was already a good platform for implementing static languages, and the DLR makes dynamic languages a first-class citizen.

Other language implementations from outside of Microsoft also use the DLR, including IronScheme[5] and IronJS[6]. In addition, Microsoft's PowerShell v3 will use the DLR instead of its own dynamic object system.

8.2 Dynamic Language Runtime Principles

The CLR is designed with statically-typed languages in mind; the knowledge of types is baked very deeply into the runtime, and one of its key assumptions is that those types do not change—that a variable never changes its type, or that a type never has any fields or members added or removed while the program is running. This is fine for languages like C# or Java, but dynamic languages, by definition, do not follow those rules. The CLR also provides a common object system for static types, which means that any .NET language can call objects written in any other .NET language with no extra effort.

Without the DLR, every dynamic language would have to provide its own object model; the various dynamic languages would not be able to call objects in another dynamic language, and C# would not be able to treat IronPython and IronRuby equally. Thus, the heart of the DLR is a standard way of implementing *dynamic objects* while still allowing an object's behaviour to be customized for a particular language by using *binders*. It also includes a mechanism known as *call-site caching* for ensuring that dynamic operations are as fast as possible, and a set of classes for building *expression trees*, which allow code to be stored as data and easily manipulated.

The CLR also provides several other features that are useful to dynamic languages, including a sophisticated garbage collector; a Just-in-Time (JIT) compiler that converts Common Intermediate Language (IL) bytecode, which is what .NET compilers output, into machine code at runtime; a runtime introspection system, which allows dynamic languages to call objects written in any static language; and finally, dynamic methods (also known as lightweight code generation) that allow code

---

[3] http://ironpython.codeplex.com/wikipage?title=IP26RC1VsCPy26Perf
[4] In October of 2010, Microsoft stopped developing IronPython and IronRuby and they became independent open-source projects.
[5] http://ironscheme.codeplex.com/
[6] https://github.com/fholm/IronJS/

to be generated at runtime and then executed with only sightly more overhead than a static method call[7].

The result of the DLR design is that languages like IronPython and IronRuby can call each other's objects (and those of any other DLR language), because they have a common dynamic object model. Support for this object model was also added to C# 4 (with the dynamic keyword) and Visual Basic 10 (in addition to VB's existing method of "late binding") so that they can perform dynamic calls on objects as well. The DLR thus makes dynamic languages first-class citizens on .NET.

Interestingly, the DLR is entirely implemented as a set of libraries and can be built and run on .NET 2.0 as well. No changes to the CLR are required to implement it.

8.3 Language Implementation Details

Every language implementation has two basic stages—*parsing* (the front end) and *code generation* (the backend). In the DLR, each language implements its own front end, which contains the language parser and syntax tree generator; the DLR provides a common backend that takes expression trees to produce Intermediate Language (IL) for the CLR to consume; the CLR will pass the IL to a Just-In-Time (JIT) compiler, which produces machine code to run on the processor. Code that is defined at runtime (and run using eval) is handled similarly, except that everything happens at the eval call site instead of when the file is loaded.

There are a few different way to implement the key pieces of a language front end, and while IronPython and IronRuby are very similar (they were developed side-by-side, after all) they differ in a few key areas. Both IronPython and IronRuby have fairly standard parser designs—both use a *tokenizer* (also known as a *lexer*) to split the text into tokens, and then the *parser* turns those tokens into an *abstract syntax tree* (AST) that represents the program. However, the languages have completely different implementations of these pieces.

8.4 Parsing

IronPython's tokenizer is in the `IronPython.Compiler.Tokenizer` class and the parser is in the `IronPython.Compiler.Parser` class. The tokenizer is a hand-written state machine that recognizes Python keywords, operators, and names and produces the corresponding tokens. Each token also carries with it any additional information (such as the value of a constant or name), as well as where in the source the token was found, to aid in debugging. The parser then takes this set of tokens and compares them to the Python grammar to see if it matches legal Python constructs.

IronPython's parser is an LL(1) *recursive descent parser*. The parser will look at the incoming token, call a function if the token is allowed and return an error if it is not. A recursive descent parser is built from a set of mutually recursive functions; these functions ultimately implement a state machine, with each new token triggering a state transition. Like the tokenizer, IronPython's parser is written by hand.

IronRuby, on the other hand, has a tokenizer and parser generated by the Gardens Point Parser Generator (GPPG). The parser is is described in the `Parser.y` file[8], which is a yacc-format file that describes the grammar of IronRuby at a high level using *rules* that describe the grammar. GPPG then

---

[7]The JVM acquired a similar mechanism with invokedynamic in Java 7.
[8]Languages/Ruby/Ruby/Compiler/Parser/Parser.y

takes `Parser.y` and creates the actual parser functions and tables; the result is a *table-based* LALR(1) parser. The generated tables are long arrays of integers, where each integer represents a state; based on the current state and the current token, the tables determine which state should be transitioned to next. While IronPython's recursive descent parser is quite easy to read, IronRuby's generated parser is not. The transition table is enormous (540 distinct states and over 45,000 transitions) and it is next to impossible to modify it by hand.

Ultimately, this is an engineering tradeoff—IronPython's parser is simple enough to modify by hand, but complex enough that it obscures the structure of the language. The IronRuby parser, on the other hand, makes it much easier to understand the structure of the language in the `Parser.y` file, but it is now dependent on a third-party tool that uses a custom (albeit well-known) domain-specific language and may have its own bugs or quirks. In this case, the IronPython team didn't want to commit to a dependency on an external tool, while the IronRuby team didn't mind.

What is clear, however, is how important state machines are to parsing, at every phase. For any parsing task, no matter how simple, a state machine is always the right answer.

The output of the parser for either language is an abstract syntax tree (AST). This describes the structure of the program at a high level, with each node mapping directly to a language construct—a statement or expression. These trees can be manipulated at runtime, often to make optimizations to the program before compilation. However, a language's AST is tied to the language; the DLR needs to operate on trees that do not contain any language-specific constructs, only general ones.

8.5 Expression Trees

An *expression tree* is also a representation of a program that can be manipulated at runtime, but in a lower-level, language-independent form. In .NET, the node types are in the `System.Linq.Expressions` namespace[9], and all of the node types are derived from the abstract `Expression` class. These expression trees cover more than just expressions, however, as there are node types for `if` statements, `try` blocks, and loops as well; in some languages (Ruby, for one) these are expressions and not statements.

There are nodes to cover almost every feature a programming language could want. However, they tend to be defined at a fairly low level—instead of having `ForExpression`, `WhileExpression`, etc., there is a single `LoopExpression` which, when combined with a `GotoExpression`, can describe any type of loop. To describe a language at a higher level, languages can define their own node types by deriving from `Expression` and overriding the `Reduce()` method, which returns another expression tree. In IronPython, the parse tree is also a DLR expression tree, but it contains many custom nodes that the DLR would not normally understand (such as `ForStatement`). These custom nodes can be reduced to expression trees that the DLR does understand (such as a combination of `LoopExpressions` and `GotoExpressions`). A custom expression node can reduce to other custom expression nodes, so the reduction proceeds recursively until only the intrinsic DLR nodes remain. One key difference between IronPython and IronRuby is that while IronPython's AST is also an expression tree, IronRuby's is not. Instead, IronRuby's AST is transformed into an expression tree before moving onto the next stage. It's arguable whether having the AST also be an expression tree is actually useful, so IronRuby did not implement it that way.

Each node type knows how to reduce itself, and it can usually only be reduced in one way. For transformations that come from code outside the tree—optimizations such as constant folding, for ex-

---

[9]The namespace is a historical artifact; expression trees were originally added in .NET 3.5 to implement LINQ—Language Integrated Query—and the DLR expression trees extended that.

ample, or IronPython's implementation of Python generators—a subclass of the `ExpressionVisitor` class is used. `ExpressionVisitor` has a `Visit()` method that calls the `Accept()` method on `Expression`, and subclasses of `Expression` override `Accept()` to call a specific `Visit()` method on `ExpressionVisitor`, such as `VisitBinary()`. This is a textbook implementation of the *Visitor pattern* from Gamma et al.—there's a fixed set of node types to visit, and an infinite number of operations that could be performed upon them. When the expression visitor visits a node, it usually recursively visits its children as well, and its children, and so on down the tree. However, an `ExpressionVisitor` can't actually modify the expression tree it is visiting, because expression trees are immutable. If the expression visitor needs to modify a node (such as removing children), it must produce a new node that replaces the old one instead, and all of its parents as well.

Once an expression tree has been created, reduced, and visited, it ultimately needs to be executed. While expression trees can be compiled directly to IL code, IronPython and IronRuby pass them to an interpreter first, because compiling directly to IL is expensive for code that may only be executed a handful of times.

8.6 Interpreting and Compilation

One of the downsides to using a JIT compiler, like .NET does, is that it imposes a time penalty when starting up because it takes time to convert the IL bytecode into machine code that the processor can run. JIT compilation makes the code much faster while running than using an interpreter, but the initial cost can be prohibitive, depending on what is being done. For example, a long-lived server process such as a web application will benefit from the JIT because the startup time is mostly irrelevant but the per-request time is critical, and it tends to run the same code repeatedly. On the other hand, a program that is run often but only for short periods of time, such as the Mercurial command-line client, would be better off with a short startup time because it likely only runs each chunk of code once, and the fact that the JIT'd code is faster doesn't overcome the fact that it takes longer to start running.

.NET can't execute IL code directly; it always gets JIT compiled into machine code, and this takes time. In particular, program startup times are one of the weak spots of the .NET Framework because much of the code needs to be JIT compiled. While there are ways to avoid the JIT penalty in static .NET programs[10], they don't work for dynamic programs. Rather than always compile directly to IL, IronRuby and IronPython will use their own interpreter (found in `Microsoft.Scripting.Interpreter`) that isn't as fast as JIT-compiled code but takes much less time to get started. The interpreter is also useful in situations where dynamic code generation is not allowed, such as on mobile platforms; otherwise the DLR languages would not be able to run at all.

Before execution, the entire expression tree must be wrapped in a function so that it can be executed. In the DLR, functions are represented as `LambdaExpression` nodes. While in most languages a lambda is an anonymous function, the DLR has no concept of names; all functions are anonymous. The `LambdaExpression` is unique in that it is the only node type that can be converted to a *delegate*, which is what .NET calls first-class functions, using its `Compile()` method. A delegate is similar to a C function pointer—it is simply a handle to a piece of code that can be called.

Initially, the expression tree is wrapped in a `LightLambdaExpression`, which can also produce a delegate that can be executed, but rather than generate IL code (which would then invoke the JIT), it instead compiles the expression tree to a list of instructions that are then executed on the interpreter's simple VM. The interpreter is a simple stack-based one; instructions pop values off

---

[10]Native Image Generation, or NGEN—http://msdn.microsoft.com/en-us/library/6t9t5wcf.aspx.

of the stack, perform an operation, and then push the result back on the stack. Each instruction is an instance of a class derived from `Microsoft.Scripting.Interpreter.Instruction` (such as `AddInstruction` or `BranchTrueInstruction`) that has properties describing how many items it takes off of the stack, how many it will put on, and a `Run()` method that executes the instruction by popping and pushing values on the stack and returning the offset of the next instruction. The interpreter takes the list of instructions and executes them one by one, jumping forward or backwards depending on the return value of the `Run()` method.

Once a a piece of code has been executed a certain number of times, it will be converted to a full `LambdaExpression` by calling `LightLambdaExpression.Reduce()`, then compiled to a `DynamicMethod` delegate (on a background thread for a bit of parallelism), and the old delegate call site will be replaced with the newer, faster one. This greatly reduces the cost of executing functions that may only be called a few times, such as the main function of a program, while making commonly called functions run as fast as possible. By default, the compilation threshold is set at 32 executions, but this can be changed with a command-line option or by the host program, and can include disabling either compilation or the interpreter entirely.

Whether running through the interpreter or compiled to IL, the language's operations are not hard-coded by the expression tree compiler. Instead, the compiler generates call sites for each operation that may be dynamic (which is nearly all of them). These call sites give the objects a chance to implement dynamic behaviour while still keeping performance high.

8.7 Dynamic Call Sites

In a static .NET language, all of the decisions about what code should be called are made at compile time. For example, consider the following line of C#:

```
var z = x + y;
```

The compiler knows what the types of 'x' and 'y' are and whether or not they can be added. The compiler can emit the proper code for handling overloaded operators, type conversions, or whatever else might be needed to make the code run properly, based solely on the static information it knows about the types involved. Now, consider the following line of Python code:

```
z = x + y
```

The IronPython compiler has *no idea* what this might do when it encounters it, because it doesn't know what the types of x and y are[11], and even if it did know, the ability of x and y to be added could change at runtime anyway. Instead of emitting the IL code for adding numbers, the IronPython emits a *call site* that will be resolved at runtime.

A call site is a placeholder for an operation to be determined at runtime; they are implemented as instances of the `System.Runtime.CompilerServices.CallSite` class. In a dynamic language like Ruby or Python, just about every operation has a dynamic component; these dynamic operations are represented in the expression trees as `DynamicExpression` nodes, which the expression tree compiler knows to convert to a call site. When a call site is created, it is does not yet know how to perform the desired operation; however, it is created with an instance of the proper *call site binder* that is specific to the language in use, and contains all of the necessary information about how to perform the operation.

---

[11] In principle it could, but neither IronPython nor IronRuby do type inference.

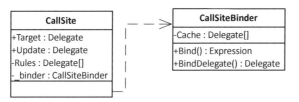

Figure 8.1: CallSite class diagram

Each language will have a different call site binder for each operation, and the binders often know many different ways to perform an operation depending on the arguments given to the call site. However, generating these rules is expensive (in particular, compiling them to a delegate for execution, which involves invoking the .NET JIT), so the call site has a multi-level *call site cache* that stores the rules that have already been created for later use.

The first level, L0, is the `CallSite.Target` property on the call site instance itself. This stores the most-recently-used rule for this call site; for a vast number of call sites, this is all that will ever be needed as they are only ever called with one set of argument types. The call site also has another cache, L1, that stores a further 10 rules. If `Target` is not valid for this call (for example, if the arguments types are different), the call site first checks its rules cache to see if it has already created the proper delegate from a previous call, and reuses that rule instead of creating a new one.

Storing rules in the cache is driven by the time it takes to actually compile a new rule compared to the time it takes to check the existing rules. Roughly speaking, it takes about 10 ns for .NET to execute a type check on a variable (checking a binary function takes 20 ns, etc.), which is the most common type of rule predicate. Compiling a simple method to add doubles, on the other hand, takes about 80 μs, or three orders of magnitude longer. The size of the caches is limited to prevent wasting memory storing every rule that gets used at a call site; for a simple addition, each variation requires about 1 KB of memory. However, profiling showed that very few call sites ever had more than 10 variations.

Finally, there is the L2 cache, which is stored on the binder instance itself. The binder instance that is associated with a call site may store some extra information with it that makes it specific to a call site, but a large number of call sites aren't unique in any way and can share the same binder instance. For example, in Python, the basic rules for addition are the same throughout the program; it depends on the two types on the either side of the +, and that's it. All of the addition operations in the program can share the same binder, and if both the L0 and L1 caches miss, the L2 cache contains a much larger number of recent rules (128) collected from across the entire program. Even if a call site is on its first execution, there's a good chance it might already find an appropriate rule in the L2 cache. To ensure that this works most effectively, IronPython and IronRuby both have a set of canonical binder instances that are used for common operations like addition.

If the L2 cache misses, the binder is asked to create an *implementation* for the call site, taking into account the types (and possibly even the values) of the arguments. In the above example, if x and y are doubles (or another native type), then the implementation simply casts them to doubles and calls the IL add instruction. The binder also produces a test that checks the arguments and ensures they are valid for the implementation. Together, the implementation and the test make a rule. In most cases, both the implementation and the test are created and stored as expression trees[12].

---

[12] The call site infrastructure does not depend on expression trees, however; it can be used with delegates alone.

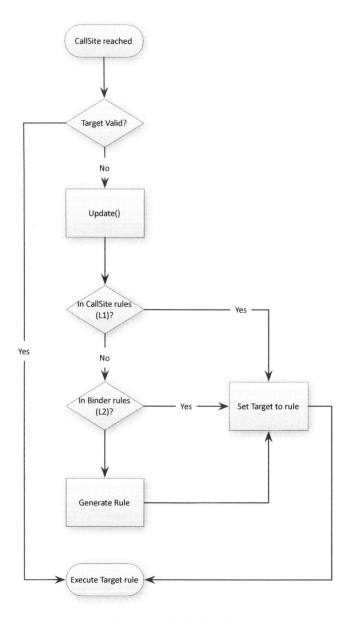

Figure 8.2: CallSite flowchart

If the expression trees were expressed in C#, the code would be similar to:

```
if(x is double && y is double) {        // check for doubles
     return (double)x + (double)y;      // execute if doubles
}
 return site.Update(site, x, y);        // not doubles, so find/create another rule
                                        // for these types
```

The binder then produces a *delegate* from the expression trees, which means the rule is compiled to IL and then to machine code. In the case of adding two numbers, this will likely become a quick type check and then a machine instruction to add the numbers. Even with all of the machinery involved, the ultimate end result is only marginally slower than static code. IronPython and IronRuby also include a set of precompiled rules for common operations like addition of primitive types, which saves time because they don't have to be created at runtime, but does cost some extra space on disk.

8.8 Meta-Object Protocol

Besides the language infrastructure, the other key part of the DLR is the ability for a language (the *host language*) to make dynamic calls on objects defined in another language (the *source language*). To make this possible, the DLR must be able to understand what operations are valid on an object, no matter the language it was written in. Python and Ruby have fairly similar object models, but JavaScript has a radically different prototype-based (as opposed class-based) type system. Instead of trying to unify the various type systems, the DLR treats them all as if they were based on Smalltalk-style *message passing*.

In a message-passing object-oriented system, objects send messages to other objects (with parameters, usually), and the object can return another object as a result. Thus, while each language has its own idea of what an object is, they can almost all be made equivalent by viewing method calls as messages that are sent between objects. Of course, even static OO languages fit this model to some extent; what makes dynamic languages different is that the method being called does not have to be known at compile time, or even exist on the object at all (e.g., Ruby's method_missing), and the target object usually has a chance to intercept the message and process it differently if necessary (e.g., Python's __getattr__).

The DLR defines the following messages:

- Get|Set|DeleteMember: operations for manipulating an object's members
- Get|Set|DeleteIndex: operations for indexed objects (such as arrays or dictionaries)
- Invoke, InvokeMember: invoke an object or member of an object
- CreateInstance: create an instance of an object
- Convert: convert an object from one type to another
- UnaryOperation, BinaryOperation: perform operator-based operations, such as negate (!) or add (+)

Taken together, these operations should be sufficient for implementing just about any language's object model.

Because the CLR is inherently statically typed, dynamic language objects must still be represented by static classes. The usual technique is to have a static class such as PythonObject and have the actual Python objects be instances of this class or its subclasses. For reasons of interoperability and performance, the DLR's mechanism is a lot more complicated. Instead of dealing with language-specific objects the DLR deals with *meta-objects*, which are subclasses of System.Dynamic.DynamicMetaObject and have methods for handling all of the above messages. Each language has its own subclasses of DynamicMetaObject that implement the language's object model, such as IronPython's MetaPythonObject. The meta classes also have corresponding concrete classes that implement the System.Dynamic.IDynamicMetaObjectProtocol interface, which is how the DLR identifies dynamic objects.

From a class that implements IDynamicMetaObjectProtocol, the DLR can get a DynamicMetaObject by calling GetMetaObject(). This DynamicMetaObject is provided by the language

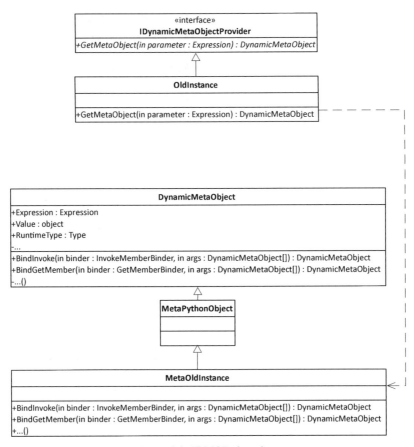

Figure 8.3: IDMOP class diagram

and implements the binding functions as required by that object. Each DynamicMetaObject also has the value and type, if available, of the underlying object. Finally, a DynamicMetaObject stores an expression tree representing the call site so far and any restrictions on that expression, similar to the call site binders.

When the DLR is compiling a call to a method on a user-defined class, it first creates a call site (i.e., an instance of the CallSite class). The call site initiates the binding process as described above in "Dynamic Call Sites", which results in it eventually calling GetMetaObject() on an instance of OldInstance[13], which returns a MetaOldInstance. Next, a binder is called (PythonGetMemberBinder.Bind()) which in turn calls MetaOldInstance.BindGetMember(); it returns a new DynamicMetaObject that describes how to look up the method name on the object. Then another binder, PythonInvokeBinder.Bind(), is called, which calls MetaOldInstance.BindInvoke(), wrapping the first DynamicMetaObject with a new one representing how to call the method that was looked up. This includes the original object, the expression tree for looking up the method name, and DynamicMetaObjects representing the arguments to the method.

Once the final DynamicMetaObject in an expression has been built, its expression tree and

---

[13]Python has old-style and new-style classes, but that's not relevant here.

restrictions are used to build a delegate which is then returned to the call site that initiated the binding. From there the code can be stored in the call site caches, making operations on objects as fast as other dynamic calls, and almost as fast as static calls.

Host languages that want to perform dynamic operations on dynamic languages must derive their binders from `DynamicMetaObjectBinder`. The `DynamicMetaObjectBinder` will first ask the target object to bind the operation (by calling `GetMetaObject()` and going through the binding process described above) before falling back on the host language's binding semantics. As a result, if an IronRuby object is accessed from an IronPython program, the binding is first attempted with Ruby (target language) semantics; if that fails, the `DynamicMetaObjectBinder` will fall back on the Python (host language) semantics. If the object being bound is not dynamic (i.e., it does not implement `IDynamicMetaObjectProvider`), such as classes from the .NET base class library, then it is accessed with the host language's semantics using .NET reflection.

Languages do have some freedom in how they implement this; IronPython's `PythonInvokeBinder` does not derive from `InvokeBinder` because it needs to do some extra processing specific to Python objects. As long as it only deals with Python objects, there are no issues; if it encounters an object that implements `IDynamicMetaObjectProvider` but is not a Python object, it forwards to a `CompatibilityInvokeBinder` class that does inherit from `InvokeBinder` and can handle foreign objects correctly.

If the fallback cannot bind the operation, it doesn't throw an exception; instead, it returns a `DynamicMetaObject` representing the error. The host language's binder will then handle this in an appropriate manner for the host language; for example, accessing a missing member on an IronPython object from a hypothetical JavaScript implementation could return `undefined`, while doing the same to a JavaScript object from IronPython would raise an `AttributeError`.

The ability for languages to work with dynamic objects is rather useless without the ability to first load and execute code written in other languages, and for this the DLR provides a common mechanism for hosting other languages.

8.9 Hosting

In addition to providing common language implementation details, the DLR also provides a shared *hosting interface*. The hosting interface is used by the host language (usually a static language like C#) to execute code written in another language such as Python or Ruby. This is a common technique that allows end users to extend an application, and the DLR takes it step further by making it trivial to use any scripting language that has a DLR implementation. There are four key parts to the hosting interface: the *runtime*, *engines*, *sources*, and *scopes*.

The `ScriptRuntime` is generally shared amongst all dynamic languages in an application. The runtime handles all of the current assembly references that are presented to the loaded languages, provides methods for quick execution of a file, and provides the methods for creating new engines. For simple scripting tasks, the runtime is the only interface that needs to be used, but the DLR also provides classes with more control over how scripts are run.

Usually, only one `ScriptEngine` is used for each scripting language. The DLR's meta-object protocol means that a program can load scripts from multiple languages, and the objects created by each language can all seamlessly interoperate. The engine wraps a language-specific `LanguageContext` (such as `PythonContext` or `RubyContext`) and is used for executing code from files or strings and performing operations on dynamic objects from languages that don't natively support the DLR (such as C# prior to .NET 4). Engines are thread-safe, and can execute multiple scripts in parallel, as long as each thread has its own scope. It also provides methods for creating script sources, which allow for more fine-grained control of script execution.

A `ScriptSource` holds a chunk of code to be executed; it binds a `SourceUnit` object, which holds the actual code, to the `ScriptEngine` that created the source. This class allows code to be compiled (which produces a `CompiledCode` object that can be cached) or executed directly. If a chunk of code is going to be executed repeatedly, it's best to compile first, and then execute the compiled code; for scripts that will only be executed once, it's best to just execute it directly.

Finally, however the code gets to be executed, a `ScriptScope` must be provided for the code to execute in. The scope is used to hold all of script's variables, and can be pre-loaded with variables from the host, if necessary. This allows a host to provide custom objects to the script when it starts running—for example, an image editor may provide a method to access the pixels of the image the script is working on. Once a script has executed, any variables it created can be read from the scope. The other main use of scopes is to provide isolation, so that multiple scripts can be loaded and executed at the same time without interfering with each other.

It's important to note that all of these classes are provided by the DLR, not the language; only the `LanguageContext` used by the engine comes from the language implementation. The language context provides all of the functionality—loading code, creating scopes, compilation, execution, and operations on dynamic objects—that is needed by a host, and the DLR hosting classes provide a more usable interface to access that functionality. Because of this, the same hosting code can be used to host any DLR-based language.

For dynamic language implementations written in C (such as the original Python and Ruby), special wrapper code must be written to access code not written in the dynamic language, and it must be repeated for each supported scripting language. While software like SWIG exists to make this easier, it's still not trivial to add a Python or Ruby scripting interface to a program and expose its object model for manipulation by external scripts. For .NET programs, however, adding scripting is as simple as setting up a runtime, loading the program's assemblies into the runtime, and using `ScriptScope.SetVariable()` to make the program's objects available to the scripts. Adding support for scripting to a .NET application can be done in a matter of minutes, which is a huge bonus of the DLR.

8.10 Assembly Layout

Because of how the DLR evolved from a separate library into part of the CLR, there are parts that are in the CLR (call sites, expression trees, binders, code generation, and dynamic meta objects) and parts that are part of IronLanguages open-source project (hosting, the interpreter, and a few other bits not discussed here). The parts that are in the CLR are also included in the IronLanguages project in `Microsoft.Scripting.Core`. The DLR parts are split into two assemblies, `Microsoft.Scripting` and `Microsoft.Dynamic`—the former contains the hosting APIs and the latter contains code for COM interop, the interpreter, and some other pieces common to dynamic languages.

The languages themselves are split in two as well: `IronPython.dll` and `IronRuby.dll` implement the languages themselves (parsers, binders, etc.) while `IronPython.Modules.dll` and `IronRuby.Libraries.dll` implement the portions of the standard library that are implemented in C in the classic Python and Ruby implementations.

8.11 Lessons Learned

The DLR is a useful example of a language-neutral platform for dynamic languages built on top of a static runtime. The techniques it uses to achieve high-performance dynamic code are tricky to implement properly, so the DLR takes these techniques and makes them available to every dynamic language implementation.

IronPython and IronRuby are good examples of how to build a language on top of the DLR. The implementations are very similar because they were developed at the same time by close teams, yet they still have significant differences in implementation. Having multiple different languages co-developed[14], along with C#'s and VB's dynamic features, made sure that the DLR design got plenty of testing during development.

The actual development of IronPython, IronRuby, and the DLR was handled very differently than most projects within Microsoft at the time—it was a very agile, iterative development model with continuous integration running from day one. This enabled them to change very quickly when they had to, which was good because the DLR became tied into C#'s dynamic features early in its development. While the DLR tests are very quick, only taking a dozen seconds or so, the language tests take far too long to run (the IronPython test suite takes about 45 minutes, even with parallel execution); improving this would have improved the iteration speed. Ultimately, these iterations converged on the current DLR design, which seems overly complicated in parts but fits together quite nicely in total.

Having the DLR tied to C# was critically important because it made sure the DLR had a place and a "purpose", but once the C# dynamic features were done the political climate changed (coinciding with an economic downturn) and the Iron languages lost their support within the company. The hosting APIs, for example, never made it into the .NET Framework (and it's highly unlikely they ever will); this means that PowerShell 3, which is also based on the DLR, uses a completely different set of hosting APIs than IronPython and IronRuby, although all of their objects can still interact as described above[15]. But, thanks to the wonder of open source licensing, they will continue to survive and even thrive.

---

[14] IronPython, IronRuby, a prototype JavaScript, and the mysterious VBx—a fully dynamic version of VB.

[15] Some of the DLR team members went on to work on the C# compiler-as-a-service library code-named "Roslyn", which bears a striking resemblance to the IronPython and IronRuby hosting APIs.

[chapter 9]

ITK
Luis Ibáñez and Brad King

9.1 What Is ITK?

ITK (the Insight Toolkit)[1] is a library for image analysis that was developed by the initiative, and mainly with the funding, of the US National Library of Medicine[2]. ITK can be thought of as a usable encyclopedia of image analysis algorithms, in particular for image filtering, image segmentation and image registration. The library was developed by a consortium involving universities, commercial companies, and many individual contributors from around the world. Development of ITK started in 1999, and recently after its 10th anniversary the library underwent a refactoring process intended to remove crusty code and to reshape it for the next decade.

9.2 Architectural Features

Software toolkits have a very synergistic relationship with their communities. They shape one another in a continuous iterative cycle. The software is continuously modified until it satisfies the needs of the community, while the community behaviors themselves are adapted based on what the software empowers or restricts them to do. In order to better understand the nature of ITK's architecture, it is therefore very useful to get a sense of what kind of problems the ITK community is usually addressing, and how they tend to go about solving them.

The Nature of the Beast

> If you did not understand the nature of the beasts,
> it would be of little use to know the mechanics of their anatomy.
> Dee Hock, *One from Many: VISA and the Rise of Chaordic Organization*

In a typical image analysis problem, a researcher or an engineer will take an input image, improve some characteristics of the image by, let's say, reducing noise or increasing contrast, and then proceed to identify some features in the image, such as corners and strong edges. This type of processing is naturally well-suited for a data pipeline architecture, as shown in Figure 9.1.

---
[1] http://www.itk.org
[2] http://www.nlm.nih.gov

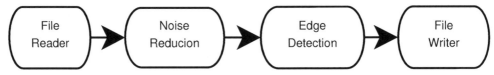

Figure 9.1: Image processing pipeline

To illustrate this point, Figure 9.2 shows an image of a brain from a magnetic resonance image (MRI), and the result of processing it with a median filter to reduce its level of noise, as well as the outcome of an edge detection filter used to identify the borders of anatomical structures.

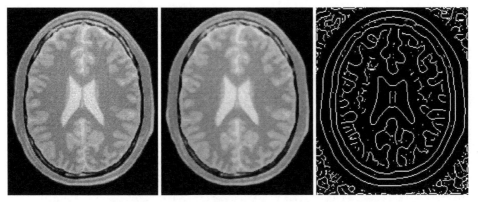

Figure 9.2: From left to right: MRI brain image, median filter, edge detection filter

For each one of these tasks, the image analysis community has developed a variety of algorithms, and continue developing new ones. Why do they continue doing this?, you may ask, and the answer is that image processing is a combination of science, engineering, art, and "cooking" skills. Claiming that there is an algorithmic combination that is the "right" answer to an image processing task is as misleading as claiming that there is such a thing as the "right" type of chocolate dessert for a dinner. Instead of pursuing perfection, the community strives to produce a rich set of tools that ensures that there will be no shortage of options to try when facing a given image processing challenge. This state of affairs, of course, comes at a price. The cost is that the image analyst has the difficult task of choosing among dozens of different tools that can be used in different combinations to achieve similar results.

The image analysis community is closely integrated with the research community. It is common to find that specific research groups become attached to the algorithmic families they have developed. This custom of "branding", and up to some level "marketing", leads to a situation where the best that the software toolkit can do for the community is to offer a very complete set of algorithmic implementations that they can try, and then mix and match to create a recipe that satisfies their needs.

These are some of the reasons why ITK was designed and implemented as a large collection of somewhat independent but coherent tools, the *image filters*, many of which can be used to solve similar problems. In this context, a certain level of "redundancy"—for example, offering three different implementations of the Gaussian filter—is not seen as a problem but as a valuable feature, because different implementations can be used interchangeably to satisfy constraints and exploit efficiencies with respect to image size, number of processors, and Gaussian kernel size that might be specific to a given imaging application.

The toolkit was also conceived as a resource that grows and renews itself continuously as new algorithms and better implementations become available, superseding existing ones, and as new tools are developed in response to the emerging needs of new medical imaging technologies.

Armed with this quick insight into the daily routine of the image analysts in the ITK community, we can now dive into the main features of the architecture:

- Modularity
- Data Pipeline
- Factories
- IO Factories
- Streaming
- Reusability
- Maintainability

Modularity

Modularity is one of the main characteristics of ITK. This is a requirement that emerges from the way people in the image analysis community work when solving their problems. Most image analysis problems put one or more input images through a combination of processing filters that enhance or extract particular pieces of information from the images. Therefore there is no single large processing object, but rather myriad small ones. This structural nature of the image processing problem logically implies implementing the software as a large collection of image processing filters that can be combined in many different ways.

It is also the case that certain types of processing filters are clustered into families, inside which some of their implementation features can be factorized. This leads to natural grouping of the image filters into modules and groups of modules.

Modularity, therefore occurs at three natural levels in ITK:

- Filter Level
- Filter Family Level
- Filter Family Group Level

At the image filter level, ITK has a collection of about 700 filters. Given that ITK is implemented in C++, this is a natural level at which every one of those filters is implemented by a C++ Class following object-oriented design patterns. At the filter family level, ITK groups filters together according to the nature of the processing that they perform. For example, all filters that are related to Fourier transforms will be put together into a Module. At the C++ level, Modules map to directories in the source tree, and to libraries once the software is compiled to its binary form. ITK has about 120 of these Modules. Each module contains:

1. The source code of the image filters that belong to that family.
2. A set of configuration files that describe how to build the module and list dependencies between this module and other modules.
3. The set of unit tests corresponding to each one of the filters.

The group level is mostly a conceptual division that has been drawn on top of the software to help locate filters in the source tree. Groups are associated with high-level concepts such as Filtering, Segmentation, Registration and IO. This hierarchical structure is illustrated in Figure 9.3. ITK currently has 124 modules, which are in turn aggregated into 13 major groups. The modules have a variety of different sizes. This size distribution, in bytes, is presented in Figure 9.4.

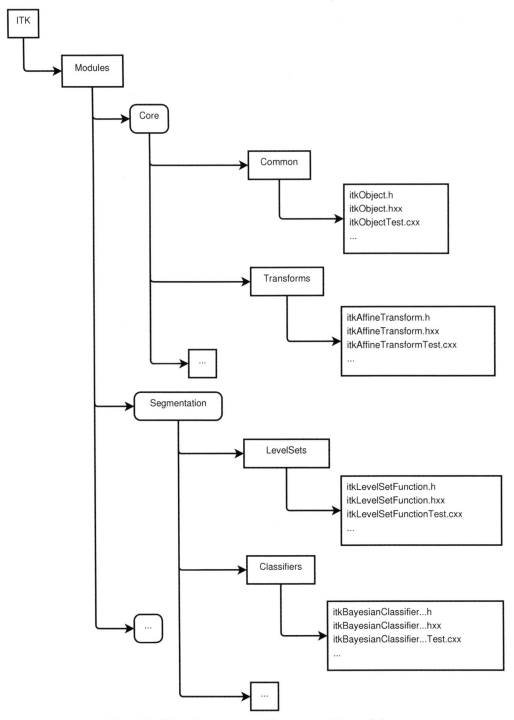

Figure 9.3: Hierarchical structure of groups, modules and classes

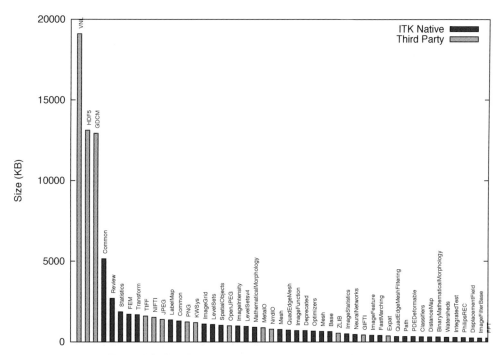

Figure 9.4: Size distribution of 50 largest ITK modules in KB

The modularization in ITK also applies to a set of third-party libraries that are not directly part of the toolkit, but that the toolkit depends upon, and that are distributed along with the rest of the code for the convenience of users. Particular examples of these third-party libraries are the image file format libraries: HDF5, PNG, TIFF, JPEG and OpenJPEG among others. The third party libraries are highlighted here because they account for about 56 percent of the size of ITK. This reflects the usual nature of open source applications that build upon existing platforms. The size distribution of the third-party libraries does not necessarily reflect the architectural organization of ITK, since we have adopted these useful libraries just as they have been developed upstream. However, the third-party code is distributed along with the toolkit, and partitioning it was one of the key driving directives for the modularization process.

The module size distribution is presented here because it is a measure of the proper modularization of the code. One can see the modularization of the code as a continuous spectrum that ranges from the extremes of having all the code in a single module, the monolithic version, to partitioning the code in a very large collection of equally sized modules. This size distribution was a tool used to monitor the progression of the modularization process, particularly to ensure that no big blocks of code were left in the same module unless true logical dependencies called for such grouping.

The modular architecture of ITK enables and facilitates:

- Reduction and clarification of cross-dependencies
- Adoption of code contributed by the community
- Evaluation of quality metrics per module (for example, code coverage)
- Building selected subsets of the toolkit
- Packaging selected subsets of the toolkit for redistribution
- Continued growth by progressive addition of new modules

The modularization process made it possible to explicitly identify and declare the dependencies between different portions of the toolkit as they were put into modules. In many cases, this exercise revealed artificial or incorrect dependencies that had been introduced in the toolkit over time, and that passed unnoticed when most of the code was put together in a few large groups.

The usefulness of evaluating quality metrics per module is twofold. First, it makes it easier to hold developers accountable for the modules which they maintain. Second, it makes it possible to engage in clean-up initiatives in which a few developers focus for a short period of time on raising the quality of a specific module. When concentrating on a small portion of the toolkit, it is easier to see the effect of the effort and to keep developers engaged and motivated.

To reiterate, we note that the structure of the toolkit reflects the organization of the community and in some cases the processes that have been adopted for the continuous growth and quality control of the software.

Data Pipeline

The staged nature of most image analysis tasks led naturally to the selection of a Data Pipeline architecture as the backbone infrastructure for data processing. The Data Pipeline enables:

- *Filter Concatenation:* A set of image filters can be concatenated one after another, composing a processing chain in which a sequence of operations are applied to the input images.
- *Parameter Exploration:* Once a processing chain is put together, it is easy to change the parameters of any filter in the chain, and to explore the effects that such change will have on the final output image.
- *Memory Streaming:* Large images can be managed by processing only sub-blocks of the image at a time. In this way, it becomes possible to process large images that otherwise would not have fit into main memory.

Figures 9.1 and 9.2 have already presented a simplified representation of a data pipeline from the image processing point of view. Image filters typically have numeric parameters that are used to regulate the behavior of the filter. Every time one of the numeric parameters is modified, the data pipeline marks its output as "dirty" and knows that this particular filter, and all the downstream ones that use its output, should be executed again. This feature of the pipeline facilitates the exploration of parameter space while using a minimum amount of processing power for each instance of an experiment.

The process of updating the pipeline can be driven in such a way that only sub-pieces of the images are processed at a time. This is a mechanism necessary to support the functionality of streaming. In practice, the process is controlled by the internal passing of a `RequestedRegion` specification from one filter downstream to its provider filter upstream. This communication is done through an internal API and it is not exposed to the application developers.

For a more concrete example, if a Gaussian blur image filter is expecting to use as input a 100x100-pixel image that is produced by a median image filter, the blur filter can ask the median filter to produce only a quarter of the image, that is, an image region of size 100x25 pixels. This request can be further propagated upstream, with the caveat that every intermediate filter may have to add an extra border to the image region size in order to produce that requested output region size. There is more on data streaming in Section 9.2.

Both a change in the parameters of a given filter, or a change in the specific requested region to be processed by that filter, will have the effect of marking the pipeline as "dirty" and indicating the need for a reexecution of that filter through the downstream filters in the pipeline.

Process and Data Objects

Two main types of objects were designed to hold the basic structure of the pipeline. They are the `DataObject` and the `ProcessObject`. The `DataObject` is the abstraction of classes that carry data; for example, images and geometrical meshes. The `ProcessObject` provides an abstraction for the image filters and mesh filters that process such data. `ProcessObjects` take `DataObjects` as input and perform some type of algorithmic transformation on them, such as the ones illustrated in Figure 9.2.

`DataObjects` are generated by `ProcessObjects`. This chain typically starts by reading a `DataObject` from disk, for example by using a `ImageFileReader` which is a type of `ProcessObject`. The `ProcessObject` that created a given `DataObject` is the only one that should modify such `DataObject`. This output `DataObject` is typically connected as input to another `ProcessObject` downstream in the pipeline.

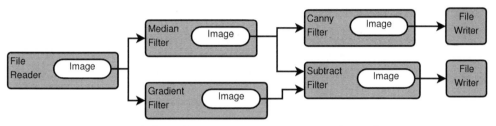

Figure 9.5: Relationship between `ProcessObjects` and `DataObjects`

This sequence is illustrated in Figure 9.5. The same `DataObject` may be passed as input to multiple `ProcessObjects`, as it is shown in the figure, where the `DataObject` is produced by the file reader at the beginning of the pipeline. In this particular case, the file reader is an instance of the `ImageFileReader` class, and the `DataObject` that it produces as output is an instance of the `Image` class. It is also common for some filters to require two `DataObjects` as input, as it is the case of the subtract filter indicated in the right side of the same figure.

The `ProcessObjects` and `DataObjects` are connected together as a side effect of constructing the pipeline. From the application developer's point of view, the pipeline is linked together by invoking a sequence of calls involving the `ProcessObjects` such as:

```
writer->SetInput( canny->GetOutput() );
canny->SetInput( median->GetOutput() );
median->SetInput( reader->GetOutput() );
```

Internally, however, what is connected as a consequence of these calls is not one `ProcessObject` to the next `ProcessObject`, but the downstream `ProcessObject` to the `DataObject` that is produced by the upstream `ProcessObject`.

The internal chained structure of the pipeline is held together by three types of connections:

- The `ProcessObject` holds a list of pointers to its output `DataObjects`. Output `DataObjects` are owned and controlled by the `ProcessObject` that produces them.
- The `ProcessObject` holds a list of pointers to its input `DataObjects`. Input `DataObjects` are owned by the upstream `ProcessObject`.
- The `DataObject` holds a pointer to its producer `ProcessObject`. That happens to be the `ProcessObject` that also owns and control this `DataObject`.

This collection of internal links is later exploited to propagate calls upstream and downstream in the pipeline. During all these interactions, the `ProcessObject` retains control and ownership of the DataObject that it generates. The filters downstream gain access to the information about a given DataObject through the pointer links that are established as a consequence of the calls to the SetInput() and GetOutput() methods, without ever taking control of that input data. For practical purposes, filters should treat their input data as read-only objects. This is enforced in the API by using the C++ const keyword in the arguments of SetInput() methods. As a general rule, ITK embraces a const-correct external API, even though internally this const-correctness is overridden by some of the pipeline operations.

The Pipeline Class Hierarchy

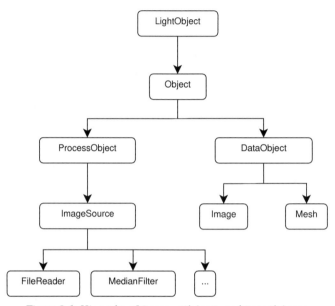

Figure 9.6: Hierarchy of ProcessObjects and DataObjects

The initial design and implementation of the Data Pipeline in ITK was derived from the Visualization Toolkit (VTK)[3], a mature project at the time when ITK development began.

Figure 9.6 shows the object-oriented hierarchy of the pipeline objects in ITK. In particular, note the relationship between the basic Object, ProcessObject, DataObject, and some of the classes in the filter family and the data family. In this abstraction, any object that is expected to be passed as input to a filter, or to be produced as output by a filter, must derive from the DataObject. All filters that produce and consume data are expected to derive from the ProcessObject. The data negotiations required to move data through the pipeline are implemented partly in the ProcessObject and partly in the DataObject.

The LightObject and Object classes are above the dichotomy of the ProcessObject and DataObject. The LightObject and Object classes provide common functionalities such as the API for communications of Events, and the support for multi-threading.

---

[3]See *The Architecture of Open Source Applications*, Volume 1

The Inner Workings of the Pipeline

Figure 9.7 presents a UML sequence diagram describing the interactions between `ProcessObjects` and `DataObjects` in a minimal pipeline composed of an `ImageFileReader`, `MedianImageFilter` and `ImageFileWriter`.

The full interaction consist of four passes:

- Update Output Information (upstream call sequence)
- Update Requested Region (upstream call sequence)
- Update Output Data (upstream call sequence)
- Generate Data (downstream call sequence)

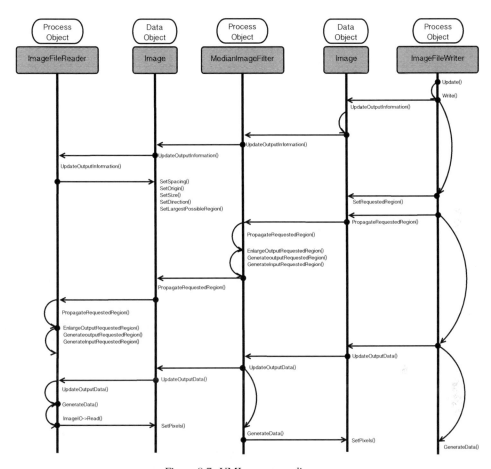

Figure 9.7: UML sequence diagram

The whole process is triggered when an application invokes the `Update()` method in the last filter of the pipeline; in this concrete example this is the `ImageFileWriter`. The `Update()` call initiates the first pass that goes in the upstream direction. That is, from the last filter in the pipeline, towards the first filter in the pipeline.

The goal of this first pass is to ask the question, "How much data can you generate for me?" This question is codified in the method `UpdateOutputInformation()`. In this method, every filter

Luis Ibáñez and Brad King   135

computes the amount of image data that can be produced as output with the given amount of data available to it as input. Given that the amount of data input must be known first before the filter can answer the question about the amount of data output, the question has to propagate to the filter upstream, until it reaches a source filter that can answer the first question by itself. In this concrete example, that source filter is the `ImageFileReader`. This filter can figure out the size of its output by gathering information from the image file that it has been assigned to read. Once the first filter of the pipeline answers the question, then the subsequent filters downstream can compute their respective amount of output one after another, until they make it to the last filter of the pipeline.

The second pass, which also travels in the upstream direction, informs filters as to the amount of output that they are requested to produce during pipeline execution. The concept of *Requested Region* is essential in supporting the streaming capabilities of ITK. It makes it possible to tell the filters in the pipeline not to generate the entire full image, but to focus instead in a subregion of the image, the Requested Region. This is very useful when the image at hand is larger than the RAM available in the system. The call propagates from the last filter to the first one, and at every intermediate filter the requested region size is modified to take into account any extra borders that a filter may need in the input so it can generate a given region size as output. In our concrete example, the median filter will typically have to add a 2-pixel border to the size of its own input. That is, if the writer requests a region of size 500 x 500 pixels to the median filter, the median filter in its turn will request a region of 502 x 502 pixels to the reader, because the median filter by default needs a 3 x 3 pixel neighborhood region to compute the value of one output pixel. The pass is encoded in the `PropagateRequestedRegion()` method.

The third pass is intended to trigger the computation on the data inside the Requested Region. This pass also goes in the upstream direction and it is codified in the `UpdateOutputData()` method. Since every filter needs its input data before it can compute its output data, the call is passed to the respective upstream filter first, hence the upstream propagation. Upon return the current filter actually proceeds to computes its data.

The fourth and final pass proceeds downstream, and consists of the actual execution of computation by every filter. The call is codified in the `GenerateData()` method. The downstream direction is not a consequence of one filter making calls on its downstream partner, but rather of the fact that the `UpdateOutputData()` calls are executing in order from the first filter to the last filter. That is, the sequence happens downstream due to timing of the calls, and not due to what filter is driving the calls. This clarification is important because the ITK pipeline is by nature a *Pull Pipeline*, in which data is requested from the end, and the logic is also controlled from the end.

Factories

One of the fundamental design requirements of ITK is to provide support for multiple platforms. This requirement emerges from the desire to maximize the impact of the toolkit by making it usable to a broad community regardless of their platform of choice. ITK adopted the *Factory* design pattern to address the challenge of supporting fundamental differences among the many hardware and software platforms, without sacrificing the fitness of a solution to each one of the individual platforms.

The Factory pattern in ITK uses class names as keys to a registry of class constructors. The registration of factories happens at run time, and can be done by simply placing dynamic libraries in specific directories that ITK applications search at start-up time. This last feature provides a natural mechanism for implementing a plugin architecture in a clean and transparent way. The outcome is to facilitate the development of extensible image analysis applications, satisfying the need to provide an ever-growing set of image analysis capabilities.

IO Factories

The factory mechanism is particularly important when performing IO.

Embracing Diversity with Facades

The image analysis community has developed a very large set of file formats to store image data. Many of these file formats are designed and implemented with specific uses in mind, and therefore are fine-tuned to specific types of images. As a consequence, on a regular basis, new image file formats are conceived and promoted across the community. Aware of this situation, the ITK development team designed an IO architecture suitable for ease of extensibility, in which it is easy to add support for more and more file formats on a regular basis.

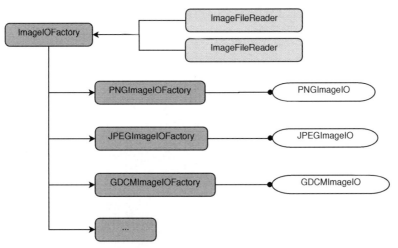

Figure 9.8: IO Factories dependencies

This IO extensible architecture is built upon the Factory mechanism described in the previous section. The main difference is that in the case of IO, the IO Factories are registered in a specialized registry that is managed by the ImageIOFactory base class, shown on the upper left corner of Figure 9.8. The actual functionality of reading and writing data from image file formats is implemented in a family of ImageIO classes, shown on the right side of Figure 9.8. These service classes are intended to be instantiated on demand when the user requests to read or write an image. The service classes are not exposed to the application code. Instead, applications are expected to interact with the facade classes:

- ImageFileReader
- ImageFileWriter

These are the two classes with which the application will invoke code such as:

```
reader->SetFileName(''image1.png'');
reader->Update();
```

or

```
writer->SetFileName(''image2.jpg'');
writer->Update();
```

In both cases the call to Update() triggers the execution of the upstream pipeline to which these ProcessObjects are connected. Both the reader and the writer behave as one filter more in a pipeline. In the particular case of the reader, the call to Update() triggers the reading of the corresponding image file into memory. In the case of the writer, the call to Update() triggers the execution of the upstream pipeline that is providing the input to the writer, and finally results in an image being written out to disk into a particular file format.

These facade classes hide from the application developer the internal differences that are inherent to the particularities of each file format. They even hide the existence of the file format itself. The facades are designed in such a way that most of the time application developers do not need to know what file formats are expected to be read by the application. The typical application will simply invoke code such as

```
std::string filename = this->GetFileNameFromGUI();
writer->SetFileName( filename );
writer->Update();
```

These calls will work fine regardless of whether the content of the filename variable is any of the following strings:

- image1.png
- image1.jpeg
- image1.tiff
- image1.dcm
- image1.mha
- image1.nii
- image1.nii.gz

where the file name extensions identify a different image file format in every case.

Know Thy Pixel Type

Despite the assistance that the file reader and writer facades provide, it is still up to the application developer to be aware of the pixel type that the application needs to process. In the context of medical imaging, it is reasonable to expect that the application developer will know whether the input image will contain a MRI, a mammogram or a CT scan, and therefore be mindful of selecting the appropriate pixel type and image dimensionality for each one of these different image modalities. This specificity of image type might not be convenient for application settings where users wants to read *any* image type, which are most commonly found in the scenarios of rapid prototyping and teaching. In the context of deploying a medical image application for production in a clinical setting, however, it is expected that the pixel type and dimension of the images will be clearly defined and specified based on the image modality to be processed. A concrete example, where an application manages 3D MRI scans, looks like:

```
typedef itk::Image< signed short, 3 > MRIImageType;
typedef itk::ImageFileWriter< MRIImageType > MRIWriterType;
MRIWriterType::Pointer writer = MRIWriterType::New();
writer->Update();
```

There is a limit, however, to how much the particularities of the image file formats can be hidden from the application developer. For example, when reading images from DICOM files, or when reading RAW images, the application developer may have to insert extra calls to further specify the characteristics of the file format at hand. DICOM files will be the most commonly found in clinical environments, while RAW images are still a necessary evil for exchanging data in the research environment.

Together But Separate

The self-contained nature of every IO Factory and ImageIO service class is also reflected in the modularization. Typically, an ImageIO class depends on a specialized library that is dedicated to managing a specific file format. That is the case for PNG, JPEG, TIFF and DICOM, for example. In those cases, the third-party library is managed as a self-contained module, and the specialized ImageIO code that interfaces ITK to that third-party library is also put in a module by itself. In this way, specific applications may disable many file formats that are not relevant to their domain, and can focus on offering only those file formats that are useful for the anticipated scenarios of that application.

Just as with standard factories, the IO factories can be loaded at run-time from dynamic libraries. This flexibility facilitates the use of specialized and in-house developed file formats without requiring all such file formats to be incorporated directly into the ITK toolkit itself. The loadable IO factories has been one of the most successful features in the architectural design of ITK. It has made it possible to easily manage a challenging situation without placing a burden on the code or obscuring its implementation. More recently, the same IO architecture has been adapted to manage the process of reading and writing files containing spatial transformations represented by the Transform class family.

Streaming

ITK was initially conceived as a set of tools for processing the images acquired by the Visible Human Project[4]. At the time, it was clear that such a large dataset would not fit in the RAM of computers that were typically available to the medical imaging research community. It is still the case that the dataset will not fit in the typical desktop computers that we use today. Therefore, one of the requirements for developing the Insight Toolkit was to enable the streaming of image data through the data pipeline. More specifically, to be able to process large images by pushing sub-blocks of the image throughout the data pipeline, and then assembling the resulting blocks on the output side of the pipeline.

This partitioning of the image domain is illustrated in Figure 9.9 for the concrete example of a median filter. The median filter computes the value of one output pixel as the statistical median of the pixel values from the input image in a neighborhood around the pixel. The size of that neighborhood is a numerical parameter of the filter. In this case we set it to 2 pixels, which means that we will take a neighborhood with a 2-pixel radius around our output pixel. This leads to a neighborhood of 5x5 pixels with the position of the output pixel in the middle, and a rectangular border of 2 pixels around it. This is usually called a Manhattan radius. When the median filter is asked to computed a particular Requested Region of the output image, it turns around and asks its upstream filter to provide a larger region that is formed by the Requested Region enlarged by a border of, in this case, 2 pixels. In the specific case of Figure 9.9, when asked for Region 2, of size 100x25 pixels, the median filter passes along that request to its upstream filter for a region of size 100x29 pixels. The 29-pixel size in the vertical direction is computed as 25 pixels plus two borders of 2-pixel radius

---

[4]http://www.nlm.nih.gov/research/visible/visible_human.html

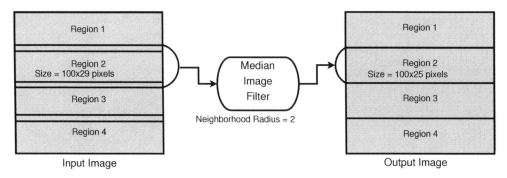

Figure 9.9: Illustration of image streaming process

each. Note that the horizontal dimension is not enlarged in this case because it is already at the maximum that the input image can provide; therefore, the enlarged request of 104 pixels (100 pixels plus two borders of 2 pixels) gets cropped to the maximum size of the image, which is 100 pixels in the horizontal dimension.

ITK filters that operate on neighborhoods will take care of the boundary conditions by using one of the three typical approaches: considering a null value outside of the image, mirroring the pixels' values across the border, or repeating the border value on the outside. In the case of the median filter, a zero-flux Neumann boundary condition is used, which simply means that the pixels outside of the region border are assumed to be a repetition of the pixel values found in the last pixels inside the border.

It is a well-kept dirty little secret of the image processing literature that most of the implementation difficulties with image filters are related to proper management of boundary conditions. This is a particular symptom of the disconnection between the theoretical training found in many textbooks and the software practice of image processing. In ITK this was managed by implementing a collection of image iterator classes and an associated family of boundary condition calculators. These two helper classes families hide from image filters the complexities of managing boundary conditions in N-dimensions.

The streaming process is driven from outside the filter, typically by the `ImageFileWriter` or the `StreamingImageFilter`. These two classes implement the streaming functionality of taking the total size of the image and partitioning it into a number of divisions requested by the application developer. Then, during their `Update()` call, they go in an iteration loop asking for each one of the intermediate pieces of the image. At that stage, they take advantage of the `SetRequestedRegion()` API described in Figure 9.7 in Section 9.2. That constrains the computation of the upstream pipeline to a subregion of the image.

The application code driving the streaming process looks like

```
median->SetInput( reader->GetOutput() );
median->SetNeighborhoodRadius( 2 );
writer->SetInput( median->GetOutput() );
writer->SetFileName( filename );
writer->SetNumberOfStreamDivisions( 4 );
writer->Update();
```

where the only new element is the `SetNumberOfStreamDivisions()` call that defines the number of pieces into which the image will be split for the purpose of streaming it through the pipeline. To match the example of Figure 9.9 we have used four as the number of regions to split the image into. This means that the `writer` is going to trigger the execution of the `median` filter four times, each time with a different Requested Region.

There are interesting similarities between the process of streaming and the process of parallelizing the execution of a given filter. Both of them rely on the possibility of dividing the image processing work into image chunks that are processed separately. In the streaming case, the image chunks are processed across time, one after another, while in the parallelization case the image chunks are assigned to different threads, which in turn are assigned to separate processor cores. At the end, it is the algorithmic nature of the filter that will determine whether it is possible to split the output image into chunks that can be computed independently based on a corresponding set of image chunks from the input image. In ITK, streaming and parallelization are actually orthogonal, in the sense that there is an API to take care of the streaming process, and a separate API dedicated to support the implementation of parallel computation base on multiple-threads and shared memory.

Streaming, unfortunately, can not be applied to all types of algorithms. Specific cases that are not suitable for streaming are:

- Iterative algorithms that, to compute a pixel value at every iteration, require as input the pixel values of its neighbors. This is the case for most PDE-solving-based algorithms, such as anisotropic diffusion, demons deformable registration, and dense level sets.
- Algorithms that require the full set of input pixel values in order to compute the value of one of the output pixels. Fourier transform and Infinite Impulse Response (IIR) filters, such as the Recursive Gaussian filter, are examples of this class.
- Region propagation or front propagation algorithms in which the modification of pixels also happens in an iterative way but for which the location of the regions or fronts can not be systematically partitioned in blocks in a predictable way. Region growing segmentation, sparse level sets, some implementations of mathematical morphology operations and some forms of watersheds are typical examples here.
- Image registration algorithms, given that they require access to the full input image data for computing metric values at every iteration of their optimization cycles.

Fortunately, on the other hand, the data pipeline structure of ITK enables support for streaming in a variety of transformation filters by taking advantage of the fact that all filters create their own output, and therefore they do not overwrite the memory of the input image. This comes at the price of memory consumption, since the pipeline has to allocate both the input and output images in memory simultaneously. Filters such as flipping, axes permutation, and geometric resampling fall in this category. In these cases, the data pipeline manages the matching of input regions to output regions by requiring that every filter provide a method called `GenerateInputRequestedRegion()` that takes as an argument a rectangular output region. This method computes the rectangular input region that will be needed by this filter to compute that specific rectangular output region. This continuous negotiation in the data pipeline makes it possible to associate, for every output block, the corresponding section of input image that is required for computation.

To be more precise here, we must say therefore that ITK supports streaming—but only in algorithms that are "streamable" in nature. That said, in the spirit of being progressive regarding the remaining algorithms, we should qualify this statement not by claiming that "it is impossible to stream such algorithms", but rather that "our typical approach to streaming is not suitable for these algorithms" at this point, and that hopefully new techniques will be devised by the community in the future to address these cases.

9.3 Lessons Learned

Reusability

The principle of reusability can also be read as "avoidance of redundancy". In the case of ITK, this has been achieved with a three-pronged approach.

- First, the adoption of object-oriented programming, and in particular the proper creation of class hierarchies where common functionalities are factorized in base classes.
- Second, the adoption of generic programming, implemented via the heavy use of C++ templates, factorizing behaviors that are identified as patterns.
- Third, the generous use of C++ macros has also permitted reuse of standard snippets of code that are needed in myriad places across the toolkit.

Many of these items may sound like platitudes and appear obvious today, but when ITK development started in 1999 some of them were not that obvious. In particular, at the time the support most C++ compilers offered for templates did not quite follow a consistent standard. Even today, decisions such as the adoption of generic programming and the use of a widely templated implementation continue to be controversial in the community. This is manifested in the communities that prefer to use ITK via the wrapping layers to Python, Tcl or Java.

Generic Programming

The adoption of generic programming was one of the defining implementation features of ITK. It was a difficult decision in 1999 when the compiler support for C++ templates was rather fragmented, and the Standard Template Library (STL) was still considered a bit exotic.

Generic programming was adopted in ITK by embracing the use of C++ templates for implementing generalization of concepts and in this way increasing code reuse. The typical example of C++ template parameterization in ITK is the Image class, that can be instantiated in the following way:

```
typedef unsigned char PixelType;
const unsigned int Dimension = 3;
typedef itk::Image< PixelType, Dimension > ImageType;
ImageType::Pointer image = ImageType::New();
```

In this expression, the application developer chooses the type to be used to represent pixels in the image, as well as the dimension of the image as a grid in space. In this particular example, we chose to use an 8-bit pixel represented in an unsigned char type, for a 3D image. Thanks to the underlying generic implementation, it is possible to instantiate images of any pixel type and any dimension in ITK.

To make it possible to write these expressions, ITK developers had to implement the Image class by being very careful with the assumptions made about the pixel type. Once the application developer has instantiated the image type, the developer can create objects of that type, or proceed to instantiate image filters whose types, in turn, depend on the image type. For example:

```
typedef itk::MedianImageFilter< ImageType, ImageType> FilterType;
FilterType::Pointer median = FilterType::New();
```

The algorithmic specificity of different image filters restricts the actual pixel types that they can support. For example, some image filters expect the image pixel type to be an integer scalar type while some other filters expect the pixel type to be a vector of floating point numbers. When instantiated with inappropriate pixel types, these filters will produce compilation errors or will result in erroneous computational results. To prevent incorrect instantiations and to facilitate the troubleshooting of compilation errors, ITK adopted the use of *concept checking* that is based on forcing the exercise of certain expected features of the types, with the goal of producing early failures combined with human-readable error messages.

C++ templates are also exploited in certain sections of the toolkit in the form of Template Metaprogramming, with the goal of increasing run-time speed performance of the code, in particular for unrolling loops that control the computation of low-dimensional vectors and matrices. Ironically, we have found over time that certain compilers have become smarter at figuring out when to unroll loops, and no longer need the help of Template MetaProgramming expressions in some cases.

Knowing When to Stop

There is also the general risk of doing "too much of a good thing", meaning, there is a risk of overusing templates, or overusing macros. It is easy to go overboard and end up creating a new language on top of C++ that is essentially based on the use of templates and macros. This is a fine line, and it demands continuous attention from the development team to make sure that the language features are properly used without being abused.

As a concrete example, the widespread use of explicitly naming types via C++ `typedefs` has proved to be particularly important. This practice plays two roles: on the one hand it provides a human-readable informative name describing the nature of the type and its purpose; on the other hand, it ensures that the type is used consistently across the toolkit. As an example, during the refactoring of the toolkit for its 4.0 version, a massive effort was invested in collecting the cases where C++ integer types such as `int`, `unsigned int`, `long` and `unsigned long` were used and to replace them with types named after the proper concept that the associated variables were representing. This was the most costly part of the task of ensuring that the toolkit was able to take advantage of 64-bit types for managing images larger than four gigabytes in all platforms. This task was of the utmost importance for promoting the use of ITK in the fields of microscopy and remote sensing, where image of tens of gigabytes in size are common.

Maintainability

The architecture satisfies the constraints that minimize maintenance cost.
- Modularity (at the class level)
- Many small files
- Code reuse
- Repeated patterns

These characteristics reduce maintenance cost in the following ways:
- Modularity (at the class level) makes it possible to enforce test-driven development techniques at the image filter level, or in general the ITK class level. Stringent testing discipline applied to small and modular pieces of code has the advantage of reducing the pools of code where bugs can hide, and with the natural decoupling that results from modularization, it is a lot easier to locate defects and eliminate them.
- Many small files facilitate the assignment of portions of the code to specific developers, and simplify the tracking of defects when they are associated with specific commits in the revision

control system. The discipline of keeping small files also leads to the enforcement of the golden rule of functions and classes: Do one thing, and do it right.
- Code reuse: When code is reused (instead of being copy-pasted and reimplemented) the code itself benefits from the higher level of scrutiny that results from being exercised in many different circumstances. It leads more eyes to look at the code, or at least at the effects of the code, and so the code benefits from Linus's Law: "Given enough eyeballs, all bugs are shallow."
- Repeated patterns simplify the work of maintainers, who in reality account for more than 75% of the cost of software development over the lifetime of a project. Using coding patterns that are consistently repeated in different places in the code makes it a lot easier for a developer to open a file and quickly understand what the code is doing, or what it is intended to do.

As the developers got involved in regular maintenance activities they were exposed to some "common failures", in particular:

- Assumptions that some filters make regarding specific pixel types for their input or output images, but that are not enforced via types or concept checking, and that are not specified in the documentation.
- Not writing for readability. This is one of the most common challenges for any software whose new algorithm implementations originate in the research community. It is common in that environment to write code that "just works", and to forget that the purpose of code is not just to be executed at run time, but to be easily read by the next developer. Typical good rules of "clean code" writing—for example, write small functions that do one thing and one thing only (the Single Responsibility Principle and the Principle of Least Surprise), adhere to proper naming of variables and functions—tend to be ignored when researchers are excited about getting their new shiny algorithm to work.
- Ignoring failure cases and error management. It is common to focus on the "nice cases" of data processing and to fail to provide code for managing all the cases that can go wrong. Adopters of the toolkit quickly run into such cases once they start developing and deploying applications in the real world.
- Insufficient testing. It requires a lot of discipline to follow the practice of test-driven development, especially the notion of writing the tests first and only implementing functionalities as you test them. It is almost always the case that bugs in the code are hiding behind the cases that were skipped while implementing the testing code.

Thanks to the communication practices of open source communities, many of these items end up being exposed through questions that are commonly asked in the mailing lists, or are directly reported as bugs by users. After dealing with many such issues, developers learn to write code that is "good for maintenance". Some of these traits apply to both coding style and the actual organization of the code. It is our view that a developer only reaches mastery after spending some time—at least a year—doing maintenance and getting exposed to "all the things that can go wrong".

The Invisible Hand

Software should look like it was written by a single person. The best developers are the ones who write code that, should they be hit by the proverbial bus, can be taken over by anybody else. We have grown to recognize that any trace of a "personal touch" is an indication of a defect introduced in the software.

In order to enforce and promote code style uniformity, the following tools have proved to be very effective:

- KWStyle[5] for automatic source code style checking. This is a simplified C++ parser that checks coding style and flags any violations.
- Gerrit[6] for regular code reviews. This tools serves two purposes: On one hand, it prevents immature code from entering the code base by distilling its errors, deficiencies and imperfections during iterative review cycles where other developers contribute to improve the code. On the other hand, it provides a virtual training camp in which new developers get to learn from more experienced developers (read "experienced" as *have made all the mistakes and know where the bodies are buried...*) how to improve the code and avoid known problems that have been observed during maintenance cycles.
- Git hooks that enforce the use of the KWStyle and Gerrit and that also perform some of their own checks. For example, ITK uses Git hooks that prevent commits of code with tabs or with trailing blank spaces.
- The team has also explored the use of Uncrustify[7] as a tool for enforcing a consistent style.

It is worth emphasizing that uniformity of style is not a simple matter of aesthetic appeal, it is really a matter of economics. Studies on the *Total Cost of Ownership* (TCO) of software projects have estimated that in the life-cycle of a project, the cost of maintenance will be about 75% of the TCO, and given that maintenance cost is applied on an annual basis, it typically surpasses the cost of initial development costs by the first five years of the life-cycle of a software project[8]. Maintenance is estimated to be about 80% of what software developers actually do, and when engaged in that activity the large majority of the developer's time is dedicated to reading someone else's code, trying to figure out what it was supposed to do[9]. Uniform style does wonders for reducing the time it takes for developers to immerse themselves in a newly open source file and understand the code before they make any modifications to it. By the same token, it reduces the chances that developers will misinterpret the code and make modifications that end up introducing new bugs when they were honestly trying to fix old bugs[10].

The key for making these tools effective is to make sure that they are:
- Available to all developers, hence our preference for Open Source tools.
- Run on a regular basis. In the case of ITK, these tools have been integrated in the Nightly and Continuous Dashboard builds managed by CDash[11].
- Run as close as possible to the point where the code is being written, so that deviations can be fixed immediately, and so developers quickly learn what kind of practices break style rules.

Refactoring

ITK started in 2000 and grew continuously until 2010. In 2011, thanks to an infusion of federal funding investment, the development team had the truly unique opportunity to embark on a refactoring effort. The funding was provided by the National Library of Medicine as part of the initiative of the American Recovery and Reinvestment Act (ARRA). This was not a minor undertaking. Imagine you have been working on a piece of software for over a decade, and you are offered the opportunity to clean it up; what would you change?

---

[5] http://public.kitware.com/KWStyle
[6] http://code.google.com/p/gerrit
[7] http://uncrustify.sourceforge.net
[8] *"Software Development Cost Estimating Handbook"*, Volume I, Naval Center for Cost Analysis, Air Force Cost Analysis Agency, 2008.
[9] *"Clean Code, A Handbook of Agile Software Craftsmanship"*, Robert C. Martin, Prentice Hall, 2009
[10] *"The Art of Readable Code"*, Dustin Boswell, Trevor Foucher, O'Reilly, 2012
[11] http://www.cdash.org/CDash/index.php?project=Insight

This opportunity for widespread refactoring is very rare. For the previous ten years, we had relied on the daily effort of performing small local refactorings, cleaning up specific corners of the toolkit as we ran into them. This continuous process of clean up and improvement takes advantage of the massive collaboration of open source communities, and it is safely enabled by the testing infrastructure driven by CDash, which regularly exercises about 84% of the code in the toolkit. Note that in contrast, the average code coverage of software industry testing is estimated to be only 50%.

Among the many things that were changed in the refactoring effort, the ones that are most relevant to the architecture are:

- Modularization was introduced in the toolkit
- Integer types were standardized
- Typedefs were fixed to allow management of images larger than 4 GB on all platforms
- The software process was revised:
    - Migrated from CVS to Git
    - Introduced code review with Gerrit
    - Introduced testing on demand with CDash@home
    - Improved method for downloading data for unit testing
- Deprecated support for obsolete compilers
- Improved support for many IO image file formats including:
    - DICOM
    - JPEG2000
    - TIFF (BigTIFF)
    - HDF5
- Introduced a framework for supporting GPU computation
- Introduced support for video processing
    - Added a bridge to OpenCV
    - Added a bridge to VXL

Maintenance based on incremental modifications—tasks such as adding features to an image filter, improving performance of a given algorithm, addressing bug reports, and improving documentation of specific image filters—works fine for the local improvement of specific C++ classes. However, a massive refactoring is needed for infrastructure modifications that affect a large number of classes across the board, such as the ones listed above. For example, the set of changes needed to support images larger than 4 GB was probably one of the largest patches ever applied to ITK. It required the modification of hundreds of classes and could not have been done incrementally without incurring in a great deal of pain. The modularization is another example of a task that could not have been done incrementally. It truly affected the entire organization of the toolkit, how its testing infrastructure works, how testing data is managed, how the toolkit is packaged and distributed, and how new contributions will be encapsulated to be added to the toolkit in the future.

Reproducibility

One of the early lessons learned in ITK was that the many papers published in the field were not as easy to implement as we were led to believe. The computational field tends to over-celebrate algorithms and to dismiss the practical work of writing software as "just an implementation detail".

That dismissive attitude is quite damaging to the field, since it diminishes the importance of the first-hand experience with the code and its proper use. The outcome is that most published papers are simply not reproducible, and when researchers and students attempt to use such techniques they end up spending a lot of time in the process and deliver *variations* of the original work. It is actually quite difficult, in practice, to verify if an implementation matches what was described in a paper.

ITK disrupted, for the good, that environment and restored a culture of DIY to a field that had grown accustomed to theoretical reasoning, and that had learned to dismiss experimental work. The new culture brought by ITK is a practical and pragmatic one in which the virtues of the software are judged by its practical results and not by the appearance of complexity that is celebrated in some scientific publications. It turns out that in practice the most effective processing methods are those that would appear to be too simple to be accepted for a scientific paper.

The culture of reproducibility is a continuation of the philosophy of test driven development, and systematically results in better software; higher clarity, readability, robustness and focus.

In order to fill the gap of lack of reproducible publications, the ITK community created the Insight Journal[12]. It is an open-access, fully online publication in which contributions are required to include code, data, parameters, and tests in order to enable verification by reproducibility. Articles are published online less than 24 hours after submission. Then they are made available for peer-review by any member of the community. Readers get full access to all the materials accompanying the article, namely source code, data, parameters, and testing scripts. The Journal has provided a productive space for sharing new code contributions which from there make their way into the code base. The Journal recently received its 500th article, and continues to be used as the official gateway for new code to be added to ITK.

---

[12] http://www.insight-journal.org

[chapter 10]

GNU Mailman
Barry Warsaw

GNU Mailman[1] is free software for managing mailing lists. Almost everybody who writes or uses free and open source software has encountered a mailing list. Mailing lists can be discussion-based or announcement-based, with all kinds of variations in between. Sometimes mailing lists are gatewayed to newsgroups on Usenet or similar services such as Gmane[2]. Mailing lists typically have archives which contain the historical record of all the messages that have been posted to the mailing list.

GNU Mailman has been around since the early 1990s, when John Viega wrote the first version to connect fans with the nascent Dave Matthews Band, the members of which he was friends with in college. This early version came to the attention of the Python community in the mid-'90s, when the center of the Python universe had moved from CWI[3], a scientific research institute in the Netherlands, to CNRI[4], the Corporation for National Research Initiatives in Reston, Virginia, USA. At CNRI we were running various Python-related mailing lists using Majordomo, a Perl-based mailing list manager. Of course, it just wouldn't do for the Python world to be maintaining so much Perl code. More importantly, because of its design, we found that modifying Majordomo for our purposes (such as to add minimal anti-spam measures) was too difficult.

Ken Manheimer was instrumental in much of the early GNU Mailman work, and many excellent developers have contributed to Mailman since then. Today, Mark Sapiro is maintaining the stable 2.1 branch, while Barry Warsaw, the author of this chapter, concentrates on the new 3.0 version.

Many of the original architectural decisions John made have lived on in the code right up until the Mailman 3 branch, and can still be seen in the stable branch. In the sections that follow, I'll describe some of the more problematic design decisions in Mailman 1 and 2, and how we've addressed them in Mailman 3.

In the early Mailman 1 days, we had a lot of problems with messages getting lost, or bugs causing messages to be re-delivered over and over again. This prompted us to articulate two overriding principles that are critical to Mailman's ongoing success:

- No message should ever be lost.
- No message should ever be delivered more than once.

In Mailman 2 we re-designed the message handling system to ensure that these two principles would always be of prime importance. This part of the system has been stable for at least a decade

---
[1] http://www.list.org
[2] http://gmane.org/
[3] http://www.cwi.nl/
[4] http://www.cnri.reston.va.us/

now, and is one of the key reasons that Mailman is as ubiquitous as it is today. Despite modernizing this subsystem in Mailman 3, the design and implementation remains largely unchanged.

10.1 The Anatomy of a Message

One of the core data structures in Mailman is the *email message*, represented by a *message* object. Many of the interfaces, functions, and methods in the system take three arguments: the mailing list object, the message object, and a metadata dictionary that is used to record and communicate state while a message is processed through the system.

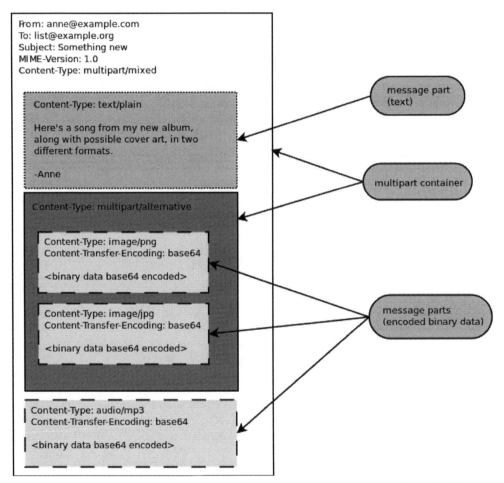

Figure 10.1: A MIME `multipart/mixed` message containing text, images, and an audio file

On the face of it, an email message is a simple object. It consists of a number of colon-separated key-value pairs, called the headers, followed by an empty line which separates the headers from the message body. This textural representation should be easy to parse, generate, reason about, and manipulate, but in fact it quickly gets quite complicated. There are countless RFCs that describe all the variations that can occur, such as handling complex data types like images, audio, and more. Email can contain ASCII English, or just about any language and character set in existence. The basic structure of an email message has been borrowed over and over again for other protocols, such as NNTP and HTTP, yet each is slightly different. Our work on Mailman has spawned several libraries just to deal with the vagaries of this format (often called "RFC822" for the founding 1982 IETF standard[5]). The email libraries originally developed for use by GNU Mailman have found their way into the Python standard library, where development continues to make them more standards-compliant and robust.

Email messages can act as containers for other types of data, as defined in the various MIME standards. A container *message part* can encode an image, some audio, or just about any type of binary or text data, including other container parts. In mail reader applications, these are known as *attachments*. Figure 10.1 shows the structure of a complex MIME message. The boxes with solid borders are the container parts, the boxes with dashed borders are Base64 encoded binary data, and the box with a dotted border is a plain text message.

Container parts can also be arbitrarily nested; these are called *multiparts* and can in fact get quite deep. But any email message, regardless of its complexity, can be modeled as a tree with a single message object at its root. Within Mailman, we often refer to this as the *message object tree*, and we pass this tree around by reference to the root message object. Figure 10.2 shows the object tree of the multipart message in Figure 10.1.

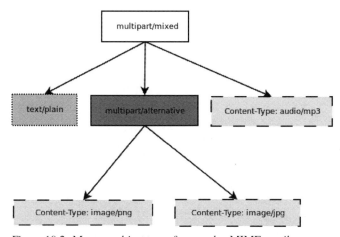

Figure 10.2: Message object tree of a complex MIME email message

Mailman will almost always modify the original message in some way. Sometimes the transformations can be fairly benign, such as adding or removing headers. Sometimes we'll completely change the structure of the message object tree, such as when the content filter removes certain content types like HTML, images, or other non-text parts. Mailman might even collapse "multipart/alternatives", where a message appears as both plain text and as some rich text type, or add additional parts containing information about the mailing list itself.

Mailman generally parses the *on the wire* bytes representation of a message just once, when it first comes into the system. From then on, it deals only with the message object tree until it's ready to send it back out to the outgoing mail server. It's at that point that Mailman flattens the tree back into a bytes representation. Along the way, Mailman pickles[6] the message object tree for quick storage to, and reconstruction from, the file system. *Pickles* are a Python technology for serializing any

---

[5] http://www.faqs.org/rfcs/rfc822.html
[6] http://docs.python.org/library/pickle.html

Python object, including all its subobjects, to a byte stream, and it's perfectly suited to optimizing the handling of email message object trees. *Unpickling* is deserializing this byte stream back into a live object. By storing these byte streams in a file, Python programs gain low-cost persistence.

10.2 The Mailing List

The *mailing list* is obviously another core object in the Mailman system, and most of the operations in Mailman are mailing list-centric, such as:

- Membership is defined in terms of a user or address being subscribed to a specific mailing list.
- Mailing lists have a large number of configuration options that are stored in the database, and which control everything from posting privileges to how messages are modified before final delivery.
- Mailing lists have owners and moderators which have greater permission to change aspects of the list, or to approve and reject questionable postings.
- Every mailing list has its own archive.
- Users post new messages to a specific mailing list.

and so on. Almost every operation in Mailman takes a mailing list as an argument—it's that fundamental. Mailing list objects have undergone a radical redesign in Mailman 3 to make them more efficient and to expand their flexibility.

One of John's earliest design decisions was how to represent a mailing list object inside the system. For this central data type, he chose a Python class with multiple base classes, each of which implements a small part of the mailing list's responsibility. These cooperating base classes, called *mixin classes*, were a clever way to organize the code so that it was easy to add entirely new functionality. By grafting on a new mixin base class, the core `MailList` class could easily accommodate something new and cool.

For example, to add an auto-responder to Mailman 2, a mixin class was created that held the data specific to that feature. The data would get automatically initialized when a new mailing list was created. The mixin class also provided the methods necessary to support the auto-responder feature. This structure was even more useful when it came to the design of the mailing `MailList` object's persistence.

Another of John's early design decisions was to use Python pickles for storing `MailList` state persistence.

In Mailman 2, the `MailList` object's state is stored in a file called `config.pck`, which is just the pickled representation of the `MailList` object's dictionary. Every Python object has an attribute dictionary called `__dict__`. So saving a mailing list object then is simply a matter of pickling its `__dict__` to a file, and loading it just involves reading the pickle from the file and reconstituting its `__dict__`.

Thus, when a new mixin class was added to implement some new functionality, all the attributes of the mixin were automatically pickled and unpickled appropriately. The only extra work we had to do was to maintain a *schema version number* to automatically upgrade older mailing list objects when new attributes were added via the mixin, since the pickled representation of older `MailList` objects would be missing the new attributes.

As convenient as this was, both the mixin architecture and pickle persistence eventually crumbled under their own weight. Site administrators often requested ways to access the mailing list configuration variables via external, non-Python systems. But the pickle protocol is entirely Python-specific, so sequestering all that useful data inside a pickle wouldn't work for them. Also, because the entire state of a mailing list was contained in the `config.pck`, and Mailman has multiple processes that need to read, modify, and write the mailing list state, we had to implement exclusive file-based and NFS-safe locks to ensure data consistency. Every time some part of Mailman wants to change the state of a mailing list, it must acquire the lock, write out the change, then release the lock. Even read operations can require a re-load of the list's `config.pck` file, since some other process may have changed it before the read operation. This serialization of operations on a mailing list turned out to be horribly slow and inefficient.

For these reasons, Mailman 3 stores all of its data in a SQL database. By default SQLite3 is used, though this is easily changed since Mailman 3 uses the Object Relational Mapper called Storm, which supports a wide variety of databases. PostgreSQL support was added with just a few lines of code, and a site administrator can enable it by changing one configuration variable.

Another, bigger problem is that in Mailman 2, each mailing list is a silo. Often operations span across many mailing lists, or even all of them. For example, a user might want to temporarily suspend all their subscriptions when they go on vacation. Or a site administrator might want to add some disclaimer to the welcome message of all of the mailing lists on her system. Even the simple matter of figuring out which mailing lists a single address is subscribed to required unpickling the state of every mailing list on the system, since membership information was kept in the `config.pck` file too.

Another problem was that each `config.pck` file lived in a directory named after the mailing list, but Mailman was originally designed without consideration for virtual domains. This lead to a very unfortunate problem where two mailing lists could not have the same name in different domains. For example, if you owned both the `example.com` and `example.org` domains, and you wanted them to act independently and allow for a different `support` mailing list in each, you cannot do this in Mailman 2, without modifications to the code, a barely supported hook, or conventional workarounds that forced a different list name under the covers, which is the approach used by large sites such as SourceForge.

This has been solved in Mailman 3 by changing the way mailing lists are identified, along with moving all the data into a traditional database. The *primary key* for the mailing list table is the *fully qualified list name* or as you'd probably recognize it, the posting address. Thus `support@example.com` and `support@example.org` are now completely independent rows in the mailing list table, and can easily co-exist in a single Mailman system.

10.3 Runners

Messages flow through the system by way of a set of independent processes called *runners*. Originally conceived as a way of predictably processing all the queued message files found in a particular directory, there are now a few runners which are simply independent, long-running processes that perform a specific task and are managed by a master process; more on that later. When a runner does manage files in a directory, it is called a *queue runner*.

Mailman is religiously single-threaded, even though there is significant parallelism to exploit. For example, Mailman can accept messages from the mail server at the same time it's sending messages out to recipients, or processing bounces, or archiving a message. Parallelism in Mailman is achieved through the use of multiple processes, in the form of these runners. For example, there is an *incoming* queue runner with the sole job of accepting (or rejecting) messages from the upstream mail server. There is an *outgoing* queue runner with the sole job of communicating with the upstream mail server over SMTP in order to send messages out to the final recipients. There's an *archiver* queue runner, a *bounce* processing queue runner, a queue runner for forwarding messages to an NNTP server, a runner for composing digests, and several others. Runners which don't manage a queue include a Local Mail Transfer Protocol (LMTP)[7] server and an administrative HTTP server.

Each queue runner is responsible for a single directory, i.e., its queue. While the typical Mailman system can perform perfectly well with a single process per queue, we use a clever algorithm for allowing parallelism within a single queue directory, without requiring any kind of cooperation or locking. The secret is in the way we name the files within the queue directory.

As mentioned above, every message that flows through the system is also accompanied by a metadata dictionary that accumulates state and allows independent components of Mailman to communicate with each other. Python's `pickle` library is able to serialize and deserialize multiple objects to a single file, so we can pickle both the message object tree and metadata dictionary into one file.

There is a core Mailman class called `Switchboard` which provides an interface for enqueuing (i.e., writing) and dequeuing (i.e., reading) the message object tree and metadata dictionary to files in a specific queue directory. Every queue directory has at least one switchboard instance, and every queue runner instance has exactly one switchboard.

Pickle files all end in the `.pck` suffix, though you may also see `.bak`, `.tmp`, and `.psv` files in a queue. These are used to ensure the two sacrosanct tenets of Mailman: no file should ever get lost, and no message should ever be delivered more than once. But things usually work properly and these files can be pretty rare.

As indicated, for really busy sites Mailman supports running more than one runner process per queue directory, completely in parallel, with no communication between them or locking necessary to process the files. It does this by naming the pickle files with a SHA1 hash, and then allowing a single queue runner to manage just a slice of the hash space. So if a site wants to run two runners on the *bounces* queue, one would process files from the top half of the hash space, and the other would process files from the bottom half of the hash space. The hashes are calculated using the contents of the pickled message object tree, the name of the mailing list that the message is destined for, and a time stamp. The SHA1 hashes are effectively random, and thus on average a two-runner queue directory will have about equal amounts of work per process. And because the hash space can be statically divided, these processes can operate on the same queue directory with no interference or communication necessary.

There's an interesting limitation to this algorithm. Since the splitting algorithm allots one or more bits of the hash to each space, the number of runners per queue directory must be a power of 2. This means there can be 1, 2, 4, or 8 runner processes per queue, but not, for example, 5. In practice this has never been a problem, since few sites will ever need more than 4 processes to handle their load.

There's another side effect of this algorithm that did cause problems during the early design of this system. Despite the unpredictability of email delivery in general, the best user experience is provided by processing the queue files in FIFO order, so that replies to a mailing list get sent out in roughly chronological order. Not making a best effort attempt at doing so can cause confusion for members. But using SHA1 hashes as file names obliterates any timestamps, and for performance reasons `stat()` calls on queue files, or unpickling the contents (e.g., to read a time stamp in the metadata) should be avoided.

Mailman's solution was to extend the file naming algorithm to include a time stamp prefix, as the number of seconds since the epoch (e.g., `<timestamp>+<sha1hash>.pck`). Each loop through the queue runner starts by doing an `os.listdir()`, which returns all the files in the queue directory.

---

[7]http://tools.ietf.org/html/rfc2033

Then for each file, it splits the file name and ignores any file names where the SHA1 hash doesn't match its slice of responsibility. The runner then sorts the remaining files based on the timestamp part of the file name. It's true that with multiple queue runners each managing different slices of the hash space, this could lead to ordering problems between the parallel runners, but in practice, the timestamp ordering is enough to preserve end-user perception of best-effort sequential delivery.

In practice this has worked extremely well for at least a decade, with only the occasional minor bug fix or elaboration to handle obscure corner cases and failure modes. It's one of the most stable parts of Mailman and was largely ported untouched from Mailman 2 to Mailman 3.

10.4 The Master Runner

With all these runner processes, Mailman needed a simple way to start and stop them consistently; thus the master watcher process was born. It must be able to handle both queue runners and runners which do not manage a queue. For example, in Mailman 3, we accept messages from the incoming upstream mail server via LMTP, which is a protocol similar to SMTP, but which operates only for local delivery and thus can be much simpler as it doesn't need to deal with the vagaries of delivering mail over an unpredictable Internet. The LMTP runner simply listens on a port, waiting for its upstream mail server to connect and send it a byte stream. It then parses this byte stream into a message object tree, creates an initial metadata dictionary, and enqueues this into a processing queue directory.

Mailman also has a runner that listens on another port and processes REST requests over HTTP. This process doesn't handle queue files at all.

A typical running Mailman system might have eight or ten processes, and they all need to be stopped and started appropriately and conveniently. They can also crash occasionally; for example, when a bug in Mailman causes an unexpected exception to occur. When this happens, the message being delivered is *shunted* to a holding area, with the state of the system at the time of the exception preserved in the message metadata. This ensures that an uncaught exception does not cause multiple deliveries of the message. In theory, the Mailman site administrator could fix the problem, and then *unshunt* the offending messages for redelivery, picking up where it left off. After shunting the problematic message, the master restarts the crashed queue runner, which begins processing the remaining messages in its queue.

When the master watcher starts, it looks in a configuration file to determine how many and which types of child runners to start. For the LMTP and REST runners, there is usually a single process. For the queue runners, as mentioned above, there can be a power-of-2 number of parallel processes. The master `fork()`s and `exec()`s all the runner processes based on the configuration file, passing in the appropriate command line arguments to each (e.g., to tell the subprocess which slice of the hash space to look at). Then the master basically sits in an infinite loop, blocking until one of its child processes exits. It keeps track of the process ID for each child, along with a count of the number of times the child has been restarted. This count prevents a catastrophic bug from causing a cascade of unstoppable restarts. There's a configuration variable which specifies how many restarts are allowed, after which an error is logged and the runner is not restarted.

When a child does exit, the master looks at both the exit code and the signal that killed the subprocess. Each runner process installs a number of signal handlers with the following semantics:

- SIGTERM: intentionally stop the subprocess. It is not restarted. SIGTERM is what `init` will kill the process with when changing run levels, and it's also the signal that Mailman itself uses to stop the subprocess.

- SIGINT: also used to intentionally stop the subprocess, it's the signal that occurs when control-C is used in a shell. The runner is not restarted.
- SIGHUP: tells the process to close and reopen its log files, but to keep running. This is used when rotating log files.
- SIGUSR1: initially stop the subprocess, but allow the master to restart the process. This is used in the restart command of init scripts.

The master also responds to all four of these signals, but it doesn't do much more than forward them to all its subprocesses. So if you sent SIGTERM to the master, all the subprocesses would get SIGTERM'd and exit. The master would know that the subprocess exited because of SIGTERM and it would know that this was an intentional stoppage, so it would not restart the runner.

To ensure that only one master is running at any time, it acquires a lock with a lifetime of about a day and a half. The master installs a SIGALRM handler, which wakes the master up once per day so that it can refresh the lock. Because the lock's lifetime is longer than the wake up interval, the lock should never time out or be broken while Mailman is running, unless of course the system crashes or the master is killed with an uncatchable signal. In those cases, the command line interface to the master process provides an option to override a stale lock.

This leads to the last bit of the master watcher story, the command line interface to it. The actual master script takes very few command line options. Both it and the queue runner scripts are intentionally kept simple. This wasn't the case in Mailman 2, where the master script was fairly complex and tried to do too much, which made it more difficult to understand and debug. In Mailman 3, the real command line interface for the master process is in the bin/mailman script, a kind of meta-script that contains a number of subcommands, in a style made popular by programs like Subversion. This reduces the number of programs that need to be installed on your shell's PATH. bin/mailman has subcommands to start, stop, and restart the master, as well as all the subprocesses, and also to cause all the log files to be reopened. The start subcommand fork()s and exec()s the master process, while the others simply send the appropriate signal to the master, which then propagates it to its subprocesses as described above. This improved separation of responsibility make it much easier to understand each individual piece.

10.5 Rules, Links, and Chains

A mailing list posting goes through several phases from the time it's first received until the time it's sent out to the list's membership. In Mailman 2, each processing step was represented by a *handler*, and a string of handlers were put together into a *pipeline*. So, when a message came into the system, Mailman would first determine which pipeline would be used to process it, and then each handler in the pipeline would be called in turn. Some handlers would do moderation functions (e.g., "Is this person allowed to post to the mailing list?"), others would do modification functions (e.g., "Which headers should I remove or add?"), and others would copy the message to other queues. A few examples of the latter are:

- A message accepted for posting would be copied to the archiver queue at some point, so that its queue runner would add the message to the archive.
- A copy of the message eventually had to end up in the outgoing queue so that it could be delivered to the upstream mail server, which has the ultimate responsibility of delivery to a list member.
- A copy of the message had to get put into a digest for people who wanted only occasional, regular traffic from the list, rather than an individual message whenever someone sent it.

The pipeline-of-handlers architecture proved to be quite powerful. It provided an easy way that people could extend and modify Mailman to do custom operations. The interface for a handler was fairly straightforward, and it was a simple matter to implement a new handler, ensuring it got added to the right pipeline in the right location to accomplish the custom operation.

One problem with this was that mixing moderation and modification in the same pipeline became problematic. The handlers had to be sequenced in the pipeline just so, or unpredictable or undesirable things would happen. For example, if the handler that added the RFC 2369[8] List-* headers came after the handler to copy the message to the digest collator, then folks receiving digests would get incorrect copies of the list posts. In different cases, it might be beneficial to moderate the message before or after modifying it. In Mailman 3, the moderation and modification operations have been split into separate subsystems for better control over the sequencing.

As described previously, the LMTP runner parses an incoming byte stream into a message object tree and creates an initial metadata dictionary for the message. It then enqueues these to one or another queue directory. Some messages may be *email commands* (e.g., to join or leave a mailing list, to get automated help, etc.) which are handled by a separate queue. Most messages are postings to the mailing list, and these get put in the *incoming* queue. The incoming queue runner processes each message sequentially through a *chain* consisting of any number of *links*. There is a built-in chain that most mailing lists use, but even this is configurable.

Figure 10.3 illustrates the default set of chains in the Mailman 3 system. Each link in the chain is illustrated by a rounded rectangle. The built-in chain is where the initial rules of moderation are applied to the incoming message, and in this chain, each link is associated with a *rule*. Rules are simply pieces of code that get passed the three typical parameters: the mailing list, the message object tree, and the metadata dictionary. Rules are not supposed to modify the message; they just make a binary decision and return a Boolean answering the question, "Did the rule match or not?". Rules can also record information in the metadata dictionary.

In the figure, solid arrows indicates message flow when the rule matches, while dotted arrows indicate message flow when the rule does not match. The outcome of each rule is recorded in the metadata dictionary so that later on, Mailman will know (and be able to report) exactly which rules matched and which ones missed. The dashed arrows indication transitions which are taken unconditionally, regardless of whether the rule matches or not.

It's important to note that the rules themselves do not dispatch based on outcome. In the built-in chain, each link is associated with an *action* which is performed when the rule matches. So for example, when the "loop" rule matches (meaning, the mailing list has seen this message before), the message is immediate handed off to the "discard" chain, which throws the message away after some bookkeeping. If the "loop" rule does not match, the next link in the chain will process the message.

In Figure 10.3, the links associated with "administrivia", "max-size", and "truth" rules have no binary decision. In case of the first two, this is because their action is *deferred*, so they simply record the match outcome and processing continues to the next link. The "any" rule then matches if any previous rule matches. This way, Mailman can report on all the reasons why a message is not allowed to be posted, instead of just the first reason. There are several more such rules not illustrated here for simplicity.

The "truth" rule is a bit different. It's always associated with the last link in the chain, and it always matches. With the combination of the penultimate "any" rule sweeping aside all previously matching messages, the last link then knows that any message making it this far is allowed to be posted to the mailing list, so it unconditionally moves the message to the "accept" chain.

---

[8]http://www.faqs.org/rfcs/rfc2369.html

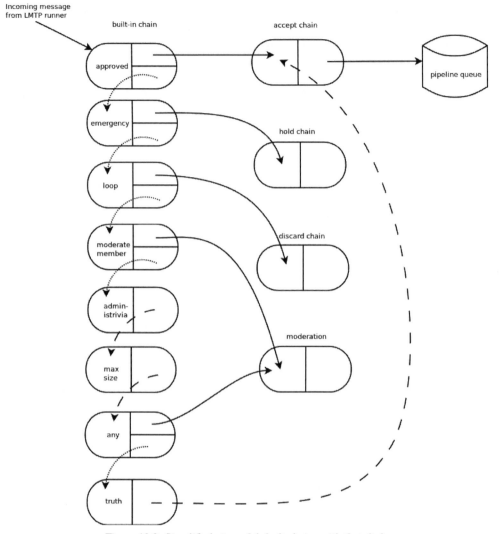

Figure 10.3: Simplified view of default chains with their links

There are a few other details of chain processing not described here, but the architecture is very flexible and extensible so that just about any type of message processing can be implemented, and sites can customize and extend rules, links, and chains.

What happens to the message when it hits the "accept" chain? The message, which is now deemed appropriate for the mailing list, is sent off to the *pipeline* queue for some modifications before it is delivered to the end recipients. This process is described in more detail in the following section.

The "hold" chain puts the message into a special bucket for the human moderator to review. The "moderation" chain does a little additional processing to decide whether the message should be accepted, held for moderator approval, discarded, or rejected. In order to reduce clutter in the diagram, the "reject" chain, which is used to bounce messages back to the original sender, is not illustrated.

10.6 Handlers and Pipelines

Once a message has made its way through the chains and rules and is accepted for posting, the message must be further processed before it can be delivered to the final recipients. For example, some headers may get added or deleted, and some messages may get some extra decorations that provide important disclaimers or information, such as how to leave the mailing list. These modifications are performed by a pipeline which contains a sequence of handlers. In a manner similar to chains and rules, pipelines and handlers are extensible, but there are a number of built-in pipelines for the common cases. Handlers have a similar interface as rules, accepting a mailing list, message object, and metadata dictionary. However, unlike rules, handlers can and do modify the message. Figure 10.4 illustrates the default pipeline and set of handlers (some handlers are omitted for simplicity).

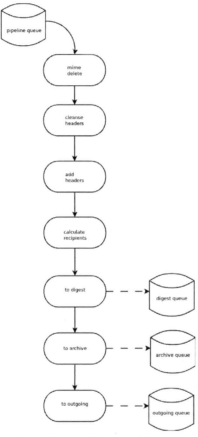

Figure 10.4: Pipeline queue handlers

For example, a posted message needs to have a Precedence: header added, which tells other automated software that this message came from a mailing list. This header is a de facto standard to prevent vacation programs from responding back to the mailing list. Adding this header (among other header modifications) is done by the "add headers" handler. Unlike rules, handler order generally doesn't matter, and messages always flow through all handlers in the pipeline.

Some handlers send copies of the message to other queues. As shown in Figure 10.4, there is a handler that makes a copy of the message for folks who want to receive digests. Copies are also sent to the archive queue for eventual delivery to the mailing list archives. Finally, the message is copied to the outgoing queue for final delivery to the mailing list's members.

10.7 VERP

"VERP" stands for "Variable Envelope Return Path", and it is a well-known technique[9] that mailing lists use to unambiguously determine bouncing recipient addresses. When an address on a mailing list is no longer active, the recipient's mail server will send a notification back to the sender. In the case of a mailing list, you want this bounce to go back to the mailing list, not to the original author of the message; the author can't do anything about the bounce, and worse, sending the bounce back to the author can leak information about who is subscribed to the mailing list. When the mailing list gets the bounce, however, it can do something useful, such as disable the bouncing address or remove it from the list's membership.

There are two general problems with this. First, even though there is a standard format for these bounces[10] (called *delivery status notifications*) many deployed mail servers do not conform to it. Instead, the body of their bounce messages can contain just about any amount of difficult-to-machine-parse gobbledygook, which makes automated parsing difficult. In fact, Mailman uses a library that contains dozens of bounce format heuristics, all of which have been seen in the wild during the 15 years of Mailman's existence.

Second, imagine the situation where a member of a mailing list has several forwards. She might be subscribed to the list with her anne@example.com address, but this might forward to person@example.org, which might further forward the message to me@example.net. When the final destination server at example.net receives the message, it will usually just send a bounce saying that me@example.net is no longer valid. But the Mailman server that sent the message only knows the member as anne@example.com, so a bounce flagging me@example.net will not contain a subscribed address, and Mailman will ignore it.

Along comes VERP, which exploits a requirement of the fundamental SMTP protocol[11] to provide unambiguous bounce detection, by returning such bounce messages to the *envelope sender*. This is not the From: field in the message body, but in fact the MAIL FROM value set during the SMTP dialog. This is preserved along the delivery route, and the ultimate receiving mail server is required, by the standards, to send the bounces to this address. Mailman uses this fact to encode the original recipient email address into the MAIL FROM value.

If the Mailman server is mylist@example.org, then the VERP-encoded envelope sender for a mailing list posting sent to anne@example.com will be:

mylist-bounce+anne=example.com@example.org

Here, the + is a local address separator, which is a format supported by most modern mail servers. So when the bounce comes back, it will actually be delivered to mylist-bounce@example.com but with the To: header still set to VERP-encoded recipient address. Mailman can then parse this To: header to decode the original recipient as anne@example.com.

While VERP is an extremely powerful tool for culling bad addresses from the mailing list, it does have one potentially important disadvantage. Using VERP requires that Mailman send out exactly one copy of the message per recipient. Without VERP, Mailman can bundle up identical copies of an

---

[9]http://cr.yp.to/proto/verp.txt
[10]http://www.faqs.org/rfcs/rfc5337.html
[11]http://www.faqs.org/rfcs/rfc5321.html

outgoing message for multiple recipients, thus reducing overall bandwidth and processing time. But VERP requires a unique MAIL FROM for each recipient, and the only way to do that is to send a unique copy of the message. Generally this is an acceptable trade-off, and in fact, once these individualized messages are being sent for VERP anyway, there are a lot of useful things Mailman can also do. For example, it can embed a URL in the footer of the message customized for each recipient which gives them a direct link to unsubscribe from the list. You could even imagine various types of mail-merge operations for customizing the body of the message for each individual recipient.

10.8 REST

One of the key architectural changes in Mailman 3 addresses a common request over the years: to allow Mailman to be more easily integrated with external systems. When I was hired by Canonical, the corporate sponsor of the Ubuntu project, in 2007 my job was originally to add mailing lists to Launchpad, a collaboration and hosting platform for software projects. I knew that Mailman 2 could do the job, but there was a requirement to use Launchpad's web user interface instead of Mailman's default user interface. Since Launchpad mailing lists were almost always going to be discussion lists, we wanted very little variability in the way they operated. List administrators would not need the plethora of options available in the typical Mailman site, and what few options they would need would be exposed through the Launchpad web user interface.

At the time, Launchpad was not free software (this changed in 2009), so we had to design the integration in such a way that Mailman 2's GPLv2 code could not infect Launchpad. This led to a number of architectural decisions during that integration design that were quite tricky and somewhat inefficient. Because Launchpad is now free software licensed under the AGPLv3, these hacks wouldn't be necessary today, but having to do it this way did provide some very valuable lessons on how a web-user-interface-less Mailman could be integrated with external systems. The vision that emerged was of a core engine that implemented mailing list operations efficiently and reliably, and that could be managed by any kind of web front-end, including ones written in Zope, Django, or PHP, or with no web user interface at all.

There were a number of technologies at the time that would allow this, and in fact Mailman's integration with Launchpad is based on XMLRPC. But XMLRPC has a number of problems that make it a less-than-ideal protocol.

Mailman 3 has adopted the Representational State Transfer (REST) model for external administrative control. REST is based on HTTP, and Mailman's default object representation is JSON. These protocols are ubiquitous and well-supported in a large variety of programming languages and environments, making it fairly easy to integrate Mailman with third party systems. REST was the perfect fit for Mailman 3, and now much of its functionality is exposed through a REST API.

This is a powerful paradigm that more applications should adopt: deliver a core engine that implements its basic functionality well, exposing a REST API to query and control it. The REST API provides yet another way of integrating with Mailman, the others being utilizing the command line interface, and writing Python code to access the internal API. This architecture is extremely flexible and can be used and integrated in ways that are beyond the initial vision of the system designers.

Not only does this design allow for much greater choices for deployment, but it even allowed the official components of the system to be designed and implemented independently. For example, the new official web user interface for Mailman 3 is technically a separate project with its own code base, driven primarily by experienced web designers. These outstanding developers are empowered to make decisions, create designs, and execute implementations without the core engine development being a bottleneck. The web user interface work feeds back into the core engine implementation by requesting additional functionality, exposed through the REST API, but they needn't wait for it, since they can mock up the server side on their end and continue experimenting and developing the web user interface while the core engine catches up.

We plan to use the REST API for many more things, including allowing the scripting of common operations and integration with IMAP or NNTP servers for alternative access to the archives.

10.9 Internationalization

GNU Mailman was one of the first Python programs to embrace internationalization. Of course, because Mailman does not usually modify the contents of email messages posted through it, those messages can be in any language of the original author's choosing. However, when interacting directly with Mailman, either through the web interface or via email commands, users would prefer to use their own natural language.

Mailman pioneered many of the internationalization technologies used in the Python world, but it is actually much more complex than most applications. In a typical desktop environment, the natural language is chosen when the user logs in, and remains static throughout the desktop session. However, Mailman is a server application, so it must be able to handle dozens of languages, separate from the language of the system on which it runs. In fact, Mailman must somehow determine the *language context* that a response is to be returned under, and translate its text to that language. Sometimes a response may even involve multiple languages; for example, if a bounce message from a Japanese user is to be forwarded to list administrators who speak German, Italian, and Catalan.

Again, Mailman pioneered some key Python technologies to handle complex language contexts such as these. It utilizes a library that manages a stack of languages which can be pushed onto and popped from as the context changes, even within the processing of a single message. It also implements an elaborate scheme for customizing its response templates based on site preferences, list owner preferences, and language choice. For example, if a list owner wants to customize a response template for one of her lists, but only for Japanese users, she would place the specific template in the appropriate place on the file system, and this would override more generic defaults.

10.10 Lessons Learned

While this article has provided an overview of Mailman 3's architecture and insight into how that architecture has evolved over the 15 years of its existence (through three major rewrites), there are lots of other interesting architectural decisions in Mailman which I can't cover. These include the configuration subsystem, the testing infrastructure, the database layer, the programmatic use of formal interfaces, archiving, mailing list styles, the email commands and command-line interface, and integration with the outgoing mail server. Contact us on the mailman-developers mailing list[12] if you're interested in more details.

Here are some lessons we've learned while rewriting a popular, established, and stable piece of the open source ecosystem.

- Use test driven development (TDD). There really is no other way! Mailman 2 largely lacks an automated test suite, and while it's true that not all of the Mailman 3 code base is covered by its test suite, most of it is, and all new code is required to be accompanied by tests, using either

---

[12]http://mail.python.org/mailman/listinfo/mailman-developers

unittests or doctests. Doing TDD is the only way to gain the confidence that the changes you make today do not introduce regressions in existing code. Yes, TDD can sometimes take longer, but think of it as an investment in the future quality of your code. In that way, *not* having a good test suite means you're just wasting your time. Remember the mantra: untested code is broken code.

- Get your bytes/strings story straight from the beginning. In Python 3, a sharp distinction is made between Unicode text strings and byte arrays, which, while initially painful, is a huge benefit to writing correct code. Python 2 blurred this line by having both Unicode and 8-bit ASCII strings, with some automated coercions between them. While appearing to be a useful convenience, problems with this fuzzy line are the number one cause of bugs in Mailman 2. This is not helped by the fact that email is notoriously difficult to classify into strings and bytes. Technically, the on-the-wire representation of an email is as a sequence of bytes, but these bytes are almost always ASCII, and there is a strong temptation to manipulate message components as text. The email standards themselves describe how human-readable, non-ASCII text can be safely encoded, so even things like finding a `Re:` prefix in a `Subject:` header will be text operations, not byte operations. Mailman's principle is to convert all incoming data from bytes to Unicode as early as possible, deal with the text as Unicode internally, and only convert it back to bytes on the way out. It's critical to be crystal clear from the start when you're dealing with bytes and when you're dealing with text, since it's very difficult to retrofit this fundamental model shift later.

- Internationalize your application from the start. Do you want your application to be used only by the minority of the world that speaks English? Think about how many fantastic users this ignores! It's not hard to set up internationalization, and there are lots of good tools for making this easy, many of which were pioneered in Mailman. Don't worry about the translations to start with; if your application is accessible to the world's wealth of languages, you will have volunteer translators knocking down your door to help.

GNU Mailman is a vibrant project with a healthy user base, and lots of opportunities for contributions. Here are some resources you can use if you think you'd like to help us out, which I hope you do!

Primary web site	`http://www.list.org`
Project wiki	`http://wiki.list.org`
Developer mailing list	`mailman-developers@python.org`
Users mailing list	`mailman-users@python.org`
Freenode IRC channel	`#mailman`

A Final Note

While this chapter was being written, we learned with sadness of the passing of Tokio Kikuchi[13], a Japanese professor who contributed heavily to Mailman, and was especially knowledgeable about internationalization and the idiosyncrasies of Japanese mail user agents. He will be greatly missed.

---

[13]`http://wiki.list.org/display/COM/TokioKikuchi`

[chapter 11]

matplotlib
John Hunter and Michael Droettboom

matplotlib is a Python-based plotting library with full support for 2D and limited support for 3D graphics, widely used in the Python scientific computing community. The library targets a broad range of use cases. It can embed graphics in the user interface toolkit of your choice, and currently supports interactive graphics on all major desktop operating systems using the GTK+, Qt, Tk, FLTK, wxWidgets and Cocoa toolkits. It can be called interactively from the interactive Python shell to produce graphics with simple, procedural commands, much like Mathematica, IDL or MATLAB. matplotlib can also be embedded in a headless webserver to provide hardcopy in both raster-based formats like Portable Network Graphics (PNG) and vector formats like PostScript, Portable Document Format (PDF) and Scalable Vector Graphics (SVG) that look great on paper.

11.1 The Dongle Problem

matplotlib's origin dates to an attempt by one of us (John Hunter) to free himself and his fellow epilepsy researchers from a proprietary software package for doing electrocorticography (ECoG) analysis. The laboratory in which he worked had only one license for the software, and the various graduate students, medical students, postdocs, interns, and investigators took turns sharing the hardware key dongle. MATLAB is widely used in the biomedical community for data analysis and visualization, so Hunter set out, with some success, to replace the proprietary software with a MATLAB-based version that could be utilized and extended by multiple investigators. MATLAB, however, naturally views the world as an array of floating point numbers, and the complexities of real-world hospital records for epilepsy surgery patients with multiple data modalities (CT, MRI, ECoG, EEG) warehoused on different servers pushed MATLAB to its limits as a data management system. Unsatisfied with the suitability of MATLAB for this task, Hunter began working on a new Python application built on top of the user interface toolkit GTK+, which was at the time the leading desktop windowing system for Linux.

matplotlib was thus originally developed as an EEG/ECoG visualization tool for this GTK+ application, and this use case directed its original architecture. matplotlib was originally designed to serve a second purpose as well: as a replacement for interactive command-driven graphics generation, something that MATLAB does very well. The MATLAB design makes the simple task of loading a data file and plotting very straightforward, where a full object-oriented API would be too syntactically heavy. So matplotlib also provides a stateful scripting interface for quick and easy generation of graphics similar to MATLAB's. Because matplotlib is a library, users have access to all of the rich built-in Python data structures such as lists, dictionaries, sets and more.

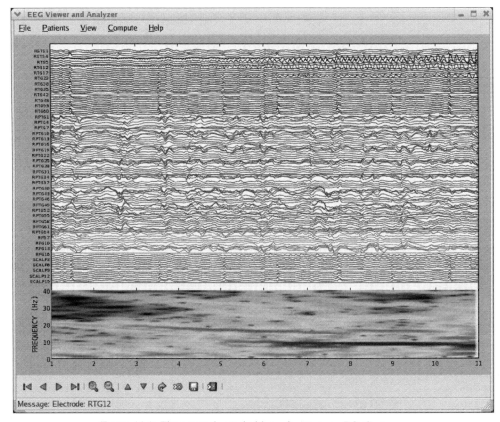

Figure 11.1: The original matplotlib application: an ECoG viewer

11.2 Overview of matplotlib Architecture

The top-level matplotlib object that contains and manages all of the elements in a given graphic is called the Figure. One of the core architectural tasks matplotlib must solve is implementing a framework for representing and manipulating the Figure that is segregated from the act of rendering the Figure to a user interface window or hardcopy. This enables us to build increasingly sophisticated features and logic into the Figures, while keeping the "backends", or output devices, relatively simple. matplotlib encapsulates not just the drawing interfaces to allow rendering to multiple devices, but also the basic event handling and windowing of most popular user interface toolkits. Because of this, users can create fairly rich interactive graphics and toolkits incorporating mouse and keyboard input that can be plugged without modification into the six user interface toolkits we support.

The architecture to accomplish this is logically separated into three layers, which can be viewed as a stack. Each layer that sits above another layer knows how to talk to the layer below it, but the lower layer is not aware of the layers above it. The three layers from bottom to top are: backend, artist, and scripting.

Backend Layer

At the bottom of the stack is the *backend* layer, which provides concrete implementations of the abstract interface classes:

- FigureCanvas encapsulates the concept of a surface to draw onto (e.g. "the paper").
- Renderer does the drawing (e.g. "the paintbrush").
- Event handles user inputs such as keyboard and mouse events.

For a user interface toolkit such as Qt, the FigureCanvas has a concrete implementation which knows how to insert itself into a native Qt window (QtGui.QMainWindow), transfer the matplotlib Renderer commands onto the canvas (QtGui.QPainter), and translate native Qt events into the matplotlib Event framework, which signals the callback dispatcher to generate the events so upstream listeners can handle them. The abstract base classes reside in matplotlib.backend_bases and all of the derived classes live in dedicated modules like matplotlib.backends.backend_qt4agg. For a pure image backend dedicated to producing hardcopy output like PDF, PNG, SVG, or PS, the FigureCanvas implementation might simply set up a file-like object into which the default headers, fonts, and macro functions are defined, as well as the individual objects (lines, text, rectangles, etc.) that the Renderer creates.

The job of the Renderer is to provide a low-level drawing interface for putting ink onto the canvas. As mentioned above, the original matplotlib application was an ECoG viewer in a GTK+ application, and much of the original design was inspired by the GDK/GTK+ API available at that time. The original Renderer API was motivated by the GDK Drawable interface, which implements such primitive methods as draw_point, draw_line, draw_rectangle, draw_image, draw_polygon, and draw_glyphs. Each additional backend we implemented—the earliest were the PostScript backend and the GD backend—implemented the GDK Drawable API and translated these into native backend-dependent drawing commands. As we discuss below, this unnecessarily complicated the implementation of new backends with a large proliferation of methods, and this API has subsequently been dramatically simplified, resulting in a simple process for porting matplotlib to a new user interface toolkit or file specification.

One of the design decisions that has worked quite well for matplotlib is support for a core pixel-based renderer using the C++ template library Anti-Grain Geometry or "agg" [She06]. This is a high-performance library for rendering anti-aliased 2D graphics that produces attractive images. matplotlib provides support for inserting pixel buffers rendered by the agg backend into each user interface toolkit we support, so one can get pixel-exact graphics across UIs and operating systems. Because the PNG output matplotlib produces also uses the agg renderer, the hardcopy is identical to the screen display, so what you see is what you get across UIs, operating systems and PNG output.

The matplotlib Event framework maps underlying UI events like key-press-event or mouse-motion-event to the matplotlib classes KeyEvent or MouseEvent. Users can connect to these events to callback functions and interact with their figure and data; for example, to pick a data point or group of points, or manipulate some aspect of the figure or its constituents. The following code sample illustrates how to toggle all of the lines in an Axes window when the user types 't'.

```
import numpy as np
import matplotlib.pyplot as plt

def on_press(event):
    if event.inaxes is None: return
    for line in event.inaxes.lines:
        if event.key=='t':
```

```
        visible = line.get_visible()
        line.set_visible(not visible)
    event.inaxes.figure.canvas.draw()

fig, ax = plt.subplots(1)

fig.canvas.mpl_connect('key_press_event', on_press)

ax.plot(np.random.rand(2, 20))

plt.show()
```

The abstraction of the underlying UI toolkit's event framework allows both matplotlib developers and end-users to write UI event-handling code in a "write once run everywhere" fashion. For example, the interactive panning and zooming of matplotlib figures that works across all user interface toolkits is implemented in the matplotlib event framework.

Artist Layer

The `Artist` hierarchy is the middle layer of the matplotlib stack, and is the place where much of the heavy lifting happens. Continuing with the analogy that the `FigureCanvas` from the backend is the paper, the `Artist` is the object that knows how to take the `Renderer` (the paintbrush) and put ink on the canvas. Everything you see in a matplotlib `Figure` is an `Artist` instance; the title, the lines, the tick labels, the images, and so on all correspond to individual `Artist` instances (see Figure 11.3). The base class is `matplotlib.artist.Artist`, which contains attributes that every `Artist` shares: the transformation which translates the artist coordinate system to the canvas coordinate system (discussed in more detail below), the visibility, the clip box which defines the region the artist can paint into, the label, and the interface to handle user interaction such as "picking"; that is, detecting when a mouse click happens over the artist.

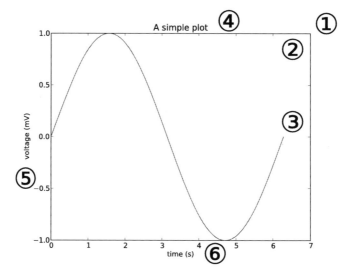

Figure 11.2: A figure

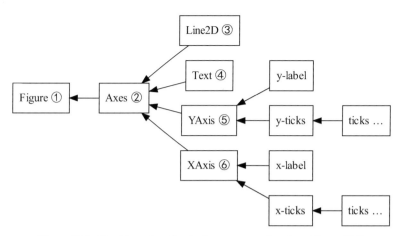

Figure 11.3: The hierarchy of artist instances used to draw Figure 11.2.

The coupling between the Artist hierarchy and the backend happens in the draw method. For example, in the mockup class below where we create SomeArtist which subclasses Artist, the essential method that SomeArtist must implement is draw, which is passed a renderer from the backend. The Artist doesn't know what kind of backend the renderer is going to draw onto (PDF, SVG, GTK+ DrawingArea, etc.) but it does know the Renderer API and will call the appropriate method (draw_text or draw_path). Since the Renderer has a pointer to its canvas and knows how to paint onto it, the draw method transforms the abstract representation of the Artist to colors in a pixel buffer, paths in an SVG file, or any other concrete representation.

```
class SomeArtist(Artist):
    'An example Artist that implements the draw method'

    def draw(self, renderer):
        """Call the appropriate renderer methods to paint self onto canvas"""
        if not self.get_visible():   return

        # create some objects and use renderer to draw self here
        renderer.draw_path(graphics_context, path, transform)
```

There are two types of Artists in the hierarchy. *Primitive* artists represent the kinds of objects you see in a plot: Line2D, Rectangle, Circle, and Text. *Composite* artists are collections of Artists such as the Axis, Tick, Axes, and Figure. Each composite artist may contain other composite artists as well as primitive artists. For example, the Figure contains one or more composite Axes and the background of the Figure is a primitive Rectangle.

The most important composite artist is the Axes, which is where most of the matplotlib API plotting methods are defined. Not only does the Axes contain most of the graphical elements that make up the background of the plot—the ticks, the axis lines, the grid, the patch of color which is the plot background—it contains numerous helper methods that create primitive artists and add them to the Axes instance. For example, Table 11.1 shows a small sampling of Axes methods that create plot objects and store them in the Axes instance.

method	creates	stored in
Axes.imshow	one or more `matplotlib.image.AxesImages`	Axes.images
Axes.hist	many `matplotlib.patch.Rectangles`	Axes.patches
Axes.plot	one or more `matplotlib.lines.Line2Ds`	Axes.lines

Table 11.1: Sampling of Axes methods and the Artist instances they create

Below is a simple Python script illustrating the architecture above. It defines the backend, connects a Figure to it, uses the array library numpy to create 10,000 normally distributed random numbers, and plots a histogram of these.

```
# Import the FigureCanvas from the backend of your choice
#   and attach the Figure artist to it.
from matplotlib.backends.backend_agg import FigureCanvasAgg as FigureCanvas
from matplotlib.figure import Figure
fig = Figure()
canvas = FigureCanvas(fig)

# Import the numpy library to generate the random numbers.
import numpy as np
x = np.random.randn(10000)

# Now use a figure method to create an Axes artist; the Axes artist is
#   added automatically to the figure container fig.axes.
# Here "111" is from the MATLAB convention: create a grid with 1 row and 1
#   column, and use the first cell in that grid for the location of the new
#   Axes.
ax = fig.add_subplot(111)

# Call the Axes method hist to generate the histogram; hist creates a
#   sequence of Rectangle artists for each histogram bar and adds them
#   to the Axes container.  Here "100" means create 100 bins.
ax.hist(x, 100)

# Decorate the figure with a title and save it.
ax.set_title('Normal distribution with $\mu=0,\ \sigma=1$')
fig.savefig('matplotlib_histogram.png')
```

Scripting Layer (pyplot)

The script using the API above works very well, especially for programmers, and is usually the appropriate programming paradigm when writing a web application server, a UI application, or perhaps a script to be shared with other developers. For everyday purposes, particularly for interactive exploratory work by bench scientists who are not professional programmers, it is a bit syntactically heavy. Most special-purpose languages for data analysis and visualization provide a lighter scripting interface to simplify common tasks, and matplotlib does so as well in its `matplotlib.pyplot` interface. The same code above, using pyplot, reads

```
import matplotlib.pyplot as plt
import numpy as np
```

```
x = np.random.randn(10000)
plt.hist(x, 100)
plt.title(r'Normal distribution with $\mu=0, \sigma=1$')
plt.savefig('matplotlib_histogram.png')
plt.show()
```

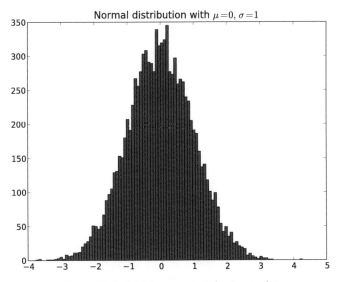

Figure 11.4: A histogram created using pyplot

pyplot is a stateful interface that handles much of the boilerplate for creating figures and axes and connecting them to the backend of your choice, and maintains module-level internal data structures representing the current figure and axes to which to direct plotting commands.

Let's dissect the important lines in the script to see how this internal state is managed.

- `import matplotlib.pyplot as plt`: When the pyplot module is loaded, it parses a local configuration file in which the user states, among many other things, their preference for a default backend. This might be a user interface backend like QtAgg, in which case the script above will import the GUI framework and launch a Qt window with the plot embedded, or it might be a pure image backend like Agg, in which case the script will generate the hard-copy output and exit.
- `plt.hist(x, 100)`: This is the first plotting command in the script. pyplot will check its internal data structures to see if there is a current Figure instance. If so, it will extract the current Axes and direct plotting to the Axes.hist API call. In this case there is none, so it will create a Figure and Axes, set these as current, and direct the plotting to Axes.hist.
- `plt.title(r'Normal distribution with $\mu=0, \sigma=1$')`: As above, pyplot will look to see if there is a current Figure and Axes. Finding that there is, it will not create new instances but will direct the call to the existing Axes instance method Axes.set_title.
- `plt.show()`: This will force the Figure to render, and if the user has indicated a default GUI backend in their configuration file, will start the GUI mainloop and raise any figures created to the screen.

A somewhat stripped-down and simplified version of pyplot's frequently used line plotting function matplotlib.pyplot.plot is shown below to illustrate how a pyplot function wraps functionality in matplotlib's object-oriented core. All other pyplot scripting interface functions follow the same design.

```
@autogen_docstring(Axes.plot)
def plot(*args, **kwargs):
    ax = gca()

    ret = ax.plot(*args, **kwargs)
    draw_if_interactive()

    return ret
```

The Python decorator @autogen_docstring(Axes.plot) extracts the documentation string from the corresponding API method and attaches a properly formatted version to the pyplot.plot method; we have a dedicated module matplotlib.docstring to handle this docstring magic. The *args and **kwargs in the documentation signature are special conventions in Python to mean all the arguments and keyword arguments that are passed to the method. This allows us to forward them on to the corresponding API method. The call ax = gca() invokes the stateful machinery to "get current Axes" (each Python interpreter can have only one "current axes"), and will create the Figure and Axes if necessary. The call to ret = ax.plot(*args, **kwargs) forwards the function call and its arguments to the appropriate Axes method, and stores the return value to be returned later. Thus the pyplot interface is a fairly thin wrapper around the core Artist API which tries to avoid as much code duplication as possible by exposing the API function, call signature and docstring in the scripting interface with a minimal amount of boilerplate code.

11.3 Backend Refactoring

Over time, the drawing API of the output backends grew a large number of methods, including:

draw_arc, draw_image, draw_line_collection, draw_line, draw_lines, draw_point, draw_quad_mesh, draw_polygon_collection, draw_polygon, draw_rectangle, draw_regpoly_collection

Unfortunately, having more backend methods meant it took much longer to write a new backend, and as new features were added to the core, updating the existing backends took considerable work. Since each of the backends was implemented by a single developer who was expert in a particular output file format, it sometimes took a long time for a new feature to arrive in all of the backends, causing confusion for the user about which features were available where.

For matplotlib version 0.98, the backends were refactored to require only the minimum necessary functionality in the backends themselves, with everything else moved into the core. The number of required methods in the backend API was reduced considerably, to only:

- draw_path: Draws compound polygons, made up of line and Bézier segments. This interfaces replaces many of the old methods: draw_arc, draw_line, draw_lines, and draw_rectangle.
- draw_image: Draws raster images.
- draw_text: Draws text with the given font properties.
- get_text_width_height_descent: Given a string of text, return its metrics.

It's possible to implement all of the drawing necessary for a new backend using only these methods.[1] This is useful for getting a new backend up and running more easily. However, in some cases, a backend may want to override the behavior of the core in order to create more efficient output. For example, when drawing markers (small symbols used to indicate the vertices in a line plot), it is more space-efficient to write the marker's shape only once to the file, and then repeat it as a "stamp" everywhere it is used. In that case, the backend can implement a draw_markers method. If it's implemented, the backend writes out the marker shape once and then writes out a much shorter command to reuse it in a number of locations. If it's not implemented, the core simply draws the marker multiple times using multiple calls to draw_path.

The full list of optional backend API methods is:

- draw_markers: Draws a set of markers.
- draw_path_collection: Draws a collection of paths.
- draw_quad_mesh: Draws a quadrilateral mesh.

11.4 Transforms

matplotlib spends a lot of time transforming coordinates from one system to another. These coordinate systems include:

- **data:** the original raw data values
- **axes:** the space defined by a particular axes rectangle
- **figure:** the space containing the entire figure
- **display:** the physical coordinates used in the output (e.g. points in PostScript, pixels in PNG)

Every Artist has a transformation node that knows how to transform from one coordinate system to another. These transformation nodes are connected together in a directed graph, where each node is dependent on its parent. By following the edges to the root of the graph, coordinates in data space can be transformed all the way to coordinates in the final output file. Most transformations are invertible, as well. This makes it possible to click on an element of the plot and return its coordinate in data space. The transform graph sets up dependencies between transformation nodes: when a parent node's transformation changes, such as when an Axes's limits are changed, any transformations related to that Axes are invalidated since they will need to be redrawn. Transformations related to other Axes in the figure, of course, may be left alone, preventing unnecessary recomputations and contributing to better interactive performance.

Transform nodes may be either simple affine transformations and non-affine transformations. Affine transformations are the family of transformations that preserve straight lines and ratios of distances, including rotation, translation, scale and skew. Two-dimensional affine transformations are represented using a 3×3 affine transformation matrix. The transformed point $(x\prime, y\prime)$ is obtained by matrix-multiplying the original point (x, y) by this matrix:

$$\begin{bmatrix} x' \\ y' \\ 1 \end{bmatrix} = \begin{bmatrix} s_x & \theta_x & t_x \\ \theta_y & s_y & t_y \\ 0 & 0 & 1 \end{bmatrix} \begin{bmatrix} x \\ y \\ 1 \end{bmatrix}$$

Two-dimensional coordinates can then easily be transformed by simply multiplying them by the transformation matrix. Affine transformations also have the useful property that they can be composed

---

[1] We could also go one step further and draw text using draw_path, removing the need for the draw_text method, but we haven't gotten around to making that simplification. Of course, a backend would still be free to implement its own draw_text method to output "real" text.

together using matrix multiplication. This means that to perform a series of affine transformations, the transformation matrices can first be multiplied together only once, and the resulting matrix can be used to transform coordinates. matplotlib's transformation framework automatically composes (freezes) affine transformation matrices together before transforming coordinates to reduce the amount of computation. Having fast affine transformations is important, because it makes interactive panning and zooming in a GUI window more efficient.

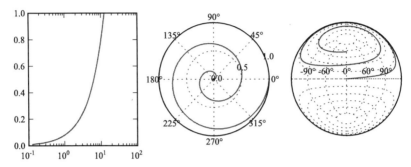

Figure 11.5: The same data plotted with three different non-affine transformations: logarithmic, polar and Lambert

Non-affine transformations in matplotlib are defined using Python functions, so they are truly arbitrary. Within the matplotlib core, non-affine transformations are used for logarithmic scaling, polar plots and geographical projections (Figure 11.5). These non-affine transformations can be freely mixed with affine ones in the transformation graph. matplotlib will automatically simplify the affine portion and only fall back to the arbitrary functions for the non-affine portion.

From these simple pieces, matplotlib can do some pretty advanced things. A blended transformation is a special transformation node that uses one transformation for the x axis and another for the y axis. This is of course only possible if the given transformations are "separable", meaning the x and y coordinates are independent, but the transformations themselves may be either affine or non-affine. This is used, for example, to plot logarithmic plots where either or both of the x and y axes may have a logarithmic scale. Having a blended transformation node allow the available scales to be combined in arbitrary ways. Another thing the transform graph allows is the sharing of axes. It is possible to "link" the limits of one plot to another and ensure that when one is panned or zoomed, the other is updated to match. In this case, the same transform node is simply shared between two axes, which may even be on two different figures. Figure 11.6 shows an example transformation graph with some of these advanced features at work. axes1 has a logarithmic x axis; axes1 and axes2 share the same y axis.

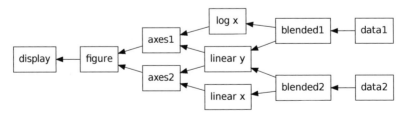

Figure 11.6: An example transformation graph

11.5 The Polyline Pipeline

When plotting line plots, there are a number of steps that are performed to get from the raw data to the line drawn on screen. In an earlier version of matplotlib, all of these steps were tangled together. They have since been refactored so they are discrete steps in a "path conversion" pipeline. This allows each backend to choose which parts of the pipeline to perform, since some are only useful in certain contexts.

Figure 11.7: A close-up view of the effect of pixel snapping. On the left, without pixel snapping; on the right, with pixel snapping.

- **Transformation:** The coordinates are transformed from data coordinates to figure coordinates. If this is a purely affine transformation, as described above, this is as simple as a matrix multiplication. If this involves arbitrary transformations, transformation functions are called to transform the coordinates into figure space.
- **Handle missing data:** The data array may have portions where the data is missing or invalid. The user may indicate this either by setting those values to NaN, or using numpy masked arrays. Vector output formats, such as PDF, and rendering libraries, such as Agg, do not often have a concept of missing data when plotting a polyline, so this step of the pipeline must skip over the missing data segments using MOVETO commands, which tell the renderer to pick up the pen and begin drawing again at a new point.
- **Clipping:** Points outside of the boundaries of the figure can increase the file size by including many invisible points. More importantly, very large or very small coordinate values can cause overflow errors in the rendering of the output file, which results in completely garbled output. This step of the pipeline clips the polyline as it enters and exits the edges of the figure to prevent both of these problems.
- **Snapping:** Perfectly vertical and horizontal lines can look fuzzy due to antialiasing when their centers are not aligned to the center of a pixel (see Figure 11.7). The snapping step of the pipeline first determines whether the entire polyline is made up of horizontal and vertical segments (such as an axis-aligned rectangle), and if so, rounds each resulting vertex to the nearest pixel center. This step is only used for raster backends, since vector backends should continue to have exact data points. Some renderers of vector file formats, such as Adobe Acrobat, perform pixel snapping when viewed on screen.
- **Simplification:** When plotting really dense plots, many of the points on the line may not actually be visible. This is particularly true of plots representing a noisy waveform. Including these points in the plot increases file size, and may even hit limits on the number of points allowed in the file format. Therefore, any points that lie exactly on the line between their two neighboring points are removed (see Figure 11.8). The determination depends on a threshold based on what would be visible at a given resolution specified by the user.

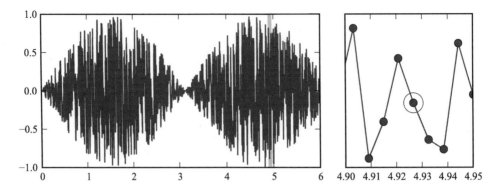

Figure 11.8: The figure on the right is a close-up of the figure on the left. The circled vertex is automatically removed by the path simplification algorithm, since it lies exactly on the line between its neighboring vertices, and therefore is redundant.

11.6 Math Text

Since the users of matplotlib are often scientists, it is useful to put richly formatted math expressions directly on the plot. Perhaps the most widely used syntax for math expressions is from Donald Knuth's TeX typesetting system. It's a way to turn input in a plain-text language like this:

`\sqrt{\frac{\delta x}{\delta y}}`

into a properly formatted math expression like this:

$$\sqrt{\frac{\delta x}{\delta y}}$$

matplotlib provides two ways to render math expressions. The first, `usetex`, uses a full copy of TeX on the user's machine to render the math expression. TeX outputs the location of the characters and lines in the expression in its native DVI (device independent) format. matplotlib then parses the DVI file and converts it to a set of drawing commands that one of its output backends then renders directly onto the plot. This approach handles a great deal of obscure math syntax. However, it requires that the user have a full and working installation of TeX. Therefore, matplotlib also includes its own internal math rendering engine, called `mathtext`.

`mathtext` is a direct port of the TeX math-rendering engine, glued onto a much simpler parser written using the `pyparsing` [McG07] parsing framework. This port was written based on the published copy of the TeX source code [Knu86]. The simple parser builds up a tree of *boxes* and *glue* (in TeX nomenclature), that are then laid out by the layout engine. While the complete TeX math rendering engine is included, the large set of third-party TeX and LaTeX math libraries is not. Features in such libraries are ported on an as-needed basis, with an emphasis on frequently used and non-discipline-specific features first. This makes for a nice, lightweight way to render most math expressions.

11.7 Regression Testing

Historically, matplotlib has not had a large number of low-level unit tests. Occasionally, if a serious bug was reported, a script to reproduce it would be added to a directory of such files in the source tree. The lack of automated tests created all of the usual problems, most importantly regressions in features that previously worked. (We probably don't need to sell you on the idea that automated testing is a good thing.) Of course, with so much code and so many configuration options and interchangeable pieces (e.g., the backends), it is arguable that low-level unit tests alone would ever be enough; instead we've followed the belief that it is most cost-effective to test all of the pieces working together in concert.

To this end, as a first effort, a script was written that generated a number of plots exercising various features of matplotlib, particularly those that were hard to get right. This made it a little easier to detect when a new change caused inadvertent breakage, but the correctness of the images still needed to be verified by hand. Since this required a lot of manual effort, it wasn't done very often.

As a second pass, this general approach was automated. The current matplotlib testing script generates a number of plots, but instead of requiring manual intervention, those plots are automatically compared to baseline images. All of the tests are run inside of the nose testing framework, which makes it very easy to generate a report of which tests failed.

Complicating matters is that the image comparison cannot be exact. Subtle changes in versions of the Freetype font-rendering library can make the output of text slightly different across different machines. These differences are not enough to be considered "wrong", but are enough to throw off any exact bit-for-bit comparison. Instead, the testing framework computes the histogram of both images, and calculates the root-mean-square of their difference. If that difference is greater than a given threshold, the images are considered too different and the comparison test fails. When tests fail, difference images are generated which show where on the plot a change has occurred (see Figure 11.9). The developer can then decide whether the failure is due to an intentional change and update the baseline image to match the new image, or decide the image is in fact incorrect and track down and fix the bug that caused the change.

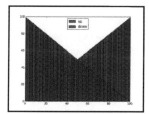 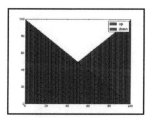 

Figure 11.9: A regression test image comparison. From left to right: a) The expected image, b) the result of broken legend placement, c) the difference between the two images.

Since different backends can contribute different bugs, the testing framework tests multiple backends for each plot: PNG, PDF and SVG. For the vector formats, we don't compare the vector information directly, since there are multiple ways to represent something that has the same end result when rasterized. The vector backends should be free to change the specifics of their output to increase efficiency without causing all of the tests to fail. Therefore, for vector backends, the testing framework first renders the file to a raster using an external tool (Ghostscript for PDF and Inkscape for SVG) and then uses those rasters for comparison.

Using this approach, we were able to bootstrap a reasonably effective testing framework from scratch more easily than if we had gone on to write many low-level unit tests. Still, it is not perfect; the code coverage of the tests is not very complete, and it takes a long time to run all of the tests.[2] Therefore, some regressions do still fall through the cracks, but overall the quality of the releases has improved considerably since the testing framework was implemented.

11.8 Lessons Learned

One of the important lessons from the development of matplotlib is, as Le Corbusier said, "Good architects borrow". The early authors of matplotlib were largely scientists, self-taught programmers trying to get their work done, not formally trained computer scientists. Thus we did not get the internal design right on the first try. The decision to implement a user-facing scripting layer largely compatible with the MATLAB API benefited the project in three significant ways: it provided a time-tested interface to create and customize graphics, it made for an easy transition to matplotlib from the large base of MATLAB users, and—most importantly for us in the context of matplotlib architecture—it freed developers to refactor the internal object-oriented API several times with minimal impact to most users because the scripting interface was unchanged. While we have had API users (as opposed to scripting users) from the outset, most of them are power users or developers able to adapt to API changes. The scripting users, on the other hand, can write code once and pretty much assume it is stable for all subsequent releases.

For the internal drawing API, while we did borrow from GDK, we did not spend enough effort determining whether this was the right drawing API, and had to expend considerable effort subsequently after many backends were written around this API to extend the functionality around a simpler and more flexible drawing API. We would have been well-served by adopting the PDF drawing specification [Ent11b], which itself was developed from decades of experience Adobe had with its PostScript specification; it would have given us mostly out-of-the-box compatibility with PDF itself, the Quartz Core Graphics framework, and the Enthought Enable Kiva drawing kit [Ent11a].

One of the curses of Python is that it is such an easy and expressive language that developers often find it easier to re-invent and re-implement functionality that exists in other packages than work to integrate code from other packages. matplotlib could have benefited in early development from expending more effort on integration with existing modules and APIs such as Enthought's Kiva and Enable toolkits which solve many similar problems, rather than reinventing functionality. Integration with existing functionality is, however, a double-edged sword, as it can make builds and releases more complex and reduce flexibility in internal development.

---

[2] Around 15 minutes on a 2.33 GHz Intel Core 2 E6550.

MediaWiki
Sumana Harihareswara and Guillaume Paumier

From the start, MediaWiki was developed specifically to be Wikipedia's software. Developers have worked to facilitate reuse by third-party users, but Wikipedia's influence and bias have shaped MediaWiki's architecture throughout its history.

Wikipedia is one of the top ten websites in the world, currently getting about 400 million unique visitors a month. It gets over 100,000 hits per second. Wikipedia isn't commercially supported by ads; it is entirely supported by a non-profit organization, the Wikimedia Foundation, which relies on donations as its primary funding model. This means that MediaWiki must not only run a top-ten website, but also do so on a shoestring budget. To meet these demands, MediaWiki has a heavy bias towards performance, caching and optimization. Expensive features that can't be enabled on Wikipedia are either reverted or disabled through a configuration variable; there is an endless balance between performance and features.

The influence of Wikipedia on MediaWiki's architecture isn't limited to performance. Unlike generic content management systems (CMSes), MediaWiki was originally written for a very specific purpose: supporting a community that creates and curates freely reusable knowledge on an open platform. This means, for example, that MediaWiki doesn't include regular features found in corporate CMSes, like a publication workflow or access control lists, but does offer a variety of tools to handle spam and vandalism.

So, from the start, the needs and actions of a constantly evolving community of Wikipedia participants have affected MediaWiki's development, and vice versa. The architecture of MediaWiki has been driven many times by initiatives started or requested by the community, such as the creation of Wikimedia Commons, or the Flagged Revisions feature. Developers made major architectural changes because the way that MediaWiki was used by Wikipedians made it necessary.

MediaWiki has also gained a solid external user base by being open source software from the beginning. Third-party reusers know that, as long as such a high-profile website as Wikipedia uses MediaWiki, the software will be maintained and improved. MediaWiki used to be really focused on Wikimedia sites, but efforts have been made to make it more generic and better accommodate the needs of these third-party users. For example, MediaWiki now ships with an excellent web-based installer, making the installation process much less painful than when everything had to be done via the command line and the software contained hardcoded paths for Wikipedia.

Still, MediaWiki is and remains Wikipedia's software, and this shows throughout its history and architecture.

This chapter is organized as follows:

- *Historical Overview* gives a short overview of the history of MediaWiki, or rather its prehistory, and the circumstances of its creation.
- *MediaWiki Code Base and Practices* explains the choice of PHP, the importance and implementation of secure code, and how general configuration is handled.
- *Database and Text Storage* dives into the distributed data storage system, and how its structure evolved to accommodate growth.
- *Requests, Caching and Delivery* follows the execution of a web request through the components of MediaWiki it activates. This section includes a description of the different caching layers, and the asset delivery system.
- *Languages* details the pervasive internationalization and localization system, why it matters, and how it is implemented.
- *Users* presents how users are represented in the software, and how user permissions work.
- *Content* details how content is structured, formatted and processed to generate the final HTML. A subsection focuses on how MediaWiki handles media files.
- *Customizing and Extending MediaWiki* explains how JavaScript, CSS, extensions, and skins can be used to customize a wiki, and how they modify its appearance and behavior. A subsection presents the software's machine-readable web API.

12.1 Historical Overview

Phase I: UseModWiki

Wikipedia was launched in January 2001. At the time, it was mostly an experiment to try to boost the production of content for Nupedia, a free-content, but peer-reviewed, encyclopedia created by Jimmy Wales. Because it was an experiment, Wikipedia was originally powered by UseModWiki, an existing GPL wiki engine written in Perl, using CamelCase and storing all pages in individual text files with no history of changes made.

It soon appeared that CamelCase wasn't really appropriate for naming encyclopedia articles. In late January 2001, UseModWiki developer and Wikipedia participant Clifford Adams added a new feature to UseModWiki: free links; i.e., the ability to link to pages with a special syntax (double square brackets), instead of automatic CamelCase linking. A few weeks later, Wikipedia upgraded to the new version of UseModWiki supporting free links, and enabled them.

While this initial phase isn't about MediaWiki per se, it provides some context and shows that, even before MediaWiki was created, Wikipedia started to shape the features of the software that powered it. UseModWiki also influenced some of MediaWiki's features; for example, its markup language. The Nostalgia Wikipedia[1] contains a complete copy of the Wikipedia database from December 2001, when Wikipedia still used UseModWiki.

Phase II: The PHP Script

In 2001, Wikipedia was not yet a top ten website; it was an obscure project sitting in a dark corner of the Interwebs, unknown to most search engines, and hosted on a single server. Still, performance was already an issue, notably because UseModWiki stored its content in a flat file database. At the

---

[1] http://nostalgia.wikipedia.org

time, Wikipedians were worried about being inundated with traffic following articles in the New York Times, Slashdot and Wired.

So in summer 2001, Wikipedia participant Magnus Manske (then a university student) started to work on a dedicated Wikipedia wiki engine in his free time. He aimed to improve Wikipedia's performance using a database-driven app, and to develop Wikipedia-specific features that couldn't be provided by a "generic" wiki engine. Written in PHP and MySQL-backed, the new engine was simply called the "PHP script", "PHP wiki", "Wikipedia software" or "phase II".

The PHP script was made available in August 2001, shared on SourceForge in September, and tested until late 2001. As Wikipedia suffered from recurring performance issues because of increasing traffic, the English language Wikipedia eventually switched from UseModWiki to the PHP script in January 2002. Other language versions also created in 2001 were slowly upgraded as well, although some of them would remain powered by UseModWiki until 2004.

As PHP software using a MySQL database, the PHP script was the first iteration of what would later become MediaWiki. It introduced many critical features still in use today, like namespaces to organize content (including talk pages), skins, and special pages (including maintenance reports, a contributions list and a user watchlist).

Phase III: MediaWiki

Despite the improvements from the PHP script and database backend, the combination of increasing traffic, expensive features and limited hardware continued to cause performance issues on Wikipedia. In 2002, Lee Daniel Crocker rewrote the code again, calling the new software "Phase III"[2]. Because the site was experiencing frequent difficulties, Lee thought there "wasn't much time to sit down and properly architect and develop a solution", so he "just reorganized the existing architecture for better performance and hacked all the code". Profiling features were added to track down slow functions.

The Phase III software kept the same basic interface, and was designed to look and behave as much like the Phase II software as possible. A few new features were also added, like a new file upload system, side-by-side diffs of content changes, and interwiki links.

Other features were added over 2002, like new maintenance special pages, and the "edit on double click" option. Performance issues quickly reappeared, though. For example, in November 2002, administrators had to temporarily disable the "view count" and "site" statistics which were causing two database writes on every page view. They would also occasionally switch the site to read-only mode to maintain the service for readers, and disable expensive maintenance pages during high-access times because of table locking problems.

In early 2003, developers discussed whether they should properly re-engineer and re-architect the software from scratch, before the fire-fighting became unmanageable, or continue to tweak and improve the existing code base. They chose the latter solution, mostly because most developers were sufficiently happy with the code base, and confident enough that further iterative improvements would be enough to keep up with the growth of the site.

In June 2003, administrators added a second server, the first database server separate from the web server. (The new machine was also the web server for non-English Wikipedia sites.) Load-balancing between the two servers would be set up later that year. Admins also enabled a new page-caching system that used the file system to cache rendered, ready-to-output pages for anonymous users.

June 2003 is also when Jimmy Wales created the non-profit Wikimedia Foundation to support Wikipedia and manage its infrastructure and day-to-day operations. The "Wikipedia software" was

---

[2] http://article.gmane.org/gmane.science.linguistics.wikipedia.technical/2794

officially named "MediaWiki" in July, as wordplay on the Wikimedia Foundation's name. What was thought at the time to be a clever pun would confuse generations of users and developers.

New features were added in July, like the automatically generated table of contents and the ability to edit page sections, both still in use today. The first release under the name "MediaWiki" happened in August 2003, concluding the long genesis of an application whose overall structure would remain fairly stable from there on.

12.2 MediaWiki Code Base and Practices

PHP

PHP was chosen as the framework for Wikipedia's "Phase II" software in 2001; MediaWiki has grown organically since then, and is still evolving. Most MediaWiki developers are volunteers contributing in their free time, and there were very few of them in the early years. Some software design decisions or omissions may seem wrong in retrospect, but it's hard to criticize the founders for not implementing some abstraction which is now found to be critical, when the initial code base was so small, and the time taken to develop it so short.

For example, MediaWiki uses unprefixed class names, which can cause conflicts when PHP core and PECL (PHP Extension Community Library) developers add new classes: MediaWiki `Namespace` class had to be renamed to `MWNamespace` to be compatible with PHP 5.3. Consistently using a prefix for all classes (e.g., "MW") would have made it easier to embed MediaWiki inside another application or library.

Relying on PHP was probably not the best choice for performance, since it has not benefitted from improvements that some other dynamic languages have seen. Using Java would have been much better for performance, and simplified execution scaling for back-end maintenance tasks. On the other hand, PHP is very popular, which facilitates recruiting new developers.

Even if MediaWiki still contains "ugly" legacy code, major improvements have been made over the years, and new architectural elements have been introduced to MediaWiki throughout its history. They include the `Parser`, `SpecialPage`, and `Database` classes, the `Image` class and the `FileRepo` class hierarchy, `ResourceLoader`, and the `Action` hierarchy. MediaWiki started without any of these things, but all of them support features that have been around since the beginning. Many developers are interested primarily in feature development and architecture is often left behind, only to catch up later as the cost of working within an inadequate architecture becomes apparent.

Security

Because MediaWiki is the platform for high-profile sites such as Wikipedia, core developers and code reviewers have enforced strict security rules[3]. To make it easier to write secure code, MediaWiki gives developers wrappers around HTML output and database queries to handle escaping. To sanitize user input, a develop uses the `WebRequest` class, which analyzes data passed in the URL or via a POSTed form. It removes "magic quotes" and slashes, strips illegal input characters and normalizes Unicode sequences. Cross-site request forgery (CSRF) is avoided by using tokens, and cross-site scripting (XSS) by validating inputs and escaping outputs, usually with PHP's `htmlspecialchars()` function. MediaWiki also provides (and uses) an XHTML sanitizer with the `Sanitizer` class, and database functions that prevent SQL injection.

---

[3] See https://www.mediawiki.org/wiki/Security_for_developers for a detailed guide.

Configuration

MediaWiki offers hundreds of configuration settings, stored in global PHP variables. Their default value is set in `DefaultSettings.php`, and the system administrator can override them by editing `LocalSettings.php`.

MediaWiki used to over-depend on global variables, including for configuration and context processing. Globals cause serious security implications with PHP's `register_globals` function (which MediaWiki hasn't needed since version 1.2). This system also limits potential abstractions for configuration, and makes it more difficult to optimize the start-up process. Moreover, the configuration namespace is shared with variables used for registration and object context, leading to potential conflicts. From a user perspective, global configuration variables have also made MediaWiki seem difficult to configure and maintain. MediaWiki development has been a story of slowly moving context out of global variables and into objects. Storing processing context in object member variables allows those objects to be reused in a much more flexible way.

12.3 Database and Text Storage

MediaWiki has been using a relational database backend since the Phase II software. The default (and best-supported) database management system (DBMS) for MediaWiki is MySQL, which is the one that all Wikimedia sites use, but other DBMSes (such as PostgreSQL, Oracle, and SQLite) have community-supported implementations. A sysadmin can choose a DBMS while installing MediaWiki, and MediaWiki provides both a database abstraction and a query abstraction layer that simplify database access for developers.

The current layout contains dozens of tables. Many are about the wiki's content (e.g., `page`, `revision`, `category`, and `recentchanges`). Other tables include data about users (`user`, `user_groups`), media files (`image`, `filearchive`), caching (`objectcache`, `l10n_cache`, `querycache`) and internal tools (`job` for the job queue), among others[4]. (See Figure 12.1.) Indices and summary tables are used extensively in MediaWiki, since SQL queries that scan huge numbers of rows can be very expensive, particularly on Wikimedia sites. Unindexed queries are usually discouraged.

The database went through dozens of schema changes over the years, the most notable being the decoupling of text storage and revision tracking in MediaWiki 1.5.

In the 1.4 model, the content was stored in two important tables, `cur` (containing the text and metadata of the current revision of the page) and `old` (containing previous revisions); deleted pages were kept in `archive`. When an edit was made, the previously current revision was copied to the `old` table, and the new edit was saved to `cur`. When a page was renamed, the page title had to be updated in the metadata of all the `old` revisions, which could be a long operation. When a page was deleted, its entries in both the `cur` and `old` tables had to be copied to the `archive` table before being deleted; this meant moving the text of all revisions, which could be very large and thus take time.

In the 1.5 model, revision metadata and revision text were split: the `cur` and `old` tables were replaced with `page` (pages' metadata), `revision` (metadata for all revisions, old or current) and `text` (text of all revisions, old, current or deleted). Now, when an edit is made, revision metadata don't need to be copied around tables: inserting a new entry and updating the `page_latest` pointer is enough. Also, the revision metadata don't include the page title anymore, only its ID: this removes the need for renaming all revisions when a page is renamed

---

[4]Complete documentation of the database layout in MediaWiki is available at https://www.mediawiki.org/wiki/Manual:Database_layout.

```
cur:                         page:
    cur_id                       page_id
    cur_namespace                page_namespace
    cur_title                    page_title
    cur_text                     page_restrictions
    cur_comment                  page_counter
    cur_user                     page_is_redirect
    cur_user_text                page_is_new
    cur_timestamp                page_random
    cur_restrictions             page_touched
    cur_counter                  page_latest
    cur_is_redirect
    cur_minor_edit
    cur_is_new
    cur_random              revision:
    cur_touched                  rev_id
    inverse_timestamp            rev_page
                                 rev_comment
old:                             rev_user
    old_id                       rev_user_text
    old_namespace                rev_timestamp
    old_title                    inverse_timestamp
    old_text                     rev_minor_edit
    old_comment
    old_user
    old_user_text           text:
    old_timestamp                old_id
    old_minor_edit               old_text
    old_flags                    old_flags
    inverse_timestamp
```

Figure 12.1: Main content tables in MediaWiki 1.4 and 1.5

The `revision` table stores metadata for each revision, but not their text; instead, they contain a text ID pointing to the `text` table, which contains the actual text. When a page is deleted, the text of all revisions of the page stays there and doesn't need to be moved to another table. The `text` table is composed of a mapping of IDs to text blobs; a `flags` field indicates if the text blob is gzipped (for space savings) or if the text blob is only a pointer to external text storage. Wikimedia sites use a MySQL-backed external storage cluster with blobs of a few dozen revisions. The first revision of the blob is stored in full, and following revisions to the same page are stored as diffs relative to the previous revision; the blobs are then gzipped. Because the revisions are grouped per page, they tend to be similar, so the diffs are relatively small and gzip works well. The compression ratio achieved on Wikimedia sites nears 98%.

On the hardware side, MediaWiki has built-in support for load balancing, added as early as 2004 in MediaWiki 1.2 (when Wikipedia got its second server—a big deal at the time). The load balancer (MediaWiki's PHP code that decides which server to connect to) is now a critical part of Wikimedia's infrastructure, which explains its influence on some algorithm decisions in the code. The system administrator can specify, in MediaWiki's configuration, that there is one master database server and any number of slave database servers; a weight can be assigned to each server. The load balancer will send all writes to the master, and will balance reads according to the weights. It also keeps track of the replication lag of each slave. If a slave's replication lag exceeds 30 seconds, it will not receive any read queries to allow it to catch up; if all slaves are lagged more than 30 seconds, MediaWiki will automatically put itself in read-only mode.

MediaWiki's "chronology protector" ensures that replication lag never causes a user to see a page that claims an action they've just performed hasn't happened yet: for instance, if a user renames a page, another user may still see the old name, but the one who renamed will always see the new name, because he's the one who renamed it. This is done by storing the master's position in the user's session if a request they made resulted in a write query. The next time the user makes a read request, the load balancer reads this position from the session, and tries to select a slave that has caught up to that replication position to serve the request. If none is available, it will wait until one is. It may appear to other users as though the action hasn't happened yet, but the chronology remains consistent for each user.

12.4 Requests, Caching and Delivery

Execution Workflow of a Web Request

`index.php` is the main entry point for MediaWiki, and handles most requests processed by the application servers (i.e., requests that were not served by the *caching* infrastructure; see below). The code executed from `index.php` performs security checks, loads default configuration settings from `includes/DefaultSettings.php`, guesses configuration with `includes/Setup.php` and then applies site settings contained in `LocalSettings.php`. Next it instantiates a `MediaWiki` object (`$mediawiki`), and creates a `Title` object (`$wgTitle`) depending on the title and action parameters from the request.

`index.php` can take a variety of action parameters in the URL request; the default action is `view`, which shows the regular view of an article's content. For example, the request `https://en.wikipedia.org/w/index.php?title=Apple\&action=view` displays the content of the article "Apple" on the English Wikipedia[5]. Other frequent actions include `edit` (to open an article for editing), `submit` (to preview or save an article), `history` (to show an article's history) and `watch` (to add an article to the user's watchlist). Administrative actions include `delete` (to delete an article) and `protect` (to prevent edits to an article).

`MediaWiki::performRequest()` is then called to handle most of the URL request. It checks for bad titles, read restrictions, local interwiki redirects, and redirect loops, and determines whether the request is for a normal or a special page.

Normal page requests are handed over to `MediaWiki::initializeArticle()`, to create an `Article` object for the page (`$wgArticle`), and then to `MediaWiki::performAction()`, which handles "standard" actions. Once the action has been completed, `MediaWiki::finalCleanup()` finalizes the request by committing database transactions, outputting the HTML and launching deferred updates through the job queue. `MediaWiki::restInPeace()` commits the deferred updates and closes the task gracefully.

If the page requested is a Special page (i.e., not a regular wiki content page, but a special software-related page such as `Statistics`), `SpecialPageFactory::executePath` is called instead of `initializeArticle()`; the corresponding PHP script is then called. Special pages can do all sorts of magical things, and each has a specific purpose, usually independent of any one article or its content. Special pages include various kinds of reports (recent changes, logs, uncategorized pages) and wiki administration tools (user blocks, user rights changes), among others. Their execution workflow depends on their function.

Many functions contain profiling code, which makes it possible to follow the execution workflow for debugging if profiling is enabled. Profiling is done by calling the `wfProfileIn` and `wfProfileOut` functions to respectively start and stop profiling a function; both functions take the function's name as a parameter. On Wikimedia sites, profiling is done for a percentage of all

---

[5]View requests are usually prettified with URL rewriting, in this example to `https://en.wikipedia.org/wiki/Apple`.

requests, to preserve performance. MediaWiki sends UDP packets to a central server that collects them and produces profiling data.

Caching

MediaWiki itself is improved for performance because it plays a central role on Wikimedia sites, but it is also part of a larger operational ecosystem that has influenced its architecture. Wikimedia's caching infrastructure (structured in layers) has imposed limitations in MediaWiki; developers worked around the issues, not by trying to shape Wikimedia's extensively optimized caching infrastructure around MediaWiki, but rather by making MediaWiki more flexible, so it could work within that infrastructure without compromising on performance and caching needs. For example, by default MediaWiki displays the user's IP in the top-right corner of the interface (for left-to-right languages) as a reminder that that's how they're known to the software when they're not logged in. The `$wgShowIPinHeader` configuration variable allows the system administrator to disable this feature, thus making the page content independent of the user: all anonymous visitors can then be served the exact same version of each page.

The first level of caching (used on Wikimedia sites) consists of reverse caching proxies (Squids) that intercept and serve most requests before they make it to the MediaWiki application servers. Squids contain static versions of entire rendered pages, served for simple reads to users who aren't logged in to the site. MediaWiki natively supports Squid and Varnish, and integrates with this caching layer by, for example, notifying them to purge a page from the cache when it has been changed. For logged-in users, and other requests that can't be served by Squids, Squid forwards the requests to the web server (Apache).

The second level of caching happens when MediaWiki renders and assembles the page from multiple objects, many of which can be cached to minimize future calls. Such objects include the page's interface (sidebar, menus, UI text) and the content proper, parsed from wikitext. The in-memory object cache has been available in MediaWiki since the early 1.1 version (2003), and is particularly important to avoid re-parsing long and complex pages.

Login session data can also be stored in memcached, which lets sessions work transparently on multiple front-end web servers in a load-balancing setup (Wikimedia heavily relies on load balancing, using LVS with PyBal).

Since version 1.16, MediaWiki uses a dedicated object cache for localized UI text; this was added after noticing that a large part of the objects cached in memcached consisted of UI messages localized into the user's language. The system is based on fast fetches of individual messages from constant databases (CDB), e.g., files with key-value pairs. CDBs minimize memory overhead and start-up time in the typical case; they're also used for the interwiki cache.

The last caching layer consists of the PHP opcode cache, commonly enabled to speed up PHP applications. Compilation can be a lengthy process; to avoid compiling PHP scripts into opcode every time they're invoked, a PHP accelerator can be used to store the compiled opcode and execute it directly without compilation. MediaWiki will "just work" with many accelerators such as APC, PHP accelerator and eAccelerator.

Because of its Wikimedia bias, MediaWiki is optimized for this complete, multi-layer, distributed caching infrastructure. Nonetheless, it also natively supports alternate setups for smaller sites. For example, it offers an optional simplistic file caching system that stores the output of fully rendered pages, like Squid does. Also, MediaWiki's abstract object caching layer lets it store the cached objects in several places, including the file system, the database, or the opcode cache.

ResourceLoader

As in many web applications, MediaWiki's interface has become more interactive and responsive over the years, mostly through the use of JavaScript. Usability efforts initiated in 2008, as well as advanced media handling (e.g., online editing of video files), called for dedicated front-end performance improvements.

To optimize the delivery of JavaScript and CSS assets, the ResourceLoader module was developed to optimize delivery of JS and CSS. Started in 2009, it was completed in 2011 and has been a core feature of MediaWiki since version 1.17. ResourceLoader works by loading JS and CSS assets on demand, thus reducing loading and parsing time when features are unused, for example by older browsers. It also minifies the code, groups resources to save requests, and can embed images as data URIs[6].

12.5 Languages

Context and Rationale

A central part of effectively contributing and disseminating free knowledge to all is to provide it in as many languages as possible. Wikipedia is available in more than 280 languages, and encyclopedia articles in English represent less than 20% of all articles. Because Wikipedia and its sister sites exist in so many languages, it is important not only to provide the content in the readers' native language, but also to provide a localized interface, and effective input and conversion tools, so that participants can contribute content.

For this reason, localization and internationalization (l10n and i18n) are central components of MediaWiki. The i18n system is pervasive, and impacts many parts of the software; it's also one of the most flexible and feature-rich[7]. Translator convenience is usually preferred to developer convenience, but this is believed to be an acceptable cost.

MediaWiki is currently localized in more than 350 languages, including non-Latin and right-to-left (RTL) languages, with varying levels of completion. The interface and content can be in different languages, and have mixed directionality.

Content Language

MediaWiki originally used per-language encoding, which led to a lot of issues; for example, foreign scripts could not be used in page titles. UTF-8 was adopted instead. Support for character sets other than UTF-8 was dropped in 2005, along with the major database schema change in MediaWiki 1.5; content must now be encoded in UTF-8.

Characters not available on the editor's keyboard can be customized and inserted via MediaWiki's Edittools, an interface message that appears below the edit window; its JavaScript version automatically inserts the character clicked into the edit window. The WikiEditor extension for MediaWiki, developed as part of a usability effort, merges special characters with the edit toolbar. Another extension, called Narayam, provides additional input methods and key mapping features for non-ASCII characters.

---

[6]For more on ResourceLoader, see https://www.mediawiki.org/wiki/ResourceLoader for the official documentation, and the talk *Low Hanging Fruit vs. Micro-optimization: Creative Techniques for Loading Web Pages Faster* given by Trevor Parscal and Roan Kattouw at OSCON 2011.

[7]For an exhaustive guide to internationalization and localization in MediaWiki, see https://www.mediawiki.org/wiki/Localisation.

Interface Language

Interface messages have been stored in PHP arrays of key-values pairs since the Phase III software was created. Each message is identified by a unique key, which is assigned different values across languages. Keys are determined by developers, who are encouraged to use prefixes for extensions; for example, message keys for the UploadWizard extension will start with `mwe-upwiz-`, where `mwe` stands for *MediaWiki extension*.

MediaWiki messages can embed parameters provided by the software, which will often influence the grammar of the message. In order to support virtually any possible language, MediaWiki's localization system has been improved and complexified over time to accommodate languages' specific traits and exceptions, often considered oddities by English speakers.

For example, adjectives are invariable words in English, but languages like French require adjective agreement with nouns. If the user specified their gender in their preferences, the `GENDER:` switch can be used in interface messages to appropriately address them. Other switches include `PLURAL:`, for "simple" plurals and languages like Arabic with dual, trial or paucal numbers, and `GRAMMAR:`, providing grammatical transformation functions for languages like Finnish whose grammatical cases cause alterations or inflections.

Localizing Messages

Localized interface messages for MediaWiki reside in `MessagesXx.php` files, where `Xx` is the ISO-639 code of the language (e.g. `MessagesFr.php` for French); default messages are in English and stored in `MessagesEn.php`. MediaWiki extensions use a similar system, or host all localized messages in an `<Extension-name>.i18n.php` file. Along with translations, Message files also include language-dependent information such as date formats.

Contributing translations used to be done by submitting PHP patches for the `MessagesXx.php` files. In December 2003, MediaWiki 1.1 introduced "database messages", a subset of wiki pages in the MediaWiki namespace containing interface messages. The content of the wiki page `MediaWiki:<Message-key>` is the message's text, and overrides its value in the PHP file. Localized versions of the message are at `MediaWiki:<Message-key>/<language-code>`; for example, `MediaWiki:Rollbacklink/de`.

This feature has allowed power users to translate (and customize) interface messages locally on their wiki, but the process doesn't update i18n files shipping with MediaWiki. In 2006, Niklas Laxström created a special, heavily hacked MediaWiki website (now hosted at `http://translatewiki.net`) where translators can easily localize interface messages in all languages simply by editing a wiki page. The `MessagesXx.php` files are then updated in the MediaWiki code repository, where they can be automatically fetched by any wiki, and updated using the LocalisationUpdate extension. On Wikimedia sites, database messages are now only used for customization, and not for localization any more. MediaWiki extensions and some related programs, such as bots, are also localized at translatewiki.net.

To help translators understand the context and meaning of an interface message, it is considered a good practice in MediaWiki to provide documentation for every message. This documentation is stored in a special Message file, with the qqq language code which doesn't correspond to a real language. The documentation for each message is then displayed in the translation interface on translatewiki.net. Another helpful tool is the qqx language code; when used with the `&uselang` parameter to display a wiki page (e.g., `https://en.wikipedia.org/wiki/Special:`

RecentChanges?uselang=qqx), MediaWiki will display the message keys instead of their values in the user interface; this is very useful to identify which message to translate or change.

Registered users can set their own interface language in their preferences, to override the site's default interface language. MediaWiki also supports fallback languages: if a message isn't available in the chosen language, it will be displayed in the closest possible language, and not necessarily in English. For example, the fallback language for Breton is French.

12.6 Users

Users are represented in the code using instances of the User class, which encapsulates all of the user-specific settings (user id, name, rights, password, email address, etc.). Client classes use accessors to access these fields; they do all the work of determining whether the user is logged in, and whether the requested option can be satisfied from cookies or whether a database query is needed. Most of the settings needed for rendering normal pages are set in the cookie to minimize use of the database.

MediaWiki provides a very granular permissions system, with a user permission for, basically, every possible action. For example, to perform the "Rollback" action (i.e., to "quickly rollback the edits of the last user who edited a particular page"), a user needs the rollback permission, included by default in MediaWiki's sysop user group. But it can also be added to other user groups, or have a dedicated user group only providing this permission (this is the case on the English Wikipedia, with the Rollbackers group). Customization of user rights is done by editing the $wgGroupPermissions array in LocalSettings.php; for instance, $wgGroupPermissions['user']['movefile'] = true; allows all registered users to rename files. A user can belong to several groups, and inherits the highest rights associated with each of them.

However, MediaWiki's user permissions system was really designed with Wikipedia in mind: a site whose content is accessible to all, and where only certain actions are restricted to some users. MediaWiki lacks a unified, pervasive permissions concept; it doesn't provide traditional CMS features like restricting read or write access by topic or type of content. A few MediaWiki extensions provide such features to some extent.

12.7 Content

Content Structure

The concept of namespaces was used in the UseModWiki era of Wikipedia, where talk pages were at the title "<article name>/Talk". Namespaces were formally introduced in Magnus Manske's first "PHP script". They were reimplemented a few times over the years, but have kept the same function: to separate different kinds of content. They consist of a prefix separated from the page title by a colon (e.g. Talk: or File: and Template:); the main content namespace has no prefix. Wikipedia users quickly adopted them, and they provided the community with different spaces to evolve. Namespaces have proven to be an important feature of MediaWiki, as they create the necessary preconditions for a wiki's community and set up meta-level discussions, community processes, portals, user profiles, etc.

The default configuration for MediaWiki's main content namespace is to be flat (no subpages), because it's how Wikipedia works, but it is trivial to enable subpages. They are enabled in other namespaces (e.g., User:, where people can, for instance, work on draft articles) and display breadcrumbs.

Namespaces separate content by type; within the same namespace, pages can be organized by topic using categories, a pseudo-hierarchical organization scheme introduced in MediaWiki 1.3.

Content Processing: MediaWiki Markup Language and Parser

The user-generated content stored by MediaWiki isn't in HTML, but in a markup language specific to MediaWiki, sometimes called "wikitext". It allows users to make formatting changes (e.g. bold, italic using quotes), add links (using square brackets), include templates, insert context-dependent content (like a date or signature), and make an incredible number of other magical things happen[8].

To display a page, this content needs to be parsed, assembled from all the external or dynamic pieces it calls, and converted to proper HTML. The parser is one of the most essential parts of MediaWiki, which makes it difficult to change or improve. Because hundreds of millions of wiki pages worldwide depend on the parser to continue outputting HTML the way it always has, it has to remain extremely stable.

The markup language wasn't formally specced from the beginning; it started based on Use-ModWiki's markup, then morphed and evolved as needs demanded. In the absence of a formal specification, the MediaWiki markup language has become a complex and idiosyncratic language, basically only compatible with MediaWiki's parser; it can't be represented as a formal grammar. The current parser's specification is jokingly referred to as "whatever the parser spits out from wikitext, plus a few hundred test cases".

There have been many attempts at alternative parsers, but none has succeeded so far. In 2004 an experimental tokenizer was written by Jens Frank to parse wikitext, and enabled on Wikipedia; it had to be disabled three days later because of the poor performance of PHP array memory allocations. Since then, most of the parsing has been done with a huge pile of regular expressions, and a ton of helper functions. The wiki markup, and all the special cases the parser needs to support, have also become considerably more complex, making future attempts even more difficult.

A notable improvement was Tim Starling's preprocessor rewrite in MediaWiki 1.12, whose main motivation was to improve the parsing performance on pages with complex templates. The preprocessor converts wikitext to an XML DOM tree representing parts of the document (template invocations, parser functions, tag hooks, section headings, and a few other structures), but can skip "dead branches", such as unfollowed `#switch` cases and unused defaults for template arguments, in template expansion. The parser then iterates through the DOM structure and converts its content to HTML.

Recent work on a visual editor for MediaWiki has made it necessary to improve the parsing process (and make it faster), so work has resumed on the parser and intermediate layers between MediaWiki markup and final HTML (see *Future*, below).

Magic Words and Templates

MediaWiki offers "magic words" that modify the general behavior of the page or include dynamic content into it. They consist of: behavior switches like `__NOTOC__` (to hide the automatic table of content) or `__NOINDEX__` (to tell search engines not to index the page); variables like `CURRENTTIME` or `SITENAME`; and parser functions, i.e., magic words that can take parameters, like `lc:<string>` (to output `<string>` in lowercase). Constructs like `GENDER:`, `PLURAL:` and `GRAMMAR:`, used to localize the UI, are parser functions.

---

[8]Detailed documentation is available at `https://www.mediawiki.org/wiki/Markup_spec` and the associated pages.

The most common way to include content from other pages in a MediaWiki page is to use templates. Templates were really intended to be used to include the same content on different pages, e.g., navigation panels or maintenance banners on Wikipedia articles; having the ability to create partial page layouts and reuse them in thousands of articles with central maintenance made a huge impact on sites like Wikipedia.

However, templates have also been used (and abused) by users for a completely different purpose. MediaWiki 1.3 made it possible for templates to take parameters that change their output; the ability to add a default parameter (introduced in MediaWiki 1.6) enabled the construction of a functional programming language implemented on top of PHP, which was ultimately one of the most costly features in terms of performance.

Tim Starling then developed additional parser functions (the ParserFunctions extension), as a stopgap measure against insane constructs created by Wikipedia users with templates. This set of functions included logical structures like `#if` and `#switch`, and other functions like `#expr` (to evaluate mathematical expressions) and `#time` (for time formatting).

Soon enough, Wikipedia users started to create even more complex templates using the new functions, which considerably degraded the parsing performance on template-heavy pages. The new preprocessor introduced in MediaWiki 1.12 (a major architectural change) was implemented to partly remedy this issue. Recently, MediaWiki developers have discussed the possibility of using an actual scripting language, perhaps Lua, to improve performance.

Media Files

Users upload files through the `Special:Upload` page; administrators can configure the allowed file types through an extension whitelist. Once uploaded, files are stored in a folder on the file system, and thumbnails in a dedicated `thumb` directory.

Because of Wikimedia's educational mission, MediaWiki supports file types that may be uncommon in other web applications or CMSes, like SVG vector images, and multipage PDFs and DjVus. They are rendered as PNG files, and can be thumbnailed and displayed inline, as are more common image files like GIFs, JPGs and PNGs.

When a file is uploaded, it is assigned a `File:` page containing information entered by the uploader; this is free text and usually includes copyright information (author, license) and items describing or classifying the content of the file (description, location, date, categories, etc.). While private wikis may not care much about this information, on media libraries like Wikimedia Commons it are critical to organise the collection and ensure the legality of sharing these files. It has been argued that most of these metadata should, in fact, be stored in a queryable structure like a database table. This would considerably facilitate search, but also attribution and reuse by third parties—for example, through the API.

Most Wikimedia sites also allow "local" uploads to each wiki, but the community tries to store freely licensed media files in Wikimedia's free media library, Wikimedia Commons. Any Wikimedia site can display a file hosted on Commons as if it were hosted locally. This custom avoids having to upload a file to every wiki to use it there.

As a consequence, MediaWiki natively supports foreign media repositories, i.e., the ability to access media files hosted on another wiki through its API and the `ForeignAPIRepo` system. Since version 1.16, any MediaWiki website can easily use files from Wikimedia Commons through the `InstantCommons` feature. When using a foreign repository, thumbnails are stored locally to save bandwidth. However, it is not (yet) possible to upload to a foreign media repository from another wiki.

12.8 Customizing and Extending MediaWiki

Levels

MediaWiki's architecture provides different ways to customize and extend the software. This can be done at different levels of access:

- System administrators can install extensions and skins, and configure the wiki's separate helper programs (e.g., for image thumbnailing and TeX rendering) and global settings (see *Configuration* above).
- Wiki sysops (sometimes called "administrators" too) can edit site-wide gadgets, JavaScript and CSS settings.
- Any registered user can customize their own experience and interface using their preferences (for existing settings, skins and gadgets) or make their own modifications (using their personal JS and CSS pages).

External programs can also communicate with MediaWiki through its machine API, if it's enabled, basically making any feature and data accessible to the user.

JavaScript and CSS

MediaWiki can read and apply site-wide or skin-wide JavaScript and CSS using custom wiki pages; these pages are in the `MediaWiki:` namespace, and thus can only be edited by sysops; for example, JavaScript modifications from `MediaWiki:Common.js` apply to all skins, CSS from `MediaWiki:Common.css` applies to all skins, but `MediaWiki:Vector.css` only applies to users with the Vector skin.

Users can do the same types of changes, which will only apply to their own interface, by editing subpages of their user page (e.g. `User:<Username>/common.js` for JavaScript on all skins, `User:<Username>/common.css` for CSS on all skins, or `User:<Username>/vector.css` for CSS modifications that only apply to the Vector skin).

If the Gadgets extension is installed, sysops can also edit gadgets, i.e., snippets of JavaScript code, providing features that can be turned on and off by users in their preferences. Upcoming developments on gadgets will make it possible to share gadgets across wikis, thus avoiding duplication.

This set of tools has had a huge impact and greatly increased the democratization of MediaWiki's software development. Individual users are empowered to add features for themselves; power users can share them with others, both informally and through globally configurable sysop-controlled systems. This framework is ideal for small, self-contained modifications, and presents a lower barrier to entry than heavier code modifications done through hooks and extensions.

Extensions and Skins

When JavaScript and CSS modifications are not enough, MediaWiki provides a system of hooks that let third-party developers run custom PHP code before, after, or instead of MediaWiki code for particular events[9]. MediaWiki extensions use hooks to plug into the code.

Before hooks existed in MediaWiki, adding custom PHP code meant modifying the core code, which was neither easy nor recommended. The first hooks were proposed and added in 2004 by Evan Prodromou; many more have been added over the years when needed. Using hooks, it is even possible to extend MediaWiki's wiki markup with additional capabilities using tag extensions.

---

[9] MediaWiki hooks are referenced at https://www.mediawiki.org/wiki/Manual:Hooks.

The extension system isn't perfect; extension registration is based on code execution at startup, rather than cacheable data, which limits abstraction and optimization and hurts MediaWiki's performance. But overall, the extension architecture is now a fairly flexible infrastructure that has helped make specialized code more modular, keeping the core software from expanding (too) much, and making it easier for third-party users to build custom functionality on top of MediaWiki.

Conversely, it's very difficult to write a new skin for MediaWiki without reinventing the wheel. In MediaWiki, skins are PHP classes each extending the parent Skin class; they contain functions that gather the information needed to generate the HTML. The long-lived "MonoBook" skin was difficult to customize because it contained a lot of browser-specific CSS to support old browsers; editing the template or CSS required many subsequent changes to reflect the change for all browsers and platforms.

API

The other main entry point for MediaWiki, besides index.php, is api.php, used to access its machine-readable web query API (Application Programming Interface).

Wikipedia users originally created "bots" that worked by screen scraping the HTML content served by MediaWiki; this method was very unreliable and broke many times. To improve this situation, developers introduced a read-only interface (located at query.php), which then evolved into a full-fledged read and write machine API providing direct, high-level access to the data contained in the MediaWiki database[10].

Client programs can use the API to login, get data, and post changes. The API supports thin web-based JavaScript clients and end-user applications. Almost anything that can be done via the web interface can basically be done through the API. Client libraries implementing the MediaWiki API are available in many languages, including Python and .NET.

12.9 Future

What started as a summer project done by a single volunteer PHP developer has grown into MediaWiki, a mature, stable wiki engine powering a top-ten website with a ridiculously small operational infrastructure. This has been made possible by constant optimization for performance, iterative architectural changes and a team of awesome developers.

The evolution of web technologies, and the growth of Wikipedia, call for ongoing improvements and new features, some of which require major changes to MediaWiki's architecture. This is, for example, the case for the ongoing visual editor project, which has prompted renewed work on the parser and on the wiki markup language, the DOM and final HTML conversion.

MediaWiki is a tool used for very different purposes. Within Wikimedia projects, for instance, it's used to create and curate an encyclopedia (Wikipedia), to power a huge media library (Wikimedia Commons), to transcribe scanned reference texts (Wikisource), and so on. In other contexts, MediaWiki is used as a corporate CMS, or as a data repository, sometimes combined with a semantic framework. These specialized uses that weren't planned for will probably continue to drive constant adjustments to the software's internal structure. As such, MediaWiki's architecture is very much alive, just like the immense community of users it supports.

---

[10]Exhaustive documentation of the API is available at https://www.mediawiki.org/wiki/API.

12.10 Further Reading

- MediaWiki documentation and support: `https://www.mediawiki.org`.
- Automatically generated MediaWiki documentation: `http://svn.wikimedia.org/doc/`.
- Domas Mituzas, *Wikipedia: site internals, configuration, code examples and management issues*, MySQL Users conference, 2007. Full text available at `http://dom.as/talks/`.

12.11 Acknowledgments

This chapter was created collaboratively. Guillaume Paumier wrote most of the content by organizing the input provided by MediaWiki users and core developers. Sumana Harihareswara coordinated the interviews and input-gathering phases. Many thanks to Antoine Musso, Brion Vibber, Chad Horohoe, Tim Starling, Roan Kattouw, Sam Reed, Siebrand Mazeland, Erik Möller, Magnus Manske, Rob Lanphier, Amir Aharoni, Federico Leva, Graham Pearce and others for providing input and/or reviewing the content.

[chapter 13]

Moodle
Tim Hunt

Moodle is a web application used in educational settings. While this chapter will try to give an overview of all aspects of how Moodle works, it focuses on those areas where Moodle's design is particularly interesting:

- The way the application is divided into plugins;
- The permission system, which controls which users can perform which actions in different parts of the system;
- The way output is generated, so that different themes (skins) can be used to give different appearances, and so that the interface can be localised.
- The database abstraction layer.

Moodle[1] provides a place online where students and teachers can come together to teach and learn. A Moodle site is divided into *courses*. A course has *users* enrolled in it with different roles, such as *Student* or *Teacher*. Each course comprises a number of *resources* and *activities*. A resource might be a PDF file, a page of HTML within Moodle, or a link to something elsewhere on the web. An activity might be a forum, a quiz or a wiki. Within the course, these resources and activities will be structured in some way. For example they may be grouped into logical topics, or into weeks on a calendar.

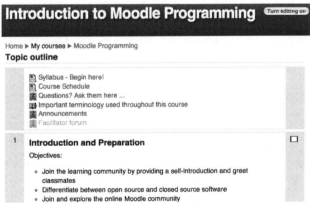

Figure 13.1: Moodle course

---

[1] http://moodle.org/

Moodle can be used as a standalone application. Should you wish to teach courses on software architecture (for example) you could download Moodle to your web host, install it, start creating courses, and wait for students to come and self-register. Alternatively, if you are a large institution, Moodle would be just one of the systems you run. You would probably also have the infrastructure shown in Figure 13.2.

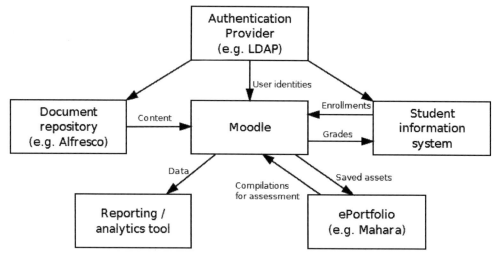

Figure 13.2: Typical university systems architecture

- An authentication/identity provider (for example LDAP) to control user accounts across all your systems.
- A student information system; that is, a database of all your students, which program of study they are on, and hence which courses they need to complete; and their transcript—a high-level summary of the results of the courses they have completed. This would also deal with other administrative functions, like tracking whether they have paid their fees.
- A document repository (for example, Alfresco); to store files, and track workflow as users collaborate to create files.
- An ePortfolio; this is a place where students can assemble assets, either to build a CV (resume), or to provide evidence that they have met the requirements of a practice-based course.
- A reporting or analytics tool; to generate high-level information about what is going on in your institution.

Moodle focuses on providing an online space for teaching and learning, rather than any of the other systems that an educational organisation might need. Moodle provides a basic implementation of the other functionalities, so that it can function either as a stand-alone system or integrated with other systems. The role Moodle plays is normally called a virtual learning environment (VLE), or learning or course management system (LMS, CMS or even LCMS).

Moodle is open source or free software (GPL). It is written in PHP. It will run on most common web servers, on common platforms. It requires a database, and will work with MySQL, PostgreSQL, Microsoft SQL Server or Oracle.

The Moodle project was started by Martin Dougiamas in 1999, while he was working at Curtin University, Australia. Version 1.0 was released in 2002, at which time PHP4.2 and MySQL 3.23 were the technologies available. This limited the kind of architecture that was possible initially, but much has changed since then. The current release is the Moodle 2.2.x series.

13.1 An Overview of How Moodle Works

A Moodle installation comprises three parts:
1. The code, typically in a folder like `/var/www/moodle` or `~/htdocs/moodle`. This should not be writable by the web server.
2. The database, managed by one of the supported RDMSs. In fact, Moodle adds a prefix to all the table names, so it can share a database with other applications if desired.
3. The `moodledata` folder. This is a folder where Moodle stores uploaded and generated files, and so needs to be writable by the web server. For security reasons, the should be outside the web root.

These can all be on a single server. Alternatively, in a load-balanced set-up, there will be multiple copies of the code on each web server, but just one shared copy of the database and `moodledata`, probably on other servers.

The configuration information about these three parts is stored in a file called `config.php` in the root of the `moodle` folder when Moodle is installed.

Request Dispatching

Moodle is a web applications, so users interact with it using their web browser. From Moodle's point of view that means responding to HTTP requests. An important aspect of Moodle's design is, therefore, the URL namespace, and how URLs get dispatched to different scripts.

Moodle uses the standard PHP approach to this. To view the main page for a course, the URL would be `.../course/view.php?id=123`, where 123 is the unique id of the course in the database. To view a forum discussion, the URL would be something like `.../mod/forum/discuss.php?id=456789`. That is, these particular scripts, `course/view.php` or `mod/forum/discuss.php`, would handle these requests.

This is simple for the developer. To understand how Moodle handles a particular request, you look at the URL and start reading code there. It is ugly from the user's point of view. These URLs are, however, permanent. The URLs do not change if the course is renamed, or if a moderator moves a discussion to a different forum.[2]

The alternative approach one could take is to have a single entry point `.../index.php/[extra-information-to-make-the-request-unique]`. The single script `index.php` would then dispatch the requests in some way. This approach adds a layer of indirection, which is something software developers always like to do. The lack of this layer of indirection does not seem to hurt Moodle.

Plugins

Like many successful open source projects, Moodle is built out of many plugins, working together with the core of the system. This is a good approach because at allows people to change and enhance Moodle in defined ways. An important advantage of an open source system is that you can tailor it to your particular needs. Making extensive customisations to the code can, however, lead to big problems when the time comes to upgrade, even when using a good version control system. By allowing as many customisations and new features as possible to be implemented as self-contained plugins that interact with the Moodle core through a defined API, it is easier for people to customise

---

[2]This is a good property for URLs to have, as explained in Tim Berners-Lee's article *Cool URIs don't change* http://www.w3.org/Provider/Style/URI.html

Moodle to their needs, and to share customisations, while still being able to upgrade the core Moodle system.

There are various ways a system can be built as a core surrounded by plugins. Moodle has a relatively fat core, and the plugins are strongly-typed. When I say a fat core, I mean that there is a lot of functionality in the core. This contrasts with the kind of architecture where just about everything, except for a small plugin-loader stub, is a plugin.

When I say plugins are strongly typed, I mean that depending on which type of functionality you want to implement, you have to write a different type of plugin, and implement a different API. For example, a new Activity module plugin would be very different from a new Authentication plugin or a new Question type. At the last count there are about 35 different types of plugin[3]. This contrasts with the kind of architecture where all plugins use basically the same API and then, perhaps, subscribe to the subset of hooks or events they are interested in.

Generally, the trend in Moodle has been to try to shrink the core, by moving more functionality into plugins. This effort has only been somewhat successful, however, because an increasing feature-set tends to expand the core. The other trend has been to try to standardise the different types of plugin as much as possible, so that in areas of common functionality, like install and upgrade, all types of plugins work the same way.

A plugin in Moodle takes the form of a folder containing files. The plugin has a type and a name, which together make up the "Frankenstyle" component name of the plugin[4]. The plugin type and name determine the path to the plugin folder. The plugin type gives a prefix, and the foldername is the plugin name. Here are some examples:

Plugin type	**Plugin name**	**Frankenstyle**	**Folder**
mod (Activity module)	forum	mod_forum	mod/forum
mod (Activity module)	quiz	mod_quiz	mod/quiz
block (Side-block)	navigation	block_navigation	blocks/navigation
qtype (Question type)	shortanswer	qtype_shortanswer	question/type/shortanswer
quiz (Quiz report)	statistics	quiz_statistics	mod/quiz/report/statistics

The last example shows that each activity module is allowed to declare sub-plugin types. At the moment only activity modules can do this, for two reasons. If all plugins could have sub-plugins that might cause performance problems. Activity modules are the main educational activities in Moodle, and so are the most important type of plugin, thus they get special privileges.

An Example Plugin

I will explain a lot of details of the Moodle architecture by considering a specific example plugin. As is traditional, I have chosen to implement a plugin that displays "Hello world".

This plugin does not really fit naturally into any of the standard Moodle plugin types. It is just a script, with no connection to anything else, so I will choose to implement it as a "local" plugin. This is a catch-all plugin type for miscellaneous functionality that does not fit anywhere better. I will name my plugin greet, to give a Frankensyle name of local_greet, and a folder path of local/greet.[5]

Each plugin must contain a file called version.php which defines some basic metadata about the plugin. This is used by the Moodle's plugin installer system to install and upgrade the plugin. For example, local/greet/version.php contains:

---

[3]For a full list of Moodle plugin types see http://docs.moodle.org/dev/Plugins.
[4]The word "Frankenstyle" arose out of an argument in the developers' Jabber channel, but everyone liked it and it stuck.
[5]The plugin code can be downloaded from https://github.com/timhunt/moodle-local_greet.

```php
<?php
$plugin->component    = 'local_greet';
$plugin->version      = 2011102900;
$plugin->requires     = 2011102700;
$plugin->maturity     = MATURITY_STABLE;
```

It may seem redundant to include the component name, since this can be deduced from the path, but the installer uses this to verify that the plugin has been installed in the right place. The version field is the version of this plugin. Maturity is ALPHA, BETA, RC (release candidate), or STABLE. Requires is the minimum version of Moodle that this plugin is compatible with. If necessary, one can also document other plugins that this one depends on.

Here is the main script for this simple plugin (stored in `local/greet/index.php`):

```php
<?php
require_once(dirname(__FILE__) . '/../../config.php');      // 1

require_login();                                             // 2
$context = context_system::instance();                       // 3
require_capability('local/greet:begreeted', $context);       // 4

$name = optional_param('name', '', PARAM_TEXT);              // 5
if (!$name) {
    $name = fullname($USER);                                 // 6
}

add_to_log(SITEID, 'local_greet', 'begreeted',
        'local/greet/index.php?name=' . urlencode($name));   // 7

$PAGE->set_context($context);                                // 8
$PAGE->set_url(new moodle_url('/local/greet/index.php'),
        array('name' => $name));                             // 9
$PAGE->set_title(get_string('welcome', 'local_greet'));      // 10

echo $OUTPUT->header();                                      // 11
echo $OUTPUT->box(get_string('greet', 'local_greet',
        format_string($name)));                              // 12
echo $OUTPUT->footer();                                      // 13
```

Line 1: Bootstrapping Moodle

```php
require_once(dirname(__FILE__) . '/../../config.php');      // 1
```

The single line of this script that does the most work is the first. I said above that `config.php` contains the details Moodle needs to connect to the database and find the moodledata folder. It ends, however, with the line `require_once('lib/setup.php')`. This:

1. loads all the standard Moodle libraries using `require_once`;
2. starts the session handling;
3. connects to the database; and
4. sets up a number of global variables, which we shall meet later.

Line 2: Checking the User Is Logged In

```
require_login();                                              // 2
```

This line causes Moodle to check that the current user is logged in, using whatever authentication plugin the administrator has configured. If not, the user will be redirected to the log-in form, and this function will never return.

A script that was more integrated into Moodle would pass more arguments here, to say which course or activity this page is part of, and then `require_login` would also verify that the user is enrolled in, or otherwise allowed to access this course, and is allowed to see this activity. If not, an appropriate error would be displayed.

13.2 Moodle's Roles and Permissions System

The next two lines of code show how to check that the user has permission to do something. As you can see, from the developer's point of view, the API is very simple. Behind the scenes, however, there is a sophisticated access system which gives the administrator great flexibility to control who can do what.

Line 3: Getting the Context

```
$context = context_system::instance();                        // 3
```

In Moodle, users can have different permissions in different places. For example, a user might be a Teacher in one course, and a Student in another, and so have different permissions in each place. These places are called *contexts*. Contexts in Moodle form a hierarchy rather like a folder hierarchy in a file-system. At the top level is the System context (and, since this script is not very well integrated into Moodle, it uses that context).

Within the System context are a number of contexts for the different categories that have been created to organise courses. These can be nested, with one category containing other categories. Category contexts can also contain Course contexts. Finally, each activity in a course will have its own Module context.

Line 4: Checking the User Has Permission to Use This Script

```
require_capability('local/greet:begreeted', $context);        // 4
```

Having got the context—the relevant area of Moodle—the permission can be checked. Each bit of functionality that a user may or may not have is called a *capability*. Checking a capability provides more fine-grained access control than the basic checks performed by `require_login`. Our simple example plugin has just one capability: `local/greet:begreeted`.

The check is done using the `require_capability` function, which takes the capability name and the context. Like other `require_...` functions, it will not return if the user does not have the capability. It will display an error instead. In other places the non-fatal `has_capability` function, which returns a Boolean would be used, for example, to determine whether to display a link to this script from another page.

How does the administrator configure which user has which permission? Here is the calculation that `has_capability` performs (at least conceptually):

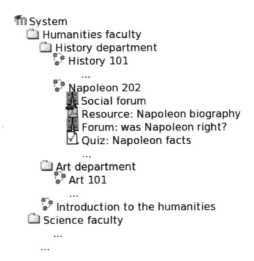

Figure 13.3: Contexts

1. Start from the current Context.
2. Get a list of the Roles that the user has in this Context.
3. Then work out what the Permission is for each Role in this Context.
4. Aggregate those permissions to get a final answer.

Defining Capabilities

As the example shows, a plugin can define new capabilities relating to the particular functionality it provides. Inside each Moodle plugin there is a sub-folder of the code called db. This contains all the information required to install or upgrade the plugin. One of those bits of information is a file called access.php that defines the capabilities. Here is the access.php file for our plugin, which lives in local/greet/db/access.php:

```
<?php
$capabilities = array('local/greet:begreeted' => array(
    'captype' => 'read',
    'contextlevel' => CONTEXT_SYSTEM,
    'archetypes' => array('guest' => CAP_ALLOW, 'user' => CAP_ALLOW)
));
```

This gives some metadata about each capability which are used when constructing the permissions management user interface. It also give default permissions for common types of role.

Roles

The next part of the Moodle permissions system is roles. A *role* is really just a named set of permissions. When you are logged into Moodle, you will have the "Authenticated user" role in the System context, and since the System context is the root of the hierarchy, that role will apply everywhere.

Within a particular course, you may be a Student, and that role assignment will apply in the Course context and all the Module contexts within it. In another course, however, you may have a different role. For example, Mr Gradgrind may be Teacher in the "Facts, Facts, Facts" course, but a Student in the professional development course "Facts Aren't Everything". Finally, a user might be given the Moderator role in one particular forum (Module context).

Permissions

A role defines a *permission* for each capability. For example the Teacher role will probably ALLOW moodle/course:manage, but the Student role will not. However, both Student and Teacher will allow mod/forum:startdiscussion.

The roles are normally defined globally, but they can be re-defined in each context. For example, one particular wiki can be made read-only to students by overriding the permission for the mod/wiki:edit capability for the Student role in that wiki (Module) context, to PREVENT.

There are four Permissions:

- NOT SET/INHERIT (default)
- ALLOW
- PREVENT
- PROHIBIT

In a given context, a role will have one of these four permissions for each capability. One difference between PROHIBIT and PREVENT is that a PROHIBIT cannot be overridden in sub-contexts.

Permission Aggregation

Finally the permissions for all the roles the user has in this context are aggregated.

- If any role gives the permission PROHIBIT for this capability, return false.
- Otherwise, if any role gives ALLOW for this capability, return true.
- Otherwise return false.

A use case for PROHIBIT is this: Suppose a user has been making abusive posts in a number of forums, and we want to stop them immediately. We can create a Naughty user role, which sets mod/forum:post and other such capabilities to PROHIBIT. We can then assign this role to the abusive user in the System context. That way, we can be sure that the user will not be able to post any more in any forum. (We would then talk to the student, and having reached a satisfactory outcome, remove that role assignment so that they may use the system again.)

So, Moodle's permissions system gives administrators a huge amount of flexibility. They can define whichever roles they like with different permissions for each capability; they can alter the role definitions in sub-contexts; and then they can assign different roles to users in different contexts.

13.3 Back to Our Example Script

The next part of the script illustrates some miscellaneous points:

Line 5: Get Data From the Request

```
$name = optional_param('name', '', PARAM_TEXT);                    // 5
```

Something that every web application has to do is get data from a request (GET or POST variables) without being susceptible to SQL injection or cross-site scripting attacks. Moodle provides two ways to do this.

The simple method is the one shown here. It gets a single variable given the parameter name (here name) a default value, and the expected type. The expected type is used to clean the input of all unexpected characters. There are numerous types like PARAM_INT, PARAM_ALPHANUM, PARAM_EMAIL, and so on.

There is also a similar required_param function, which like other require_... functions stops execution and displays an error message if the expected parameter is not found.

The other mechanism Moodle has for getting data from the request is a fully fledged forms library. This is a wrapper around the HTML QuickForm library from PEAR[6]. This seemed like a good choice when it was selected, but is now no longer maintained. At some time in the future we will have to tackle moving to a new forms library, which many of us look forwards to, because QuickForm has several irritating design issues. For now, however, it is adequate. Forms can be defined as a collection of fields of various types (e.g. text box, select drop-down, date-selector) with client- and server- side validation (including use of the same PARAM_... types).

Line 6: Global Variables

```
if (!$name) {
    $name = fullname($USER);                              // 6
}
```

This snippet shows the first of the global variables Moodle provides. $USER makes accessible the information about the user accessing this script. Other globals include:

- $CFG: holds the commonly used configuration settings.
- $DB: the database connection.
- $SESSION: a wrapper around the PHP session.
- $COURSE: the course the current request relates to.

and several others, some of which we will encounter below.

You may have read the words "global variable" with horror. Note, however, that PHP processes a single request at a time. Therefore these variables are not as global as all that. In fact, PHP global variables can be seen as an implementation of the thread-scoped registry pattern[7] and this is the way in which Moodle uses them. It is very convenient in that it makes commonly used objects available throughout the code, without requiring them to be passed to every function and method. It is only infrequently abused.

Nothing is Simple

This line also serves to make a point about the problem domain: nothing is ever simple. To display a user's name is more complicated than simply concatenating $USER->firstname, ' ', and $USER->lastname. The school may have policies about showing either of those parts, and different cultures have different conventions for which order to show names. Therefore, there are several configurations settings and a function to assemble the full name according to the rules.

---

[6]For non-PHP programmers, PEAR is PHP's equivalent of CPAN.
[7]See Martin Fowler's *Patterns of Enterprise Application Architecture*.

Dates are a similar problem. Different users may be in different time-zones. Moodle stores all dates as Unix time-stamps, which are integers, and so work in all databases. There is then a userdate function to display the time-stamp to the user using the appropriate timezone and locale settings.

Line 7: Logging

```
add_to_log(SITEID, 'local_greet', 'begreeted',
        'local/greet/index.php?name=' . urlencode($name));    // 7
```

All significant actions in Moodle are logged. Logs are written to a table in the database. This is a trade-off. It makes sophisticated analysis quite easy, and indeed various reports based on the logs are included with Moodle. On a large and busy site, however, it is a performance problem. The log table gets huge, which makes backing up the database more difficult, and makes queries on the log table slow. There can also be write contention on the log table. These problems can be mitigated in various ways, for example by batching writes, or archiving or deleting old records to remove them from the main database.

13.4 Generating Output

Output is mainly handled via two global objects.

Line 8: The $PAGE Global

```
$PAGE->set_context($context);                                 // 8
```

$PAGE stores the information about the page to be output. This information is then readily available to the code that generates the HTML. This script needs to explicitly specify the current context. (In other situations, this might have been set automatically by require_login.) The URL for this page must also be set explicitly. This may seem redundant, but the rationale for requiring it is that you might get to a particular page using any number of different URLs, but the URL passed to set_url should be the canonical URL for the page—a good permalink, if you like. The page title is also set. This will end up in the head element of the HTML.

Line 9: Moodle URL

```
$PAGE->set_url(new moodle_url('/local/greet/index.php'),
        array('name' => $name));                              // 9
```

I just wanted to flag this nice little helper class which makes manipulating URLs much easier. As an aside, recall that the add_to_log function call above did not use this helper class. Indeed, the log API cannot accept moodle_url objects. This sort of inconsistency is a typical sign of a code-base as old as Moodle's.

Line 10: Internationalisation

```
$PAGE->set_title(get_string('welcome', 'local_greet'));       // 10
```

Moodle uses its own system to allow the interface to be translated into any language. There may now be good PHP internationalisation libraries, but in 2002 when it was first implemented there was not one available that was adequate. The system is based around the get_string function. Strings are identified by a key and the plugin Frankenstyle name. As can be seen on line 12, it is possible to interpolate values into the string. (Multiple values are handled using PHP arrays or objects.)

The strings are looked up in language files that are just plain PHP arrays. Here is the language file local/greet/lang/en/local_greet.php for our plugin:

```
<?php
$string['greet:begreeted'] = 'Be greeted by the hello world example';
$string['welcome'] = 'Welcome';
$string['greet'] = 'Hello, {$a}!';
$string['pluginname'] = 'Hello world example';
```

Note that, as well as the two string used in our script, there are also strings to give a name to the capability, and the name of the plugin as it appears in the user interface.

The different languages are identified by the two-letter country code (en here). Languages packs may derive from other language packs. For example the fr_ca (French Canadian) language pack declares fr (French) as the parent language, and thus only has to define those strings that differ from the French. Since Moodle originated in Australia, en means British English, and en_us (American English) is derived from it.

Again, the simple get_string API for plugin developers hides a lot of complexity, including working out the current language (which may depend on the current user's preferences, or the settings for the particular course they are currently in), and then searching through all the language packs and parent language packs to find the string.

Producing the language pack files, and co-ordinating the translation effort is managed at http://lang.moodle.org/, which is Moodle with a custom plugin[8]. It uses both Git and the database as a backend to store the language files with full version history.

Line 11: Starting Output

echo $OUTPUT->header();   // 11

This is another innocuous-looking line that does much more than it seems. The point is that before any output can be done, the applicable theme (skin) must be worked out. This may depend on a combination of the page context and the user's preferences. $PAGE->context was, however, only set on line 8, so the $OUTPUT global could not have been initialised at the start of the script. In order to solve this problem, some PHP magic is used to create the proper $OUTPUT object based on the information in $PAGE the first time any output method is called.

Another thing to consider is that every page in Moodle may contain *blocks*. These are extra configurable bits of content that are normally displayed to the left or right of the main content. (They are a type of plugin.) Again, the exact collection of blocks to display depends, in a flexible way (that the administrator can control) on the page context and some other aspects of the page identity. Therefore, another part of preparing for output is a call to $PAGE->blocks->load_blocks().

Once all the necessary information has been worked out, the theme plugin (that controls the overall look of the page) is called to generate the overall page layout, including whatever standard header and footer is desired. This call is also responsible for adding the output from the blocks

---

[8] local_amos, http://docs.moodle.org/22/en/AMOS.

at the appropriate place in the HTML. In the middle of the layout there will be a div where the specific content for this page goes. The HTML of this layout is generated, and then split in half after the start of the main content div. The first half is returned, and the rest is stored to be returned by $OUTPUT->footer().

Line 12: Outputting the Body of the Page

```
echo $OUTPUT->box(get_string('greet', 'local_greet',
        format_string($name)));                                  // 12
```

This line outputs the body of the page. Here it simply displays the greeting in a box. The greeting is, again, a localised string, this time with a value substituted into a placeholder. The core renderer $OUTPUT provides many convenience methods like box to describe the required output in quite high-level terms. Different themes can control what HTML is actually output to make the box.

The content that originally came from the user ($name) is output though the format_string function. This is the other part of providing XSS protection. It also enables the user of text filters (another plugin type). An example filter would be the LaTeX filter, which replaces input like $$x + 1$$ with an image of the equation. I will mention, but not explain, that there are actually three different functions (s, format_string, and format_text) depending on the particular type of content being output.

Line 13: Finishing Output

```
echo $OUTPUT->footer();                                          // 13
```

Finally, the footer of the page is output. This example does not show it, but Moodle tracks all the JavaScript that is required by the page, and outputs all the necessary script tags in the footer. This is standard good practice. It allows users to see the page without waiting for all the JavaScript to load. A developer would include JavaScript using API calls like $PAGE->requires->js('/local/greet/cooleffect.js').

Should This Script Mix Logic and Output?

Obviously, putting the output code directly in index.php, even if at a high level of abstraction, limits the flexibility that themes have to control the output. This is another sign of the age of the Moodle code-base. The $OUTPUT global was introduced in 2010 as a stepping stone on the way from the old code, where the output and controller code were in the same file, to a design where all the view code was properly separated. This also explains the rather ugly way that the entire page layout is generated, then split in half, so that any output from the script itself can be placed between the header and the footer. Once the view code has been separated out of the script, into what Moodle calls a renderer, the theme can then choose to completely (or partially) override the view code for a given script.

A small refactoring can move all the output code out of our index.php and into a renderer. The end of index.php (lines 11 to 13) would change to:

```
$output = $PAGE->get_renderer('local_greet');
echo $output->greeting_page($name);
```

and there would be a new file local/greet/renderer.php:

```
<?php
class local_greet_renderer extends plugin_renderer_base {
    public function greeting_page($name) {
        $output = '';
        $output .= $this->header();
        $output .= $this->box(get_string('greet', 'local_greet', $name));
        $output .= $this->footer();
        return $output;
    }
}
```

If the theme wished to completely change this output, it would define a subclass of this renderer that overrides the `greeting_page` method. `$PAGE->get_renderer()` determines the appropriate renderer class to instantiate depending on the current theme. Thus, the output (view) code is fully separated from the controller code in `index.php`, and the plugin has been refactored from typical legacy Moodle code to a clean MVC architecture.

13.5 Database Abstraction

The "Hello world" script was sufficiently simple that it did not need to access the database, although several of the Moodle library calls used did do database queries. I will now briefly describe the Moodle database layer.

Moodle used to use the ADOdb library as the basis of its database abstraction layer, but there were issues for us, and the extra layer of library code had a noticeable impact on performance. Therefore, in Moodle 2.0 we switched to our own abstraction layer, which is a thin wrapper around the various PHP database libraries.

The `moodle_database` Class

The heart of the library is the `moodle_database` class. This defines the interface provided by the $DB global variable, which gives access to the database connection. A typical usage might be:

```
$course = $DB->get_record('course', array('id' => $courseid));
```

That translates into the SQL:

```
SELECT * FROM mdl_course WHERE id = $courseid;
```

and returns the data as a plain PHP object with public fields, so you could access $course->id, $course->fullname, etc.

Simple methods like this deal with basic queries, and simple updates and inserts. Sometimes it is necessary to do more complex SQL, for example to run reports. In that case, there are methods to execute arbitrary SQL:

```
$courseswithactivitycounts = $DB->get_records_sql(
    'SELECT c.id, ' . $DB->sql_concat('shortname', "' '", 'fullname') . ' AS coursename,
        COUNT(1) AS activitycount
    FROM {course} c
    JOIN {course_modules} cm ON cm.course = c.id
```

```
WHERE c.category = :categoryid
GROUP BY c.id, c.shortname, c.fullname ORDER BY c.shortname, c.fullname',
array('categoryid' => $category));
```

Some things to note there:

- The table names are wrapped in {} so that the library can find them and prepend the table name prefix.
- The library uses placeholders to insert values into the SQL. In some cases this uses the facilities of the underlying database driver. In other cases the values have to be escaped and inserted into the SQL using string manipulation. The library supports both named placeholders (as above) and anonymous ones, using ? as the placeholder.
- For queries to work on all our supported databases a safe subset of standard SQL must be used. For example, you can see that I have used the AS keyword for column aliases, but not for table aliases. Both of these usage rules are necessary.
- Even so, there are some situations where no subset of standard SQL will work on all our supported databases; for example, every database has a different way to concatenate strings. In these cases there are compatibility functions to generate the correct SQL.

Defining the Database Structure

Another area where database management systems differ a lot is in the SQL syntax required to define tables. To get around this problem, each Moodle plugin (and Moodle core) defines the required database tables in an XML file. The Moodle install system parses the `install.xml` files and uses the information they contain to create the required tables and indexes. There is a developer tool called XMLDB built into Moodle to help create and edit these install files.

If the database structure needs to change between two releases of Moodle (or of a plugin) then the developer is responsible for writing code (using an additional database object that provides DDL methods) to update the database structure, while preserving all the users' data. Thus, Moodle will always self-update from one release to the next, simplifying maintenance for administrators.

One contentious point, stemming from the fact that Moodle started out using MySQL 3, is that the Moodle database does not use foreign keys. This allows some buggy behaviour to remain undetected even though modern databases would be capable of detecting the problem. The difficulty is that people have been running Moodle sites without foreign keys for years, so there is almost certainly inconsistent data present. Adding the keys now would be impossible, without a very difficult clean-up job. Even so, since the XMLDB system was added to Moodle 1.7 (in 2006!) the install.xml files have contained the definitions of the foreign keys that should exist, and we are still hoping, one day, to do all the work necessary to allow us to create them during the install process.

13.6 What Has Not Been Covered

I hope I have given you a good overview of how Moodle works. Due to lack of space I have had to omit several interesting topics, including how authentication, enrolment and grade plugins allow Moodle to interoperate with student information systems, and the interesting content-addressed way that Moodle stores uploaded files. Details of these, and other aspects of Moodle's design, can be found in the developer documentation[9].

---
[9] http://docs.moodle.org/dev/

13.7 Lessons Learned

One interesting aspect of working on Moodle is that it came out of a research project. Moodle enables (but does not enforce) a social constructivist pedagogy[10]. That is, we learn best by actually creating something, and we learn from each other as a community. Martin Dougiamas's PhD question did not ask whether this was an effective model for education, but rather whether it is an effective model for running an open source project. That is, can we view the Moodle project as an attempt to learn how to build and use a VLE, and an attempt to learn that by actually building and using Moodle as a community where teachers, developers, administrators and students all teach and learn from each other? I find this a good model for thinking about an open source software development project. The main place where developers and users learn from each other is in discussions in the Moodle project forums, and in the bug database.

Perhaps the most important consequence of this learning approach is that you should not be afraid to start by implementing the simplest possible solution first. For example, early versions of Moodle had just a few hard-coded roles like Teacher, Student and Administrator. That was enough for many years, but eventually the limitations had to be addressed. When the time came to design the Roles system for Moodle 1.7, there was a lot of experience in the community about how people were using Moodle, and many little feature requests that showed what people needed to be able to adjust using a more flexible access control system. This all helped design the Roles system to be as simple as possible, but as complex as necessary. (In fact, the first version of the roles system ended up slightly too complex, and it was subsequently simplified a little in Moodle 2.0.)

If you take the view that programming is a problem-solving exercise, then you might think that Moodle got the design wrong the first time, and later had to waste time correcting it. I suggest that is an unhelpful viewpoint when trying to solve complex real-world problems. At the time Moodle started, no-one knew enough to design the roles system we now have. If you take the learning viewpoint, then the various stages Moodle went through to reach the current design were necessary and inevitable.

For this perspective to work, it must be possible to change almost any aspect of a system's architecture once you have learned more. I think Moodle shows that this is possible. For example, we found a way for code to be gradually refactored from legacy scripts to a cleaner MVC architecture. This requires effort, but it seems that when necessary, the resources to implement these changes can be found in open source projects. From the user's point of view, the system gradually evolves with each major release.

---

[10]http://docs.moodle.org/22/en/Pedagogy

nginx
Andrew Alexeev

nginx (pronounced "engine x") is a free open source web server written by Igor Sysoev, a Russian software engineer. Since its public launch in 2004, nginx has focused on high performance, high concurrency and low memory usage. Additional features on top of the web server functionality, like load balancing, caching, access and bandwidth control, and the ability to integrate efficiently with a variety of applications, have helped to make nginx a good choice for modern website architectures. Currently nginx is the second most popular open source web server on the Internet.

14.1 Why Is High Concurrency Important?

These days the Internet is so widespread and ubiquitous it's hard to imagine it wasn't exactly there, as we know it, a decade ago. It has greatly evolved, from simple HTML producing clickable text, based on NCSA and then on Apache web servers, to an always-on communication medium used by more than 2 billion users worldwide. With the proliferation of permanently connected PCs, mobile devices and recently tablets, the Internet landscape is rapidly changing and entire economies have become digitally wired. Online services have become much more elaborate with a clear bias towards instantly available live information and entertainment. Security aspects of running online business have also significantly changed. Accordingly, websites are now much more complex than before, and generally require a lot more engineering efforts to be robust and scalable.

One of the biggest challenges for a website architect has always been concurrency. Since the beginning of web services, the level of concurrency has been continuously growing. It's not uncommon for a popular website to serve hundreds of thousands and even millions of simultaneous users. A decade ago, the major cause of concurrency was slow clients—users with ADSL or dial-up connections. Nowadays, concurrency is caused by a combination of mobile clients and newer application architectures which are typically based on maintaining a persistent connection that allows the client to be updated with news, tweets, friend feeds, and so on. Another important factor contributing to increased concurrency is the changed behavior of modern browsers, which open four to six simultaneous connections to a website to improve page load speed.

To illustrate the problem with slow clients, imagine a simple Apache-based web server which produces a relatively short 100 KB response—a web page with text or an image. It can be merely a fraction of a second to generate or retrieve this page, but it takes 10 seconds to transmit it to a client with a bandwidth of 80 kbps (10 KB/s). Essentially, the web server would relatively quickly pull 100 KB of content, and then it would be busy for 10 seconds slowly sending this content to the client before freeing its connection. Now imagine that you have 1,000 simultaneously connected clients who have requested similar content. If only 1 MB of additional memory is allocated per client, it would result in 1000 MB (about 1 GB) of extra memory devoted to serving just 1000 clients 100 KB of content. In reality, a typical web server based on Apache commonly allocates more than 1 MB of additional memory per connection, and regrettably tens of kbps is still often the effective speed of mobile communications. Although the situation with sending content to a slow client might be, to some extent, improved by increasing the size of operating system kernel socket buffers, it's not a general solution to the problem and can have undesirable side effects.

With persistent connections the problem of handling concurrency is even more pronounced, because to avoid latency associated with establling new HTTP connections, clients would stay connected, and for each connected client there's a certain amount of memory allocated by the web server.

Consequently, to handle the increased workloads associated with growing audiences and hence higher levels of concurrency—and to be able to continuously do so—a website should be based on a number of very efficient building blocks. While the other parts of the equation such as hardware (CPU, memory, disks), network capacity, application and data storage architectures are obviously important, it is in the web server software that client connections are accepted and processed. Thus, the web server should be able to scale nonlinearly with the growing number of simultaneous connections and requests per second.

Isn't Apache Suitable?

Apache, the web server software that still largely dominates the Internet today, has its roots in the beginning of the 1990s. Originally, its architecture matched the then-existing operating systems and hardware, but also the state of the Internet, where a website was typically a standalone physical server running a single instance of Apache. By the beginning of the 2000s it was obvious that the standalone web server model could not be easily replicated to satisfy the needs of growing web services. Although Apache provided a solid foundation for future development, it was architected to spawn a copy of itself for each new connection, which was not suitable for nonlinear scalability of a website. Eventually Apache became a general purpose web server focusing on having many different features, a variety of third-party extensions, and universal applicability to practically any kind of web application development. However, nothing comes without a price and the downside to having such a rich and universal combination of tools in a single piece of software is less scalability because of increased CPU and memory usage per connection.

Thus, when server hardware, operating systems and network resources ceased to be major constraints for website growth, web developers worldwide started to look around for a more efficient means of running web servers. Around ten years ago, Daniel Kegel, a prominent software engineer, proclaimed that "it's time for web servers to handle ten thousand clients simultaneously"[1] and predicted what we now call Internet cloud services. Kegel's C10K manifest spurred a number of attempts to solve the problem of web server optimization to handle a large number of clients at the same time, and nginx turned out to be one of the most successful ones.

Aimed at solving the C10K problem of 10,000 simultaneous connections, nginx was written with a different architecture in mind—one which is much more suitable for nonlinear scalability in both the number of simultaneous connections and requests per second. nginx is event-based, so it does not follow Apache's style of spawning new processes or threads for each web page request. The end result is that even as load increases, memory and CPU usage remain manageable. nginx can now deliver tens of thousands of concurrent connections on a server with typical hardware.

---

[1] http://www.kegel.com/c10k.html

When the first version of nginx was released, it was meant to be deployed alongside Apache such that static content like HTML, CSS, JavaScript and images were handled by nginx to offload concurrency and latency processing from Apache-based application servers. Over the course of its development, nginx has added integration with applications through the use of FastCGI, uswgi or SCGI protocols, and with distributed memory object caching systems like *memcached*. Other useful functionality like reverse proxy with load balancing and caching was added as well. These additional features have shaped nginx into an efficient combination of tools to build a scalable web infrastructure upon.

In February 2012, the Apache 2.4.x branch was released to the public. Although this latest release of Apache has added new multi-processing core modules and new proxy modules aimed at enhancing scalability and performance, it's too soon to tell if its performance, concurrency and resource utilization are now on par with, or better than, pure event-driven web servers. It would be very nice to see Apache application servers scale better with the new version, though, as it could potentially alleviate bottlenecks on the backend side which still often remain unsolved in typical nginx-plus-Apache web configurations.

Are There More Advantages to Using nginx?

Handling high concurrency with high performance and efficiency has always been the key benefit of deploying nginx. However, there are now even more interesting benefits.

In the last few years, web architects have embraced the idea of decoupling and separating their application infrastructure from the web server. However, what would previously exist in the form of a LAMP (Linux, Apache, MySQL, PHP, Python or Perl)-based website, might now become not merely a LEMP-based one ('E' standing for 'Engine x'), but more and more often an exercise in pushing the web server to the edge of the infrastructure and integrating the same or a revamped set of applications and database tools around it in a different way.

nginx is very well suited for this, as it provides the key features necessary to conveniently offload concurrency, latency processing, SSL (secure sockets layer), static content, compression and caching, connections and requests throttling, and even HTTP media streaming from the application layer to a much more efficient edge web server layer. It also allows integrating directly with memcached/Redis or other "NoSQL" solutions, to boost performance when serving a large number of concurrent users.

With recent flavors of development kits and programming languages gaining wide use, more and more companies are changing their application development and deployment habits. nginx has become one of the most important components of these changing paradigms, and it has already helped many companies start and develop their web services quickly and within their budgets.

The first lines of nginx were written in 2002. In 2004 it was released to the public under the two-clause BSD license. The number of nginx users has been growing ever since, contributing ideas, and submitting bug reports, suggestions and observations that have been immensely helpful and beneficial for the entire community.

The nginx codebase is original and was written entirely from scratch in the C programming language. nginx has been ported to many architectures and operating systems, including Linux, FreeBSD, Solaris, Mac OS X, AIX and Microsoft Windows. nginx has its own libraries and with its standard modules does not use much beyond the system's C library, except for zlib, PCRE and OpenSSL which can be optionally excluded from a build if not needed or because of potential license conflicts.

A few words about the Windows version of nginx. While nginx works in a Windows environment, the Windows version of nginx is more like a proof-of-concept rather than a fully functional port.

There are certain limitations of the nginx and Windows kernel architectures that do not interact well at this time. The known issues of the nginx version for Windows include a much lower number of concurrent connections, decreased performance, no caching and no bandwidth policing. Future versions of nginx for Windows will match the mainstream functionality more closely.

14.2 Overview of nginx Architecture

Traditional process- or thread-based models of handling concurrent connections involve handling each connection with a separate process or thread, and blocking on network or input/output operations. Depending on the application, it can be very inefficient in terms of memory and CPU consumption. Spawning a separate process or thread requires preparation of a new runtime environment, including allocation of heap and stack memory, and the creation of a new execution context. Additional CPU time is also spent creating these items, which can eventually lead to poor performance due to thread thrashing on excessive context switching. All of these complications manifest themselves in older web server architectures like Apache's. This is a tradeoff between offering a rich set of generally applicable features and optimized usage of server resources.

From the very beginning, nginx was meant to be a specialized tool to achieve more performance, density and economical use of server resources while enabling dynamic growth of a website, so it has followed a different model. It was actually inspired by the ongoing development of advanced event-based mechanisms in a variety of operating systems. What resulted is a modular, event-driven, asynchronous, single-threaded, non-blocking architecture which became the foundation of nginx code.

nginx uses multiplexing and event notifications heavily, and dedicates specific tasks to separate processes. Connections are processed in a highly efficient run-loop in a limited number of single-threaded processes called `workers`. Within each `worker` nginx can handle many thousands of concurrent connections and requests per second.

Code Structure

The nginx `worker` code includes the core and the functional modules. The core of nginx is responsible for maintaining a tight run-loop and executing appropriate sections of modules' code on each stage of request processing. Modules constitute most of the presentation and application layer functionality. Modules read from and write to the network and storage, transform content, do outbound filtering, apply server-side include actions and pass the requests to the upstream servers when proxying is activated.

nginx's modular architecture generally allows developers to extend the set of web server features without modifying the nginx core. nginx modules come in slightly different incarnations, namely core modules, event modules, phase handlers, protocols, variable handlers, filters, upstreams and load balancers. At this time, nginx doesn't support dynamically loaded modules; i.e., modules are compiled along with the core at build stage. However, support for loadable modules and ABI is planned for the future major releases. More detailed information about the roles of different modules can be found in Section 14.4.

While handling a variety of actions associated with accepting, processing and managing network connections and content retrieval, nginx uses event notification mechanisms and a number of disk I/O performance enhancements in Linux, Solaris and BSD-based operating systems, like `kqueue`, `epoll`, and `event ports`. The goal is to provide as many hints to the operating system as possible, in regards to obtaining timely asynchronous feedback for inbound and outbound traffic, disk operations, reading from or writing to sockets, timeouts and so on. The usage of different methods for multiplexing and advanced I/O operations is heavily optimized for every Unix-based operating system nginx runs on.

A high-level overview of nginx architecture is presented in Figure 14.1.

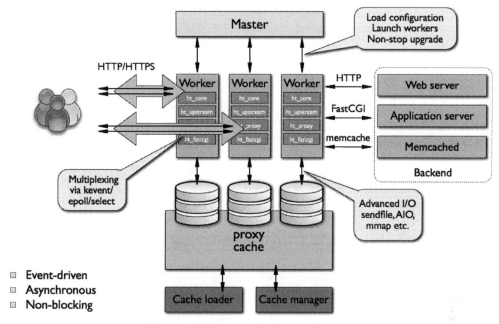

Figure 14.1: Diagram of nginx's architecture

Workers Model

As previously mentioned, nginx doesn't spawn a process or thread for every connection. Instead, worker processes accept new requests from a shared "listen" socket and execute a highly efficient run-loop inside each worker to process thousands of connections per worker. There's no specialized arbitration or distribution of connections to the workers in nginx; this work is done by the OS kernel mechanisms. Upon startup, an initial set of listening sockets is created. workers then continuously accept, read from and write to the sockets while processing HTTP requests and responses.

The run-loop is the most complicated part of the nginx worker code. It includes comprehensive inner calls and relies heavily on the idea of asynchronous task handling. Asynchronous operations are implemented through modularity, event notifications, extensive use of callback functions and fine-tuned timers. Overall, the key principle is to be as non-blocking as possible. The only situation where nginx can still block is when there's not enough disk storage performance for a worker process.

Because nginx does not fork a process or thread per connection, memory usage is very conservative and extremely efficient in the vast majority of cases. nginx conserves CPU cycles as well because there's no ongoing create-destroy pattern for processes or threads. What nginx does is check the state of the network and storage, initialize new connections, add them to the run-loop, and process asynchronously until completion, at which point the connection is deallocated and removed from the run-loop. Combined with the careful use of syscalls and an accurate implementation of supporting interfaces like pool and slab memory allocators, nginx typically achieves moderate-to-low CPU usage even under extreme workloads.

Because nginx spawns several workers to handle connections, it scales well across multiple cores. Generally, a separate worker per core allows full utilization of multicore architectures, and prevents thread thrashing and lock-ups. There's no resource starvation and the resource controlling mechanisms are isolated within single-threaded worker processes. This model also allows more scalability across physical storage devices, facilitates more disk utilization and avoids blocking on disk I/O. As a result, server resources are utilized more efficiently with the workload shared across several workers.

With some disk use and CPU load patterns, the number of nginx workers should be adjusted. The rules are somewhat basic here, and system administrators should try a couple of configurations for their workloads. General recommendations might be the following: if the load pattern is CPU intensive—for instance, handling a lot of TCP/IP, doing SSL, or compression—the number of nginx workers should match the number of CPU cores; if the load is mostly disk I/O bound—for instance, serving different sets of content from storage, or heavy proxying—the number of workers might be one and a half to two times the number of cores. Some engineers choose the number of workers based on the number of individual storage units instead, though efficiency of this approach depends on the type and configuration of disk storage.

One major problem that the developers of nginx will be solving in upcoming versions is how to avoid most of the blocking on disk I/O. At the moment, if there's not enough storage performance to serve disk operations generated by a particular worker, that worker may still block on reading/writing from disk. A number of mechanisms and configuration file directives exist to mitigate such disk I/O blocking scenarios. Most notably, combinations of options like sendfile and AIO typically produce a lot of headroom for disk performance. An nginx installation should be planned based on the data set, the amount of memory available for nginx, and the underlying storage architecture.

Another problem with the existing worker model is related to limited support for embedded scripting. For one, with the standard nginx distribution, only embedding Perl scripts is supported. There is a simple explanation for that: the key problem is the possibility of an embedded script to block on any operation or exit unexpectedly. Both types of behavior would immediately lead to a situation where the worker is hung, affecting many thousands of connections at once. More work is planned to make embedded scripting with nginx simpler, more reliable and suitable for a broader range of applications.

nginx Process Roles

nginx runs several processes in memory; there is a single master process and several worker processes. There are also a couple of special purpose processes, specifically a cache loader and cache manager. All processes are single-threaded in version 1.x of nginx. All processes primarily use shared-memory mechanisms for inter-process communication. The master process is run as the root user. The cache loader, cache manager and workers run as an unprivileged user.

The master process is responsible for the following tasks:

- Reading and validating configuration
- Creating, binding and closing sockets
- Starting, terminating and maintaining the configured number of worker processes
- Reconfiguring without service interruption
- Controlling non-stop binary upgrades (starting new binary and rolling back if necessary)
- Re-opening log files

- Compiling embedded Perl scripts

The worker processes accept, handle and process connections from clients, provide reverse proxying and filtering functionality and do almost everything else that nginx is capable of. In regards to monitoring the behavior of an nginx instance, a system administrator should keep an eye on workers as they are the processes reflecting the actual day-to-day operations of a web server.

The cache loader process is responsible for checking the on-disk cache items and populating nginx's in-memory database with cache metadata. Essentially, the cache loader prepares nginx instances to work with files already stored on disk in a specially allocated directory structure. It traverses the directories, checks cache content metadata, updates the relevant entries in shared memory and then exits when everything is clean and ready for use.

The cache manager is mostly responsible for cache expiration and invalidation. It stays in memory during normal nginx operation and it is restarted by the master process in the case of failure.

Brief Overview of nginx Caching

Caching in nginx is implemented in the form of hierarchical data storage on a filesystem. Cache keys are configurable, and different request-specific parameters can be used to control what gets into the cache. Cache keys and cache metadata are stored in the shared memory segments, which the cache loader, cache manager and workers can access. Currently there is not any in-memory caching of files, other than optimizations implied by the operating system's virtual filesystem mechanisms. Each cached response is placed in a different file on the filesystem. The hierarchy (levels and naming details) are controlled through nginx configuration directives. When a response is written to the cache directory structure, the path and the name of the file are derived from an MD5 hash of the proxy URL.

The process for placing content in the cache is as follows: When nginx reads the response from an upstream server, the content is first written to a temporary file outside of the cache directory structure. When nginx finishes processing the request it renames the temporary file and moves it to the cache directory. If the temporary files directory for proxying is on another file system, the file will be copied, thus it's recommended to keep both temporary and cache directories on the same file system. It is also quite safe to delete files from the cache directory structure when they need to be explicitly purged. There are third-party extensions for nginx which make it possible to control cached content remotely, and more work is planned to integrate this functionality in the main distribution.

14.3 nginx Configuration

nginx's configuration system was inspired by Igor Sysoev's experiences with Apache. His main insight was that a scalable configuration system is essential for a web server. The main scaling problem was encountered when maintaining large complicated configurations with lots of virtual servers, directories, locations and datasets. In a relatively big web setup it can be a nightmare if not done properly both at the application level and by the system engineer himself.

As a result, nginx configuration was designed to simplify day-to-day operations and to provide an easy means for further expansion of web server configuration.

nginx configuration is kept in a number of plain text files which typically reside in /usr/local-/etc/nginx or /etc/nginx. The main configuration file is usually called nginx.conf. To keep it uncluttered, parts of the configuration can be put in separate files which can be automatically included in the main one. However, it should be noted here that nginx does not currently support

Apache-style distributed configurations (i.e., .htaccess files). All of the configuration relevant to nginx web server behavior should reside in a centralized set of configuration files.

The configuration files are initially read and verified by the master process. A compiled read-only form of the nginx configuration is available to the worker processes as they are forked from the master process. Configuration structures are automatically shared by the usual virtual memory management mechanisms.

nginx configuration has several different contexts for main, http, server, upstream, location (and also mail for mail proxy) blocks of directives. Contexts never overlap. For instance, there is no such thing as putting a location block in the main block of directives. Also, to avoid unnecessary ambiguity there isn't anything like a "global web server" configuration. nginx configuration is meant to be clean and logical, allowing users to maintain complicated configuration files that comprise thousands of directives. In a private conversation, Sysoev said, "Locations, directories, and other blocks in the global server configuration are the features I never liked in Apache, so this is the reason why they were never implemented in nginx."

Configuration syntax, formatting and definitions follow a so-called C-style convention. This particular approach to making configuration files is already being used by a variety of open source and commercial software applications. By design, C-style configuration is well-suited for nested descriptions, being logical and easy to create, read and maintain, and liked by many engineers. C-style configuration of nginx can also be easily automated.

While some of the nginx directives resemble certain parts of Apache configuration, setting up an nginx instance is quite a different experience. For instance, rewrite rules are supported by nginx, though it would require an administrator to manually adapt a legacy Apache rewrite configuration to match nginx style. The implementation of the rewrite engine differs too.

In general, nginx settings also provide support for several original mechanisms that can be very useful as part of a lean web server configuration. It makes sense to briefly mention variables and the try_files directive, which are somewhat unique to nginx. Variables in nginx were developed to provide an additional even-more-powerful mechanism to control run-time configuration of a web server. Variables are optimized for quick evaluation and are internally pre-compiled to indices. Evaluation is done on demand; i.e., the value of a variable is typically calculated only once and cached for the lifetime of a particular request. Variables can be used with different configuration directives, providing additional flexibility for describing conditional request processing behavior.

The try_files directive was initially meant to gradually replace conditional if configuration statements in a more proper way, and it was designed to quickly and efficiently try/match against different URI-to-content mappings. Overall, the try_files directive works well and can be extremely efficient and useful. It is recommended that the reader thoroughly check the try_files directive and adopt its use whenever applicable[2].

14.4 nginx Internals

As was mentioned before, the nginx codebase consists of a core and a number of modules. The core of nginx is responsible for providing the foundation of the web server, web and mail reverse proxy functionalities; it enables the use of underlying network protocols, builds the necessary run-time environment, and ensures seamless interaction between different modules. However, most of the protocol- and application-specific features are done by nginx modules, not the core.

---

[2] See http://nginx.org/en/docs/http/ngx_http_core_module.html#try_files for more details.

Internally, nginx processes connections through a pipeline, or chain, of modules. In other words, for every operation there's a module which is doing the relevant work; e.g., compression, modifying content, executing server-side includes, communicating to the upstream application servers through FastCGI or uwsgi protocols, or talking to memcached.

There are a couple of nginx modules that sit somewhere between the core and the real "functional" modules. These modules are `http` and `mail`. These two modules provide an additional level of abstraction between the core and lower-level components. In these modules, the handling of the sequence of events associated with a respective application layer protocol like HTTP, SMTP or IMAP is implemented. In combination with the nginx core, these upper-level modules are responsible for maintaining the right order of calls to the respective functional modules. While the HTTP protocol is currently implemented as part of the `http` module, there are plans to separate it into a functional module in the future, due to the need to support other protocols like SPDY[3].

The functional modules can be divided into event modules, phase handlers, output filters, variable handlers, protocols, upstreams and load balancers. Most of these modules complement the HTTP functionality of nginx, though event modules and protocols are also used for `mail`. Event modules provide a particular OS-dependent event notification mechanism like kqueue or epoll. The event module that nginx uses depends on the operating system capabilities and build configuration. Protocol modules allow nginx to communicate through HTTPS, TLS/SSL, SMTP, POP3 and IMAP.

A typical HTTP request processing cycle looks like the following:

1. Client sends HTTP request
2. nginx core chooses the appropriate phase handler based on the configured location matching the request
3. If configured to do so, a load balancer picks an upstream server for proxying
4. Phase handler does its job and passes each output buffer to the first filter
5. First filter passes the output to the second filter
6. Second filter passes the output to third (and so on)
7. Final response is sent to the client

nginx module invocation is extremely customizable. It is performed through a series of callbacks using pointers to the executable functions. However, the downside of this is that it may place a big burden on programmers who would like to write their own modules, because they must define exactly how and when the module should run. Both the nginx API and developers' documentation are being improved and made more available to alleviate this.

Some examples of where a module can attach are:

- Before the configuration file is read and processed
- For each configuration directive for the location and the server where it appears
- When the main configuration is initialized
- When the server (i.e., host/port) is initialized
- When the server configuration is merged with the main configuration
- When the location configuration is initialized or merged with its parent server configuration
- When the master process starts or exits
- When a new worker process starts or exits
- When handling a request
- When filtering the response header and the body
- When picking, initiating and re-initiating a request to an upstream server

---

[3] See "SPDY: An experimental protocol for a faster web" at http://www.chromium.org/spdy/spdy-whitepaper

- When processing the response from an upstream server
- When finishing an interaction with an upstream server

Inside a worker, the sequence of actions leading to the run-loop where the response is generated looks like the following:

1. Begin `ngx_worker_process_cycle()`
2. Process events with OS specific mechanisms (such as `epoll` or `kqueue`)
3. Accept events and dispatch the relevant actions
4. Process/proxy request header and body
5. Generate response content (header, body) and stream it to the client
6. Finalize request
7. Re-initialize timers and events

The run-loop itself (steps 5 and 6) ensures incremental generation of a response and streaming it to the client.

A more detailed view of processing an HTTP request might look like this:

1. Initialize request processing
2. Process header
3. Process body
4. Call the associated handler
5. Run through the processing phases

Which brings us to the phases. When nginx handles an HTTP request, it passes it through a number of processing phases. At each phase there are handlers to call. In general, phase handlers process a request and produce the relevant output. Phase handlers are attached to the locations defined in the configuration file.

Phase handlers typically do four things: get the location configuration, generate an appropriate response, send the header, and send the body. A handler has one argument: a specific structure describing the request. A request structure has a lot of useful information about the client request, such as the request method, URI, and header.

When the HTTP request header is read, nginx does a lookup of the associated virtual server configuration. If the virtual server is found, the request goes through six phases:

1. Server rewrite phase
2. Location phase
3. Location rewrite phase (which can bring the request back to the previous phase)
4. Access control phase
5. `try_files` phase
6. Log phase

In an attempt to generate the necessary content in response to the request, nginx passes the request to a suitable content handler. Depending on the exact location configuration, nginx may try so-called unconditional handlers first, like `perl`, `proxy_pass`, `flv`, `mp4`, etc. If the request does not match any of the above content handlers, it is picked by one of the following handlers, in this exact order: `random index`, `index`, `autoindex`, `gzip_static`, `static`.

Indexing module details can be found in the nginx documentation, but these are the modules which handle requests with a trailing slash. If a specialized module like `mp4` or `autoindex` isn't appropriate, the content is considered to be just a file or directory on disk (that is, static) and is served by the `static` content handler. For a directory it would automatically rewrite the URI so that the trailing slash is always there (and then issue an HTTP redirect).

The content handlers' content is then passed to the filters. Filters are also attached to locations, and there can be several filters configured for a location. Filters do the task of manipulating the output produced by a handler. The order of filter execution is determined at compile time. For the out-of-the-box filters it's predefined, and for a third-party filter it can be configured at the build stage. In the existing nginx implementation, filters can only do outbound changes and there is currently no mechanism to write and attach filters to do input content transformation. Input filtering will appear in future versions of nginx.

Filters follow a particular design pattern. A filter gets called, starts working, and calls the next filter until the final filter in the chain is called. After that, nginx finalizes the response. Filters don't have to wait for the previous filter to finish. The next filter in a chain can start its own work as soon as the input from the previous one is available (functionally much like the Unix pipeline). In turn, the output response being generated can be passed to the client before the entire response from the upstream server is received.

There are header filters and body filters; nginx feeds the header and the body of the response to the associated filters separately.

A header filter consists of three basic steps:

1. Decide whether to operate on this response
2. Operate on the response
3. Call the next filter

Body filters transform the generated content. Examples of body filters include:

- Server-side includes
- XSLT filtering
- Image filtering (for instance, resizing images on the fly)
- Charset modification
- `gzip` compression
- Chunked encoding

After the filter chain, the response is passed to the writer. Along with the writer there are a couple of additional special purpose filters, namely the `copy` filter, and the `postpone` filter. The copy filter is responsible for filling memory buffers with the relevant response content which might be stored in a proxy temporary directory. The `postpone` filter is used for subrequests.

Subrequests are a very important mechanism for request/response processing. Subrequests are also one of the most powerful aspects of nginx. With subrequests nginx can return the results from a different URL than the one the client originally requested. Some web frameworks call this an internal redirect. However, nginx goes further—not only can filters perform multiple subrequests and combine the outputs into a single response, but subrequests can also be nested and hierarchical. A subrequest can perform its own sub-subrequest, and a sub-subrequest can initiate sub-sub-subrequests. Subrequests can map to files on the hard disk, other handlers, or upstream servers. Subrequests are most useful for inserting additional content based on data from the original response. For example, the SSI (server-side include) module uses a filter to parse the contents of the returned document, and then replaces `include` directives with the contents of specified URLs. Or, it can be an example of making a filter that treats the entire contents of a document as a URL to be retrieved, and then appends the new document to the URL itself.

Upstream and load balancers are also worth describing briefly. Upstreams are used to implement what can be identified as a content handler which is a reverse proxy (`proxy_pass` handler). Upstream modules mostly prepare the request to be sent to an upstream server (or "backend") and receive the response from the upstream server. There are no calls to output filters here. What an upstream module does exactly is set callbacks to be invoked when the upstream server is ready to be written to and read from. Callbacks implementing the following functionality exist:

- Crafting a request buffer (or a chain of them) to be sent to the upstream server
- Re-initializing/resetting the connection to the upstream server (which happens right before creating the request again)
- Processing the first bits of an upstream response and saving pointers to the payload received from the upstream server
- Aborting requests (which happens when the client terminates prematurely)
- Finalizing the request when nginx finishes reading from the upstream server
- Trimming the response body (e.g. removing a trailer)

Load balancer modules attach to the proxy_pass handler to provide the ability to choose an upstream server when more than one upstream server is eligible. A load balancer registers an enabling configuration file directive, provides additional upstream initialization functions (to resolve upstream names in DNS, etc.), initializes the connection structures, decides where to route the requests, updates stats information. Currently nginx supports two standard disciplines for load balancing to upstream servers: round-robin and ip-hash.

Upstream and load balancing handling mechanisms include algorithms to detect failed upstream servers and to re-route new requests to the remaining ones—though a lot of additional work is planned to enhance this functionality. In general, more work on load balancers is planned, and in the next versions of nginx the mechanisms for distributing the load across different upstream servers as well as health checks will be greatly improved.

There are also a couple of other interesting modules which provide an additional set of variables for use in the configuration file. While the variables in nginx are created and updated across different modules, there are two modules that are entirely dedicated to variables: geo and map. The geo module is used to facilitate tracking of clients based on their IP addresses. This module can create arbitrary variables that depend on the client's IP address. The other module, map, allows for the creation of variables from other variables, essentially providing the ability to do flexible mappings of hostnames and other run-time variables. This kind of module may be called the variable handler.

Memory allocation mechanisms implemented inside a single nginx worker were, to some extent, inspired by Apache. A high-level description of nginx memory management would be the following: For each connection, the necessary memory buffers are dynamically allocated, linked, used for storing and manipulating the header and body of the request and the response, and then freed upon connection release. It is very important to note that nginx tries to avoid copying data in memory as much as possible and most of the data is passed along by pointer values, not by calling memcpy.

Going a bit deeper, when the response is generated by a module, the retrieved content is put in a memory buffer which is then added to a buffer chain link. Subsequent processing works with this buffer chain link as well. Buffer chains are quite complicated in nginx because there are several processing scenarios which differ depending on the module type. For instance, it can be quite tricky to manage the buffers precisely while implementing a body filter module. Such a module can only operate on one buffer (chain link) at a time and it must decide whether to overwrite the input buffer, replace the buffer with a newly allocated buffer, or insert a new buffer before or after the buffer in question. To complicate things, sometimes a module will receive several buffers so that it has an incomplete buffer chain that it must operate on. However, at this time nginx provides only a low-level API for manipulating buffer chains, so before doing any actual implementation a third-party module developer should become really fluent with this arcane part of nginx.

A note on the above approach is that there are memory buffers allocated for the entire life of a connection, thus for long-lived connections some extra memory is kept. At the same time, on an idle keepalive connection, nginx spends just 550 bytes of memory. A possible optimization for future releases of nginx would be to reuse and share memory buffers for long-lived connections.

The task of managing memory allocation is done by the nginx pool allocator. Shared memory areas are used to accept mutex, cache metadata, the SSL session cache and the information associated with bandwidth policing and management (limits). There is a slab allocator implemented in nginx to manage shared memory allocation. To allow simultaneous safe use of shared memory, a number of locking mechanisms are available (mutexes and semaphores). In order to organize complex data structures, nginx also provides a red-black tree implementation. Red-black trees are used to keep cache metadata in shared memory, track non-regex location definitions and for a couple of other tasks.

Unfortunately, all of the above was never described in a consistent and simple manner, making the job of developing third-party extensions for nginx quite complicated. Although some good documents on nginx internals exist—for instance, those produced by Evan Miller—such documents required a huge reverse engineering effort, and the implementation of nginx modules is still a black art for many.

Despite certain difficulties associated with third-party module development, the nginx user community recently saw a lot of useful third-party modules. There is, for instance, an embedded Lua interpreter module for nginx, additional modules for load balancing, full WebDAV support, advanced cache control and other interesting third-party work that the authors of this chapter encourage and will support in the future.

14.5 Lessons Learned

When Igor Sysoev started to write nginx, most of the software enabling the Internet already existed, and the architecture of such software typically followed definitions of legacy server and network hardware, operating systems, and old Internet architecture in general. However, this didn't prevent Igor from thinking he might be able to improve things in the web servers area. So, while the first lesson might seem obvious, it is this: there is always room for improvement.

With the idea of better web software in mind, Igor spent a lot of time developing the initial code structure and studying different ways of optimizing the code for a variety of operating systems. Ten years later he is developing a prototype of nginx version 2.0, taking into account the years of active development on version 1. It is clear that the initial prototype of a new architecture, and the initial code structure, are vitally important for the future of a software product.

Another point worth mentioning is that development should be focused. The Windows version of nginx is probably a good example of how it is worth avoiding the dilution of development efforts on something that is neither the developer's core competence or the target application. It is equally applicable to the rewrite engine that appeared during several attempts to enhance nginx with more features for backward compatibility with the existing legacy setups.

Last but not least, it is worth mentioning that despite the fact that the nginx developer community is not very large, third-party modules and extensions for nginx have always been a very important part of its popularity. The work done by Evan Miller, Piotr Sikora, Valery Kholodkov, Zhang Yichun (agentzh) and other talented software engineers has been much appreciated by the nginx user community and its original developers.

[chapter 15]

Open MPI
Jeffrey M. Squyres

15.1 Background

Open MPI [GFB+04] is an open source software implementation of The Message Passing Interface (MPI) standard. Before the architecture and innards of Open MPI will make any sense, a little background on the MPI standard must be discussed.

The Message Passing Interface (MPI)

The MPI standard is created and maintained by the MPI Forum[1], an open group consisting of parallel computing experts from both industry and academia. MPI defines an API that is used for a specific type of portable, high-performance inter-process communication (IPC): *message passing*. Specifically, the MPI document describes the reliable transfer of discrete, typed messages between MPI processes. Although the definition of an "MPI process" is subject to interpretation on a given platform, it usually corresponds to the operating system's concept of a process (e.g., a POSIX process). MPI is specifically intended to be implemented as middleware, meaning that upper-level applications call MPI functions to perform message passing.

MPI defines a high-level API, meaning that it abstracts away whatever underlying transport is actually used to pass messages between processes. The idea is that sending-process X can effectively say "take this array of 1,073 double precision values and send them to process Y". The corresponding receiving-process Y effectively says "receive an array of 1,073 double precision values from process X." A miracle occurs, and the array of 1,073 double precision values arrives in Y's waiting buffer.

Notice what is absent in this exchange: there is no concept of a connection occurring, no stream of bytes to interpret, and no network addresses exchanged. MPI abstracts all of that away, not only to hide such complexity from the upper-level application, but also to make the application portable across different environments and underlying message passing transports. Specifically, a correct MPI application is source-compatible across a wide variety of platforms and network types.

MPI defines not only point-to-point communication (e.g., send and receive), it also defines other communication patterns, such as *collective* communication. Collective operations are where multiple processes are involved in a single communication action. Reliable broadcast, for example, is where one process has a message at the beginning of the operation, and at the end of the operation, all

---
[1]http://www.mpi-forum.org/

processes in a group have the message. MPI also defines other concepts and communications patterns that are not described here.[2]

Uses of MPI

There are many implementations of the MPI standard that support a wide variety of platforms, operating systems, and network types. Some implementations are open source, some are closed source. Open MPI, as its name implies, is one of the open source implementations. Typical MPI transport networks include (but are not limited to): various protocols over Ethernet (e.g., TCP, iWARP, UDP, raw Ethernet frames, etc.), shared memory, and InfiniBand.

MPI implementations are typically used in so-called "high-performance computing" (HPC) environments. MPI essentially provides the IPC for simulation codes, computational algorithms, and other "big number crunching" types of applications. The input data sets on which these codes operate typically represent too much computational work for just one server; MPI jobs are spread out across tens, hundreds, or even thousands of servers, all working in concert to solve one computational problem.

That is, the applications using MPI are both parallel in nature and highly compute-intensive. It is not unusual for all the processor cores in an MPI job to run at 100% utilization. To be clear, MPI jobs typically run in dedicated environments where the MPI processes are the *only* application running on the machine (in addition to bare-bones operating system functionality, of course).

As such, MPI implementations are typically focused on providing extremely high performance, measured by metrics such as:

- Extremely low latency for short message passing. As an example, a 1-byte message can be sent from a user-level Linux process on one server, through an InfiniBand switch, and received at the target user-level Linux process on a different server in a little over 1 microsecond (i.e., 0.000001 second).
- Extremely high message network injection rate for short messages. Some vendors have MPI implementations (paired with specified hardware) that can inject up to 28 million messages per second into the network.
- Quick ramp-up (as a function of message size) to the maximum bandwidth supported by the underlying transport.
- Low resource utilization. All resources used by MPI (e.g., memory, cache, and bus bandwidth) cannot be used by the application. MPI implementations therefore try to maintain a balance of low resource utilization while still providing high performance.

Open MPI

The first version of the MPI standard, MPI-1.0, was published in 1994 [Mes93]. MPI-2.0, a set of additions on top of MPI-1, was completed in 1996 [GGHL+96].

In the first decade after MPI-1 was published, a variety of MPI implementations sprung up. Many were provided by vendors for their proprietary network interconnects. Many other implementations arose from the research and academic communities. Such implementations were typically "research-quality," meaning that their purpose was to investigate various high-performance networking concepts and provide proofs-of-concept of their work. However, some were high enough quality that they gained popularity and a number of users.

---

[2] As of this writing, the most recent version of the MPI standard is MPI-2.2 [For09]. Draft versions of the upcoming MPI-3 standard have been published; it may be finalized as early as late 2012.

Open MPI represents the union of four research/academic, open source MPI implementations: LAM/MPI, LA/MPI (Los Alamos MPI), and FT-MPI (Fault-Tolerant MPI). The members of the PACX-MPI team joined the Open MPI group shortly after its inception.

The members of these four development teams decided to collaborate when we had the collective realization that, aside from minor differences in optimizations and features, our software code bases were quite similar. Each of the four code bases had their own strengths and weaknesses, but on the whole, they more-or-less did the same things. So why compete? Why not pool our resources, work together, and make an *even better* MPI implementation?

After much discussion, the decision was made to abandon our four existing code bases and take only the best *ideas* from the prior projects. This decision was mainly predicated upon the following premises:

- Even though many of the underlying algorithms and techniques were similar among the four code bases, they each had radically different implementation architectures, and would be incredible difficult (if not impossible) to merge.
- Each of the four also had their own (significant) strengths and (significant) weaknesses. Specifically, there were features and architecture decisions from each of the four that were desirable to carry forward. Likewise, there were poorly optimized and badly designed code in each of the four that were desirable to leave behind.
- The members of the four developer groups had not worked directly together before. Starting with an entirely new code base (rather than advancing one of the existing code bases) put all developers on equal ground.

Thus, Open MPI was born. Its first Subversion commit was on November 22, 2003.

15.2 Architecture

For a variety of reasons (mostly related to either performance or portability), C and C++ were the only two possibilities for the primary implementation language. C++ was eventually discarded because different C++ compilers tend to lay out structs/classes in memory according to different optimization algorithms, leading to different on-the-wire network representations. C was therefore chosen as the primary implementation language, which influenced several architectural design decisions.

When Open MPI was started, we knew that it would be a large, complex code base:

- In 2003, the current version of the MPI standard, MPI-2.0, defined over 300 API functions.
- Each of the four prior projects were large in themselves. For example, LAM/MPI had over 1,900 files of source code, comprising over 300,000 lines of code (including comments and blanks).
- We wanted Open MPI to support more features, environments, and networks than all four prior projects put together.

We therefore spent a good deal of time designing an architecture that focused on three things:

1. Grouping similar functionality together in distinct abstraction layers
2. Using run-time loadable plugins and run-time parameters to choose between multiple different implementations of the same behavior
3. Not allowing abstraction to get in the way of performance

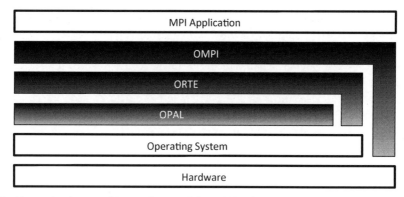

Figure 15.1: Abstraction layer architectural view of Open MPI showing its three main layers: OPAL, ORTE, and OMPI

Abstraction Layer Architecture

Open MPI has three main abstraction layers, shown in Figure 15.1:

- *Open, Portable Access Layer (OPAL)*: OPAL is the bottom layer of Open MPI's abstractions. Its abstractions are focused on individual processes (versus parallel jobs). It provides utility and glue code such as generic linked lists, string manipulation, debugging controls, and other mundane—yet necessary—functionality.

    OPAL also provides Open MPI's core portability between different operating systems, such as discovering IP interfaces, sharing memory between processes on the same server, processor and memory affinity, high-precision timers, etc.

- *Open MPI Run-Time Environment (ORTE)*[3]: An MPI implementation must provide not only the required message passing API, but also an accompanying run-time system to launch, monitor, and kill parallel jobs. In Open MPI's case, a parallel job is comprised of one or more processes that may span multiple operating system instances, and are bound together to act as a single, cohesive unit.

    In simple environments with little or no distributed computational support, ORTE uses `rsh` or `ssh` to launch the individual processes in parallel jobs. More advanced, HPC-dedicated environments typically have schedulers and resource managers for fairly sharing computational resources between many users. Such environments usually provide specialized APIs to launch and regulate processes on compute servers. ORTE supports a wide variety of such managed environments, such as (but not limited to): Torque/PBS Pro, SLURM, Oracle Grid Engine, and LSF.

- *Open MPI (OMPI)*: The MPI layer is the highest abstraction layer, and is the only one exposed to applications. The MPI API is implemented in this layer, as are all the message passing semantics defined by the MPI standard.

    Since portability is a primary requirement, the MPI layer supports a wide variety of network types and underlying protocols. Some networks are similar in their underlying characteristics and abstractions; some are not.

Although each abstraction is layered on top of the one below it, for performance reasons the ORTE and OMPI layers can bypass the underlying abstraction layers and interact directly with the

---

[3]Pronounced "or-tay".

operating system and/or hardware when needed (as depicted in Figure 15.1). For example, the OMPI layer uses OS-bypass methods to communicate with certain types of NIC hardware to obtain maximum networking performance.

Each layer is built into a standalone library. The ORTE library depends on the OPAL library; the OMPI library depends on the ORTE library. Separating the layers into their own libraries has acted as a wonderful tool for preventing abstraction violations. Specifically, applications will fail to link if one layer incorrectly attempts to use a symbol in a higher layer. Over the years, this abstraction enforcement mechanism has saved many developers from inadvertently blurring the lines between the three layers.

Plugin Architecture

Although the initial members of the Open MPI collaboration shared a similar core goal (produce a portable, high-performance implementation of the MPI standard), our organizational backgrounds, opinions, and agendas were—and still are—wildly different. We therefore spent a considerable amount of time designing an architecture that would allow us to be different, even while sharing a common code base.

Run-time loadable *components* were a natural choice (a.k.a., dynamic shared objects, or "DSOs", or "plugins"). Components enforce a common API but place few limitations on the implementation of that API. Specifically: the same interface behavior can be implemented multiple different ways. Users can then choose, at run time, which plugin(s) to use. This even allows third parties to independently develop and distribute their own Open MPI plugins outside of the core Open MPI package. Allowing arbitrary extensibility is quite a liberating policy, both within the immediate set of Open MPI developers and in the greater Open MPI community.

This run-time flexibility is a key component of the Open MPI design philosophy and is deeply integrated throughout the entire architecture. Case in point: the Open MPI v1.5 series includes 155 plugins. To list just a few examples, there are plugins for different memcpy() implementations, plugins for how to launch processes on remote servers, and plugins for how to communicate on different types of underlying networks.

One of the major benefits of using plugins is that multiple groups of developers have freedom to experiment with alternate implementations without affecting the core of Open MPI. This was a critical feature, particularly in the early days of the Open MPI project. Sometimes the developers didn't always know what was the right way to implement something, or sometimes they just disagreed. In both cases, each party would implement their solution in a component, allowing the rest of the developer community to easily compare and contrast. Code comparisons can be done without components, of course, but the component concept helps guarantee that all implementations expose exactly the same external API, and therefore provide exactly the same required semantics.

As a direct result of the flexibility that it provides, the component concept is utilized heavily throughout all three layers of Open MPI; in each layer there are many different types of components. Each type of component is enclosed in a *framework*. A component belongs to exactly one framework, and a framework supports exactly one kind of component. Figure 15.2 is a template of Open MPI's architectural layout; it shows a few of Open MPI's frameworks and some of the components that they contain. (The rest of Open MPI's frameworks and components are laid out in the same manner.) Open MPI's set of layers, frameworks, and components is referred to as the Modular Component Architecture (MCA).

Finally, another major advantage of using frameworks and components is their inherent composability. With over 40 frameworks in Open MPI v1.5, giving users the ability to mix-n-match different

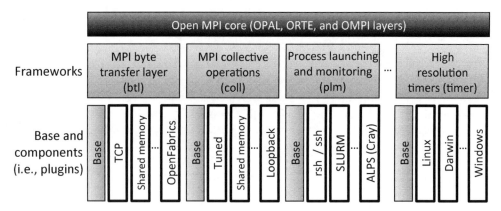

Figure 15.2: Framework architectural view of Open MPI, showing just a few of Open MPI's frameworks and components (i.e., plugins). Each framework contains a *base* and one or more components. This structure is replicated in each of the layers shown in Figure 15.1. The sample frameworks listed in this figure are spread across all three layers: btl and coll are in the OMPI layer, plm is in the ORTE layer, and timer is in the OPAL layer.

plugins of different types allows them to create a software stack that is effectively tailored to their individual system.

Plugin Frameworks

Each framework is fully self-contained in its own subdirectory in the Open MPI source code tree. The name of the subdirectory is the same name as the framework; for example, the memory framework is in the memory directory. Framework directories contain at least the following three items:

1. *Component interface definition:* A header file named <framework>.h will be located in the top-level framework directory (e.g., the Memory framework contains memory/memory.h). This well-known header file defines the interfaces that each component in the framework must support. This header includes function pointer typedefs for the interface functions, structs for marshaling these function pointers, and any other necessary types, attribute fields, macros, declarations, etc.
2. *Base code*: The base subdirectory contains the glue code that provides the core functionality of the framework. For example, the memory framework's base directory is memory/base. The base is typically comprised of logistical grunt work such as finding and opening components at run-time, common utility functionality that may be utilized by multiple components, etc.
3. *Components*: All other subdirectories in the framework directory are assumed to be components. Just like the framework, the names of the components are the same names as their subdirectories (e.g., the memory/posix subdirectory contains the POSIX component in the Memory framework).

Similar to how each framework defines the interfaces to which its components must adhere, frameworks also define other operational aspects, such as how they bootstrap themselves, how they pick components to use, and how they are shut down. Two common examples of how frameworks differ in their setup are many-of-many versus one-of-many frameworks, and static versus dynamic frameworks.

Many-of-many frameworks. Some frameworks have functionality that can be implemented multiple different ways in the same process. For example, Open MPI's point-to-point network framework will load multiple driver plugins to allow a single process to send and receive messages on multiple network types.

Such frameworks will typically open all components that they can find and then query each component, effectively asking, "Do you want to run?" The components determine whether they want to run by examining the system on which they are running. For example, a point-to-point network component will look to see if the network type it supports is both available and active on the system. If it is not, the component will reply "No, I do not want to run", causing the framework to close and unload that component. If that network type *is* available, the component will reply "Yes, I want to run", causing the framework to keep the component open for further use.

One-of-many frameworks. Other frameworks provide functionality for which it does not make sense to have more than one implementation available at run-time. For example, the creation of a consistent checkpoint of a parallel job—meaning that the job is effectively "frozen" and can be arbitrarily resumed later—must be performed using the same back-end checkpointing system for each process in the job. The plugin that interfaces to the desired back-end checkpointing system is the *only* checkpoint plugin that must be loaded in each process—all others are unnecessary.

Dynamic frameworks. Most frameworks allow their components to be loaded at run-time via DSOs. This is the most flexible method of finding and loading components; it allows features such as explicitly *not* loading certain components, loading third-party components that were not included in the main-line Open MPI distribution, etc.

Static frameworks. Some one-of-many frameworks have additional constraints that force their one-and-only-one component to be selected at compile time (versus run time). Statically linking one-of-many components allows direct invocation of its member functions (versus invocation via function pointer), which may be important in highly performance-sensitive functionality. One example is the memcpy framework, which provides platform-optimized memcpy() implementations.

Additionally, some frameworks provide functionality that may need to be utilized before Open MPI is fully initialized. For example, the use of some network stacks require complicated memory registration models, which, in turn, require replacing the C library's default memory management routines. Since memory management is intrinsic to an entire process, replacing the default scheme can only be done pre-main. Therefore, such components must be statically linked into Open MPI processes so that they can be available for pre-main hooks, long before MPI has even been initialized.

Plugin Components

Open MPI plugins are divided into two parts: a *component* struct and a *module* struct. The component struct and the functions to which it refers are typically collectively referred to as "the component." Similarly, "the module" collectively refers to the module struct and its functions. The division is somewhat analogous to C++ classes and objects. There is only one component per process; it describes the overall plugin with some fields that are common to all components (regardless of framework). If the component elects to run, it is used to generate one or more modules, which typically perform the bulk of the functionality required by the framework.

Throughout the next few sections, we'll build up the structures necessary for the TCP component in the BTL (byte transfer layer) framework. The BTL framework effects point-to-point message transfers; the TCP component, not surprisingly, uses TCP as its underlying transport for message passing.

Component struct. Regardless of framework, each component contains a well-known, statically allocated and initialized component struct. The struct must be named according to the template mca_<framework>_<component>_component. For example, the TCP network driver component's struct in the BTL framework is named mca_btl_tcp_component.

Having templated component symbols both guarantees that there will be no name collisions between components, and allows the MCA core to find any arbitrary component struct via dlsym(2) (or the appropriate equivalent in each supported operating system).

The base component struct contains some logistical information, such as the component's formal name, version, framework version adherence, etc. This data is used for debugging purposes, inventory listing, and run-time compliance and compatibility checking.

```
struct mca_base_component_2_0_0_t {
    /* Component struct version number */
    int mca_major_version, mca_minor_version, mca_release_version;

    /* The string name of the framework that this component belongs to,
       and the framework's API version that this component adheres to */
    char mca_type_name[MCA_BASE_MAX_TYPE_NAME_LEN + 1];
    int mca_type_major_version, mca_type_minor_version,
        mca_type_release_version;

    /* This component's name and version number */
    char mca_component_name[MCA_BASE_MAX_COMPONENT_NAME_LEN + 1];
    int mca_component_major_version, mca_component_minor_version,
        mca_component_release_version;

    /* Function pointers */
    mca_base_open_component_1_0_0_fn_t mca_open_component;
    mca_base_close_component_1_0_0_fn_t mca_close_component;
    mca_base_query_component_2_0_0_fn_t mca_query_component;
    mca_base_register_component_params_2_0_0_fn_t
        mca_register_component_params;
};
```

The base component struct is the core of the TCP BTL component; it contains the following function pointers:

- *Open.* The *open* call is the initial query function invoked on a component. It allows a component to initialize itself, look around the system where it is running, and determine whether it wants to run. If a component can always be run, it can provide a NULL open function pointer.

  The TCP BTL component *open* function mainly initializes some data structures and ensures that invalid parameters were not set by the user.

- *Close.* When a framework decides that a component is no longer needed, it calls the *close* function to allow the component to release any resources that it has allocated. The close function is invoked on all remaining components when processes are shutting down. However, *close* can also be invoked on components that are rejected at run time so that they can be closed and ignored for the duration of the process.

The TCP BTL component *close* function closes listening sockets and frees resources (e.g., receiving buffers).

- *Query*. This call is a generalized "Do you want to run?" function. Not all frameworks utilize this specific call—some need more specialized query functions.

  The BTL framework does not use the generic *query* function (it defines its own; see below), so the TCP BTL does not fill it in.

- *Parameter registration*. This function is typically the first function called on a component. It allows the component to register any relevant run-time, user-settable parameters. Run-time parameters are discussed further below.

  The TCP BTL component *register* function creates a variety of user-settable run-time parameters, such as one which allows the user to specify which IP interface(s) to use.

The component structure can also be extended on a per-framework and/or per-component basis. Frameworks typically create a new component struct with the component base struct as the first member. This nesting allows frameworks to add their own attributes and function pointers. For example, a framework that needs a more specialized query function (as compared to the *query* function provided on the basic component) can add a function pointer in its framework-specific component struct.

The MPI `btl` framework, which provides point-to-point MPI messaging functionality, uses this technique.

```
struct mca_btl_base_component_2_0_0_t {
    /* Base component struct */
    mca_base_component_t btl_version;
    /* Base component data block */
    mca_base_component_data_t btl_data;

    /* btl-framework specific query functions */
    mca_btl_base_component_init_fn_t btl_init;
    mca_btl_base_component_progress_fn_t btl_progress;
};
```

As an example of the TCP BTL framework query functions, the TCP BTL component `btl_init` function does several things:

- Creates a listening socket for each "up" IPv4 and IPv6 interface
- Creates a module for each "up" IP interface
- Registers the tuple (`IP address, port`) for each "up" IP interface with a central repository so that other MPI processes know how to contact it

Similarly, plugins can extend the framework-specific component struct with their own members. The `tcp` component in the `btl` framework does this; it caches many data members in its component struct.

```
struct mca_btl_tcp_component_t {
    /* btl framework-specific component struct */
    mca_btl_base_component_2_0_0_t super;
```

```
    /* Some of the TCP BTL component's specific data members */
    /* Number of TCP interfaces on this server */
    uint32_t tcp_addr_count;

    /* IPv4 listening socket descriptor */
    int tcp_listen_sd;

    /* ...and many more not shown here */
};
```

This struct-nesting technique is effectively a simple emulation of C++ single inheritance: a pointer to an instance of a `struct mca_btl_tcp_component_t` can be cast to any of the three types such that it can be used by an abstraction layer than does not understand the "derived" types.

That being said, casting is generally frowned upon in Open MPI because it can lead to incredibly subtle, difficult-to-find bugs. An exception was made for this C++-emulation technique because it has well-defined behaviors and helps enforce abstraction barriers.

Module struct. Module structs are individually defined by each framework; there is little commonality between them. Depending on the framework, components generate one or more module struct instances to indicate that they want to be used.

For example, in the BTL framework, one module usually corresponds to a single network device. If an MPI process is running on a Linux server with three "up" Ethernet devices, the TCP BTL component will generate three TCP BTL modules; one corresponding to each Linux Ethernet device. Each module will then be wholly responsible for all sending and receiving to and from its Ethernet device.

Tying it all together. Figure 15.3 shows the nesting of the structures in the TCP BTL component, and how it generates one module for each of the three Ethernet devices.

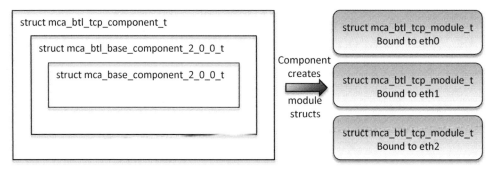

Figure 15.3: The left side shows the nesting of structures in the TCP BTL component. The right side shows how the component generates one module struct for each "up" Ethernet interface.

Composing BTL modules this way allows the upper-layer MPI progression engine both to treat all network devices equally, and to perform user-level channel bonding.

For example, consider sending a large message across the three-device configuration described above. Assume that each of the three Ethernet devices can be used to reach the intended receiver (reachability is determined by TCP networks and netmasks, and some well-defined heuristics). In this case, the sender will split the large message into multiple fragments. Each fragment will be assigned—in a round-robin fashion—to one of the TCP BTL modules (each module will therefore be assigned roughly one third of the fragments). Each module then sends its fragments over its corresponding Ethernet device.

This may seem like a complex scheme, but it is surprisingly effective. By pipelining the sends of a large message across the multiple TCP BTL modules, typical HPC environments (e.g., where each Ethernet device is on a separate PCI bus) can sustain nearly maximum bandwidth speeds across multiple Ethernet devices.

Run-Time Parameters

Developers commonly make decisions when writing code, such as:
- Should I use algorithm A or algorithm B?
- How large of a buffer should I preallocate?
- How long should the timeout be?
- At what message size should I change network protocols?
- ...and so on.

Users tend to assume that the developers will answer such questions in a way that is generally suitable for most types of systems. However, the HPC community is full of scientist and engineer power users who want to aggressively tweak their hardware and software stacks to eke out every possible compute cycle. Although these users typically do not want to tinker with the actual code of their MPI implementation, they *do* want to tinker by selecting different internal algorithms, choosing different resource consumption patterns, or forcing specific network protocols in different circumstances.

Therefore, the MCA parameter system was included when designing Open MPI; the system is a flexible mechanism that allows users to change internal Open MPI parameter values at run time. Specifically, developers register string and integer MCA parameters throughout the Open MPI code base, along with an associated default value and descriptive string defining what the parameter is and how it is used. The general rule of thumb is that rather than hard-coding constants, developers use run-time-settable MCA parameters, thereby allowing power users to tweak run-time behavior.

There are a number of MCA parameters in the base code of the three abstraction layers, but the bulk of Open MPI's MCA parameters are located in individual components. For example, the TCL BTL plugin has a parameter that specifies whether only TCPv4 interfaces, only TCPv6 interfaces, or both types of interfaces should be used. Alternatively, another TCP BTL parameter can be set to specify exactly which Ethernet devices to use.

Users can discover what parameters are available via a user-level command line tool (`ompi_info`). Parameter values can be set in multiple ways: on the command line, via environment variables, via the Windows registry, or in system- or user-level INI-style files.

The MCA parameter system complements the idea of run-time plugin selection flexibility, and has proved to be quite valuable to users. Although Open MPI developers try hard to choose reasonable defaults for a wide variety of situations, every HPC environment is different. There are inevitably environments where Open MPI's default parameter values will be unsuitable—and possibly even detrimental to performance. The MCA parameter system allows users to be proactive and tweak Open MPI's behavior for their environment. Not only does this alleviate many upstream requests for changes and/or bug reports, it allows users to experiment with the parameter space to find the best configuration for their specific system.

15.3 Lessons Learned

With such a varied group of core Open MPI members, it is inevitable that we would each learn *something*, and that as a group, we would learn many things. The following list describes just a few of these lessons.

Performance

Message-passing performance and resource utilization are the king and queen of high-performance computing. Open MPI was specifically designed in such a way that it could operate at the very bleeding edge of high performance: incredibly low latencies for sending short messages, extremely high short message injection rates on supported networks, fast ramp-ups to maximum bandwidth for large messages, etc. Abstraction is good (for many reasons), but it must be designed with care so that it does not get in the way of performance. Or, put differently: carefully choose abstractions that lend themselves to shallow, performant call stacks (versus deep, feature-rich API call stacks).

That being said, we also had to accept that in some cases, abstraction—not architecture—must be thrown out the window. Case in point: Open MPI has hand-coded assembly for some of its most performance-critical operations, such as shared memory locking and atomic operations.

It is worth noting that Figures 15.1 and 15.2 show two different *architectural* views of Open MPI. They do not represent the run-time call stacks or calling invocation layering for the high performance code sections.

Lesson learned: It is acceptable (albeit undesirable) and unfortunately sometimes necessary to have gross, complex code in the name of performance (e.g., the aforementioned assembly code). However, it is *always* preferable to spend time trying to figure out how to have good abstractions to discretize and hide complexity whenever possible. A few weeks of design can save literally hundreds or thousands of developer-hours of maintenance on tangled, subtle, spaghetti code.

Standing on the Shoulders of Giants

We actively tried to avoid re-inventing code in Open MPI that someone else has already written (when such code is compatible with Open MPI's BSD licensing). Specifically, we have no compunctions about either directly re-using or interfacing to someone else's code.

There is no place for the "not invented here" religion when trying to solve highly complex engineering problems; it only makes good logistical sense to re-use external code whenever possible. Such re-use frees developers to focus on the problems unique to Open MPI; there is no sense re-solving a problem that someone else has solved already.

A good example of this kind of code re-use is the GNU Libtool Libltdl package. Libltdl is a small library that provides a portable API for opening DSOs and finding symbols in them. Libltdl is supported on a wide variety of operating systems and environments, including Microsoft Windows.

Open MPI *could* have provided this functionality itself—but why? Libltdl is a fine piece of software, is actively maintained, is compatible with Open MPI's license, and provides exactly the functionality that was needed. Given these points, there is no realistic gain for Open MPI developers to re-write this functionality.

Lesson learned: When a suitable solution exists elsewhere, do not hesitate to integrate it and stop wasting time trying to re-invent it.

Optimize for the Common Case

Another guiding architectural principle has been to optimize for the common case. For example, emphasis is placed on splitting many operations into two phases: setup and repeated action. The assumption is that setup may be expensive (meaning: slow). So do it *once* and get it over with. Optimize for the much more common case: repeated operation.

For example, `malloc()` can be slow, especially if pages need to be allocated from the operating system. So instead of allocating just enough bytes for a single incoming network message, allocate enough space for a *bunch* of incoming messages, divide the result up into individual message buffers, and set up a freelist to maintain them. In this way, the *first* request for a message buffer may be slow, but *successive* requests will be much faster because they will just be de-queues from a freelist.

Lesson learned: Split common operations into (at least) two phases: setup and repeated action. Not only will the code perform better, it may be easier to maintain over time because the distinct actions are separated.

Miscellaneous

There are too many more lessons learned to describe in detail here; the following are a few more lessons that can be summed up briefly:

- We were fortunate to draw upon 15+ years of HPC research and make designs that have (mostly) successfully carried us for more than eight years. When embarking on a new software project, *look to the past*. Be sure to understand what has already been done, *why* it was done, and what its strengths and weaknesses were.
- The concept of components—allowing multiple different implementations of the same functionality—has saved us many times, both technically and politically. Plugins are good.
- Similarly, we continually add and remove frameworks as necessary. When developers start arguing about the "right" way to implement a new feature, add a framework that fronts components that implement that feature. Or when newer ideas come along that obsolete older frameworks, don't hesitate to delete such kruft.

Conclusion

If we had to list the three *most* important things that we've learned from the Open MPI project, I think they would be as follows:

- One size does not fit all (users). The run-time plugin and companion MCA parameter system allow users flexibility that is necessary in the world of portable software. Complex software systems cannot (always) magically adapt to a given system; providing user-level controls allows a human to figure out—and override— when the software behaves sub-optimally.
- Differences are good. Developer disagreements are good. Embrace challenges to the status quo; do not get complacent. A plucky grad student saying "Hey, check this out..." can lead to the basis of a whole new feature or a major evolution of the product.
- Although outside the scope of this book, people and community matter. A lot.

OSCAR
Jennifer Ruttan

Since their initial adoption, EMR (electronic medical record) systems have attempted to bridge the gap between the physical and digital worlds of patient care. Governments in countries around the world have attempted to come up with a solution that enables better care for patients at a lower cost while reducing the paper trail that medicine typically generates. Many governments have been very successful in their attempts to create such a system—some, like that of the Canadian province of Ontario, have not (some may remember the so-called "eHealth Scandal" in Ontario that, according to the Auditor General, cost taxpayers $1 billion CAD).

An EMR permits the digitization of a patient chart, and when used properly should make it easier for a physician to deliver care. A good system should provide a physician a bird's eye view of a patient's current and ongoing conditions, their prescription history, their recent lab results, history of their previous visits, and so on. OSCAR (Open Source Clinical Application Resource), an approximately ten-year-old project of McMaster University in Hamilton, Ontario, Canada, is the open source community's attempt to provide such a system to physicians at low or no cost.

OSCAR has many subsystems that provide functionality on a component-by-component basis. For example, oscarEncounter provides an interface for interacting with a patient's chart directly; Rx3 is a prescription module that checks for allergies and drug interactions automatically and allows a physician to directly fax a prescription to a pharmacy from the UI; the Integrator is a component to enable data sharing between multiple compatible EMRs. All of these separate components come together to build the typical OSCAR user experience.

OSCAR won't be for every physician; for example, a specialist may not find all the features of the system useful, and it is not easily customizable. However, it offers a complete set of features for a general physician interacting with patients on a day-to-day basis.

In addition, OSCAR is CMS 3.0 certified (and has applied for CMS 4.0 certification)—which allows physicians to receive funding for installing it in their clinic[1]. Receiving CMS certification involves passing a set of requirements from the Government of Ontario and paying a fee.

This chapter will discuss the architecture of OSCAR in fairly general terms, describing the hierarchy, major components, and most importantly the impact that past decisions have made on the project. As a conclusion and to wrap up, there will be a discussion on how OSCAR might have been designed today if there was an opportunity to do so.

---

[1] See https://www.emradvisor.ca/ for details.

16.1 System Hierarchy

As a Tomcat web application, OSCAR generally follows the typical model-view-controller design pattern. This means that the model code (Data Access Objects, or DAOs) is separate from the controller code (servlets) and those are separated from the views (Java Server Pages, or JSPs). The most significant difference between the two is that servlets are classes and JSPs are HTML pages marked up with Java code. Data gets placed into memory when a servlet executes and the JSP reads that same data, usually done via reads and writes to the attributes of the request object. Just about every JSP page in OSCAR has this kind of design.

16.2 Past Decision Making

I mentioned that OSCAR is a fairly old project. This has implications for how effectively the MVC pattern has been applied. In short, there are sections of the code that completely disregard the pattern as they were written before tighter enforcement of the MVC pattern began. Some of the most common features are written this way; for example, performing many actions related to demographics (patient records) are done via the `demographiccontrol.jsp` file—this includes creating patients and updating their data.

OSCAR's age is a hurdle for tackling many of the problems that are facing the source tree today. Indeed, there has been significant effort made to improve the situation, including enforcing design rules via a code review process. This is an approach that the community at present has decided will allow better collaboration in the future, and will prevent poor code from becoming part of the code base, which has been a problem in the past.

This is by no means a restriction on how we could design parts of the system now; it does, however, make it more complicated when deciding to fix bugs in a dated part of OSCAR. Do you, as somebody tasked to fix a bug in the Demographic Creation function, fix the bug with code in the same style as it currently exists? Or do you re-write the module completely so that it closely follows the MVC design pattern?

As developers we must carefully weigh our options in situations like those. There is no guarantee that if you re-architect a part of the system you will not create new bugs, and when patient data is on the line, we must make the decision carefully.

16.3 Version Control

A CVS repository was used for much of OSCAR's life. Commits weren't often checked for consistency and it was possible to commit code that could break the build. It was tough for developers to keep up with changes—especially new developers joining the project late in its lifecycle. A new developer could see something that they would want to change, make the change, and get it into the source branch several weeks before anybody would notice that something significant had been modified (this was especially prevalent during long holidays, such as Christmas break, when not many people were watching the source tree).

Things have changed; OSCAR's source tree is now controlled by git. Any commits to the main branch have to pass code-style checking and unit testing, successfully compile, and be code reviewed by the developers (much of this is handled by the combination of Hudson[2] and Gerrit[3]). The project

---
[2] A continuous integration server: http://hudson-ci.org/
[3] A code review tool: http://code.google.com/p/gerrit/

has become much more tightly controlled. Many or all of the issues caused by poor handling of the source tree have been solved.

16.4 Data Models/DAOs

When looking through the OSCAR source, you may notice that there are many different ways to access the database: you can use a direct connection to the database via a class called DBHandler, use a legacy Hibernate model, or use a generic JPA model. As new and easier database access models became available, they were integrated into OSCAR. The result is that there is now a slightly noisy picture of how OSCAR interacts with data in MySQL, and the differences between the three types of data access methods are best described with examples.

EForms (DBHandler)

The EForm system allows users to create their own forms to attach to patient records—this feature is usually used to replace a paper-based form with a digital version. On each creation of a form of a particular type, the form's template file is loaded; then the data in the form is stored in the database for each instance. Each instance is attached to a patient record.

EForms allow you to pull in certain types of data from a patient chart or other area of the system via free-form SQL queries (which are defined in a file called apconfig.xml). This can be extremely useful, as a form can load and then immediately be populated with demographic or other relevant information without intervention from the user; for example, you wouldn't have to type in a patient's name, age, date of birth, hometown, phone number, or the last note that was recorded for that patient.

A design decision was made, when originally developing the EForm module, to use raw database queries to populate a POJO (plain-old Java object) called EForm in the controller that is then passed to the view layer to display data on the screen, sort of like a JavaBean. Using a POJO in this case is actually closer in design to the Hibernate or JPA architecture, as I'll discuss in the next sections.

All of the functionality regarding saving EForm instances and templates is done via raw SQL queries run through the DBHandler class. Ultimately, DBHandler is a wrapper for a simple JDBC object and does not scrutinize a query before sending it to the SQL server. It should be added here that DBHandler is a potential security flaw as it allows unchecked SQL to be sent to the server. Any class that uses DBHandler must implement its own checking to make sure that SQL injection doesn't occur.

Depending on the type of application you're writing, direct access of a database is sometimes fine. In certain cases, it can even speed development up. Using this method to access the database doesn't conform to the model-view-controller design pattern, though: if you're going to change your database structure (the model), you have to change the SQL query elsewhere (in the controller). Sometimes, adding certain columns or changing their type in OSCAR's database tables requires this kind of invasive procedure just to implement small features.

It may not surprise you to find out that the DBHandler object is one of the oldest pieces of code still intact in the source. I personally don't know where it originated from but I consider it to be the most "primitive" of database access types that exist in the OSCAR source. No new code is permitted to use this class, and if code is committed that uses it, the commit will be rejected automatically.

Demographic Records (Hibernate)

A demographic record contains general metadata about a patient; for example, their name, age, address, language, and sex; consider it to be the result of an intake form that a patient fills out during their first visit to a doctor. All of this data is retrieved and displayed as part of OSCAR's Master Record for a specific demographic.

Using Hibernate to access the database is far safer than using `DBHandler`. For one, you have to explicitly define which columns match to which fields in your model object (in this case, the Demographic class). If you want to perform complex joins, they have to be done as prepared statements. Finally, you will only ever receive an object of the type you ask for when performing a query, which is very convenient.

The process of working with a Hibernate-style DAO and Model pair is quite simple. In the case of the Demographic object, there's a file called `Demographic.hbm.xml` that describes the mapping between object field and database column. The file describes which table to look at and what type of object to return. When OSCAR starts, this file will be read and a sanity check occurs to make sure that this kind of mapping can actually be made (server startup fails if it can't). Once running, you grab an instance of the `DemographicDao` object and run queries against it.

The best part about using Hibernate over `DBHandler` is that all of the queries to the server are prepared statements. This restricts you from running free-form SQL during runtime, but it also prevents any type of SQL injection attack. Hibernate will often build large queries to grab the data, and it doesn't always perform in an extremely efficient way.

In the previous section I mentioned an example of the EForm module using `DBHandler` to populate a POJO. This is the next logical step to preventing that kind of code from being written. If the model has to change, only the `.hbm.xml` file and the model class have to change (a new field and getter/setter for the new column), and doing so won't impact the rest of the application.

While newer than `DBHandler`, the Hibernate method is also starting to show its age. It's not always convenient to use and requires a big configuration file for each table you want to access. Setting up a new object pair takes time and if you do it incorrectly OSCAR won't even start. For this reason, nobody should be writing new code that uses pure Hibernate, either. Instead, generic JPA is being embraced in new development.

Integrator Consent (JPA)

The newest form of database access is done via generic JPA. If the OSCAR project decided to switch from Hibernate to another database access API, conforming to the JPA standard for DAOs and Model objects would make it very easy to migrate. Unfortunately, because this is so "new" to the OSCAR project, there are almost no areas of the system that actually use this method to get data.

In any case, let me explain how it works. Instead of a `.hbm.xml` file, you add annotations to your Model and DAO objects. These annotations describe the table to look in, column mappings for fields, and join queries. Everything is contained inside the two files and nothing else is necessary for their operation. Hibernate still runs behind the scenes, though, in actually retrieving the data from the database.

All of the Integrator's models are written using JPA—and they are pretty good examples of both the new style of database access as well as demonstrating that as a new technology to be implemented into OSCAR, it hasn't been used in very many places yet. The Integrator is a relatively new addition to the source. It makes quite a lot of sense to use this new data access model as opposed to Hibernate.

Touching on a now-common theme in this section of the chapter, the annotated POJOs that JPA uses allow for a far more streamlined experience. For example, during the Integrator's build process, an SQL file is created that scts up all of the tables for you—an enormously useful thing to have. With that ability, it's impossible to create mismatching tables and model objects (as you can do with any other type of database access method) and you never have to worry about naming of columns and tables. There are no direct SQL queries, so it's not possible to create SQL injection attacks. In short, it "just works".

The way that JPA works can be considered to be fairly similar to the way that ActiveRecord works in Ruby on Rails. The model class defines the data type and the database stores it; what happens in between that—getting data in and out—is not up to the user.

Issues with Hibernate and JPA

Both Hibernate and JPA offer some significant benefits in typical use cases. For simple retrieval and storage, they really cut time out of development and debugging.

However, that doesn't mean that their implementation into OSCAR has been without issue. Because the user doesn't define the SQL between the database and the POJO referencing a specific row, Hibernate gets to choose the best way to do it. The "best way" can manifest itself in a couple of ways: Hibernate can choose to just retrieve the simple data from the row, or it can perform a join and retrieve a lot of information at once. Sometimes these joins get out of hand.

Here's another example: The `casemgmt_note` table stores all patient notes. Each note object stores lots of metadata about the note—but it also stores a list of all of the issues that the note deals with (issues can be things like, "smoking cessation" or "diabetes", which describe the contents of the note). The list of issues is represented in the note object as a `List<CaseManagementIssue>`. In order to get that list, the `casemgmt_note` table is joined with the `casemgmt_issue_notes` table (which acts as a mapping table) and finally the `casemgmt_issue` table.

When you want to write a custom query in Hibernate, which this situation requires, you don't write standard SQL—you write HQL (Hibernate Query Language) that is then translated to SQL (by inserting internal column names for all the fields to be selected) before parameters are inserted and the query is sent to the database server. In this specific case, the query was written with basic joins with no join columns—meaning that when the query was eventually translated to SQL, it was so large that it wasn't immediately obvious what the query was gathering. Additionally, in almost all cases, this never created a large enough temporary table for it to matter. For most users, this query actually runs quickly enough that it's not noticeable. However, this query is unbelievably inefficient.

Let's step back for a second. When you perform a join on two tables, the server has to create a temporary table in memory. In the most generic type of joins, the number of rows is equal to the number of rows in the first table multiplied by the number of rows in the second table. So if your table has 500,000 rows, and you join it with a table that has 10,000,000 rows, you've just created a 5×10^{12} row temporary table in memory, which the select statement is then run against and that temporary table is discarded.

In one extreme case that we ran into, the join across three tables caused a temporary table to be created that was around 7×10^{12} rows in length, of which about 1000 rows were eventually selected. This operation took about 5 minutes and locked the `casemgmt_note` table while it was running.

The problem was solved, eventually, through the use of a prepared statement that restricted the scope of the first table before joining with the other two. The newer, far more efficient query brought the number of rows to select down to a very manageable 300,000 and enormously improved performance of the notes retrieval operation (down to about 0.1 seconds to perform the same select statement).

The moral of the story is simply that while Hibernate does a fairly good job, unless the join is very explicitly defined and controlled (either in the .hbm.xml file or a join annotation in the object class for a JPA model), it can very quickly get out of control. Dealing with objects instead of SQL queries requires you to leave the actual implementation of the query up to the database access library and only really allows you to control definition. Unless you're careful with how you define things, it can all fall apart under extreme conditions. Furthermore, if you're a database programmer with lots of SQL knowledge, it won't really help much when designing a JPA-enabled class, and it removes some of the control that you would have if you were writing an SQL statement manually. Ultimately, a good knowledge of both SQL and JPA annotations and how they affect queries is required.

16.5 Permissions

CAISI (Client Access to Integrated Services and Information) was originally a standalone product—a fork of OSCAR—to help manage homeless shelters in Toronto. A decision was eventually made to merge the code from CAISI into the main source branch. The original CAISI project may no longer exist, but what it gave to OSCAR is very important: its permission model.

The permissions model in OSCAR is extremely powerful and can be used to create just about as many roles and permission sets as possible. *Providers* belong to *programs* (as *staff*) where they have a specific *role*. Each *program* takes place at a *facility*. Each *role* has a description (for example, "doctor", "nurse", "social worker", and so on) and a set of attached global permissions. The permissions are written in a format that makes them very easy to understand: "read nurse notes" may be a permission that a doctor role may have, but the nurse role may not have the "read doctor notes" permission.

This format may be easy to understand, but under the hood it requires quite a bit of heavy lifting to actually check for these types of permissions. The name of the role that the current provider has is checked against its list of permissions for a match with the action that they are trying to perform. For example, a provider attempting to read a doctor's notes would cause "read doctor notes" to be checked for each and every note written by a doctor.

Another problem is the reliance on English for permission definition. Anybody using OSCAR in a language other than English would still need to write their permissions in a format such as "read *[role]* notes", using the English words "read", "write", "notes", and so on.

CAISI's permission model is a significant part of OSCAR, but it's not the only model in place. Before CAISI was implemented, another role-based (but not program-based) system was developed and is still in use in many parts of the system today.

For this second system, providers are assigned one or many roles (for example, "doctor", "nurse", "admin", and so on). They can be assigned as many roles as necessary—the roles' permissions stack on top of each other. These permissions are generally used for restricting access to parts of the system, as opposed to CAISI's permissions which restrict access to certain pieces of data on a patient's chart. For example, a user has to have the "_admin" "read" permission on a role that they have assigned to them to be able to access the Admin panel. Having the "read" permission will exempt them from being able to perform administrative tasks, however. They'll need the "write" permission as well for that.

Both of these systems accomplish roughly the same goal; it's due to CAISI's merge later in the project lifecycle that they both exist. They don't always exist happily together, so in reality it can be a lot easier to just focus on using one for day-to-day operations of OSCAR. You can generally date code in OSCAR by knowing which permissions model preceded which other permissions model: *Provider Type* then *Provider Roles* then *CAISI Programs/Roles*

The oldest type of permissions model, "Provider Type", is so dated that it's actually not used in most parts of the system and is in fact defaulted to "doctor" during new provider creation—having it as any other value (such as "receptionist") causes significant issues throughout the system. It's easier and more fine-grained to control permissions via Provider Roles instead.

16.6   Integrator

OSCAR's Integrator component is a separate web application that independent OSCAR instances use to exchange patient, program and provider information over a secure link. It can be optionally installed as a component for an installation in an environment such as a LHN (Local Health Network) or a hospital. The easiest way to describe the Integrator is as a temporary storage facility.

Consider the following use case and argument for use of the Integrator: in Hospital X, there is an ENT (ear, nose, and throat) clinic as well as an endocrinology clinic. If an ENT doctor refers their patient to an endocrinologist upstairs, they may be required to send along patient history and records. This is inconvenient and generates more paper than is necessary—perhaps the patient is only seeing the endocrinologist once. By using the Integrator, the patient's data can be accessed on the endocrinologist's EMR, and access to the contents of the patient's chart can be revoked after the visit.

A more extreme example: if an unconscious man shows up in an ER with nothing but his health card, because the home clinic and the hospital's system are connected via the Integrator, the man's record can be pulled and it can be very quickly realized that he has been prescribed the blood thinner warfarin. Ultimately, information retrieval like this is what an EMR like OSCAR paired with the Integrator can achieve.

Technical Details

The Integrator is available in source code form only, which requires the user to retrieve and build it manually. Like OSCAR, it runs on a standard installation of Tomcat with MySQL.

When the URL where the Integrator lives is accessed, it doesn't appear to display anything useful. This component is almost purely a web service; OSCAR communicates via POST and GET requests to the Integrator URL.

As an independently developed project (initially as part of the CAISI project), the Integrator is fairly strict in adhering to the MVC design pattern. The original developers have done an excellent job of setting it up with very clearly defined lines between the models, views, and controllers. The most recently implemented type of database access layer that I mentioned earlier—generic JPA—is the only such layer in the project. (As an interesting side note: because the entire project is properly set up with JPA annotations on all the model classes, an SQL script is created at build time that can be used to initialize the structure of the database; the Integrator, therefore, doesn't ship with a stand-alone SQL script.)

Communication is handled via web service calls described in WSDL XML files that are available on the server. A client could query the Integrator to find out what kind of functions are available and adapt to it. This really means that the Integrator is compatible with any kind of EMR that somebody decides to write a client for; the data format is generic enough that it could easily be mapped to local types.

For OSCAR, though, a client library is built and included in the main source tree, for simplicity's sake. That library only ever needs to be updated if new functions become available on the Integrator. A bug fix on the Integrator doesn't require an update of that file.

Design

Data for the Integrator comes in from all of the connected EMRs at scheduled times and, once there, another EMR can request that data. None of the data on the Integrator is stored permanently, though—its database could be erased and it could be rebuilt from the client data.

The dataset sent is configured individually at each OSCAR instance which is connected to a particular Integrator, and except in situations where the entire patient database has to be sent to the Integrator server, only patient records that have been viewed since the previous push to the server are sent. The process isn't exactly like delta patching, but it's close.

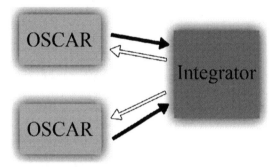

Figure 16.1: Data exchange between OSCARs and Integrator

Let me go into a little more detail about how the Integrator works with an example: a remote clinic seeing another clinic's patient. When that clinic wants to access the patient's record, the clinics first have to have been connected to the same Integrator server. The receptionist can search the Integrator for the remote patient (by name and optionally date of birth or sex) and find their record stored on the server. They initiate the copy of a limited set of the patient's demographic information and then double-check with the patient to make sure that they consent to the retrieval of their record by completing a consent form. Once completed, the Integrator server will deliver whatever information the Integrator knows about that patient—notes, prescriptions, allergies, vaccinations, documents, and so on. This data is cached locally so that the local OSCAR doesn't have to send a request to the Integrator every time it wants to see this data, but the local cache expires every hour.

After the initial setup of a remote patient by copying their demographic data to the local OSCAR, that patient is set up as any other on the system. All of the remote data that is retrieved from the Integrator is marked as such (and the clinic from which it came from is noted), but it's only temporarily cached on the local OSCAR. Any local data that is recorded is recorded just like any other patient data—to the patient record, and sent to the Integrator—but not permanently stored on any remote machine.

This has a very important implication, especially for patient consent and how that factors into the design of the Integrator. Let's say that a patient sees a remote physician and is fine with them having access to their record, but only temporarily. After their visit, they can revoke the consent for that clinic to be able to view that patient's record and the next time that clinic opens the patient's

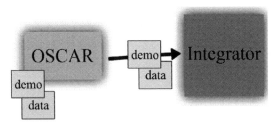

Figure 16.2: The Demographic information and associated data is sent to the Integrator during a data push from the home clinic. The record on the Integrator may not be a representation of the complete record from the home clinic as the OSCAR can choose not to send all patient data.

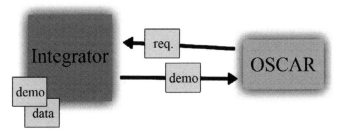

Figure 16.3: A remote OSCAR requests data from the Integrator by asking for a specific patient record. The Integrator server sends only the demographic information, which is stored permanently on the remote OSCAR.

chart there won't be any data there (with the exception of any data that was locally recorded). This ultimately gives control over how and when a record is viewed directly to the patient and is similar to walking into a clinic carrying a copy of your paper chart. They can see the chart while they're interacting with you, but you take it home with you when you leave.

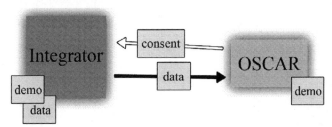

Figure 16.4: A remote clinic can see the contents of a patient chart by asking for the data; if the appropriate consent is present, the data is sent. The data is never stored permanently on the remote OSCAR.

Another very important ability is for physicians to decide what kinds of data they want to share with the other connected clinics via their Integrator server. A clinic can choose to share all of a demographic record or only parts of it, such as notes but not documents, allergies but not prescriptions, and so on. Ultimately it's up to the group of physicians who set up the Integrator server to decide what kinds of data they're comfortable with sharing with each other.

As I mentioned before, the Integrator is only a temporary storage warehouse and no data is ever stored permanently there. This is another very important decision that was made during development; it allows clinics to back out of sharing any and all data via the Integrator very easily—and in fact if necessary the entire Integrator database can be wiped. If the database is wiped, no user of a client will ever notice because the data will be accurately reconstructed from the original data on all of the various connected clients. An implication is that the OSCAR provider needs to trust the Integrator provider to have wiped the database when they say so—it is therefore best to deploy an Integrator to a group of physicians already in a legal organization such as a Family Health Organization or Family Health Team; the Integrator server would be housed at one of these physician's clinics.

Data Format

The Integrator's client libraries are built via `wsdl2java`, which creates a set of classes representing the appropriate data types the web service communicates in. There are classes for each data type as well as classes representing keys for each of these data types.

It's outside the scope of this chapter to describe how to build the Integrator's client library. What's important to know is that once the library is built, it must be included with the rest of the JARs in OSCAR. This JAR contains everything necessary to set up the Integrator connection and access all of the data types that the Integrator server will return to OSCAR, such as CachedDemographic, CachedDemographicNote, and CachedProvider, among many others. In addition to the data types that are returned, there are "WS" classes that are used for the retrieval of such lists of data in the first place—the most frequently used being DemographicWs.

Dealing with the Integrator data can sometimes be a little tricky. OSCAR doesn't have anything truly built-in to handle this kind of data, so what usually happens is when retrieving a certain kind of patient data (for example, notes for a patient's chart) the Integrator client is asked to retrieve data from the server. That data is then manually transformed into a local class representing that data (in the case of notes, it's a `CaseManagementNote`). A Boolean flag is set inside the class to indicate that it's a piece of remote content and that is used to change how the data is displayed to the user on the screen. On the opposite end, `CaisiIntegratorUpdateTask` handles taking local OSCAR data, converting it into the Integrator's data format, and then sending that data to the Integrator server.

This design may not be as efficient or as clean as possible, but it does enable older parts of the system to become "compatible" with Integrator-delivered data without much modification. In addition, keeping the view as simple as possible by referring to only one type of class improves the readability of the JSP file and makes it easier to debug in the event of an error.

16.7 Lessons Learned

As you can probably imagine, OSCAR has its share of issues when it comes to overall design. It does, however, provide a complete feature set that most users will find no issues with. That's ultimately the goal of the project: provide a good solution that works in most situations.

I can't speak for the entire OSCAR community, so this section will be highly subjective and from my point of view. I feel that there are some important takeaways from an architectural discussion about the project.

First, it's clear that poor source control in the past has caused the architecture of the system to become highly chaotic in parts, especially in areas where the controllers and the views blend together. The way that the project was run in the past didn't prevent this from happening, but the process has changed since and hopefully we won't have to deal with such a problem again.

Next, because the project is so old, it's difficult to upgrade (or even change) libraries without causing significant disruption throughout the code base. That's exactly what has happened, though. I often find it difficult to figure out what's necessary and what isn't when I'm looking in the library folder. In addition to that, sometimes when libraries undergo major upgrades they break backwards compatibility (changing package names is a common offense). There are often several libraries included with OSCAR that all accomplish the same task—this goes back to poor source control, but also the fact that that there has been no list or documentation describing which library is required by which component.

Additionally, OSCAR is a little inflexible when it comes to adding new features to existing subsystems. For example, if you want to add a new box to the E-Chart, you'll have to create a new JSP page and a new servlet, modify the layout of the E-Chart (in a few places), and modify the configuration file of the application so that your servlet can load.

Next, due to the lack of documentation, sometimes it is nearly impossible to figure out how a part of the system works—the original contributor may not even be part of the project anymore—and often the only tool you have to figure it out is a debugger. As a project of this age, this is costing the community the potential for new contributors to get involved. However, it's something that, as a collaborative effort, the community is working on.

Finally, OSCAR is a repository for medical information and its security is compromised by the inclusion of the `DBHandler` class (discussed in a previous section). I personally feel that freeform database queries that accept parameters should never be acceptable in an EMR because it's so easy to perform SQL injection attacks. While it's good that no new code is permitted that uses this class, it should be a priority of the development team to remove all instances of its use.

All of that may sound like some harsh criticism of the project. In the past, all of these problems have been significant and, like I said, prevent the community from growing as the barrier to entry is so high. This is something that is changing, so in the future, these issues won't be so much of a hindrance.

In looking back over the project's history (and especially over the past few versions) we can come up with a better design for how the application would be built. The system still has to provide a base level of functionality (mandated by the Ontario government for certification as an EMR), so that all has to be baked in by default. But if OSCAR were to be redesigned today, it should be designed in a truly modular fashion that would allow modules to be treated as plugins; if you didn't like the default E-Form module, you could write your own (or even another module entirely). It should be able to speak to more systems (or more systems should be able to speak to it), including the medical hardware that you see in increasing use throughout the industry, such as devices for measuring visual acuity. This also means that it would be easy to adapt OSCAR to the requirements of local and federal governments around the world for storing medical data. Since every region has a different set of laws and requirements, this kind of design would be crucial for making sure that OSCAR develops a worldwide userbase.

I also believe that security should be the most important feature of all. An EMR is only as secure as its least secure component, so there should be focus on abstracting away as much data access as possible from the application so that it stores and retrieves data in a sandbox-style environment through a main data access layer API that has been audited by a third-party and found to be adequate for storing medical information. Other EMRs can hide behind obscurity and proprietary code as a security measure (which isn't really a security measure at all), but being open source, OSCAR should lead the charge with better data protection.

I stand firmly as a believer in the OSCAR project. We have hundreds of users that we know about (and the many hundreds that we don't), and we receive valuable feedback from the physicians who are interacting with our project on a daily basis. Through the development of new processes and new features, we hope to grow the installed base and to support users from other regions. It is our intention to make sure that what we deliver is something that improves the lives of the physicians who use OSCAR as well as the lives of their patients, by creating better tools to help manage healthcare.

Processing.js
Mike Kamermans

Originally developed by Ben Fry and Casey Reas, the Processing programming language started as an open source programming language (based on Java) to help the electronic arts and visual design communities learn the basics of computer programming in a visual context. Offering a highly simplified model for 2D and 3D graphics compared to most programming languages, it quickly became well-suited for a wide range of activities, from teaching programming through writing small visualisations to creating multi-wall art installations, and became able to perform a wide variety of tasks, from simply reading in a sequence of strings to acting as the de facto IDE for programming and operating the popular "Arduino" open source hardware prototyping boards. Continuing to gain popularity, Processing has firmly taken its place as an easy to learn, widely used programming language for all things visual, and so much more.

The basic Processing program, called a "sketch", consists of two functions: setup and draw. The first is the main program entry point, and can contain any amount of initialization instructions. After finishing setup, Processing programs can do one of two things: 1) call draw, and schedule another call to draw at a fixed interval upon completion; or 2) call draw, and wait for input events from the user. By default, Processing does the former; calling noLoop results in the latter. This allows for two modes to present sketches, namely a fixed framerate graphical environment, and an interactive, event-based updating graphical environment. In both cases, user events are monitored and can be handled either in their own event handlers, or for certain events that set persistent global values, directly in the draw function.

Processing.js is a sister project of Processing, designed to bring it to the web without the need for Java or plugins. It started as an attempt by John Resig to see if the Processing language could be ported to the web, by using the—at the time brand new—HTML5 <canvas> element as a graphical context, with a proof of concept library released to the public in 2008. Written with the idea in mind that "your code should just work", Processing.js has been refined over the years to make data visualisations, digital art, interactive animations, educational graphs, video games, etc. work using web standards and without any plugins. You write code using the Processing language, either in the Processing IDE or your favourite editor of choice, include it on a web page using a <canvas> element, and Processing.js does the rest, rendering everything in the <canvas> element and letting users interact with the graphics in the same way they would with a normal standalone Processing program.

17.1 How Does It Work?

Processing.js is a bit unusual as an open source project, in that the code base is a single file called `processing.js` which contains the code for Processing, the single object that makes up the entire library. In terms of how the code is structured, we constantly shuffle things around inside this object as we try to clean it up a little bit with every release. Its design is relatively straightforward, and its function can be described in a single sentence: it rewrites Processing source code into pure JavaScript source code, and every Processing API function call is mapped to a corresponding function in the JavaScript Processing object, which effects the same thing on a `<canvas>` element as the Processing call would effect on a Java Applet canvas.

For speed, we have two separate code paths for 2D and 3D functions, and when a sketch is loaded, either one or the other is used for resolving function wrappers so that we don't add bloat to running instances. However, in terms of data structures and code flow, knowing JavaScript means you can read `processing.js`, with the possible exception of the syntax parser.

Unifying Java and JavaScript

Rewriting Processing source code into JavaScript source code means that you can simply tell the browser to execute the rewritten source, and if you rewrote it correctly, things just work. But, making sure the rewrite is correct has taken, and still occasionally takes, quite a bit of effort. Processing syntax is based on Java, which means that Processing.js has to essentially transform Java source code into JavaScript source code. Initially, this was achieved by treating the Java source code as a string, and iteratively replacing substrings of Java with their JavaScript equivalents[1]. For a small syntax set, this is fine, but as time went on and complexity added to complexity, this approach started to break down. Consequently, the parser was completely rewritten to build an Abstract Syntax Tree (AST) instead, first breaking down the Java source code into functional blocks, and then mapping each of those blocks to their corresponding JavaScript syntax. The result is that, at the cost of readability[2], Processing.js now effectively contains an on-the-fly Java-to-JavaScript transcompiler.

Here is the code for a Processing sketch:

```
void setup() {
  size(200,200);
  noCursor();
  noStroke();
  smooth(); }

void draw() {
  fill(255,10);
  rect(-1,-1,width+1,height+1);
  float f = frameCount*PI/frameRate;
  float d = 10+abs(60*sin(f));
  fill(0,100,0,50);
  ellipse(mouseX, mouseY, d,d); }
```

---

[1] For those interested in an early incarnation of the parser, it can be found at https://github.com/jeresig/processing-js/blob/51d280c516c0530cd9e63531076dfa147406e6b2/processing.js, running from line 37 to line 266.

[2] Readers are welcome to peruse https://github.com/jeresig/processing-js/blob/v1.3.0/processing.js#L17649, up to line 19217.

And here is its Processing.js conversion:

```
function($p) {
    function setup() {
        $p.size(200, 200);
        $p.noCursor();
        $p.noStroke();
        $p.smooth(); }
    $p.setup = setup;

    function draw() {
        $p.fill(255, 10);
        $p.rect(-1, -1, $p.width + 1, $p.height + 1);
        var f = $p.frameCount * $p.PI / $p.__frameRate;
        var d = 10 + $p.abs(60 * $p.sin(f));
        $p.fill(0, 100, 0, 50);
        $p.ellipse($p.mouseX, $p.mouseY, d, d); }
    $p.draw = draw; }
```

This sounds like a great thing, but there are a few problems when converting Java syntax to JavaScript syntax:

1. Java programs are isolated entities. JavaScript programs share the world with a web page.
2. Java is strongly typed. JavaScript is not.
3. Java is a class/instance based object-oriented language. JavaScript is not.
4. Java has distinct variables and methods. JavaScript does not.
5. Java allows method overloading. JavaScript does not.
6. Java allows importing compiled code. JavaScript has no idea what that even means.

Dealing with these problems has been a tradeoff between what users need, and what we can do given web technologies. The following sections will discuss each of these issues in greater detail.

17.2 Significant Differences

Java programs have their own threads; JavaScript can lock up your browser.

Java programs are isolated entities, running in their own thread in the greater pool of applications on your system. JavaScript programs, on the other hand, live inside a browser, and compete with each other in a way that desktop applications don't. When a Java program loads a file, the program waits until the resource is done loading, and operation resumes as intended. In a setting where the program is an isolated entity on its own, this is fine. The operating system stays responsive because it's responsible for thread scheduling, and even if the program takes an hour to load all its data, you can still use your computer. On a web page, this is not how things work. If you have a JavaScript "program" waiting for a resource to be done loading, it will lock its process until that resource is available. If you're using a browser that uses one process per tab, it will lock up your tab, and the rest of the browser is still usable. If you're using a browser that doesn't, your entire browser will seem frozen. So, regardless of what the process represents, the page the script runs on won't be usable until the resource is done loading, and it's entirely possible that your JavaScript will lock up the entire browser.

This is unacceptable on the modern web, where resources are transferred asynchronously, and the page is expected to function normally while resources are loaded in the background. While this is great for traditional web pages, for web applications this is a real brain twister: how do you make JavaScript idle, waiting for a resource to load, when there is no explicit mechanism to make JavaScript idle? While there is no explicit threading in JavaScript, there is an event model, and there is an XMLHTTPRequest object for requesting arbitrary (not just XML or HTML) data from arbitrary URLS. This object comes with several different status events, and we can use it to asynchronously get data while the browser stays responsive. Which is great in programs in which you control the source code: you make it simply stop after scheduling the data request, and make it pick up execution when the data is available. However, this is near impossible for code that was written based on the idea of synchronous resource loading. Injecting "idling" in programs that are supposed to run at a fixed framerate is not an option, so we have to come up with alternative approaches.

For some things, we decided to force synchronous waiting anyway. Loading a file with strings, for instance, uses a synchronous XMLHTTPRequest, and will halt execution of the page until the data is available. For other things, we had to get creative. Loading images, for instance, uses the browser's built-in mechanism for loading images; we build a new Image in JavaScript, set its src attribute to the image URL, and the browser does the rest, notifying us that the image is ready through the onload event. This doesn't even rely on an XMLHTTPRequest, it simply exploits the browser's capabilities.

To make matters easier when you already know which images you are loading, we added preload directives so that the sketch does not start execution until preloading is complete. A user can indicate any number of images to preload via a comment block at the start of the sketch; Processing.js then tracks outstanding image loading. The onload event for an image tells us that it is done transferring and is considered ready to be rendered (rather than simply having been downloaded but not decoded to a pixel array in memory yet), after which we can populate the corresponding Processing PImage object with the correct values (width, height, pixel data, etc.) and clear the image from the list. Once the list is empty, the sketch gets executed, and images used during its lifetime will not require waiting.

Here is an example of preload directives:

```
/* @pjs preload="./worldmap.jpg"; */

PImage img;

void setup() {
  size(640,480);
  noLoop();
  img = loadImage("worldmap.jpg"); }

void draw() {
  image(img,0,0); }
```

For other things, we've had to build more complicated "wait for me" systems. Fonts, unlike images, do not have built-in browser loading (or at least not a system as functional as image loading). While it is possible to load a font using a CSS @font-face rule and rely on the browser to make it all happen, there are no JavaScript events that can be used to determine that a font finished loading. We are slowly seeing events getting added to browsers to generate JavaScript events for font download completion, but these events come "too early", as the browser may need anywhere from a few to a few hundred more milliseconds to actually parse the font for use on the page after download. Thus, acting on these events will still lead to either no font being applied, or the wrong font being applied if there is a known fallback font. Rather than relying on these events, we embed a tiny TrueType font that only contains the letter "A" with impossibly small metrics, and instruct the browser to load this font via an @font-face rule with a data URI that contains the font's bytecode as a BASE64 string. This font is so small that we can rely on it being immediately available. For any other font load instruction we compare text metrics between the desired font and this tiny font. A hidden <div> is set up with text styled using the desired font, with our tiny font as fallback. As long as the text in that <div> is impossibly small, we know the desired font is not available yet, and we simply poll at set intervals until the text has sensible metrics.

Java is strongly typed; JavaScript is not.

In Java, the number 2 and the number 2.0 are different values, and they will do different things during mathematical operations. For instance, the code i = 1/2 will result in i being 0, because the numbers are treated as integers, whereas i = 1/2.0, i = 1.0/2, and even i = 1./2. will all result in i being 0.5, because the numbers are considered decimal fractions with a non-zero integer part, and a zero fractional part. Even if the intended data type is a floating point number, if the arithmetic uses only integers, the result will be an integer. This lets you write fairly creative math statements in Java, and consequently in Processing, but these will generate potentially wildly different results when ported to Processing.js, as JavaScript only knows "numbers". As far as JavaScript is concerned, 2 and 2.0 are the same number, and this can give rise to very interesting bugs when running a sketch using Processing.js.

This might sound like a big issue, and at first we were convinced it would be, but you can't argue with real world feedback: it turns out this is almost never an issue for people who put their sketches online using Processing.js. Rather than solving this in some cool and creative way, the resolution of this problem was actually remarkably straightforward; we didn't solve it, and as a design choice, we don't intend to ever revisit that decision. Short of adding a symbol table with strong typing so that we can fake types in JavaScript and switch functionality based on type, this incompatibility cannot properly be solved without leaving much harder to find edge case bugs, and so rather than adding bulk to the code and slowdown to execution, we left this quirk in. It is a well-documented quirk, and "good code" won't try to take advantage of Java's implicit number type casting. That said, sometimes you will forget, and the result can be quite interesting.

Java is a class/instance-based object-oriented language, with separate variable and method spaces; JavaScript is not.

JavaScript uses prototype objects, and the inheritance model that comes with it. This means all objects are essentially key/value pairs where each key is a string, and values are either primitives, arrays, objects, or functions. On the inheritance side, prototypes can extend other prototypes, but there is no real concept of "superclass" and "subclass". In order to make "proper" Java-style object-oriented code work, we had to implement classical inheritance for JavaScript in Processing.js, without making it super slow (we think we succeeded in that respect). We also had to come up with a way to prevent variable names and function names from stepping on each other. Because of the key/value nature of JavaScript objects, defining a variable called line, followed by a function like line(x1,y1,x2,y2) will leave you with an object that uses whatever was declared last for a key. JavaScript first sets object.line = "some value" for you, and then sets object.line = function(x1,y1,x2,y2){...}, overriding what you thought your variable line was.

It would have slowed down the library a lot to create separate administration for variables and methods/functions, so again the documentation explains that it's a bad idea to use variables and functions with the same name. If everyone wrote "proper" code, this wouldn't be much of a problem, as you want to name variables and functions based on what they're for, or what they do, but the real world does things differently. Sometimes your code won't work, and it's because we decided that having your code break due to a naming conflict is preferable to your code always working, but always being slow. A second reason for not implementing variable and function separation was that this could break JavaScript code used inside Processing sketches. Closures and the scope chain for JavaScript rely on the key/value nature of objects, so driving a wedge in that by writing our own administration would have also severely impacted performance in terms of Just-In-Time compilation and compression based on functional closures.

Java allows method overloading; JavaScript does not.

One of Java's more powerful features is that you can define a function, let's say add(int,int), and then define another function with the same name, but a different number of arguments, e.g. add(int,int,int), or with different argument types, e.g. add(ComplexNumber,ComplexNumber). Calling add with two or three integer arguments will automatically call the appropriate function, and calling add with floats or Car objects will generate an error. JavaScript, on the other hand, does not support this. In JavaScript, a function is a property, and you can dereference it (in which case JavaScript will give you a value based on type coercion, which in this case returns true when the property points to a function definition, or false when it doesn't), or you can call it as a function using the execution operators (which you will know as parentheses with zero or more arguments between them). If you define a function as add(x,y) and then call it as add(1,2,3,4,5,6), JavaScript is okay with that. It will set x to 1 and y to 2 and simply ignore the rest of the arguments. In order to make overloading work, we rewrite functions with the same name but different argument count to a numbered function, so that function(a,b,c) in the source becomes function$3(a,b,c) in the rewritten code, and function(a,b,c,d) becomes function$4(a,b,c,d), ensuring the correct code paths.

We also mostly solved overloading of functions with the same number but differently typed arguments, as long as the argument types can be seen as *different* by JavaScript. JavaScript can tell the functional type of properties using the typeof operator, which will return either number, string, object or function depending on what a property represents. Declaring var x = 3 followed by x = '6' will cause typeof x to report number after the initial declaration, and string after reassignment. As long as functions with the same argument count differ in argument type, we rename them and switch based on the result of the typeof operation. This does not work when the functions take arguments of type object, so for these functions we have an additional check involving the instanceof operator (which returns the name of the function that was used to create the object) to make function overloading work. In fact, the only place where we cannot successfully transcompile overloaded functions is where the argument count is the same between functions, and the argument types are different numerical types. As JavaScript only has one numerical type, declaring functions such as add(int x, int y), add(float x, float y) and add(double x, double y) will clash. Everything else, however, will work just fine.

Java allows importing compiled code.

Sometimes, plain Processing is not enough, and additional functionality is introduced in the form of a Processing library. These take the form of a `.jarchive` with compiled Java code, and offer things like networking, audio, video, hardware interfacing and other exotic functions not covered by Processing itself.

This is a problem, because compiled Java code is Java byte code. This has given us many headaches: how do we support library imports without writing a Java byte code decompiler? After about a year of discussions, we settled on what may seem the simplest solution. Rather than trying to also cover Processing libraries, we decided to support the import keyword in sketches, and create a Processing.js Library API, so that library developers can write a JavaScript version of their library (where feasible, given the web's nature), so that if they write a package that is used via `import processing.video`, native Processing will pick the `.jarchive`, and Processing.js will instead pick processing.video.js, thus ensuring that things "just work". This functionality is slated for Processing.js 1.4, and library imports is the last major feature that is still missing from Processing.js (we currently support the `import` keyword only in the sense that it is removed from the source code before conversion), and will be the last major step towards parity.

Why Pick JavaScript if It Can't Do Java?

This is not an unreasonable question, and it has multiple answers. The most obvious one is that JavaScript comes with the browser. You don't "install" JavaScript yourself, there's no plugin to download first; it's just there. If you want to port something to the web, you're stuck with JavaScript. Although, given the flexibility of JavaScript, "stuck with" is really not doing justice to how powerful the language is. So, one reason to pick JavaScript is "because it's already there". Pretty much every device that is of interest comes with a JavaScript-capable browser these days. The same cannot be said for Java, which is being offered less and less as a preinstalled technology, if it is available at all.

However, the proper answer is that it's not really true that JavaScript "can't do" the things that Java does; it *can*, it would just be slower. Even though out of the box JavaScript can't do some of the things Java does, it's still a Turing-complete programming language and it can be made to emulate any other programming language, at the cost of speed. We could, technically, write a full Java interpreter, with a `String` heap, separate variable and method models, class/instance object-orientation with rigid class hierarchies, and everything else under the Sun (or, these days, Oracle), but that's not what we're in it for: Processing.js is about offering a Processing-to-the-web conversion, in as little code as is necessary for that. This means that even though we decided not to make it do certain Java things, our library has one huge benefit: it can cope with embedded JavaScript really, really well.

In fact, during a meeting between the Processing.js and Processing people at Bocoup in Boston, in 2010, Ben Fry asked John Resig why he used regular expression replacement and only partial conversion instead of doing a proper parser and compiler. John's response was that it was important to him that people be able to mix Processing syntax (Java) and JavaScript without having to choose between them. That initial choice has been crucial in shaping the philosophy of Processing.js ever since. We've worked hard to keep it true in our code, and we can see a clear payoff when we look at all the "purely web" users of Processing.js, who never used Processing, and will happily mix Processing and JavaScript syntax without a problem.

The following example shows how JavaScript and Processing work together.

```
// JavaScript (would throw an error in native Processing)
var cs = { x: 50,
           y: 0,
           label: "my label",
           rotate: function(theta) {
                    var nx = this.x*cos(theta) - this.y*sin(theta);
                    var ny = this.x*sin(theta) + this.y*cos(theta);
                    this.x = nx; this.y = ny; }};

// Processing
float angle = 0;

void setup() {
  size(200,200);
  strokeWeight(15); }

void draw() {
  translate(width/2,height/2);
  angle += PI/frameRate;
  while(angle>2*PI) { angle-=2*PI; }
  jQuery('#log').text(angle); // JavaScript (error in native Processing)
  cs.rotate(angle);           // legal JavaScript as well as Processing
  stroke(random(255));
  point(cs.x, cs.y); }
```

A lot of things in Java are promises: strong typing is a content promise to the compiler, visibility is a promise on who will call methods and reference variables, interfaces are promises that instances contain the methods the interface describes, etc. Break those promises and the compiler complains. But, if you don't—and this is a one of the most important thoughts for Processing.js—then you don't need the additional code for those promises in order for a program to work. If you stick a number in a variable, and your code treats that variable as if it has a number in it, then at the end of the day var varname is just as good as int varname. Do you need typing? In Java, you do; in JavaScript, you don't, so why force it in? The same goes for other code promises. If the Processing compiler doesn't complain about your code, then we can strip all the explicit syntax for your promises and it'll still work the same.

This has made Processing.js a ridiculously useful library for data visualisation, media presentation and even entertainment. Sketches in native Processing work, but sketches that mix Java and JavaScript also work just fine, as do sketches that use pure JavaScript by treating Processing.js as a glorified canvas drawing framework. In an effort to reach parity with native Processing, without forcing Java-only syntax, the project has been taken in by an audience as wide as the web itself. We've seen activity all over the web using Processing.js. Everyone from IBM to Google has built visualisations, presentations and even games with Processing.js—Processing.js is making a difference.

Another great thing about converting Java syntax to JavaScript while leaving JavaScript untouched is that we've enabled something we hadn't even thought about ourselves: Processing.js will work with anything that will work with JavaScript. One of the really interesting things that we're now seeing, for instance, is that people are using CoffeeScript (a wonderfully simple, Ruby-like programming language that transcompiles to JavaScript) in combination with Processing.js, with really cool results. Even though we set out to build "Processing for the web" based on parsing Processing syntax, people took what we did and used it with brand new syntaxes. They could never have done that if we had made Processing.js simply be a Java interpreter. By sticking with code conversion rather than writing a code interpreter, Processing.js has given Processing a reach on the web far beyond what it would have had if it had stayed Java-only, or even if it had kept a Java-only syntax, with execution on the web taken care of by JavaScript. The uptake of our code not just by end users, but also by people who try to integrate it with their own technologies, has been both amazing and inspiring. Clearly we're doing something right, and the web seems happy with what we're doing.

The Result

As we are coming up to Processing.js 1.4.0, our work has resulted in a library that will run any sketch you give it, provided it does not rely on compiled Java library imports. If you can write it in Processing, and it runs, you can put it on a webpage and it will just run. Due to the differences in hardware access and low level implementations of different parts of the rendering pipeline there will be timing differences, but in general a sketch that runs at 60 frames per seconds in the Processing IDE will run at 60 frames per second on a modern computer, with a modern browser. We have reached a point where bug reports have started to die down, and most work is no longer about adding feature support, but more about bug fixing and code optimization.

Thanks to the efforts of many developers working to resolve over 1800 bug reports, Processing sketches run using Processing.js "just work". Even sketches that rely on library imports can be made to work, provided that the library code is at hand. Under favourable circumstances, the library is written in a way that lets you rewrite it to pure Processing code with a few search-replace operations. In this case the code can be made to work online virtually immediately. When the library does things that cannot be implemented in pure Processing, but can be implemented using plain JavaScript, more work is required to effectively emulate the library using JavaScript code, but porting is still possible. The only instances of Processing code that cannot be ported are those that rely on functionality that is inherently unavailable to browsers, such as interfacing directly with hardware devices (such as webcams or Arduino boards) or performing unattended disk writes, though even this is changing. Browsers are constantly adding functionality to allow for more elaborate applications, and limiting factors today may disappear a year from now, so that hopefully in the not too distant future, even sketches that are currently impossible to run online will become portable.

17.3 The Code Components

Processing.js is presented and developed as a large, single file, but architecturally it represents three different components: 1) the launcher, responsible for converting Processing source to Processing.js flavoured JavaScript and executing it, 2) static functionality that can be used by all sketches, and 3) sketch functionality that has to be tied to individual instances.

The Launcher

The launcher component takes care of three things: code preprocessing, code conversion, and sketch execution.

Preprocessing

In the preprocessing step, Processing.js directives are split off from the code, and acted upon. These directives come in two flavours: settings and load instructions. There is a small number of directives, keeping with the "it should just work" philosophy, and the only settings that sketch authors can change are related to page interaction. By default a sketch will keep running if the page is not in focus, but the pauseOnBlur = true directive sets up a sketch in such a way that it will halt execution when the page the sketch is running on is not in focus, resuming execution when the page is in focus again. Also by default, keyboard input is only routed to a sketch when it is focussed. This is especially important when people run multiple sketches on the same page, as keyboard input intended for one sketch should not be processed by another. However, this functionality can be disabled, routing keyboard events to every sketch that is running on a page, using the globalKeyEvents = true directive.

Load instructions take the form of the aforementioned image preloading and font preloading. Because images and fonts can be used by multiple sketches, they are loaded and tracked globally, so that different sketches don't attempt multiple loads for the same resource.

Code Conversion

The code conversion component decomposes the source code into AST nodes, such as statements and expressions, methods, variables, classes, etc. This AST then expanded to JavaScript source code that builds a sketch-equivalent program when executed. This converted source code makes heavy use of the Processing.js instance framework for setting up class relations, where classes in the Processing source code become JavaScript prototypes with special functions for determining superclasses and bindings for superclass functions and variables.

Sketch Execution

The final step in the launch process is sketch execution, which consists of determining whether or not all preloading has finished, and if it has, adding the sketch to the list of running instances and triggering its JavaScript onLoad event so that any sketch listeners can take the appropriate action. After this the Processing chain is run through: setup, then draw, and if the sketch is a looping sketch, setting up an interval call to draw with an interval length that gets closest to the desired framerate for the sketch.

Static Library

Much of Processing.js falls under the "static library" heading, representing constants, universal functions, and universal data types. A lot of these actually do double duty, being defined as global properties, but also getting aliased by instances for quicker code paths. Global constants such as key codes and color mappings are housed in the Processing object itself, set up once, and then referenced when instances are built via the Processing constructor. The same applies to self-contained helper functions, which lets us keep the code as close to "write once, run anywhere" as we can without sacrificing performance.

Processing.js has to support a large number of complex data types, not just in order to support the data types used in Processing, but also for its internal workings. These, too, are defined in the Processing constructor:

Char, an internal object used to overcome some of the behavioural quirks of Java's char datatype.
PShape, which represents shape objects.

`PShapeSVG`, an extension for `PShape` objects, which is built from and represents SVG XML.

> For `PShapeSVG`, we implemented our own SVG-to-`<canvas>`-instructions code. Since Processing does not implement full SVG support, the code we saved by not relying on an external SVG library means that we can account for every line of code relating to SVG imports. It only parses what it has to, and doesn't waste space with code that follows the spec, but is unused because native Processing does not support it.

`XMLElement`, an XML document object.

> For `XMLElement`, too, we implemented our own code, relying on the browser to first load the XML element into a Node-based structure, then traveling the node structure to build a leaner object. Again, this means we don't have any dead code sitting in Processing.js, taking up space and potentially causing bugs because a patch accidentally makes use of a function that shouldn't be there.

`PMatrix2D` and `PMatrix3D`, which perform matrix operations in 2D and 3D mode.

`PImage`, which represents an image resource.

> This is effectively a wrapper of the Image object, with some additional functions and properties so that its API matches the Processing API.

`PFont`, which represents a font resource.

> There is no Font object defined for JavaScript (at least for now), so rather than actually storing the font as an object, our `PFont` implementation loads a font via the browser, computes its metrics based on how the browser renders text with it, and then caches the resultant `PFont` object. For speed, `PFont`s have a reference to the canvas that was used to determine the font properties, in case `textWidth` must be calculated, but because we track `PFont` objects based on name/size pair, if a sketch uses a lot of distinct text sizes, or fonts in general, this will consume too much memory. As such, `PFont`s will clear their cached canvas and instead call a generic `textWidth` computation function when the cache grows too large. As a secondary memory preservation strategy, if the font cache continues to grow after clearing the cached canvas for each `PFont`, font caching is disabled entirely, and font changes in the sketch simply build new throwaway `PFont` objects for every change in font name, text size or text leading.

`DrawingShared`, `Drawing2D`, and `Drawing3D`, which house all the graphics functions.

> The `DrawingShared` object is actually the biggest speed trap in Processing.js. It determines if a sketch is launching in 2D or 3D mode, and then rebinds all graphics functions to either the `Drawing2D` or `Drawing3D` object. This ensures short code path for graphics instructions, as 2D Processing sketches cannot used 3D functions, and vice versa. By only binding one of the two sets of graphics functions, we gain speed from not having to switch on the graphics mode in every function to determine the code path, and we save space by not binding the graphics functions that are guaranteed not to be used.

`ArrayList`, a container that emulates Java's `ArrayList`.

`HashMap`, a container that emulates Java's `HashMap`.

> `ArrayList`, and `HashMap` in particular, are special data structures because of how Java implements them. These containers rely on the Java concepts of equality and hashing, and all objects in Java have an `equals` and a `hashCode` method that allow them to be stored in lists and maps.
>
> For non-hashing containers, objects are resolved based on equality rather than identity. Thus, `list.remove(myobject)` iterates through the list looking for an element for which `element.equals(myobject)`, rather than `element == myobject`, is true. Because all objects must have an `equals` method, we implemented a "virtual equals" function on the JavaScript

side of things. This function takes two objects as arguments, checks whether either of them implements their own `equals` function, and if so, falls through to that function. If they don't, and the passed objects are primitives, primitive equality is checked. If they're not, then there is no equality.

For hashing containers, things are even more interesting, as hashing containers act as shortcut trees. The container actually wraps a variable number of lists, each tied to a specific hash code. Objects are found based on first finding the container that matches their hash code, in which the object is then searched for based on equality evaluation. As all objects in Java have a `hashCode` method, we also wrote a "virtual hashcode" function, which takes a single object as an argument. The function checks whether the object implements its own `hashCode` function, and if so falls through to that function. If it doesn't, the hash code is computed based on the same hashing algorithm that is used in Java.

Administration

The final piece of functionality in the static code library is the instance list of all sketches that are currently running on the page. This instance list stores sketches based on the canvas they have been loaded in, so that users can call `Processing.getInstanceById('canvasid')` and get a reference to their sketch for page interaction purposes.

Instance Code

Instance code takes the form of `p.functor = function(arg, ...)` definitions for the Processing API, and `p.constant = ...` for sketch state variables (where p is our reference to the sketch being set up). Neither of these are located in dedicated code blocks. Rather, the code is organized based on function, so that instance code relating to PShape operations is defined near the PShape object, and instance code for graphics functions are defined near, or in, the Drawing2D and Drawing3D objects.

In order to keep things fast, a lot of code that could be written as static code with an instance wrapper is actually implemented as purely instance code. For instance, the `lerpColor(c1, c2, ratio)` function, which determines the color corresponding to the linear interpolation of two colors, is defined as an instance function. Rather than having `p.lerpColor(c1, c2, ratio)` acting as a wrapper for some static function `Processing.lerpColor(c1, c2, ratio)`, the fact that nothing else in Processing.js relies on `lerpColor` means that code execution is faster if we write it as a pure instance function. While this does "bloat" the instance object, most functions for which we insist on an instance function rather than a wrapper to the static library are small. Thus, at the expense of memory we create really fast code paths. While the full Processing object will take up a one-time memory slice worth around 5 MB when initially set up, the prerequisite code for individual sketches only takes up about 500 KB.

17.4 Developing Processing.js

Processing.js is worked on intensively, which we can only do because our development approach sticks to a few basic rules. As these rules influence the architecture of Processing.js, it's worth having a brief look at them before closing this chapter.

Make It Work

Writing code that works sounds like a tautological premise; you write code, and by the time you're done your code either works, because that's what you set out to do, or it doesn't, and you're not done yet. However, "make it work" comes with a corollary: Make it work, and when you're done, prove it.

If there is one thing above all other things that has allowed Processing.js to grow at the pace it has, it is the presence of tests. Any ticket that requires touching the code, be it either by writing new code or rewriting old code, cannot be marked as resolved until there is a unit or reference test that allows others to verify not only that the code works the way it should, but also that it breaks when it should. For most code, this typically involves a unit test—a short bit of code that calls a function and simply tests whether the function returns the correct values, for both legal and illegal function calls. Not only does this allow us to test code contributions, it also lets us perform regression tests.

Before any code is accepted and merged into our stable development branch, the modified Processing.js library is validated against an ever-growing battery of unit tests. Big fixes and performance tests in particular are prone to passing their own unit tests, but breaking parts that worked fine before the rewrite. Having tests for every function in the API, as well as internal functions, means that as Processing.js grows, we don't accidentally break compatibility with previous versions. Barring destructive API changes, if none of the tests failed before a code contribution or modification, none of the tests are allowed to fail with the new code in.

The following is an example of a unit test verifying inline object creation.

```
interface I {
  int getX();
  void test(); }

I i = new I() {
  int x = 5;
  public int getX() {
    return x; }
  public void test() {
    x++; }};

i.test();

_checkEqual(i.getX(), 6);
_checkEqual(i instanceof I, true);
_checkEqual(i instanceof Object, true);
```

In addition to regular code unit tests, we also have visual reference (or "ref") tests. As Processing.js is a port of a visual programming language, some tests cannot be performed using just unit tests. Testing to see whether an ellipse gets drawn on the correct pixels, or whether a single-pixel-wide vertical line is drawn crisp or smoothed cannot be determined without a visual reference. Because all mainstream browsers implement the <canvas> element and Canvas2D API with subtle differences, these things can only be tested by running code in a browser and verifying that the resulting sketch looks the same as what native Processing generates. To make life easier for developers, we use an automated test suite for this, where new test cases are run through Processing, generating "what it should look like" data to be used for pixel comparison. This data is then stored as a comment inside the sketch that generated it, forming a test, and these tests are then run by Processing.js on a visual reference test page which executes each test and performs pixel comparisons between "what it should look like" and "what it looks like". If the pixels are off, the test fails, and the developer is presented with three images: what it should look like, how Processing.js rendered it, and the difference between the two, marking problem areas as red pixels, and correct areas as white. Much like unit tests, these tests must pass before any code contribution can be accepted.

Make It Fast

In an open source project, making things work is only the first step in the life of a function. Once things work, you want to make sure things work fast. Based on the "if you can't measure it, you can't improve it" principle, most functions in Processing.js don't just come with unit or ref tests, but also with performance (or "perf") tests. Small bits of code that simply call a function, without testing the correctness of the function, are run several hundred times in a row, and their run time is recorded on a special performance test web page. This lets us quantify how well (or not!) Processing.js performs in browsers that support HTML5's `<canvas>` element. Every time an optimization patch passes unit and ref testing, it is run through our performance test page. JavaScript is a curious beast, and beautiful code can, in fact, run several orders of magnitude slower than code that contains the same lines several times over, with inline code rather than function calls. This makes performance testing crucial. We have been able to speed up certain parts of the library by three orders of magnitude simply by discovering hot loops during perf testing, reducing the number of function calls by inlining code, and by making functions return the moment they know what their return value should be, rather than having only a single return at the very end of the function.

Another way in which we try to make Processing.js fast is by looking at what runs it. As Processing.js is highly dependent on the efficiency of JavaScript engines, it makes sense to also look at which features various engines offer to speed things up. Especially now that browsers are starting to support hardware accelerated graphics, instant speed boosts are possible when engines offer new and more efficient data types and functions to perform the low level operations that Processing.js depends on. For instance, JavaScript technically has no static typing, but graphics hardware programming environments do. By exposing the data structures used to talk to the hardware directly to JavaScript, it is possible to significantly speed up sections of code if we know that they will only use specific values.

Make It Small

There are two ways to make code small. First, write compact code. If you're manipulating a variable multiple times, compact it to a single manipulation (if possible). If you access an object variable multiple times, cache it. If you call a function multiple times, cache the result. Return once you have all the information you need, and generally apply all the tricks a code optimiser would apply yourself. JavaScript is a particularly nice language for this, since it comes with an incredible amount of flexibility. For example, rather than using:

```
if ((result = functionresult)!==null) {
  var = result;
} else {
  var = default;
}
```

in JavaScript this becomes:

```
var = functionresult || default
```

There is also another form of small code, and that's in terms of runtime code. Because JavaScript lets you change function bindings on the fly, running code becomes much smaller if you can say "bind the function for line2D to the function call for `line`" once you know that a program runs in 2D rather than 3D mode, so that you don't have to perform:

```
if(mode==2D) { line2D() } else { line3D() }
```

for every function call that might be either in 2D or 3D mode.

Finally, there is the process of minification. There are a number of good systems that let you compress your JavaScript code by renaming variables, stripping whitespace, and applying certain code optimisations that are hard to do by hand while still keeping the code readable. Examples of these are the YUI minifier and Google's closure compiler. We use these technologies in Processing.js to offer end users bandwidth convenience—minification after stripping comments can shrink the library by as much as 50%, and taking advantage of modern browser/server interaction for gzipped content, we can offer the entire Processing.js library in gzipped form in 65 KB.

If All Else Fails, Tell People

Not everything that can currently be done in Processing can be done in the browser. Security models prevent certain things like saving files to the hard disk and performing USB or serial port I/O, and a lack of typing in JavaScript can have unexpected consequences (such as all math being floating point math). Sometimes we're faced with the choice between adding an incredible amount of code to enable an edge case, or mark the ticket as a "wontfix" issue. In such cases, a new ticket gets filed, typically titled "Add documentation that explains why...".

In order to make sure these things aren't lost, we have documentation for people who start using Processing.js with a Processing background, and for people who start using Processing.js with a JavaScript background, covering the differences between what is expected, and what actually happens. Certain things just deserve special mention, because no matter how much work we put into Processing.js, there are certain things we cannot add without sacrificing usability. A good architecture doesn't just cover the way things are, it also covers why; without that, you'll just end up having the same discussions about what the code looks like and whether it should be different every time the team changes.

17.5   Lessons Learned

The most important lesson we learned while writing Processing.js is that when porting a language, what matters is that the result is correct, not whether or not the code used in your port is similar to the original. Even though Java and JavaScript syntax are fairly similar, and modifying Java code to legal JavaScript code is fairly easy, it often pays to look at what JavaScript can natively do and exploit that to get the same functional result. Taking advantage of the lack of typing by recycling variables, using certain built-in functions that are fast in JavaScript but slow in Java, or avoiding patterns that are fast in Java but slow in JavaScript means your code may look radically different, but has the exact same effect. You often hear people say not to reinvent the wheel, but that only applies to working with a single programming language. When you're porting, reinvent as many wheels as you need to obtain the performance you require.

Another important lesson is to return early, return often, and branch as little as possible. An if/then statement followed by a return can be made (sometimes drastically) faster by using an if-return/return construction instead, using the return statement as a conditional shortcut. While it's conceptually pretty to aggregate your entire function state before calling the ultimate return statement for that function, it also means your code path may traverse code that is entirely unrelated to what you will be returning. Don't waste cycles; return when you have all the information you need.

A third lesson concerns testing your code. In Processing.js we had the benefit of starting with very good documentation outlining how Processing was "supposed" to work, and a large set of test cases, most of which started out as "known fail". This allowed us to do two things: 1) write code against tests, and 2) create tests before writing code. The usual process, in which code is written and then test cases are written for that code, actually creates biased tests. Rather than testing whether or not your code does what it should do, according to the specification, you are only testing whether your code is bug-free. In Processing.js, we instead start by creating test cases based on what the functional requirements for some function or set of functions is, based on the documentation for it. With these unbiased tests, we can then write code that is functionally complete, rather than simply bug-free but possibly deficient.

The last lesson is also the most general one: apply the rules of agile development to individual fixes as well. No one benefits from you retreating into dev mode and not being heard from for three days straight while you write the perfect solution. Rather, get your solutions to the point where they work, and not even necessarily for all test cases, then ask for feedback. Working alone, with a test suite for catching errors, is no guarantee of good or complete code. No amount of automated testing is going to point out that you forgot to write tests for certain edge cases, or that there is a better algorithm than the one you picked, or that you could have reordered your statements to make the code better suited for JIT compilation. Treat fixes like releases: present fixes early, update often, and work feedback into your improvements.

[chapter 18]

Puppet
Luke Kanies

18.1 Introduction

Puppet is an open source IT management tool written in Ruby, used for datacenter automation and server management at Google, Twitter, the New York Stock Exchange, and many others. It is primarily maintained by Puppet Labs, which also founded the project. Puppet can manage as few as 2 machines and as many as 50,000, on teams with one system administrator or hundreds.

Puppet is a tool for configuring and maintaining your computers; in its simple configuration language, you explain to Puppet how you want your machines configured, and it changes them as needed to match your specification. As you change that specification over time—such as with package updates, new users, or configuration updates—Puppet will automatically update your machines to match. If they are already configured as desired, then Puppet does nothing.

In general, Puppet does everything it can to use existing system features to do its work; e.g., on Red Hat it will use yum for packages and init.d for services, but on OS X it will use dmg for packages and launchd for services. One of the guiding goals in Puppet is to have the work it does make sense whether you are looking at Puppet code or the system itself, so following system standards is critical.

Puppet comes from multiple traditions of other tools. In the open source world, it is most influenced by CFEngine, which was the first open source general-purpose configuration tool, and ISconf, whose use of make for all work inspired the focus on explicit dependencies throughout the system. In the commercial world, Puppet is a response to BladeLogic and Opsware (both since acquired by larger companies), each of which was successful in the market when Puppet was begun, but each of which was focused on selling to executives at large companies rather than building great tools directly for system administrators. Puppet is meant to solve similar problems to these tools, but it is focused on a very different user.

For a simple example of how to use Puppet, here is a snippet of code that will make sure the secure shell service (SSH) is installed and configured properly:

```
class ssh {
    package { ssh: ensure => installed }
    file { "/etc/ssh/sshd_config":
        source => 'puppet:///modules/ssh/sshd_config',
        ensure => present,
        require => Package[ssh]
    }
    service { sshd:
```

```
        ensure => running,
        require => [File["/etc/ssh/sshd_config"], Package[ssh]]
    }
}
```

This makes sure the package is installed, the file is in place, and the service is running. Note that we've specified dependencies between the resources, so that we always perform any work in the right order. This class could then be associated with any host to apply this configuration to it. Notice that the building blocks of a Puppet configuration are structured objects, in this case package, file, and service. We call these objects *resources* in Puppet, and everything in a Puppet configuration comes down to these resources and the dependencies between them.

A normal Puppet site will have tens or even hundreds of these code snippets, which we call *classes*; we store these classes on disk in files called manifests, and collect them in related groups called *modules*. For instance, you might have an ssh module with this ssh class plus any other related classes, along with modules for mysql, apache, and sudo.

Most Puppet interactions are via the command line or long-running HTTP services, but there are graphical interfaces for some things such as report processing. Puppet Labs also produces commercial products around Puppet, which tend more toward graphical web-based interfaces.

Puppet's first prototype was written in the summer of 2004, and it was turned into a full-time focus in February of 2005. It was initially designed and written by Luke Kanies, a sysadmin who had a lot of experience writing small tools, but none writing tools greater than 10,000 lines of code. In essence, Luke learned to be a programmer while writing Puppet, and that shows in its architecture in both positive and negative ways.

Puppet was first and foremost built to be a tool for sysadmins, to make their lives easier and allow them to work faster, more efficiently, and with fewer errors. The first key innovation meant to deliver on this was the resources mentioned above, which are Puppet's primitives; they would both be portable across most operating systems and also abstract away implementation detail, allowing the user to focus on outcomes rather than how to achieve them. This set of primitives was implemented in Puppet's Resource Abstraction Layer.

Puppet resources must be unique on a given host. You can only have one package named "ssh", one service named "sshd", and one file named "/etc/ssh/sshd_config". This prevents different parts of your configurations from conflicting with each other, and you find out about those conflicts very early in the configuration process. We refer to these resources by their type and title; e.g., Package[ssh] and Service[sshd]. You can have a package and a service with the same name because they are different types, but not two packages or services with the same name.

The second key innovation in Puppet provides the ability to directly specify dependencies between resources. Previous tools focused on the individual work to be done, rather than how the various bits of work were related; Puppet was the first tool to explicitly say that dependencies are a first-class part of your configurations and must be modeled that way. It builds a graph of resources and their dependencies as one of the core data types, and essentially everything in Puppet hangs off of this graph (called a Catalog) and its vertices and edges.

The last major component in Puppet is its configuration language. This language is declarative, and is meant to be more configuration data than full programming—it most resembles Nagios's configuration format, but is also heavily influenced by CFEngine and Ruby.

Beyond the functional components, Puppet has had two guiding principles throughout its development: it should be as simple as possible, always preferring usability even at the expense of capability; and it should be built as a framework first and application second, so that others could build their own applications on Puppet's internals as desired. It was understood that Puppet's framework needed a killer application to be adopted widely, but the framework was always the focus, not the application. Most people think of Puppet as being that application, rather than the framework behind it.

When Puppet's prototype was first built, Luke was essentially a decent Perl programmer with a lot of shell experience and some C experience, mostly working in CFEngine. The odd thing is he had experience building parsers for simple languages, having built two as part of smaller tools and also having rewritten CFEngine's parser from scratch in an effort to make it more maintainable (this code was never submitted to the project, because of small incompatibilities).

A dynamic language was easily decided on for Puppet's implementation, based on much higher developer productivity and time to market, but choosing the language proved difficult. Initial prototypes in Perl went nowhere, so other languages were sought for experimentation. Python was tried, but Luke found the language quite at odds with how he thought about the world. Based on what amounted to a rumor of utility heard from a friend, Luke tried Ruby, and in four hours had built a usable prototype. When Puppet became a full-time effort in 2005 Ruby was a complete unknown, so the decision to stick with it was a big risk, but again programmer productivity was deemed the primary driver in language choice. The major distinguishing feature in Ruby, at least as opposed to Perl, was how easy it was to build non-hierarchical class relationships, but it also mapped very well to Luke's brain, which turned out to be critical.

18.2 Architectural Overview

This chapter is primarily about the architecture of Puppet's implementation (that is, the code that we've used to make Puppet do the things it's supposed to do) but it's worth briefly discussing its application architecture (that is, how the parts communicate), so that the implementation makes some sense.

Puppet has been built with two modes in mind: A client/server mode with a central server and agents running on separate hosts, or a serverless mode where a single process does all of the work. To ensure consistency between these modes, Puppet has always had network transparency internally, so that the two modes used the same code paths whether they went over the network or not. Each executable can configure local or remote service access as appropriate, but otherwise they behave identically. Note also that you can use the serverless mode in what amounts to a client/server configuration, by pulling all configuration files to each client and having it parse them directly. This section will focus on the client/server mode, because it's more easily understood as separate components, but keep in mind that this is all true of the serverless mode, too.

One of the defining choices in Puppet's application architecture is that clients should not get access to raw Puppet modules; instead, they get a configuration compiled just for them. This provides multiple benefits: First, you follow the principle of least privilege, in that each host only knows exactly what it needs to know (how it should be configured), but it does not know how any other servers are configured. Second, you can completely separate the rights needed to compile a configuration (which might include access to central data stores) from the need to apply that configuration. Third, you can run hosts in a disconnected mode where they repeatedly apply a configuration with no contact to a central server, which means you remain in compliance even if the server is down or the client is disconnected (such as would be the case in a mobile installation, or when the clients are in a DMZ).

Given this choice, the workflow becomes relatively straightforward:

1. The Puppet agent process collects information about the host it is running on, which it passes to the server.

2. The parser uses that system information and Puppet modules on local disk to compile a configuration for that particular host and returns it to the agent.
3. The agent applies that configuration locally, thus affecting the local state of the host, and files the resulting report with the server.

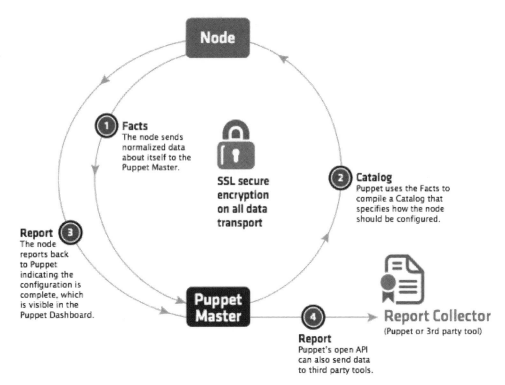

Figure 18.1: Puppet dataflow

Thus, the agent has access to its own system information, its configuration, and each report it generates. The server has copies of all of this data, plus access to all of the Puppet modules, and any back-end databases and services that might be needed to compile the configuration.

Beyond the components that go into this workflow, which we'll address next, there are many data types that Puppet uses for internal communication. These data types are critical, because they're how all communication is done and they're public types which any other tools can consume or produce.

The most important data types are:

Facts: System data collected on each machine and used to compile configurations.
Manifest: Files containing Puppet code, generally organized into collections called "modules".
Catalog: A graph of a given host's resources to be managed and the dependencies between them.
Report: The collection of all events generated during application of a given Catalog.

Beyond Facts, Manifests, Catalogs, and Reports, Puppet supports data types for files, certificates (which it uses for authentication), and others.

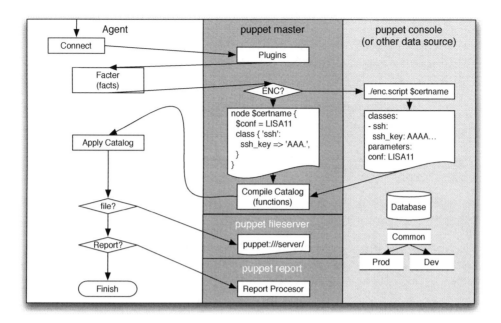

Figure 18.2: Orchestration of data flow between Puppet processes and components

18.3 Component Analysis

Agent

The first component encountered in a Puppet run is the agent process. This was traditionally a separate executable called puppetd, but in version 2.6 we reduced down to one executable so now it is invoked with puppet agent, akin to how Git works. The agent has little functionality of its own; it is primarily configuration and code that implements the client-side aspects of the above-described workflow.

Facter

The next component after the agent is an external tool called Facter, which is a very simple tool used to discover information about the host it is running on. This is data like the operating system, IP address, and host name, but Facter is easily extensible so many organizations add their own plugins to discover custom data. The agent sends the data discovered by Facter to the server, at which point it takes over the workflow.

External Node Classifier

On the server, the first component encountered is what we call the External Node Classifier, or ENC. The ENC accepts the host name and returns a simple data structure containing the high-level configuration for that host. The ENC is generally a separate service or application: either another open source project, such as Puppet Dashboard or Foreman, or integration with existing data stores, such as LDAP. The purpose of the ENC is to specify what functional classes a given host belongs to, and what parameters should be used to configure those classes. For example, a given host might be in the `debian` and `webserver` classes, and have the parameter `datacenter` set to `atlanta`.

Note that as of Puppet 2.7, the ENC is not a required component; users can instead directly specify node configurations in Puppet code. Support for an ENC was added about 2 years after Puppet was launched because we realized that classifying hosts is fundamentally different than configuring them, and it made more sense to split these problems into separate tools than to extend the language to support both facilities. The ENC is always recommended, and at some point soon will become a required component (at which point Puppet will ship with a sufficiently useful one that that requirement will not be a burden).

Once the server receives classification information from the ENC and system information from Facter (via the agent), it bundles all of the information into a Node object and passes it on to the Compiler.

Compiler

As mentioned above, Puppet has a custom language built for specifying system configurations. Its compiler is really three chunks: A Yacc-style parser generator and a custom lexer; a group of classes used to create our Abstract Syntax Tree (AST); and the Compiler class that handles the interactions of all of these classes and also functions as the API to this part of the system.

The most complicated thing about the compiler is the fact that most Puppet configuration code is lazily loaded on first reference (to reduce both load times and irrelevant logging about missing-but-unneeded dependencies), which means there aren't really explicit calls to load and parse the code.

Puppet's parser uses a normal Yacc[1]-style parser generator (built using the open source Racc[2] tool). Unfortunately, there were no open source lexer generators when Puppet was begun, so it uses a custom lexer.

Because we use an AST in Puppet, every statement in the Puppet grammar evaluates to an instance of a Puppet AST class (e.g., `Puppet::Parser::AST::Statement`), rather than taking action directly, and these AST instances are collected into a tree as the grammar tree is reduced. This AST provides a performance benefit when a single server is compiling configurations for many different nodes, because we can parse once but compile many times. It also gives us the opportunity to perform some introspection of the AST, which provides us information and capability we wouldn't have if parsing operated directly.

Very few approachable AST examples were available when Puppet was begun, so there has been a lot of evolution in it, and we've arrived at what seems a relatively unique formulation. Rather than creating a single AST for the entire configuration, we create many small ASTs, keyed off their name. For instance, this code:

```
class ssh {
    package { ssh: ensure => present }
}
```

creates a new AST containing a single `Puppet::Parser::AST::Resource` instance, and stores that AST by the name "ssh" in the hash of all classes for this particular environment. (I've left out details about other constructs akin to classes, but they are unnecessary for this discussion.)

---

[1] http://dinosaur.compilertools.net/
[2] https://github.com/tenderlove/racc

Given the AST and a Node object (from the ENC), the compiler takes the classes specified in the node object (if there are any), looks them up and evaluates them. In the course of this evaluation, the compiler is building up a tree of variable scopes; every class gets its own scope which is attached to the creating scope. This amounts to dynamic scoping in Puppet: if one class includes another class, then the included class can look up variables directly in the including class. This has always been a nightmare, and we have been on the path to getting rid of this capability.

The Scope tree is temporary and is discarded once compiling is done, but the artifact of compiling is also built up gradually over the course of the compilation. We call this artifact a Catalog, but it is just a graph of resources and their relationships. Nothing of the variables, control structures, or function calls survive into the catalog; it's plain data, and can be trivially converted to JSON, YAML, or just about anything else.

During compilation, we create containment relationships; a class "contains" all of the resources that come with that class (e.g., the ssh package above is contained by the ssh class). A class might contain a definition, which itself contains either yet more definitions, or individual resources. A catalog tends to be a very horizontal, disconnected graph: many classes, each no more than a couple of levels deep.

One of the awkward aspects of this graph is that it also contains "dependency" relationships, such as a service requiring a package (maybe because the package installation actually creates the service), but these dependency relationships are actually specified as parameter values on the resources, rather than as edges in the structure of the graph. Our graph class (called SimpleGraph, for historical reasons) does not support having both containment and dependency edges in the same graph, so we have to convert between them for various purposes.

Transaction

Once the catalog is entirely constructed (assuming there is no failure), it is passed on to the Transaction. In a system with a separate client and server, the Transaction runs on the client, which pulls the Catalog down via HTTP as in Figure 18.2.

Puppet's transaction class provides the framework for actually affecting the system, whereas everything else we've discussed just builds up and passes around objects. Unlike transactions in more common systems such as databases, Puppet transactions do not have behaviors like atomicity.

The transaction performs a relatively straightforward task: walk the graph in the order specified by the various relationships, and make sure each resource is in sync. As mentioned above, it has to convert the graph from containment edges (e.g., Class[ssh] contains Package[ssh] and Service[sshd]) to dependency edges (e.g., Service[sshd] depends on Package[ssh]), and then it does a standard topological sort of the graph, selecting each resource in turn.

For a given resource, we perform a simple three-step process: retrieve the current state of that resource, compare it to the desired state, and make any changes necessary to fix discrepancies. For instance, given this code:

```
file { "/etc/motd":
    ensure => file,
    content => "Welcome to the machine",
    mode => 644
}
```

the transaction checks the content and mode of /etc/motd, and if they don't match the specified state, it will fix either or both of them. If /etc/motd is somehow a directory, then it will back up all of the files in that directory, remove it, and replace it with a file that has the appropriate content and mode.

This process of making changes is actually handled by a simple ResourceHarness class that defines the entire interface between Transaction and Resource. This reduces the number of connections between the classes, and makes it easier to make changes to either independently.

Resource Abstraction Layer

The Transaction class is the heart of getting work done with Puppet, but all of the work is actually done by the Resource Abstraction Layer (RAL), which also happens to be the most interesting component in Puppet, architecturally speaking.

The RAL was the first component created in Puppet and, other than the language, it most clearly defines what the user can do. The job of the RAL is to define what it means to be a resource and how resources can get work done on the system, and Puppet's language is specifically built to specify resources as modeled by the RAL. Because of this, it's also the most important component in the system, and the hardest to change. There are plenty of things we would like to fix in the RAL, and we've made a lot of critical improvements to it over the years (the most crucial being the addition of Providers), but there is still a lot of work to do to the RAL in the long term.

In the Compiler subsystem, we model resources and resource types with separate classes (named, conveniently, Puppet::Resource and Puppet::Resource::Type). Our goal is to have these classes also form the heart of the RAL, but for now these two behaviors (resource and type) are modeled within a single class, Puppet::Type. (The class is named poorly because it significantly predates our use of the term Resource, and at the time we were directly serializing memory structures when communicating between hosts, so it was actually quite complicated to change class names.)

When Puppet::Type was first created, it seemed reasonable to put resource and resource type behaviors in the same class; after all, resources are just instances of resource types. Over time, however, it became clear that the relationship between a resource and its resource type aren't modeled well in a traditional inheritance structure. Resource types define what parameters a resource can have, but not whether it accepts parameters (they all do), for instance. Thus, our base class of Puppet::Type has class-level behaviors that determine how resource types behave, and instance-level behaviors that determine how resource instances behave. It additionally has the responsibility of managing registration and retrieval of resource types; if you want the "user" type, you call Puppet::Type.type(:user).

This mix of behaviors makes Puppet::Type quite difficult to maintain. The whole class is less than 2,000 lines of code, but working at three levels—resource, resource type, and resource type manager—makes it convoluted. This is obviously why it's a major target for being refactored, but it's more plumbing than user-facing, so it's always been hard to justify effort here rather than directly in features.

Beyond Puppet::Type, there are two major kinds of classes in the RAL, the most interesting of which are what we call Providers. When the RAL was first developed, each resource type mixed the definition of a parameter with code that knew how to manage it. For instance, we would define the "content" parameter, and then provide a method that could read the content of a file, and another method that could change the content:

```
Puppet::Type.newtype(:file) do
    ...
    newproperty(:content) do
        def retrieve
            File.read(@resource[:name])
        end
```

```
        def sync
            File.open(@resource[:name], "w") { |f| f.print @resource[:content] }
        end
    end
end
```

This example is simplified considerably (e.g., we use checksums internally, rather than the full content strings), but you get the idea.

This became impossible to manage as we needed to support multiple varieties of a given resource type. Puppet now supports more than 30 kinds of package management, and it would have been impossible to support all of those within a single Package resource type. Instead, we provide a clean interface between the definition of the resource type—essentially, what the name of the resource type is and what properties it supports—from how you manage that type of resource. Providers define getter and setter methods for all of a resource type's properties, named in obvious ways. For example, this is how a provider of the above property would look:

```
Puppet::Type.newtype(:file) do
    newproperty(:content)
end
Puppet::Type.type(:file).provide(:posix) do
    def content
        File.read(@resource[:name])
    end
    def content=(str)
        File.open(@resource[:name], "w") { |f| f.print(str) }
    end
end
```

This is a touch more code in the simplest cases, but is much easier to understand and maintain, especially as either the number of properties or number of providers increases.

I said at the beginning of this section that the Transaction doesn't actually affect the system directly, and it instead relies on the RAL for that. Now it's clear that it's the providers that do the actual work. In fact, in general the providers are the only part of Puppet that actually touch the system. The transaction asks for a file's content, and the provider collects it; the transaction specifies that a file's content should be changed, and the provider changes it. Note, however, that the provider never decides to affect the system—the Transaction owns the decisions, and the provider does the work. This gives the Transaction complete control without requiring that it understand anything about files, users, or packages, and this separation is what enables Puppet to have a full simulation mode where we can largely guarantee the system won't be affected.

The second major class type in the RAL is responsible for the parameters themselves. We actually support three kinds of parameters: metaparameters, which affect all resource types (e.g., whether you should run in simulation mode); parameters, which are values that aren't reflected on disk (e.g., whether you should follow links in files); and properties, which model aspects of the resource that you can change on disk (e.g., a file's content, or whether a service is running). The difference between properties and parameters is especially confusing to people, but if you just think of properties as having getter and setter methods in the providers, it's relatively straightforward.

Reporting

As the transaction walks the graph and uses the RAL to change the system's configuration, it progressively builds a report. This report largely consists of the events generated by changes to the system. These events, in turn, are comprehensive reflections of what work was done: they retain a timestamp the resource changed, the previous value, the new value, any message generated, and whether the change succeeded or failed (or was in simulation mode).

The events are wrapped in a ResourceStatus object that maps to each resource. Thus, for a given Transaction, you know all of the resources that are run, and you know any changes that happen, along with all of the metadata you might need about those changes.

Once the transaction is complete, some basic metrics are calculated and stored in the report, and then it is sent off to the server (if configured). With the report sent, the configuration process is complete, and the agent goes back to sleep or the process just ends.

18.4 Infrastructure

Now that we have a thorough understanding of what Puppet does and how, it's worth spending a little time on the pieces that don't show up as capabilities but are still critical to getting the job done.

Plugins

One of the great things about Puppet is that it is very extensible. There are at least 12 different kinds of extensibility in Puppet, and most of these are meant to be usable by just about anyone. For example, you can create custom plugins for these areas:

- resource types and custom providers
- report handlers, such as for storing reports in a custom database
- Indirector plugins for interacting with existing data stores
- facts for discovering extra information about your hosts

However, Puppet's distributed nature means that agents need a way to retrieve and load new plugins. Thus, at the start of every Puppet run, the first thing we do is download all plugins that the server has available. These might include new resource types or providers, new facts, or even new report processors.

This makes it possible to heavily upgrade Puppet agents without ever changing the core Puppet packages. This is especially useful for highly customized Puppet installations.

Indirector

You've probably detected by now that we have a tradition of bad class names in Puppet, and according to most people, this one takes the cake. The Indirector is a relatively standard Inversion of Control framework with significant extensibility. Inversion of Control systems allow you to separate development of functionality from how you control which functionality you use. In Puppet's case, this allows us to have many plugins that provide very different functionality, such as reaching the compiler via HTTP or loading it in-process, and switch between them with a small configuration change rather than a code change. In other words, Puppet's Indirector is basically an implementation of a service locator, as described on the Wikipedia page for "Inversion of Control". All of the hand-offs from one class to another go through the Indirector, via a standard REST-like interface (e.g., we support find, search, save, and destroy as methods), and switching Puppet from serverless to client/server is largely a question of configuring the agent to use an HTTP endpoint for retrieving catalogs, rather than using a compiler endpoint.

Because it is an Inversion of Control framework where configuration is stringently separated from the code paths, this class can also be difficult to understand, especially when you're debugging why a given code path was used.

Networking

Puppet's prototype was written in the summer of 2004, when the big networking question was whether to use XMLRPC or SOAP. We chose XMLRPC, and it worked fine but had most of the problems everyone else had: it didn't encourage standard interfaces between components, and it tended to get overcomplicated very quickly as a result. We also had significant memory problems, because the encoding needed for XMLRPC resulted in every object appearing at least twice in memory, which quickly gets expensive for large files.

For our 0.25 release (begun in 2008), we began the process of switching all networking to a REST-like model, but we chose a much more complicated route than just changing out the networking. We developed the Indirector as the standard framework for inter-component communication, and built REST endpoints as just one option. It took two releases to fully support REST, and we have not quite finished converting to using JSON (instead of YAML) for all serialization. We undertook switching to JSON for two major reasons: first, YAML processing Ruby is painfully slow, and pure Ruby processing of JSON is a lot faster; second, most of the web seems to be moving to JSON, and it tends to be implemented more portably than YAML. Certainly in the case of Puppet, the first use of YAML was not portable across languages, and was often not portable across different versions of Puppet, because it was essentially serialization of internal Ruby objects.

Our next major release of Puppet will finally remove all of the XMLRPC support.

18.5 Lessons Learned

In terms of implementation, we're proudest of the various kinds of separation that exist in Puppet: the language is completely separate from the RAL, the Transaction cannot directly touch the system, and the RAL can't decide to do work on its own. This gives the application developer a lot of control over application workflow, along with a lot of access to information about what is happening and why.

Puppet's extensibility and configurability are also major assets, because anyone can build on top of Puppet quite easily without having to hack the core. We've always built our own capabilities on the same interfaces we recommend our users use.

Puppet's simplicity and ease of use have always been its major draw. It's still too difficult to get running, but it's miles easier than any of the other tools on the market. This simplicity comes with a lot of engineering costs, especially in the form of maintenance and extra design work, but it's worth it to allow users to focus on their problems instead of the tool.

Puppet's configurability is a real feature, but we took it a bit too far. There are too many ways you can wire Puppet together, and it's too easy to build a workflow on top of Puppet that will make you miserable. One of our major near-term goals is to dramatically reduce the knobs you can turn in a Puppet configuration, so the user cannot so easily configure it poorly, and so we can more easily upgrade it over time without worrying about obscure edge cases.

We also just generally changed too slowly. There are major refactors we've been wanting to do for years but have never quite tackled. This has meant a more stable system for our users in the short term, but also a more difficult-to-maintain system, and one that's much harder to contribute to.

Lastly, it took us too long to realize that our goals of simplicity were best expressed in the language of design. Once we began speaking about design rather than just simplicity, we acquired a much better framework for making decisions about adding or removing features, with a better means of communicating the reasoning behind those decisions.

18.6 Conclusion

Puppet is both a simple system and a complex one. It has many moving parts, but they're wired together quite loosely, and each of them has changed pretty dramatically since its founding in 2005. It is a framework that can be used for all manner of configuration problems, but as an application it is simple and approachable.

Our future success rests on that framework becoming more solid and more simple, and that application staying approachable while it gains capability.

[chapter 19]

PyPy
Benjamin Peterson

PyPy is a Python implementation and a dynamic language implementation framework.
   This chapter assumes familiarity with some basic interpreter and compiler concepts like bytecode and constant folding.

19.1   A Little History

Python is a high-level, dynamic programming language. It was invented by the Dutch programmer Guido van Rossum in the late 1980s. Guido's original implementation is a traditional bytecode interpreter written in C, and consequently known as CPython. There are now many other Python implementations. Among the most notable are Jython, which is written in Java and allows for interfacing with Java code, IronPython, which is written in C# and interfaces with Microsoft's .NET framework, and PyPy, the subject of this chapter. CPython is still the most widely used implementation and currently the only one to support Python 3, the next generation of the Python language. This chapter will explain the design decisions in PyPy that make it different from other Python implementations and indeed from any other dynamic language implementation.

19.2   Overview of PyPy

PyPy, except for a negligible number of C stubs, is written completely in Python. The PyPy source tree contains two major components: the Python interpreter and the RPython translation toolchain. The Python interpreter is the programmer-facing runtime that people using PyPy as a Python implementation invoke. It is actually written in a subset of Python called Restricted Python (usually abbreviated RPython). The purpose of writing the Python interpreter in RPython is so the interpreter can be fed to the second major part of PyPy, the RPython translation toolchain. The RPython translator takes RPython code and converts it to a chosen lower-level language, most commonly C. This allows PyPy to be a self-hosting implementation, meaning it is written in the language it implements. As we shall see throughout this chapter, the RPython translator also makes PyPy a general dynamic language implementation framework.
   PyPy's powerful abstractions make it the most flexible Python implementation. It has nearly 200 configuration options, which vary from selecting different garbage collector implementations to altering parameters of various translation optimizations.

19.3 The Python Interpreter

Since RPython is a strict subset of Python, the PyPy Python interpreter can be run on top of another Python implementation untranslated. This is, of course, extremely slow but it makes it possible to quickly test changes in the interpreter. It also enables normal Python debugging tools to be used to debug the interpreter. Most of PyPy's interpreter tests can be run both on the untranslated interpreter and the translated interpreter. This allows quick testing during development as well as assurance that the translated interpreter behaves the same as the untranslated one.

For the most part, the details of the PyPy Python interpreter are quite similiar to that of CPython; PyPy and CPython use nearly identical bytecode and data structures during interpretation. The primary difference between the two is PyPy has a clever abstraction called *object spaces* (or objspaces for short). An objspace encapsulates all the knowledge needed to represent and manipulate Python data types. For example, performing a binary operation on two Python objects or fetching an attribute of an object is handled completely by the objspace. This frees the interpreter from having to know anything about the implementation details of Python objects. The bytecode interpreter treats Python objects as black boxes and calls objspace methods whenever it needs to manipulate them. For example, here is a rough implementation of the BINARY_ADD opcode, which is called when two objects are combined with the + operator. Notice how the operands are not inspected by the interpreter; all handling is delegated immediately to the objspace.

```
def BINARY_ADD(space, frame):
    object1 = frame.pop() # pop left operand off stack
    object2 = frame.pop() # pop right operand off stack
    result = space.add(object1, object2) # perform operation
    frame.push(result) # record result on stack
```

The objspace abstraction has numerous advantages. It allows new data type implementations to be swapped in and out without modifying the interpreter. Also, since the sole way to manipulate objects is through the objspace, the objspace can intercept, proxy, or record operations on objects. Using the powerful abstraction of objspaces, PyPy has experimented with *thunking*, where results can be lazily but completely transparently computed on demand, and *tainting*, where any operation on an object will raise an exception (useful for passing sensitive data through untrusted code). The most important application of objspaces, however, will be discussed in Section 19.4.

The objspace used in a vanilla PyPy interpreter is called the *standard objspace* (std objspace for short). In addition to the abstraction provided by the objspace system, the standard objspace provides another level of indirection; a single data type may have multiple implementations. Operations on data types are then dispatched using multimethods. This allows picking the most efficient representation for a given piece of data. For example, the Python long type (ostensibly a bigint data type) can be represented as a standard machine-word-sized integer when it is small enough. The memory and computationally more expensive arbitrary-precision long implementation need only be used when necessary. There's even an implementation of Python integers available using tagged pointers. Container types can also be specialized to certain data types. For example, PyPy has a dictionary (Python's hash table data type) implementation specialized for string keys. The fact that the same data type can be represented by different implementations is completely transparent to application-level code; a dictionary specialized to strings is identical to a generic dictionary and will degenerate gracefully if non-string keys are put into it.

PyPy distinguishes between interpreter-level (interp-level) and application-level (app-level) code. Interp-level code, which most of the interpreter is written in, must be in RPython and is translated.

It directly works with the objspace and wrapped Python objects. App-level code is always run by the PyPy bytecode interpreter. As simple as interp-level RPython code is, compared to C or Java, PyPy developers have found it easiest to use pure app-level code for some parts of the interpreter. Consequently, PyPy has support for embedding app-level code in the interpreter. For example, the functionality of the Python `print` statement, which writes objects to standard output, is implemented in app-level Python. Builtin modules can also be written partially in interp-level code and partially in app-level code.

19.4 The RPython Translator

The RPython translator is a toolchain of several lowering phases that rewrite RPython to a target language, typically C. The higher-level phases of translation are shown in Figure 19.1. The translator is itself written in (unrestricted) Python and intimately linked to the PyPy Python interpreter for reasons that will be illuminated shortly.

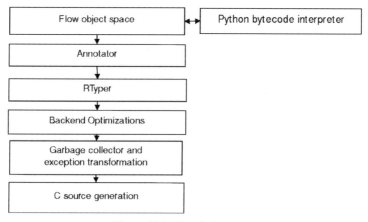

Figure 19.1: Translation steps

The first thing the translator does is load the RPython program into its process. (This is done with the normal Python module loading support.) RPython imposes a set of restrictions on normal, dynamic Python. For example, functions cannot be created at runtime, and a single variable cannot have the possibility of holding incompatible types, such as an integer and a object instance. When the program is initially loaded by the translator, though, it is running on a normal Python interpreter and can use all of Python's dynamic features. PyPy's Python interpreter, a huge RPython program, makes heavy use of this feature for metaprogramming. For example, it generates code for standard objspace multimethod dispatch. The only requirement is that the program is valid RPython by the time the translator starts the next phase of translation.

The translator builds flow graphs of the RPython program through a process called *abstract interpretation*. Abstract interpretation reuses the PyPy Python interpreter to interpret RPython programs with a special objspace called the *flow objspace*. Recall that the Python interpreter treats objects in a program like black boxes, calling out to the objspace to perform any operation. The flow objspace, instead of the standard set of Python objects, has only two objects: variables and constants. Variables represent values not known during translation, and constants, not surprisingly, represent immutable values that are known. The flow objspace has a basic facility for constant folding; if it is asked to do an operation where all the arguments are constants, it will statically evaluate it. What is immutable and must be constant in RPython is broader than in standard Python. For example, modules, which are emphatically mutable in Python, are constants in the flow objspace because they don't exist in RPython and must be constant-folded out by the flow objspace. As the Python interpreter interprets the bytecode of RPython functions, the flow objspace records the operations it is asked to perform. It takes care to record all branches of conditional control flow constructs. The end result of abstract interpretation for a function is a flow-graph consisting of linked blocks, where each block has one or more operations.

An example of the flow-graph generating process is in order. Consider a simple factorial function:

```
def factorial(n):
    if n == 1:
        return 1
    return n * factorial(n - 1)
```

The flow-graph for the function looks like Figure 19.2.

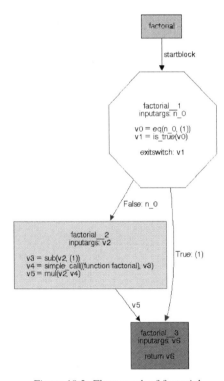

Figure 19.2: Flow-graph of factorial

The factorial function has been divided into blocks containing the operations the flowspace recorded. Each block has input arguments and a list of operations on the variables and constants. The first block has an exit switch at the end, which determines which block control-flow will pass to after the first block is run. The exit switch can be based on the value of some variable or whether an exception occurred in the last operation of the block. Control-flow follows the lines between the blocks.

The flow-graph generated in the flow objspace is in static single assignment form, or SSA, an intermediate representation commonly used in compilers. The key feature of SSA is that every variable is only assigned once. This property simplifies the implementation of many compiler transformations and optimizations.

After a function graph is generated, the annotation phase begins. The annotator assigns a type to the results and arguments of each operation. For example, the factorial function above will be annotated to accept and return an integer.

The next phase is called RTyping. RTyping uses type information from the annotator to expand each high-level flow-graph operation into low-level ones. It is the first part of translation where the target backend matters. The backend chooses a type system for the RTyper to specialize the program to. The RTyper currently has two type systems: A low-level typesystem for backends like C and one for higher-level typesystems with classes. High-level Python operations and types are transformed into the level of the type system. For example, an add operation with operands annotated as integers will generate a int_add operation with the low-level type system. More complicated operations like hash table lookups generate function calls.

After RTyping, some optimizations on the low-level flow-graph are performed. They are mostly of the traditional compiler variety like constant folding, store sinking, and dead code removal.

Python code typically has frequent dynamic memory allocations. RPython, being a Python derivative, inherits this allocation intensive pattern. In many cases, though, allocations are temporary and local to a function. *Malloc removal* is an optimization that addresses these cases. Malloc removal removes these allocations by "flattening" the previously dynamically allocated object into component scalars when possible.

To see how malloc removals works, consider the following function that computes the Euclidean distance between two points on the plane in a roundabout fashion:

```
def distance(x1, y1, x2, y2):
    p1 = (x1, y1)
    p2 = (x2, y2)
    return math.hypot(p1[0] - p2[0], p1[1] - p2[1])
```

When initially RTyped, the body of the function has the following operations:

```
v60 = malloc((GcStruct tuple2))
v61 = setfield(v60, ('item0'), x1_1)
v62 = setfield(v60, ('item1'), y1_1)
v63 = malloc((GcStruct tuple2))
v64 = setfield(v63, ('item0'), x2_1)
v65 = setfield(v63, ('item1'), y2_1)
v66 = getfield(v60, ('item0'))
v67 = getfield(v63, ('item0'))
v68 = int_sub(v66, v67)
v69 = getfield(v60, ('item1'))
v70 = getfield(v63, ('item1'))
v71 = int_sub(v69, v70)
v72 = cast_int_to_float(v68)
v73 = cast_int_to_float(v71)
v74 = direct_call(math_hypot, v72, v73)
```

This code is suboptimal in several ways. Two tuples that never escape the function are allocated. Additionally, there is unnecessary indirection accessing the tuple fields.

Running malloc removal produces the following concise code:

```
v53 = int_sub(x1_0, x2_0)
v56 = int_sub(y1_0, y2_0)
v57 = cast_int_to_float(v53)
v58 = cast_int_to_float(v56)
v59 = direct_call(math_hypot, v57, v58)
```

The tuple allocations have been completely removed and the indirections flattened out. Later, we will see how a technique similar to malloc removal is used on application-level Python in the PyPy JIT (Section 19.5).

PyPy also does function inlining. As in lower-level languages, inlining improves performance in RPython. Somewhat surprisingly, it also reduces the size of the final binary. This is because it allows more constant folding and malloc removal to take place, which reduces overall code size.

The program, now in optimized, low-level flow-graphs, is passed to the backend to generate sources. Before it can generate C code, the C backend must perform some additional transformations. One of these is exception transformation, where exception handling is rewritten to use manual stack unwinding. Another is the insertion of stack depth checks. These raise an exception at runtime if the recursion is too deep. Places where stack depth checks are needed are found by computing cycles in the call graph of the program.

Another one of the transformations performed by the C backend is adding garbage collection (GC). RPython, like Python, is a garbage-collected language, but C is not, so a garbage collector has to be added. To do this, a garbage collection transformer converts the flow-graphs of the program into a garbage-collected program. PyPy's GC transformers provide an excellent demonstration of how translation abstracts away mundane details. In CPython, which uses reference counting, the C code of the interpreter must carefully keep track of references to Python objects it is manipulating. This not only hardcodes the garbage collection scheme in the entire codebase but is prone to subtle human errors. PyPy's GC transformer solves both problems; it allows different garbage collection schemes to be swapped in and out seamlessly. It is trivial to evaluate a garbage collector implementation (of which PyPy has many), simply by tweaking a configuration option at translation. Modulo transformer bugs, the GC transformer also never makes reference mistakes or forgets to inform the GC when an object is no longer in use. The power of the GC abstraction allows GC implementations that would be practically impossible to hardcode in an interpreter. For example, several of PyPy's GC implementations require a *write barrier*. A write barrier is a check which must be performed every time a GC-managed object is placed in another GC-managed array or structure. The process of inserting write barriers would be laborious and fraught with mistakes if done manually, but is trivial when done automatically by the GC transformer.

The C backend can finally emit C source code. The generated C code, being generated from low-level flow-graphs, is an ugly mess of gotos and obscurely named variables. An advantage of writing C is that the C compiler can do most of the complicated static transformation work required to make a final binary-like loop optimizations and register allocation.

19.5 The PyPy JIT

Python, like most dynamic languages, has traditionally traded efficiency for flexibility. The architecture of PyPy, being especially rich in flexibility and abstraction, makes very fast interpretation difficult. The powerful objspace and multimethod abstractions in the std objspace do not come without a cost. Consequently, the vanilla PyPy interpreter performs up to 4 times slower than CPython. To remedy not only this but Python's reputation as a sluggish language, PyPy has a just-in-time compiler (commonly written JIT). The JIT compiles frequently used codepaths into assembly during the runtime of the program.

The PyPy JIT takes advantage of PyPy's unique translation architecture described in Section 19.4. PyPy actually has no *Python-specific* JIT; it has a JIT generator. JIT generation is implemented as simply another optional pass during translation. A interpreter desiring JIT generation need only make two special function calls called *jit hints*.

PyPy's JIT is a *tracing JIT*. This means it detects "hot" (meaning frequently run) loops to optimize by compiling to assembly. When the JIT has decided it is going to compile a loop, it records operations in one iteration of the loop, a process called *tracing*. These operations are subsequently compiled to machine code.

As mentioned above, the JIT generator requires only two hints in the interpreter to generate a JIT: `merge_point` and `can_enter_jit`. `can_enter_jit` tells the JIT where in the interpreter a loop starts. In the Python interpreter, this is the end of the `JUMP_ABSOLUTE` bytecode. (`JUMP_ABSOLUTE` makes the interpreter jump to the head of the app-level loop.) `merge_point` tells the JIT where it is safe to return to the interpreter from the JIT. This is the beginning of the bytecode dispatch loop in the Python interpreter.

The JIT generator is invoked after the RTyping phase of translation. Recall that at this point, the program's flow-graphs consist of low-level operations nearly ready for target code generation. The JIT generator locates the hints mentioned above in the interpreter and replaces them with calls to invoke the JIT during runtime. The JIT generator then writes a serialized representation of the flow-graphs of every function that the interpreter wants jitted. These serialized flow-graphs are called jitcodes. The entire interpreter is now described in terms of low-level RPython operations. The jitcodes are saved in the final binary for use at runtime.

At runtime, the JIT maintains a counter for every loop that is executed in the program. When a loop's counter exceeds a configurable threshold, the JIT is invoked and tracing begins. The key object in tracing is the *meta-interpreter*. The meta-interpreter executes the jitcodes created in translation. It is thus interpreting the main interpreter, hence the name. As it traces the loop, it creates a list of the operations it is executing and records them in JIT intermediate representation (IR), another operation format. This list is called the *trace* of the loop. When the meta-interpreter encounters a call to a jitted function (one for which jitcode exists), the meta-interpreter enters it and records its operations to original trace. Thus, the tracing has the effect of flattening out the call stack; the only calls in the trace are to interpreter functions that are outside the knowledge of jit.

The meta-interpreter is forced to specialize the trace to properties of the loop iteration it is tracing. For example, when the meta-interpreter encounters a conditional in the jitcode, it naturally must choose one path based on the state of the program. When it makes a choice based on runtime information, the meta-interpreter records an IR operation called a *guard*. In the case of a conditional, this will be a `guard_true` or `guard_false` operation on the condition variable. Most arithmetic operations also have guards, which ensure the operation did not overflow. Essentially, guards codify assumptions the meta-interpreter is making as it traces. When assembly is generated, the guards will protect assembly from being run in a context it is not specialized for. Tracing ends when the meta-interpreter reaches the same `can_enter_jit` operation with which it started tracing. The loop IR can now be passed to the optimizer.

The JIT optimizer features a few classical compiler optimizations and many optimizations specialized for dynamic languages. Among the most important of the latter are *virtuals* and *virtualizables*.

Virtuals are objects which are known not to escape the trace, meaning they are not passed as arguments to external, non-jitted function calls. Structures and constant length arrays can be virtuals. Virtuals do not have to be allocated, and their data can be stored directly in registers and on the stack. (This is much like the static malloc removal phase described in the section about translation backend optimizations.) The virtuals optimization strips away the indirection and memory allocation inefficiencies in the Python interpreter. For example, by becoming virtual, boxed Python integer objects are unboxed into simple word-sized integers and can be stored directly in machine registers.

A virtualizable acts much like a virtual but may escape the trace (that is, be passed to non-jitted functions). In the Python interpreter the frame object, which holds variable values and the instruction pointer, is marked virtualizable. This allows stack manipulations and other operations on the frame to be optimized out. Although virtuals and virtualizables are similar, they share nothing in implementation. Virtualizables are handled during tracing by the meta-interpreter. This is unlike virtuals, which are handled during trace optimization. The reason for this is virtualizables require special treatment, since they may escape the trace. Specifically, the meta-interpreter has to ensure that non-jitted functions that may use the virtualizable don't actually try to fetch its fields. This is because in jitted code, the fields of virtualizable are stored in the stack and registers, so the actual virtualizable may be out of date with respect to its current values in the jitted code. During JIT generation, code which accesses a virtualizable is rewritten to check if jitted assembly is running. If it is, the JIT is asked to update the fields from data in assembly. Additionally when the external call returns to jitted code, execution bails back to the interpreter.

After optimization, the trace is ready to be assembled. Since the JIT IR is already quite low-level, assembly generation is not too difficult. Most IR operations correspond to only a few x86 assembly operations. The register allocator is a simple linear algorithm. At the moment, the increased time that would be spent in the backend with a more sophisticated register allocation algorithm in exchange for generating slightly better code has not been justified. The trickiest portions of assembly generation are garbage collector integration and guard recovery. The GC has to be made aware of stack roots in the generated JIT code. This is accomplished by special support in the GC for dynamic root maps.

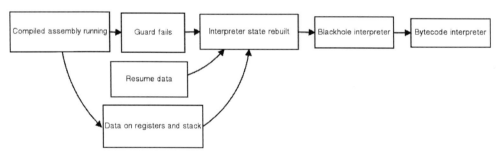

Figure 19.3: Bailing back to the interpreter on guard failure

When a guard fails, the compiled assembly is no longer valid and control must return to the bytecode interpreter. This bailing out is one of the most difficult parts of JIT implementation, since the interpreter state has to be reconstructed from the register and stack state at the point the guard failed. For each guard, the assembler writes a compact description of where all the values needed to reconstruct the interpreter state are. At guard failure, execution jumps to a function which decodes this description and passes the recovery values to a higher level be reconstructed. The failing guard may be in the middle of the execution of a complicated opcode, so the interpreter can not just start with the next opcode. To solve this, PyPy uses a *blackhole interpreter*. The blackhole interpreter executes jitcodes starting from the point of guard failure until the next merge point is reached. There, the real interpreter can resume. The blackhole interpreter is so named because unlike the meta-interpreter, it doesn't record any of the operations it executes. The process of guard failure is depicted in Figure 19.3.

As described up to this point, the JIT would be essentially useless on any loop with a frequently changing condition, because a guard failure would prevent assembly from running very many iterations. Every guard has a failure counter. After the failure count has passed a certain threshold, the JIT starts tracing from the point of guard failure instead of bailing back to the interpreter. This new sub-trace is called a *bridge*. When the tracing reaches the end of the loop, the bridge is optimized and compiled and the original loop is patched at the guard to jump to the new bridge instead of the failure code. This way, loops with dynamic conditions can be jitted.

How successful have the techniques used in the PyPy JIT proven? At the time of this writing, PyPy is a geometric average of five times faster than CPython on a comprehensive suite of benchmarks. With the JIT, app-level Python has the possibility of being faster than interp-level code. PyPy developers have recently had the excellent problem of having to write interp-level loops in app-level Python for performance.

Most importantly, the fact that the JIT is not specific to Python means it can be applied to any interpreter written within the PyPy framework. This need not necessarily be a language interpreter. For example, the JIT is used for Python's regular expression engine. NumPy is a powerful array module for Python used in numerical computing and scientific research. PyPy has an experimental reimplementation of NumPy. It harnesses the power of the PyPy JIT to speed up operations on arrays. While the NumPy implementation is still in its early stages, initial performance results look promising.

19.6 Design Drawbacks

While it beats C any day, writing in RPython can be a frustrating experience. Its implicit typing is difficult to get used to at first. Not all Python language features are supported and others are arbitrarily restricted. RPython is not specified formally anywhere and what the translator accepts can vary from day to day as RPython is adapted to PyPy's needs. The author of this chapter often manages to create programs that churn in the translator for half an hour, only to fail with an obscure error.

The fact that the RPython translator is a whole-program analyzer creates some practical problems. The smallest change anywhere in translated code requires retranslating the entire interpreter. That currently takes about 40 minutes on a fast, modern system. The delay is especially annoying for testing how changes affect the JIT, since measuring performance requires a translated interpreter. The requirement that the whole program be present at translation means modules containing RPython cannot be built and loaded separately from the core interpreter.

The levels of abstraction in PyPy are not always as clear cut as in theory. While technically the JIT generator should be able to produce an excellent JIT for a language given only the two hints mentioned above, the reality is that it behaves better on some code than others. The Python interpreter has seen a lot of work towards making it more "jit-friendly", including many more JIT hints and even new data structures optimized for the JIT.

The many layers of PyPy can make tracking down bugs a laborious process. A Python interpreter bug could be directly in the interpreter source or buried somewhere in the semantics of RPython and the translation toolchain. Especially when a bug cannot be reproduced on the untranslated interpreter, debugging is difficult. It typically involves running GDB on the nearly unreadable generated C sources.

Translating even a restricted subset of Python to a much lower-level language like C is not an easy task. The lowering passes described in Section 19.4 are not really independent. Functions are being annotated and rtyped throughout translation, and the annotator has some knowledge of low-level types. The RPython translator is thus a tangled web of cross-dependencies. The translator could do with cleaning up in several places, but doing it is neither easy nor much fun.

19.7   A Note on Process

In part to combat its own complexity (see Section 19.6), PyPy has adopted several so-called "agile" development methodologies. By far the most important of these is test-driven development. All new features and bug fixes are required to have tests to verify their correctness. The PyPy Python interpreter is also run against CPython's regression test suite. PyPy's test driver, py.test, was spun off and is now used in many other projects. PyPy also has a continuous integration system that runs the test suite and translates the interpreter on a variety of platforms. Binaries for all platforms are produced daily and the benchmark suite is run. All these tests ensure that the various components are behaving, no matter what change is made in the complicated architecture.

There is a strong culture of experimentation in the PyPy project. Developers are encouraged to make branches in the Mercurial repository. There, ideas in development can be refined without destabilizing the main branch. Branches are not always successful, and some are abandoned. If anything though, PyPy developers are tenacious. Most famously, the current PyPy JIT is the *fifth* attempt to add a JIT to PyPy!

```
LOAD_FAST
    guard(i6 == 2)
    guard_nonnull_class(p9, ConstClass(W_IntObject), descr=<Guard25>)
    guard(i4 == 0)
LOAD_CONST
    guard(p3 == ConstPtr(ptr15))
COMPARE_OP
    i16 = ((pypy.objspace.std.intobject.W_IntObject)p9).inst_intval [pure]
    i18 = i16 < 10000
    guard(i18 is true)
POP_JUMP_IF_FALSE
LOAD_FAST
LOAD_CONST
BINARY_MODULO
    i20 = i16 == -9223372036854775808
    guard(i20 is false)
    i22 = int_mod(i16, 2)
    i24 = int_rshift(i22, 63)
    i25 = 2 & i24
    i26 = i22 + i25
POP_JUMP_IF_FALSE
    i27 = int_is_true(i26)
    guard(i27 is false)
LOAD_FAST
    guard_nonnull_class(p8, ConstClass(W_IntObject), descr=<Guard31>)
LOAD_CONST
INPLACE_ADD
    i30 = ((pypy.objspace.std.intobject.W_IntObject)p8).inst_intval [pure]
    i32 = int_add_ovf(i30, 1)
    guard_no_overflow(descr=<Guard32>)
STORE_FAST
LOAD_FAST
```

Figure 19.4: The jitviewer showing Python bytecode and associated JIT IR operations

The PyPy project also prides itself on its visualization tools. The flow-graph charts in Section 19.4 are one example. PyPy also has tools to show invocation of the garbage collector over time and view the parse trees of regular expressions. Of special interest is jitviewer, a program that allows one to visually peel back the layers of a jitted function, from Python bytecode to JIT IR to assembly. (The jitviewer is shown in Figure 19.4.) Visualization tools help developers understand how PyPy's many layers interact with each other.

19.8 Summary

The Python interpreter treats Python objects as black boxes and leaves all behavior to be defined by the objspace. Individual objspaces can provide special extended behavior to Python objects. The objspace approach also enables the abstract interpretation technique used in translation.

The RPython translator allows details like garbage collection and exception handling to be abstracted from the language interpreter. It also opens up the possibly of running PyPy on many different runtime platforms by using different backends.

One of the most important uses of the translation architecture is the JIT generator. The generality of the JIT generator allows JITs for new languages and sub-languages like regular expressions to be added. PyPy is the fastest Python implementation today because of its JIT generator.

While most of PyPy's development effort has gone into the Python interpreter, PyPy can be used for the implementation of any dynamic language. Over the years, partial interpreters for JavaScript, Prolog, Scheme, and IO have been written with PyPy.

19.9 Lessons Learned

Finally, some of lessons to take away from the PyPy project:

Repeated refactoring is often a necessary process. For example, it was originally envisioned that the C backend for the translator would be able to work off the high-level flow graphs! It took several iterations for the current multi-phase translation process to be born.

The most important lesson of PyPy is the power of abstraction. In PyPy, abstractions separate implementation concerns. For example, RPython's automatic garbage collection allows a developer working the interpreter to not worry about memory management. At the same time, abstractions have a mental cost. Working on the translation chain involves juggling the various phases of translation at once in one's head. What layer a bug resides in can also be clouded by abstractions; abstraction leakage, where swapping low-level components that should be interchangeable breaks higher-level code, is perennial problem. It is important that tests are used to verify that all parts of the system are working, so a change in one system does not break a different one. More concretely, abstractions can slow a program down by creating too much indirection.

The flexibility of (R)Python as an implementation language makes experimenting with new Python language features (or even new languages) easy. Because of its unique architecture, PyPy will play a large role in the future of Python and dynamic language implementation.

[chapter 20]

SQLAlchemy
Michael Bayer

SQLAlchemy is a database toolkit and object-relational mapping (ORM) system for the Python programming language, first introduced in 2005. From the beginning, it has sought to provide an end-to-end system for working with relational databases in Python, using the Python Database API (DBAPI) for database interactivity. Even in its earliest releases, SQLAlchemy's capabilities attracted a lot of attention. Key features include a great deal of fluency in dealing with complex SQL queries and object mappings, as well as an implementation of the "unit of work" pattern, which provides for a highly automated system of persisting data to a database.

Starting from a small, roughly implemented concept, SQLAlchemy quickly progressed through a series of transformations and reworkings, turning over new iterations of its internal architectures as well as its public API as the userbase continued to grow. By the time version 0.5 was introduced in January of 2009, SQLAlchemy had begun to assume a stable form that was already proving itself in a wide variety of production deployments. Throughout 0.6 (April, 2010) and 0.7 (May, 2011), architectural and API enhancements continued the process of producing the most efficient and stable library possible. As of this writing, SQLAlchemy is used by a large number of organizations in a variety of fields, and is considered by many to be the de facto standard for working with relational databases in Python.

20.1 The Challenge of Database Abstraction

The term "database abstraction" is often assumed to mean a system of database communication which conceals the majority of details of how data is stored and queried. The term is sometimes taken to the extreme, in that such a system should not only conceal the specifics of the relational database in use, but also the details of the relational structures themselves and even whether or not the underlying storage is relational.

The most common critiques of ORMs center on the assumption that this is the primary purpose of such a tool—to "hide" the usage of a relational database, taking over the task of constructing an interaction with the database and reducing it to an implementation detail. Central to this approach of concealment is that the ability to design and query relational structures is taken away from the developer and instead handled by an opaque library.

Those who work heavily with relational databases know that this approach is entirely impractical. Relational structures and SQL queries are vastly functional, and comprise the core of an application's design. How these structures should be designed, organized, and manipulated in queries varies not just on what data is desired, but also on the structure of information. If this utility is concealed, there's little point in using a relational database in the first place.

The issue of reconciling applications that seek concealment of an underlying relational database with the fact that relational databases require great specificity is often referred to as the "object-relational impedance mismatch" problem. SQLAlchemy takes a somewhat novel approach to this problem.

SQLAlchemy's Approach to Database Abstraction

SQLAlchemy takes the position that the developer must be willing to consider the relational form of his or her data. A system which pre-determines and conceals schema and query design decisions marginalizes the usefulness of using a relational database, leading to all of the classic problems of impedance mismatch.

At the same time, the implementation of these decisions can and should be executed through high-level patterns as much as possible. Relating an object model to a schema and persisting it via SQL queries is a highly repetitive task. Allowing tools to automate these tasks allows the development of an application that's more succinct, capable, and efficient, and can be created in a fraction of the time it would take to develop these operations manually.

To this end, SQLAlchemy refers to itself as a *toolkit*, to emphasize the role of the developer as the designer/builder of all relational structures and linkages between those structures and the application, not as a passive consumer of decisions made by a library. By exposing relational concepts, SQLAlchemy embraces the idea of "leaky abstraction", encouraging the developer to tailor a custom, yet fully automated, interaction layer between the application and the relational database. SQLAlchemy's innovation is the extent to which it allows a high degree of automation with little to no sacrifice in control over the relational database.

20.2 The Core/ORM Dichotomy

Central to SQLAlchemy's goal of providing a toolkit approach is that it exposes every layer of database interaction as a rich API, dividing the task into two main categories known as *Core* and *ORM*. The Core includes Python Database API (DBAPI) interaction, rendering of textual SQL statements understood by the database, and schema management. These features are all presented as public APIs. The ORM, or object-relational mapper, is then a specific library built on top of the Core. The ORM provided with SQLAlchemy is only one of any number of possible object abstraction layers that could be built upon the Core, and many developers and organizations build their applications on top of the Core directly.

The Core/ORM separation has always been SQLAlchemy's most defining feature, and it has both pros and cons. The explicit Core present in SQLAlchemy leads the ORM to relate database-mapped class attributes to a structure known as a `Table`, rather than directly to their string column names as expressed in the database; to produce a SELECT query using a structure called `select`, rather than piecing together object attributes directly into a string statement; and to receive result rows through a facade called `ResultProxy`, which transparently maps the `select` to each result row, rather than transferring data directly from a database cursor to a user-defined object.

Core elements may not be visible in a very simple ORM-centric application. However, as the Core is carefully integrated into the ORM to allow fluid transition between ORM and Core constructs, a more complex ORM-centric application can "move down" a level or two in order to deal with the

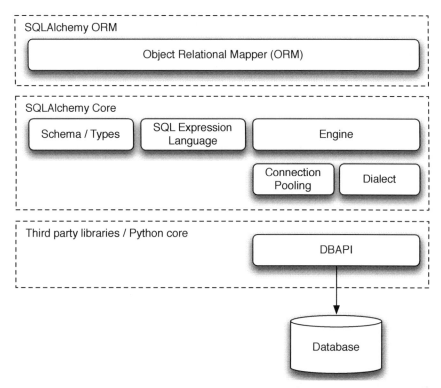

Figure 20.1: SQLAlchemy layer diagram

database in a more specific and finely tuned manner, as the situation requires. As SQLAlchemy has matured, the Core API has become less explicit in regular use as the ORM continues to provide more sophisticated and comprehensive patterns. However, the availability of the Core was also a contributor to SQLAlchemy's early success, as it allowed early users to accomplish much more than would have been possible when the ORM was still being developed.

The downside to the ORM/Core approach is that instructions must travel through more steps. Python's traditional C implementation has a significant overhead penalty for individual function calls, which are the primary cause of slowness in the runtime. Traditional methods of ameliorating this include shortening call chains through rearrangement and inlining, and replacing performance-critical areas with C code. SQLAlchemy has spent many years using both of these methods to improve performance. However, the growing acceptance of the PyPy interpreter for Python may promise to squash the remaining performance problems without the need to replace the majority of SQLAlchemy's internals with C code, as PyPy vastly reduces the impact of long call chains through just-in-time inlining and compilation.

20.3 Taming the DBAPI

At the base of SQLAlchemy is a system for interacting with the database via the DBAPI. The DBAPI itself is not an actual library, only a specification. Therefore, implementations of the DBAPI are available for a particular target database, such as MySQL or PostgreSQL, or alternatively for particular non-DBAPI database adapters, such as ODBC and JDBC.

The DBAPI presents two challenges. The first is to provide an easy-to-use yet full-featured facade around the DBAPI's rudimentary usage patterns. The second is to handle the extremely variable nature of specific DBAPI implementations as well as the underlying database engines.

The Dialect System

The interface described by the DBAPI is extremely simple. Its core components are the DBAPI module itself, the connection object, and the cursor object—a "cursor" in database parlance represents the context of a particular statement and its associated results. A simple interaction with these objects to connect and retrieve data from a database is as follows:

```
connection = dbapi.connect(user="user", pw="pw", host="host")
cursor = connection.cursor()
cursor.execute("select * from user_table where name=?", ("jack",))
print "Columns in result:", [desc[0] for desc in cursor.description]
for row in cursor.fetchall():
    print "Row:", row
cursor.close()
connection.close()
```

SQLAlchemy creates a facade around the classical DBAPI conversation. The point of entry to this facade is the `create_engine` call, from which connection and configuration information is assembled. An instance of `Engine` is produced as the result. This object then represents the gateway to the DBAPI, which itself is never exposed directly.

For simple statement executions, `Engine` offers what's known as an *implicit execution* interface. The work of acquiring and closing both a DBAPI connection and cursor are handled behind the scenes:

```
engine = create_engine("postgresql://user:pw@host/dbname")
result = engine.execute("select * from table")
print result.fetchall()
```

When SQLAlchemy 0.2 was introduced the `Connection` object was added, providing the ability to explicitly maintain the scope of the DBAPI connection:

```
conn = engine.connect()
result = conn.execute("select * from table")
print result.fetchall()
conn.close()
```

The result returned by the execute method of `Engine` or `Connection` is called a `ResultProxy`, which offers an interface similar to the DBAPI cursor but with richer behavior. The `Engine`, `Connection`, and `ResultProxy` correspond to the DBAPI module, an instance of a specific DBAPI connection, and an instance of a specific DBAPI cursor, respectively.

Behind the scenes, the `Engine` references an object called a `Dialect`. The `Dialect` is an abstract class for which many implementations exist, each one targeted at a specific DBAPI/database combination. A `Connection` created on behalf of the `Engine` will refer to this `Dialect` for all decisions, which may have varied behaviors depending on the target DBAPI and database in use.

The `Connection`, when created, will procure and maintain an actual DBAPI connection from a repository known as a `Pool` that's also associated with the `Engine`. The `Pool` is responsible for creating new DBAPI connections and, usually, maintaining them in an in-memory pool for frequent re-use.

During a statement execution, an additional object called an `ExecutionContext` is created by the `Connection`. The object lasts from the point of execution throughout the lifespan of the `ResultProxy`. It may also be available as a specific subclass for some DBAPI/database combinations.

Figure 20.2 illustrates all of these objects and their relationships to each other as well as to the DBAPI components.

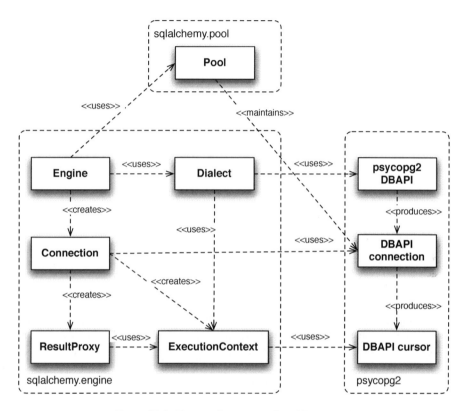

Figure 20.2: Engine, Connection, ResultProxy API

Dealing with DBAPI Variability

For the task of managing variability in DBAPI behavior, first we'll consider the scope of the problem. The DBAPI specification, currently at version two, is written as a series of API definitions which allow for a wide degree of variability in behavior, and leave a good number of areas undefined. As a result, real-life DBAPIs exhibit a great degree of variability in several areas, including when Python unicode strings are acceptable and when they are not; how the "last inserted id"—that is, an autogenerated primary key—may be acquired after an INSERT statement; and how bound parameter values may be specified and interpreted. They also have a large number of idiosyncratic type-oriented behaviors, including the handling of binary, precision numeric, date, Boolean, and unicode data.

SQLAlchemy approaches this by allowing variability in both `Dialect` and `ExecutionContext` via multi-level subclassing. Figure 20.3 illustrates the relationship between `Dialect` and

ExecutionContext when used with the psycopg2 dialect. The PGDialect class provides behaviors that are specific to the usage of the PostgreSQL database, such as the ARRAY datatype and schema catalogs; the PGDialect_psycopg2 class then provides behaviors specific to the psycopg2 DBAPI, including unicode data handlers and server-side cursor behavior.

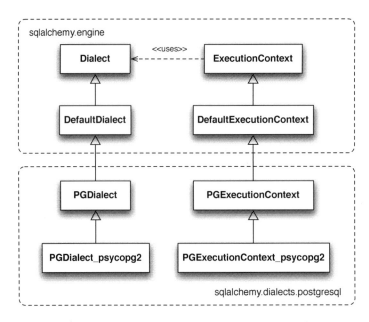

Figure 20.3: Simple Dialect/ExecutionContext hierarchy

A variant on the above pattern presents itself when dealing with a DBAPI that supports multiple databases. Examples of this include pyodbc, which deals with any number of database backends via ODBC, and zxjdbc, a Jython-only driver which deals with JDBC. The above relationship is augmented by the use of a mixin class from the sqlalchemy.connectors package which provides DBAPI behavior that is common to multiple backends. Figure 20.4 illustrates the common functionality of sqlalchemy.connectors.pyodbc shared among pyodbc-specific dialects for MySQL and Microsoft SQL Server.

The Dialect and ExecutionContext objects provide a means to define every interaction with the database and DBAPI, including how connection arguments are formatted and how special quirks during statement execution are handled. The Dialect is also a factory for SQL compilation constructs that render SQL correctly for the target database, and type objects which define how Python data should be marshaled to and from the target DBAPI and database.

20.4 Schema Definition

With database connectivity and interactivity established, the next task is to provide for the creation and manipulation of backend-agnostic SQL statements. To achieve this, we need to define first how we will refer to the tables and columns present in a database—the so-called "schema". Tables and columns represent how data is organized, and most SQL statements consist of expressions and commands referring to these structures.

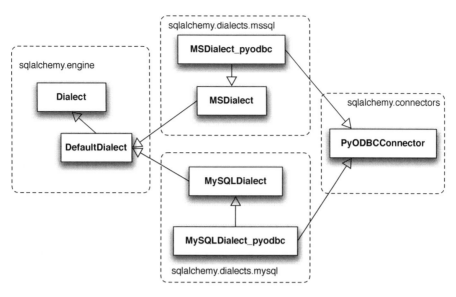

Figure 20.4: Common DBAPI behavior shared among dialect hierarchies

An ORM or data access layer needs to provide programmatic access to the SQL language; at the base is a programmatic system of describing tables and columns. This is where SQLAlchemy offers the first strong division of Core and ORM, by offering the Table and Column constructs that describe the structure of the database independently of a user's model class definition. The rationale behind the division of schema definition from object relational mapping is that the relational schema can be designed unambiguously in terms of the relational database, including platform-specific details if necessary, without being muddled by object-relational concepts—these remain a separate concern. Being independent of the ORM component also means the schema description system is just as useful for any other kind of object-relational system which may be built on the Core.

The Table and Column model falls under the scope of what's referred to as *metadata*, offering a collection object called MetaData to represent a collection of Table objects. The structure is derived mostly from Martin Fowler's description of "Metadata Mapping" in *Patterns of Enterprise Application Architecture*. Figure 20.5 illustrates some key elements of the sqlalchemy.schema package.

Table represents the name and other attributes of an actual table present in a target schema. Its collection of Column objects represents naming and typing information about individual table columns. A full array of objects describing constraints, indexes, and sequences is provided to fill in many more details, some of which impact the behavior of the engine and SQL construction system. In particular, ForeignKeyConstraint is central to determining how two tables should be joined.

Table and Column in the schema package are unique versus the rest of the package in that they are dual-inheriting, both from the sqlalchemy.schema package and the sqlalchemy.sql.expression package, serving not just as schema-level constructs, but also as core syntactical units in the SQL expression language. This relationship is illustrated in Figure 20.6.

In Figure 20.6 we can see that Table and Column inherit from the SQL world as specific forms of "things you can select from", known as a FromClause, and "things you can use in a SQL expression", known as a ColumnElement.

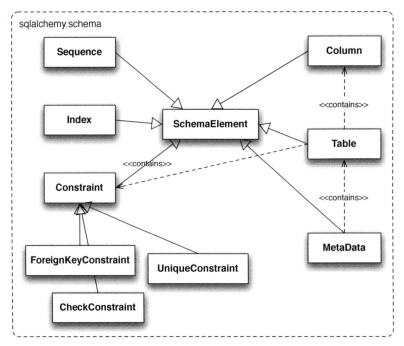

Figure 20.5: Basic sqlalchemy.schema objects

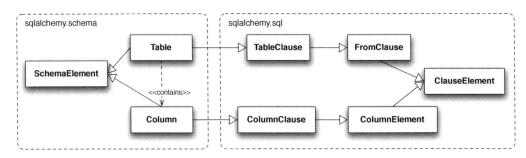

Figure 20.6: The dual lives of Table and Column

20.5 SQL Expressions

During SQLAlchemy's creation, the approach to SQL generation wasn't clear. A textual language might have been a likely candidate; this is a common approach which is at the core of well-known object-relational tools like Hibernate's HQL. For Python, however, a more intriguing choice was available: using Python objects and expressions to generatively construct expression tree structures, even re-purposing Python operators so that operators could be given SQL statement behavior.

While it may not have been the first tool to do so, full credit goes to the SQLBuilder library included in Ian Bicking's SQLObject as the inspiration for the system of Python objects and operators used by SQLAlchemy's expression language. In this approach, Python objects represent lexical portions of a SQL expression. Methods on those objects, as well as overloaded operators, generate new lexical constructs derived from them. The most common object is the "Column" object—

SQLObject would represent these on an ORM-mapped class using a namespace accessed via the `.q` attribute; SQLAlchemy named the attribute `.c`. The `.c` attribute remains today on Core selectable elements, such as those representing tables and select statements.

Expression Trees

A SQLAlchemy SQL expression construct is very much the kind of structure you'd create if you were parsing a SQL statement—it's a parse tree, except the developer creates the parse tree directly, rather than deriving it from a string. The core type of node in this parse tree is called `ClauseElement`, and Figure 20.7 illustrates the relationship of `ClauseElement` to some key classes.

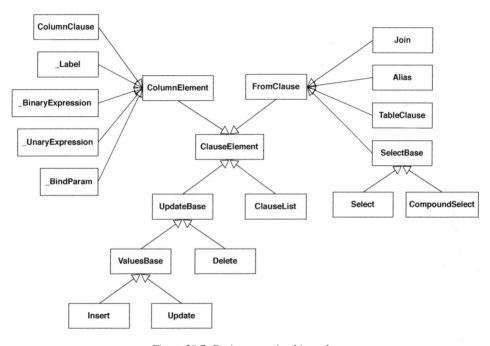

Figure 20.7: Basic expression hierarchy

Through the use of constructor functions, methods, and overloaded Python operator functions, a structure for a statement like:

```
SELECT id FROM user WHERE name = ?
```

might be constructed in Python like:

```
from sqlalchemy.sql import table, column, select
user = table('user', column('id'), column('name'))
stmt = select([user.c.id]).where(user.c.name=='ed')
```

The structure of the above `select` construct is shown in Figure 20.8. Note the representation of the literal value `'ed'` is contained within the `_BindParam` construct, thus causing it to be rendered as a bound parameter marker in the SQL string using a question mark.

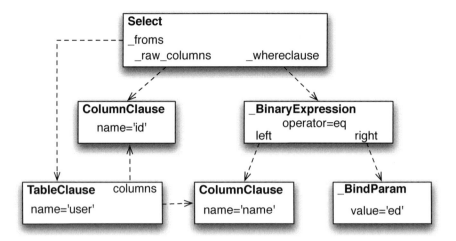

Figure 20.8: Example expression tree

From the tree diagram, one can see that a simple descending traversal through the nodes can quickly create a rendered SQL statement, as we'll see in greater detail in the section on statement compilation.

Python Operator Approach

In SQLAlchemy, an expression like this:

```
column('a') == 2
```

produces neither True nor False, but instead a SQL expression construct. The key to this is to overload operators using the Python special operator functions: e.g., methods like __eq__, __ne__, __le__, __lt__, __add__, __mul__. Column-oriented expression nodes provide overloaded Python operator behavior through the usage of a mixin called ColumnOperators. Using operator overloading, an expression column('a') == 2 is equivalent to:

```
from sqlalchemy.sql.expression import _BinaryExpression
from sqlalchemy.sql import column, bindparam
from sqlalchemy.operators import eq

_BinaryExpression(
    left=column('a'),
    right=bindparam('a', value=2, unique=True),
    operator=eq
)
```

The eq construct is actually a function originating from the Python operator built-in. Representing operators as an object (i.e., operator.eq) rather than a string (i.e., =) allows the string representation to be defined at statement compilation time, when database dialect information is known.

Compilation

The central class responsible for rendering SQL expression trees into textual SQL is the `Compiled` class. This class has two primary subclasses, `SQLCompiler` and `DDLCompiler`. `SQLCompiler` handles SQL rendering operations for SELECT, INSERT, UPDATE, and DELETE statements, collectively classified as DQL (data query language) and DML (data manipulation language), while `DDLCompiler` handles various CREATE and DROP statements, classified as DDL (data definition language). There is an additional class hierarchy focused around string representations of types, starting at `TypeCompiler`. Individual dialects then provide their own subclasses of all three compiler types to define SQL language aspects specific to the target database. Figure 20.9 provides an overview of this class hierarchy with respect to the PostgreSQL dialect.

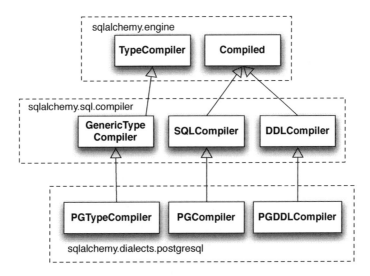

Figure 20.9: Compiler hierarchy, including PostgreSQL-specific implementation

The `Compiled` subclasses define a series of *visit* methods, each one referred to by a particular subclass of `ClauseElement`. A hierarchy of `ClauseElement` nodes is walked and a statement is constructed by recursively concatenating the string output of each visit function. As this proceeds, the `Compiled` object maintains state regarding anonymous identifier names, bound parameter names, and nesting of subqueries, among other things, all of which aim for the production of a string SQL statement as well as a final collection of bound parameters with default values. Figure 20.10 illustrates the process of visit methods resulting in textual units.

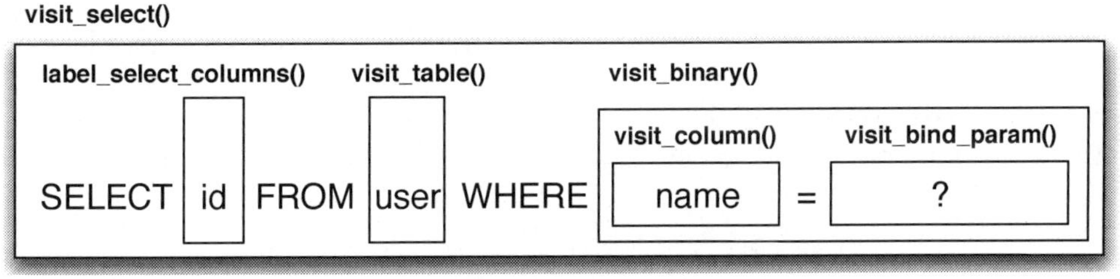

Figure 20.10: Call hierarchy of a statement compilation

A completed `Compiled` structure contains the full SQL string and collection of bound values. These are coerced by an `ExecutionContext` into the format expected by the DBAPI's execute method, which includes such considerations as the treatment of a unicode statement object, the type of collection used to store bound values, as well as specifics on how the bound values themselves should be coerced into representations appropriate to the DBAPI and target database.

20.6 Class Mapping with the ORM

We now shift our attention to the ORM. The first goal is to use the system of table metadata we've defined to allow mapping of a user-defined class to a collection of columns in a database table. The second goal is to allow the definition of relationships between user-defined classes, based on relationships between tables in a database.

SQLAlchemy refers to this as "mapping", following the well known Data Mapper pattern described in Fowler's *Patterns of Enterprise Architecture*. Overall, the SQLAlchemy ORM draws heavily from the practices detailed by Fowler. It's also heavily influenced by the famous Java relational mapper Hibernate and Ian Bicking's SQLObject product for Python.

Classical vs. Declarative

We use the term *classical mapping* to refer to SQLAlchemy's system of applying an object-relational data mapping to an existing user class. This form considers the `Table` object and the user-defined class to be two individually defined entities which are joined together via a function called `mapper`. Once `mapper` has been applied to a user-defined class, the class takes on new attributes that correspond to columns in the table:

```
class User(object):
    pass

mapper(User, user_table)

# now User has an ".id" attribute
User.id
```

`mapper` can also affix other kinds of attributes to the class, including attributes which correspond to references to other kinds of objects, as well as arbitrary SQL expressions. The process of affixing arbitrary attributes to a class is known in the Python world as "monkeypatching"; however, since we are doing it in a data-driven and non-arbitrary way, the spirit of the operation is better expressed with the term *class instrumentation*.

Modern usage of SQLAlchemy centers around the Declarative extension, which is a configurational system that resembles the common active-record-like class declaration system used by many other object-relational tools. In this system, the end user explicitly defines attributes inline with the class definition, each representing an attribute on the class that is to be mapped. The `Table` object, in most cases, is not mentioned explicitly, nor is the `mapper` function; only the class, the `Column` objects, and other ORM-related attributes are named:

```
class User(Base):
    __tablename__ = 'user'
    id = Column(Integer, primary_key=True)
```

It may appear, above, that the class instrumentation is being achieved directly by our placement of `id = Column()`, but this is not the case. The Declarative extension uses a Python metaclass, which is a handy way to run a series of operations each time a new class is first declared, to generate a new `Table` object from what's been declared, and to pass it to the mapper function along with the class. The mapper function then does its job in exactly the same way, patching its own attributes onto the class, in this case towards the `id` attribute, and replacing what was there previously. By the time the metaclass initialization is complete (that is, when the flow of execution leaves the block delineated by `User`), the `Column` object marked by `id` has been moved into a new `Table`, and `User.id` has been replaced by a new attribute specific to the mapping.

It was always intended that SQLAlchemy would have a shorthand, declarative form of configuration. However, the creation of Declarative was delayed in favor of continued work solidifying the mechanics of classical mapping. An interim extension called ActiveMapper, which later became the Elixir project, existed early on. It redefines mapping constructs in a higher-level declaration system. Declarative's goal was to reverse the direction of Elixir's heavily abstracted approach by establishing a system that preserved SQLAlchemy classical mapping concepts almost exactly, only reorganizing how they are used to be less verbose and more amenable to class-level extensions than a classical mapping would be.

Whether classical or declarative mapping is used, a mapped class takes on new behaviors that allow it to express SQL constructs in terms of its attributes. SQLAlchemy originally followed SQLObject's behavior of using a special attribute as the source of SQL column expressions, referred to by SQLAlchemy as `.c`, as in this example:

```
result = session.query(User).filter(User.c.username == 'ed').all()
```

In version 0.4, however, SQLAlchemy moved the functionality into the mapped attributes themselves:

```
result = session.query(User).filter(User.username == 'ed').all()
```

This change in attribute access proved to be a great improvement, as it allowed the column-like objects present on the class to gain additional class-specific capabilities not present on those originating directly from the underlying `Table` object. It also allowed usage integration between different kinds of class attributes, such as attributes which refer to table columns directly, attributes that refer to SQL expressions derived from those columns, and attributes that refer to a related class. Finally, it provided a symmetry between a mapped class, and an instance of that mapped class, in that the same attribute could take on different behavior depending on the type of parent. Class-bound attributes return SQL expressions while instance-bound attributes return actual data.

Anatomy of a Mapping

The `id` attribute that's been attached to our `User` class is a type of object known in Python as a *descriptor*, an object that has `__get__`, `__set__`, and `__del__` methods, which the Python runtime defers to for all class and instance operations involving this attribute. SQLAlchemy's implementation is known as an `InstrumentedAttribute`, and we'll illustrate the world behind this facade with another example. Starting with a `Table` and a user defined class, we set up a mapping that has just one mapped column, as well as a `relationship`, which defines a reference to a related class:

```
user_table = Table("user", metadata,
    Column('id', Integer, primary_key=True),
```

```
)

class User(object):
    pass

mapper(User, user_table, properties={
    'related':relationship(Address)
})
```

When the mapping is complete, the structure of objects related to the class is detailed in Figure 20.11.

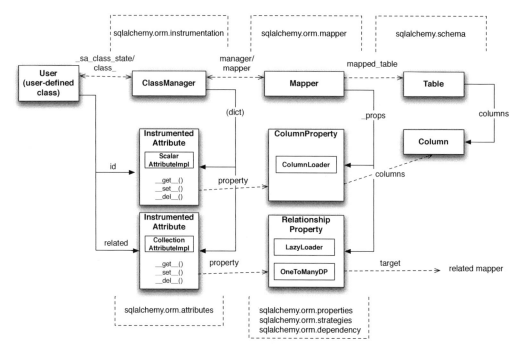

Figure 20.11: Anatomy of a mapping

The figure illustrates a SQLAlchemy mapping defined as two separate layers of interaction between the user-defined class and the table metadata to which it is mapped. Class instrumentation is pictured towards the left, while SQL and database functionality is pictured towards the right. The general pattern at play is that object composition is used to isolate behavioral roles, and object inheritance is used to distinguish amongst behavioral variances within a particular role.

Within the realm of class instrumentation, the `ClassManager` is linked to the mapped class, while its collection of `InstrumentedAttribute` objects are linked to each attribute mapped on the class. `InstrumentedAttribute` is also the public-facing Python descriptor mentioned previously, and produces SQL expressions when used in a class-based expression (e.g., `User.id==5`). When dealing with an instance of `User`, `InstrumentedAttribute` delegates the behavior of the attribute to an `AttributeImpl` object, which is one of several varieties tailored towards the type of data being represented.

Towards the mapping side, the Mapper represents the linkage of a user-defined class and a selectable unit, most typically Table. Mapper maintains a collection of per-attribute objects known as MapperProperty, which deals with the SQL representation of a particular attribute. The most common variants of MapperProperty are ColumnProperty, representing a mapped column or SQL expression, and RelationshipProperty, representing a linkage to another mapper.

MapperProperty delegates attribute loading behavior—including how the attribute renders in a SQL statement and how it is populated from a result row—to a LoaderStrategy object, of which there are several varieties. Different LoaderStrategies determine if the loading behavior of an attribute is *deferred*, *eager*, or *immediate*. A default version is chosen at mapper configuration time, with the option to use an alternate strategy at query time. RelationshipProperty also references a DependencyProcessor, which handles how inter-mapper dependencies and attribute synchronization should proceed at flush time. The choice of DependencyProcessor is based on the relational geometry of the *parent* and *target* selectables linked to the relationship.

The Mapper/RelationshipProperty structure forms a graph, where Mapper objects are nodes and RelationshipProperty objects are directed edges. Once the full set of mappers have been declared by an application, a deferred "initialization" step known as the *configuration* proceeds. It is used mainly by each RelationshipProperty to solidify the details between its *parent* and *target* mappers, including choice of AttributeImpl as well as DependencyProcessor. This graph is a key data structure used throughout the operation of the ORM. It participates in operations such as the so-called "cascade" behavior that defines how operations should propagate along object paths, in query operations where related objects and collections are "eagerly" loaded at once, as well as on the object flushing side where a dependency graph of all objects is established before firing off a series of persistence steps.

20.7 Query and Loading Behavior

SQLAlchemy initiates all object loading behavior via an object called Query. The basic state Query starts with includes the *entities*, which is the list of mapped classes and/or individual SQL expressions to be queried. It also has a reference to the Session, which represents connectivity to one or more databases, as well as a cache of data that's been accumulated with respect to transactions on those connections. Below is a rudimentary usage example:

```
from sqlalchemy.orm import Session
session = Session(engine)
query = session.query(User)
```

We create a Query that will yield instances of User, relative to a new Session we've created. Query provides a generative builder pattern in the same way as the select construct discussed previously, where additional criteria and modifiers are associated with a statement construct one method call at a time. When an iterative operation is called on the Query, it constructs a SQL expression construct representing a SELECT, emits it to the database, and then interprets the result set rows as ORM-oriented results corresponding to the initial set of entities being requested.

Query makes a hard distinction between the *SQL rendering* and the *data loading* portions of the operation. The former refers to the construction of a SELECT statement, the latter to the interpretation of SQL result rows into ORM-mapped constructs. Data loading can, in fact, proceed without a SQL rendering step, as the Query may be asked to interpret results from a textual query hand-composed by the user.

Both SQL rendering and data loading utilize a recursive descent through the graph formed by the series of lead `Mapper` objects, considering each column- or SQL-expression-holding `ColumnProperty` as a leaf node and each `RelationshipProperty` which is to be included in the query via a so-called "eager-load" as an edge leading to another Mapper node. The traversal and action to take at each node is ultimately the job of each `LoaderStrategy` associated with every `MapperProperty`, adding columns and joins to the SELECT statement being built in the SQL rendering phase, and producing Python functions that process result rows in the data loading phase.

The Python functions produced in the data loading phase each receive a database row as they are fetched, and produce a possible change in the state of a mapped attribute in memory as a result. They are produced for a particular attribute conditionally, based on examination of the first incoming row in the result set, as well as on loading options. If a load of the attribute is not to proceed, no callable function is produced.

Figure 20.12 illustrates the traversal of several `LoaderStrategy` objects in a *joined eager loading* scenario, illustrating their connection to a rendered SQL statement which occurs during the `_compile_context` method of `Query`. It also shows generation of *row population* functions which receive result rows and populate individual object attributes, a process which occurs within the `instances` method of `Query`.

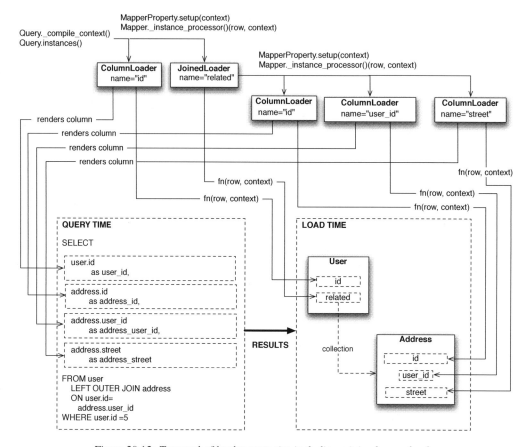

Figure 20.12: Traversal of loader strategies including a joined eager load

SQLAlchemy's early approach to populating results used a traditional traversal of fixed object methods associated with each strategy to receive each row and act accordingly. The loader callable system, first introduced in version 0.5, represented a dramatic leap in performance, as many decisions regarding row handling could be made just once up front instead of for each row, and a significant number of function calls with no net effect could be eliminated.

20.8 Session/Identity Map

In SQLAlchemy, the `Session` object presents the public interface for the actual usage of the ORM—that is, loading and persisting data. It provides the starting point for queries and persistence operations for a given database connection.

The `Session`, in addition to serving as the gateway for database connectivity, maintains an active reference to the set of all mapped entities which are present in memory relative to that `Session`. It's in this way that the `Session` implements a facade for the *identity map* and *unit of work* patterns, both identified by Fowler. The identity map maintains a database-identity-unique mapping of all objects for a particular `Session`, eliminating the problems introduced by duplicate identities. The unit of work builds on the identity map to provide a system of automating the process of persisting all changes in state to the database in the most effective manner possible. The actual persistence step is known as a "flush", and in modern SQLAlchemy this step is usually automatic.

Development History

The `Session` started out as a mostly concealed system responsible for the single task of emitting a flush. The flush process involves emitting SQL statements to the database, corresponding to changes in the state of objects tracked by the unit of work system and thereby synchronizing the current state of the database with what's in memory. The flush has always been one of the most complex operations performed by SQLAlchemy.

The invocation of *flush* started out in very early versions behind a method called `commit`, and it was a method present on an implicit, thread-local object called `objectstore`. When one used SQLAlchemy 0.1, there was no need to call `Session.add`, nor was there any concept of an explicit `Session` at all. The only user-facing steps were to create mappers, create new objects, modify existing objects loaded through queries (where the queries themselves were invoked directly from each Mapper object), and then persist all changes via the `objectstore.commit` command. The pool of objects for a set of operations was unconditionally module-global and unconditionally thread-local.

The `objectstore.commit` model was an immediate hit with the first group of users, but the rigidity of this model quickly ran into a wall. Users new to modern SQLAlchemy sometimes lament the need to define a factory, and possibly a registry, for `Session` objects, as well as the need to keep their objects organized into just one `Session` at a time, but this is far preferable to the early days when the entire system was completely implicit. The convenience of the 0.1 usage pattern is still largely present in modern SQLAlchemy, which features a session registry normally configured to use thread local scoping.

The `Session` itself was only introduced in version 0.2 of SQLAlchemy, modeled loosely after the `Session` object present in Hibernate. This version featured integrated transactional control, where the `Session` could be placed into a transaction via the `begin` method, and completed via the `commit` method. The `objectstore.commit` method was renamed to `objectstore.flush`, and new `Session` objects could be created at any time. The `Session` itself was broken off from another object called `UnitOfWork`, which remains as a private object responsible for executing the actual flush operation.

While the flush process started as a method explicitly invoked by the user, the 0.4 series of SQLAlchemy introduced the concept of *autoflush*, which meant that a flush was emitted immediately before each query. The advantage of autoflush is that the SQL statement emitted by a query always has access on the relational side to the exact state that is present in memory, as all changes have been sent over. Early versions of SQLAlchemy couldn't include this feature, because the most common pattern of usage was that the flush statement would also commit the changes permanently. But when autoflush was introduced, it was accompanied by another feature called the *transactional* `Session`, which provided a `Session` that would start out automatically in a transaction that remained until the user called `commit` explicitly. With the introduction of this feature, the `flush` method no longer committed the data that it flushed, and could safely be called on an automated basis. The `Session` could now provide a step-by-step synchronization between in-memory state and SQL query state by flushing as needed, with nothing permanently persisted until the explicit `commit` step. This behavior is, in fact, exactly the same in Hibernate for Java. However, SQLAlchemy embraced this style of usage based on the same behavior in the Storm ORM for Python, introduced when SQLAlchemy was in version 0.3.

Version 0.5 brought more transaction integration when *post-transaction expiration* was introduced; after each `commit` or `rollback`, by default all states within the `Session` are expired (erased), to be populated again when subsequent SQL statements re-select the data, or when the attributes on the remaining set of expired objects are accessed in the context of the new transaction. Originally, SQLAlchemy was constructed around the assumption that SELECT statements should be emitted as little as possible, unconditionally. The expire-on-commit behavior was slow in coming for this reason; however, it entirely solved the issue of the `Session` which contained stale data post-transaction with no simple way to load newer data without rebuilding the full set of objects already loaded. Early on, it seemed that this problem couldn't be reasonably solved, as it wasn't apparent when the `Session` should consider the current state to be stale, and thus produce an expensive new set of SELECT statements on the next access. However, once the `Session` moved to an always-in-a-transaction model, the point of transaction end became apparent as the natural point of data expiration, as the nature of a transaction with a high degree of isolation is that it *cannot* see new data until it's committed or rolled back anyway. Different databases and configurations, of course, have varied degrees of transaction isolation, including no transactions at all. These modes of usage are entirely acceptable with SQLAlchemy's expiration model; the developer only needs to be aware that a lower isolation level may expose un-isolated changes within a Session if multiple Sessions share the same rows. This is not at all different from what can occur when using two database connections directly.

Session Overview

Figure 20.13 illustrates a `Session` and the primary structures it deals with.

The public-facing portions above are the `Session` itself and the collection of user objects, each of which is an instance of a mapped class. Here we see that mapped objects keep a reference to a SQLAlchemy construct called `InstanceState`, which tracks ORM state for an individual instance including pending attribute changes and attribute expiration status. `InstanceState` is the instance-level side of the attribute instrumentation discussed in the preceding section, *Anatomy of a Mapping*, corresponding to the `ClassManager` at the class level, and maintaining the state of the mapped object's dictionary (i.e., the Python `__dict__` attribute) on behalf of the `AttributeImpl` objects associated with the class.

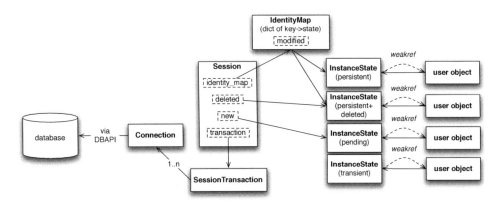

Figure 20.13: Session overview

State Tracking

The IdentityMap is a mapping of database identities to InstanceState objects, for those objects which have a database identity, which are referred to as *persistent*. The default implementation of IdentityMap works with InstanceState to self-manage its size by removing user-mapped instances once all strong references to them have been removed—in this way it works in the same way as Python's WeakValueDictionary. The Session protects the set of all objects marked as *dirty* or *deleted*, as well as pending objects marked *new*, from garbage collection, by creating strong references to those objects with pending changes. All strong references are then discarded after the flush.

InstanceState also performs the critical task of maintaining "what's changed" for the attributes of a particular object, using a move-on-change system that stores the "previous" value of a particular attribute in a dictionary called committed_state before assigning the incoming value to the object's current dictionary. At flush time, the contents of committed_state and the __dict__ associated with the object are compared to produce the set of net changes on each object.

In the case of collections, a separate collections package coordinates with the InstrumentedAttribute/InstanceState system to maintain a collection of net changes to a particular mapped collection of objects. Common Python classes such as set, list and dict are subclassed before use and augmented with history-tracking mutator methods. The collection system was reworked in 0.4 to be open ended and usable for any collection-like object.

Transactional Control

Session, in its default state of usage, maintains an open transaction for all operations which is completed when commit or rollback is called. The SessionTransaction maintains a set of zero or more Connection objects, each representing an open transaction on a particular database. SessionTransaction is a lazy-initializing object that begins with no database state present. As a particular backend is required to participate in a statement execution, a Connection corresponding to that database is added to SessionTransaction's list of connections. While a single connection at a time is common, the multiple connection scenario is supported where the specific connection used for a particular operation is determined based on configurations associated with the Table,

Mapper, or SQL construct itself involved in the operation. Multiple connections can also coordinate the transaction using two-phase behavior, for those DBAPIs which provide it.

20.9 Unit of Work

The `flush` method provided by `Session` turns over its work to a separate module called `unitofwork`. As mentioned earlier, the flush process is probably the most complex function of SQLAlchemy.

The job of the unit of work is to move all of the *pending* state present in a particular `Session` out to the database, emptying out the `new`, `dirty`, and `deleted` collections maintained by the `Session`. Once completed, the in-memory state of the `Session` and what's present in the current transaction match. The primary challenge is to determine the correct series of persistence steps, and then to perform them in the correct order. This includes determining the list of INSERT, UPDATE, and DELETE statements, including those resulting from the cascade of a related row being deleted or otherwise moved; ensuring that UPDATE statements contain only those columns which were actually modified; establishing "synchronization" operations that will copy the state of primary key columns over to referencing foreign key columns, at the point at which newly generated primary key identifiers are available; ensuring that INSERTs occur in the order in which objects were added to the `Session` and as efficiently as possible; and ensuring that UPDATE and DELETE statements occur within a deterministic ordering so as to reduce the chance of deadlocks.

History

The unit of work implementation began as a tangled system of structures that was written in an ad hoc way; its development can be compared to finding the way out of a forest without a map. Early bugs and missing behaviors were solved with bolted-on fixes, and while several refactorings improved matters through version 0.5, it was not until version 0.6 that the unit of work—by that time stable, well-understood, and covered by hundreds of tests—could be rewritten entirely from scratch. After many weeks of considering a new approach that would be driven by consistent data structures, the process of rewriting it to use this new model took only a few days, as the idea was by this time well understood. It was also greatly helped by the fact that the new implementation's behavior could be carefully cross-checked against the existing version. This process shows how the first iteration of something, however awful, is still valuable as long as it provides a working model. It further shows how total rewrites of a subsystem is often not only appropriate, but an integral part of development for hard-to-develop systems.

Topological Sort

The key paradigm behind the unit of work is that of assembling the full list of actions to be taken into a data structure, with each node representing a single step; this is known in design patterns parlance as the *command pattern*. The series of "commands" within this structure is then organized into a specific ordering using a *topological sort*. A topological sort is a process that sorts items based on a *partial ordering*, that is, only certain elements must precede others. Figure 20.14 illustrates the behavior of the topological sort.

The unit of work constructs a partial ordering based on those persistence commands which must precede others. The commands are then topologically sorted and invoked in order. The determination of which commands precede which is derived primarily from the presence of a `relationship` that

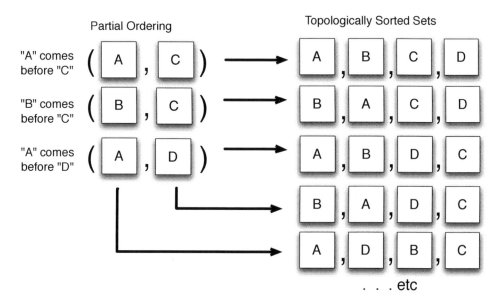

Figure 20.14: Topological sort

bridges two Mapper objects—generally, one Mapper is considered to be dependent on the other, as the relationship implies that one Mapper has a foreign key dependency on the other. Similar rules exist for many-to-many association tables, but here we focus on the case of one-to-many/many-to-one relationships. Foreign key dependencies are resolved in order to prevent constraint violations from occurring, with no reliance on needing to mark constraints as "deferred". But just as importantly, the ordering allows primary key identifiers, which on many platforms are only generated when an INSERT actually occurs, to be populated from a just-executed INSERT statement's result into the parameter list of a dependent row that's about to be inserted. For deletes, the same ordering is used in reverse—dependent rows are deleted before those on which they depend, as these rows cannot be present without the referent of their foreign key being present.

The unit of work features a system where the topological sort is performed at two different levels, based on the structure of dependencies present. The first level organizes persistence steps into buckets based on the dependencies between mappers, that is, full "buckets" of objects corresponding to a particular class. The second level breaks up zero or more of these "buckets" into smaller batches, to handle the case of reference cycles or self-referring tables. Figure 20.15 illustrates the "buckets" generated to insert a set of User objects, then a set of Address objects, where an intermediary step copies newly generated User primary key values into the user_id foreign key column of each Address object.

In the per-mapper sorting situation, any number of User and Address objects can be flushed with no impact on the complexity of steps or how many "dependencies" must be considered.

The second level of sorting organizes persistence steps based on direct dependencies between individual objects within the scope of a single mapper. The simplest example of when this occurs is a table which contains a foreign key constraint to itself; a particular row in the table needs to be inserted before another row in the same table which refers to it. Another is when a series of tables have a *reference cycle*: table A references table B, which references table C, that then references table A. Some A objects must be inserted before others so as to allow the B and C objects to also be

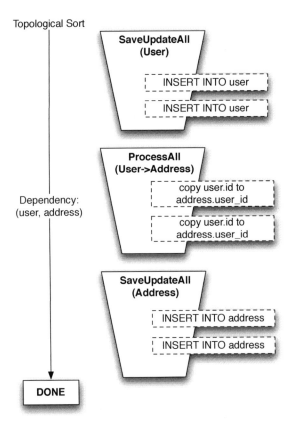

Figure 20.15: Organizing objects by mapper

inserted. The table that refers to itself is a special case of reference cycle.

To determine which operations can remain in their aggregated, per-Mapper buckets, and which will be broken into a larger set of per-object commands, a cycle detection algorithm is applied to the set of dependencies that exist between mappers, using a modified version of a cycle detection algorithm found on Guido Van Rossum's blog[1]. Those buckets involved in cycles are are then broken up into per-object operations and mixed into the collection of per-mapper buckets through the addition of new dependency rules from the per-object buckets back to the per-mapper buckets. Figure 20.16 illustrates the bucket of User objects being broken up into individual per-object commands, resulting from the addition of a new relationship from User to itself called contact.

The rationale behind the bucket structure is that it allows batching of common statements as much as possible, both reducing the number of steps required in Python and making possible more efficient interactions with the DBAPI, which can sometimes execute thousands of statements within a single Python method call. Only when a reference cycle exists between mappers does the more expensive per-object-dependency pattern kick in, and even then it only occurs for those portions of the object graph which require it.

[1] http://neopythonic.blogspot.com/2009/01/detecting-cycles-in-directed-graph.html

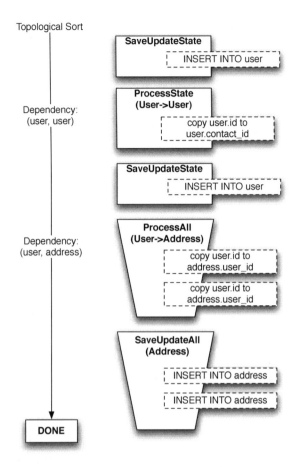

Figure 20.16: Organizing reference cycles into individual steps

20.10 Conclusion

SQLAlchemy has aimed very high since its inception, with the goal of being the most feature-rich and versatile database product possible. It has done so while maintaining its focus on relational databases, recognizing that supporting the usefulness of relational databases in a deep and comprehensive way is a major undertaking; and even now, the scope of the undertaking continues to reveal itself as larger than previously perceived.

The component-based approach is intended to extract the most value possible from each area of functionality, providing many different units that applications can use alone or in combination. This system has been challenging to create, maintain, and deliver.

The development course was intended to be slow, based on the theory that a methodical, broad-based construction of solid functionality is ultimately more valuable than fast delivery of features without foundation. It has taken a long time for SQLAlchemy to construct a consistent and well-documented user story, but throughout the process, the underlying architecture was always a step ahead, leading in some cases to the "time machine" effect where features can be added almost before users request them.

The Python language has been a reliable host (if a little finicky, particularly in the area of performance). The language's consistency and tremendously open run-time model has allowed SQLAlchemy to provide a nicer experience than that offered by similar products written in other languages.

It is the hope of the SQLAlchemy project that Python gain ever-deeper acceptance into as wide a variety of fields and industries as possible, and that the use of relational databases remains vibrant and progressive. The goal of SQLAlchemy is to demonstrate that relational databases, Python, and well-considered object models are all very much worthwhile development tools.

[chapter 21]

Twisted
Jessica McKellar

Twisted is an event-driven networking engine in Python. It was born in the early 2000s, when the writers of networked games had few scalable and no cross-platform libraries, in any language, at their disposal. The authors of Twisted tried to develop games in the existing networking landscape, struggled, saw a clear need for a scalable, event-driven, cross-platform networking framework and decided to make one happen, learning from the mistakes and hardships of past game and networked application writers.

Twisted supports many common transport and application layer protocols, including TCP, UDP, SSL/TLS, HTTP, IMAP, SSH, IRC, and FTP. Like the language in which it is written, it is "batteries-included"; Twisted comes with client and server implementations for all of its protocols, as well as utilities that make it easy to configure and deploy production-grade Twisted applications from the command line.

21.1 Why Twisted?

In 2000, glyph, the creator of Twisted, was working on a text-based multiplayer game called Twisted Reality. It was a big mess of threads, 3 per connection, in Java. There was a thread for input that would block on reads, a thread for output that would block on some kind of write, and a "logic" thread that would sleep while waiting for timers to expire or events to queue. As players moved through the virtual landscape and interacted, threads were deadlocking, caches were getting corrupted, and the locking logic was never quite right—the use of threads had made the software complicated, buggy, and hard to scale.

Seeking alternatives, he discovered Python, and in particular Python's `select` module for multiplexing I/O from stream objects like sockets and pipes[1]; at the time, Java didn't expose the operating system's `select` interface or any other asynchronous I/O API[2]. A quick prototype of the game in Python using `select` immediately proved less complex and more reliable than the threaded version.

An instant convert to Python, `select`, and event-driven programming, glyph wrote a client and server for the game in Python using the `select` API. But then he wanted to do more. Fundamentally, he wanted to be able to turn network activity into method calls on objects in the game. What if you could receive email in the game, like the Nethack mailer daemon? What if every player in the game

---

[1] The Single UNIX Specification, Version 3 (SUSv3) describes the `select` API.
[2] The `java.nio` package for non-blocking I/O was added in J2SE 1.4, released in 2002.

had a home page? Glyph found himself needing good Python IMAP and HTTP clients and servers that used `select`.

He first turned to Medusa, a platform developed in the mid-'90s for writing networking servers in Python based on the `asyncore` module[3]. `asyncore` is an asynchronous socket handler that builds a dispatcher and callback interface on top of the operating system's `select` API.

This was an inspiring find for glyph, but Medusa had two drawbacks:

1. It was on its way towards being unmaintained by 2001 when glyph started working on Twisted Reality.
2. `asyncore` is such a thin wrapper around sockets that application programmers are still required to manipulate sockets directly. This means portability is still the responsibility of the programmer. Additionally, at the time, `asyncore`'s Windows support was buggy, and glyph knew that he wanted to run a GUI client on Windows.

Glyph was facing the prospect of implementing a networking platform himself and realized that Twisted Reality had opened the door to a problem that was just as interesting as his game.

Over time, Twisted Reality the game became Twisted the networking platform, which would do what existing networking platforms in Python didn't:

- Use event-driven programming instead of multi-threaded programming.
- Be cross-platform: provide a uniform interface to the event notification systems exposed by major operating systems.
- Be "batteries-included": provide implementations of popular application-layer protocols out of the box, so that Twisted is immediately useful to developers.
- Conform to RFCs, and prove conformance with a robust test suite.
- Make it easy to use multiple networking protocols together.
- Be extensible.

21.2 The Architecture of Twisted

Twisted is an event-driven networking engine. Event-driven programming is so integral to Twisted's design philosophy that it is worth taking a moment to review what exactly event-driven programming means.

Event-driven programming is a programming paradigm in which program flow is determined by external events. It is characterized by an event loop and the use of callbacks to trigger actions when events happen. Two other common programming paradigms are (single-threaded) synchronous and multi-threaded programming.

Let's compare and contrast single-threaded, multi-threaded, and event-driven programming models with an example. Figure 21.1 shows the work done by a program over time under these three models. The program has three tasks to complete, each of which blocks while waiting for I/O to finish. Time spent blocking on I/O is greyed out.

In the single-threaded synchronous version of the program, tasks are performed serially. If one task blocks for a while on I/O, all of the other tasks have to wait until it finishes and they are executed in turn. This definite order and serial processing are easy to reason about, but the program is unnecessarily slow if the tasks don't depend on each other, yet still have to wait for each other.

In the threaded version of the program, the three tasks that block while doing work are performed in separate threads of control. These threads are managed by the operating system and may run

---

[3]http://www.nightmare.com/medusa/

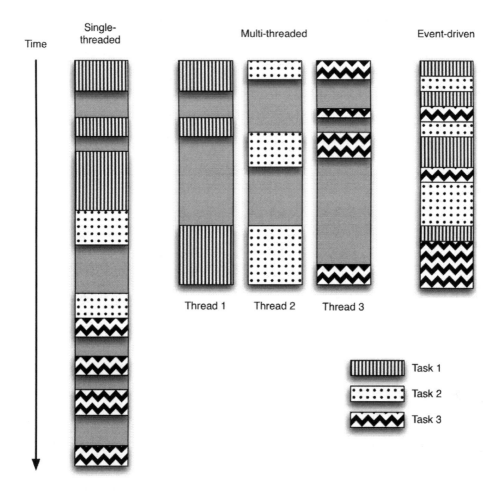

Figure 21.1: Threading models

concurrently on multiple processors or interleaved on a single processor. This allows progress to be made by some threads while others are blocking on resources. This is often more time-efficient than the analogous synchronous program, but one has to write code to protect shared resources that could be accessed concurrently from multiple threads. Multi-threaded programs can be harder to reason about because one now has to worry about thread safety via process serialization (locking), reentrancy, thread-local storage, or other mechanisms, which when implemented improperly can lead to subtle and painful bugs.

The event-driven version of the program interleaves the execution of the three tasks, but in a single thread of control. When performing I/O or other expensive operations, a callback is registered with an event loop, and then execution continues while the I/O completes. The callback describes how to handle an event once it has completed. The event loop polls for events and dispatches them as they arrive, to the callbacks that are waiting for them. This allows the program to make progress when it can without the use of additional threads. Event-driven programs can be easier to reason about than multi-threaded programs because the programmer doesn't have to worry about thread safety.

The event-driven model is often a good choice when there are:
1. many tasks, that are...
2. largely independent (so they don't have to communicate with or wait on each other), and...
3. some of these tasks block while waiting on events.

It is also a good choice when an application has to share mutable data between tasks, because no synchronization has to be performed.

Networking applications often have exactly these properties, which is what makes them such a good fit for the event-driven programming model.

Reusing Existing Applications

Many popular clients and servers for various networking protocols already existed when Twisted was created. Why did glyph not just use Apache, IRCd, BIND, OpenSSH, or any of the other pre-existing applications whose clients and servers would have to get re-implemented from scratch for Twisted?

The problem is that all of these server implementations have networking code written from scratch, typically in C, with application code coupled directly to the networking layer. This makes them very difficult to use as libraries. They have to be treated as black boxes when used together, giving a developer no chance to reuse code if he or she wanted to expose the same data over multiple protocols. Additionally, the server and client implementations are often separate applications that don't share code. Extending these applications and maintaining cross-platform client-server compatibility is harder than it needs to be.

With Twisted, the clients and servers are written in Python using a consistent interface. This makes it is easy to write new clients and servers, to share code between clients and servers, to share application logic between protocols, and to test one's code.

The Reactor

Twisted implements the *reactor* design pattern, which describes demultiplexing and dispatching events from multiple sources to their handlers in a single-threaded environment.

The core of Twisted is the reactor event loop. The reactor knows about network, file system, and timer events. It waits on and then handles these events, abstracting away platform-specific behavior and presenting interfaces to make responding to events anywhere in the network stack easy.

The reactor essentially accomplishes:

```
while True:
    timeout = time_until_next_timed_event()
    events = wait_for_events(timeout)
    events += timed_events_until(now())
    for event in events:
        event.process()
```

A reactor based on the poll API[4] is the current default on all platforms. Twisted additionally supports a number of platform-specific high-volume multiplexing APIs. Platform-specific reactors include the KQueue reactor based on FreeBSD's kqueue mechanism, an epoll-based reactor for systems supporting the epoll interface (currently Linux 2.6), and an IOCP reactor based on Windows Input/Output Completion Ports.

Examples of polling implementation-dependent details that Twisted takes care of include:

---
[4]The Single UNIX Specification, Version 3 (SUSv3) describes the poll API.

- Network and filesystem limits.
- Buffering behavior.
- How to detect a dropped connection.
- The values returned in error cases.

Twisted's reactor implementation also takes care of using the underlying non-blocking APIs correctly and handling obscure edge cases correctly. Python doesn't expose the IOCP API at all, so Twisted maintains its own implementation.

Managing Callback Chains

Callbacks are a fundamental part of event-driven programming and are the way that the reactor indicates to an application that events have completed. As event-driven programs grow, handling both the success and error cases for the events in one's application becomes increasingly complex. Failing to register an appropriate callback can leave a program blocking on event processing that will never happen, and errors might have to propagate up a chain of callbacks from the networking stack through the layers of an application.

Let's examine some of the pitfalls of event-driven programs by comparing synchronous and asynchronous versions of a toy URL fetching utility in Python-like pseudo-code:

Synchronous URL fetcher:

```
import getPage

def processPage(page):
    print page
    finishProcessing()

def logError(error):
    print error
    finishProcessing()

def finishProcessing(value):
    print "Shutting down..."
    exit(0)

url = "http://google.com"
try:
    page = getPage(url)
    processPage(page)
except Error, e:
    logError(error)
finally:
    finishProcessing()
```

Asynchronous URL fetcher:

```
from twisted.internet import reactor
import getPage

def processPage(page):
    print page
    finishProcessing()

def logError(error):
    print error
    finishProcessing()

def finishProcessing(value):
    print "Shutting down..."
    reactor.stop()

url = "http://google.com"
# getPage takes: url,
#    success callback, error callback
getPage(url, processPage, logError)

reactor.run()
```

In the asynchronous URL fetcher, `reactor.run()` starts the reactor event loop. In both the synchronous and asynchronous versions, a hypothetical `getPage` function does the work of page retrieval. `processPage` is invoked if the retrieval is successful, and `logError` is invoked if an `Exception` is raised while attempting to retrieve the page. In either case, `finishProcessing` is called afterwards.

The callback to logError in the asynchronous version mirrors the except part of the try/except block in the synchronous version. The callback to processPage mirrors else, and the unconditional callback to finishProcessing mirrors finally.

In the synchronous version, by virtue of the structure of a try/except block exactly one of logError and processPage is called, and finishProcessing is always called once; in the asynchronous version it is the programmer's responsibility to invoke the correct chain of success and error callbacks. If, through programming error, the call to finishProcessing were left out of processPage or logError along their respective callback chains, the reactor would never get stopped and the program would run forever.

This toy example hints at the complexity frustrating programmers during the first few years of Twisted's development. Twisted responded to this complexity by growing an object called a Deferred.

Deferreds

The Deferred object is an abstraction of the idea of a result that doesn't exist yet. It also helps manage the callback chains for this result. When returned by a function, a Deferred is a promise that the function will have a result *at some point*. That single returned Deferred contains references to all of the callbacks registered for an event, so only this one object needs to be passed between functions, which is much simpler to keep track of than managing callbacks individually.

Deferreds have a pair of callback chains, one for success (callbacks) and one for errors (errbacks). Deferreds start out with two empty chains. One adds pairs of callbacks and errbacks to handle successes and failures at each point in the event processing. When an asynchronous result arrives, the Deferred is "fired" and the appropriate callbacks or errbacks are invoked in the order in which they were added.

Here is a version of the asynchronous URL fetcher pseudo-code which uses Deferreds:

```
from twisted.internet import reactor
import getPage

def processPage(page):
    print page

def logError(error):
    print error

def finishProcessing(value):
    print "Shutting down..."
    reactor.stop()

url = "http://google.com"
deferred = getPage(url) # getPage returns a Deferred
deferred.addCallbacks(success, failure)
deferred.addBoth(stop)

reactor.run()
```

In this version, the same event handlers are invoked, but they are all registered with a single Deferred object instead of spread out in the code and passed as arguments to getPage.

The Deferred is created with two stages of callbacks. First, addCallbacks adds the processPage callback and logError errback to the first stage of their respective chains. Then addBoth adds finishProcessing to the second stage of both chains. Diagrammatically, the callback chains look like Figure 21.2.

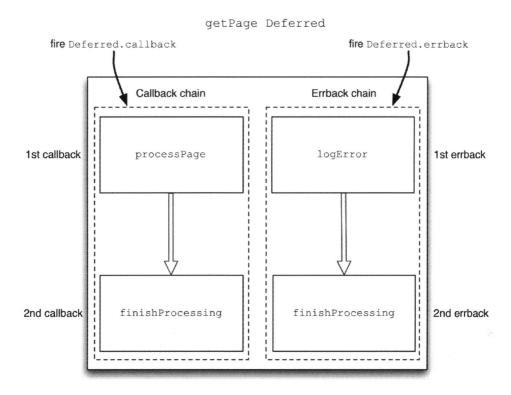

Figure 21.2: Callback chains

Deferreds can only be fired once; attempting to re-fire them will raise an Exception. This gives Deferreds semantics closer to those of the try/except blocks of their synchronous cousins, which makes processing the asynchronous events easier to reason about and avoids subtle bugs caused by callbacks being invoked more or less than once for a single event.

Understanding Deferreds is an important part of understanding the flow of Twisted programs. However, when using the high-level abstractions Twisted provides for networking protocols, one often doesn't have to use Deferreds directly at all.

The Deferred abstraction is powerful and has been borrowed by many other event-driven platforms, including jQuery, Dojo, and Mochikit.

Transports

Transports represent the connection between two endpoints communicating over a network. Transports are responsible for describing connection details, like being stream- or datagram-oriented, flow control, and reliability. TCP, UDP, and Unix sockets are examples of transports. They are designed to be "minimally functional units that are maximally reusable" and are decoupled from protocol implementations, allowing for many protocols to utilize the same type of transport. Transports implement the ITransport interface, which has the following methods:

write	Write some data to the physical connection, in sequence, in a non-blocking fashion.
writeSequence	Write a list of strings to the physical connection.
losesConnection	Write all pending data and then close the connection.
getPeer	Get the remote address of this connection.
getHost	Get the address of this side of the connection.

Decoupling transports from procotols also makes testing the two layers easier. A mock transport can simply write data to a string for inspection.

Protocols

Procotols describe how to process network events asynchronously. HTTP, DNS, and IMAP are examples of application protocols. Protocols implement the IProtocol interface, which has the following methods:

makeConnection	Make a connection to a transport and a server.
connectionMade	Called when a connection is made.
dataReceived	Called whenever data is received.
connectionLost	Called when the connection is shut down.

The relationship between the reactor, protocols, and transports is best illustrated with an example. Here are complete implementations of an echo server and client, first the server:

```
from twisted.internet import protocol, reactor

class Echo(protocol.Protocol):
    def dataReceived(self, data):
        # As soon as any data is received, write it back
        self.transport.write(data)

class EchoFactory(protocol.Factory):
    def buildProtocol(self, addr):
        return Echo()

reactor.listenTCP(8000, EchoFactory())
reactor.run()
```

And the client:

```
from twisted.internet import reactor, protocol

class EchoClient(protocol.Protocol):
    def connectionMade(self):
        self.transport.write("hello, world!")

    def dataReceived(self, data):
        print "Server said:", data
```

```
            self.transport.loseConnection()

    def connectionLost(self, reason):
        print "connection lost"

class EchoFactory(protocol.ClientFactory):
    def buildProtocol(self, addr):
        return EchoClient()

    def clientConnectionFailed(self, connector, reason):
        print "Connection failed - goodbye!"
        reactor.stop()

    def clientConnectionLost(self, connector, reason):
        print "Connection lost - goodbye!"
        reactor.stop()

reactor.connectTCP("localhost", 8000, EchoFactory())
reactor.run()
```

Running the server script starts a TCP server listening for connections on port 8000. The server uses the Echo protocol, and data is written out over a TCP transport. Running the client makes a TCP connection to the server, echoes the server response, and then terminates the connection and stops the reactor. Factories are used to produce instances of protocols for both sides of the connection. The communication is asynchronous on both sides; connectTCP takes care of registering callbacks with the reactor to get notified when data is available to read from a socket.

Applications

Twisted is an engine for producing scalable, cross-platform network servers and clients. Making it easy to deploy these applications in a standardized fashion in production environments is an important part of a platform like this getting wide-scale adoption.

To that end, Twisted developed the Twisted application infrastructure, a re-usable and configurable way to deploy a Twisted application. It allows a programmer to avoid boilerplate code by hooking an application into existing tools for customizing the way it is run, including daemonization, logging, using a custom reactor, profiling code, and more.

The application infrastructure has four main parts: Services, Applications, configuration management (via TAC files and plugins), and the twistd command-line utility. To illustrate this infrastructure, we'll turn the echo server from the previous section into an Application.

Service

A Service is anything that can be started and stopped and which adheres to the IService interface. Twisted comes with service implementations for TCP, FTP, HTTP, SSH, DNS, and many other protocols. Many Services can register with a single application.

The core of the IService interface is:

startService	Start the service. This might include loading configuration data, setting up database connections, or listening on a port.
stopService	Shut down the service. This might include saving state to disk, closing database connections, or stopping listening on a port.

Our echo service uses TCP, so we can use Twisted's default `TCPServer` implementation of this `IService` interface.

Application

An Application is the top-level service that represents the entire Twisted application. Services register themselves with an Application, and the `twistd` deployment utility described below searches for and runs Applications.

We'll create an echo Application with which the echo Service can register.

TAC Files

When managing Twisted applications in a regular Python file, the developer is responsible for writing code to start and stop the reactor and to configure the application. Under the Twisted application infrastructure, protocol implementations live in a module, Services using those protocols are registered in a Twisted Application Configuration (TAC) file, and the reactor and configuration are managed by an external utility.

To turn our echo server into an echo application, we can follow a simple algorithm:

1. Move the Protocol parts of the echo server into their own module.
2. Inside a TAC file:
    (a) Create an echo Application.
    (b) Create an instance of the `TCPServer` Service which will use our `EchoFactory`, and register it with the Application.

The code for managing the reactor will be taken care of by `twistd`, discussed below. The application code ends up looking like this:

The echo.py file:

```
from twisted.internet import protocol, reactor

class Echo(protocol.Protocol):
    def dataReceived(self, data):
        self.transport.write(data)

class EchoFactory(protocol.Factory):
    def buildProtocol(self, addr):
        return Echo()
```

The echo_server.tac file:

```
from twisted.application import internet, service
from echo import EchoFactory

application = service.Application("echo")
echoService = internet.TCPServer(8000, EchoFactory())
echoService.setServiceParent(application)
```

twistd

twistd (pronounced "twist-dee") is a cross-platform utility for deploying Twisted applications. It runs TAC files and handles starting and stopping an application. As part of Twisted's batteries-included approach to network programming, twistd comes with a number of useful configuration flags, including daemonizing the application, the location of log files, dropping privileges, running in a chroot, running under a non-default reactor, or even running the application under a profiler.

We can run our echo server Application with:

```
$ twistd -y echo_server.tac
```

In this simplest case, twistd starts a daemonized instance of the application, logging to twistd.log. After starting and stopping the application, the log looks like this:

```
2011-11-19 22:23:07-0500 [-] Log opened.
2011-11-19 22:23:07-0500 [-] twistd 11.0.0 (/usr/bin/python 2.7.1) starting up.
2011-11-19 22:23:07-0500 [-] reactor class: twisted.internet.selectreactor.SelectReactor.
2011-11-19 22:23:07-0500 [-] echo.EchoFactory starting on 8000
2011-11-19 22:23:07-0500 [-] Starting factory <echo.EchoFactory instance at 0x12d8670>
2011-11-19 22:23:20-0500 [-] Received SIGTERM, shutting down.
2011-11-19 22:23:20-0500 [-] (TCP Port 8000 Closed)
2011-11-19 22:23:20-0500 [-] Stopping factory <echo.EchoFactory instance at 0x12d8670>
2011-11-19 22:23:20-0500 [-] Main loop terminated.
2011-11-19 22:23:20-0500 [-] Server Shut Down.
```

Running a service using the Twisted application infrastructure allows developers to skip writing boilerplate code for common service functionalities like logging and daemonization. It also establishes a standard command line interface for deploying applications.

Plugins

An alternative to the TAC-based system for running Twisted applications is the plugin system. While the TAC system makes it easy to register simple hierarchies of pre-defined services within an application configuration file, the plugin system makes it easy to register custom services as subcommands of the twistd utility, and to extend the command-line interface to an application.

Using this system:

1. Only the plugin API is required to remain stable, which makes it easy for third-party developers to extend the software.
2. Plugin discoverability is codified. Plugins can be loaded and saved when a program is first run, re-discovered each time the program starts up, or polled for repeatedly at runtime, allowing the discovery of new plugins installed after the program has started.

To extend a program using the Twisted plugin system, all one has to do is create objects which implement the IPlugin interface and put them in a particular location where the plugin system knows to look for them.

Having already converted our echo server to a Twisted application, transformation into a Twisted plugin is straightforward. Alongside the echo module from before, which contains the Echo protocol and EchoFactory definitions, we add a directory called twisted, containing a subdirectory called plugins, containing our echo plugin definition. This plugin will allow us to start an echo server and specify the port to use as arguments to the twistd utility:

```
from zope.interface import implements

from twisted.python import usage
from twisted.plugin import IPlugin
from twisted.application.service import IServiceMaker
from twisted.application import internet

from echo import EchoFactory

class Options(usage.Options):
    optParameters = [["port", "p", 8000, "The port number to listen on."]]

class EchoServiceMaker(object):
    implements(IServiceMaker, IPlugin)
    tapname = "echo"
    description = "A TCP-based echo server."
    options = Options

    def makeService(self, options):
        """
        Construct a TCPServer from a factory defined in myproject.
        """
        return internet.TCPServer(int(options["port"]), EchoFactory())

serviceMaker = EchoServiceMaker()
```

Our echo server will now show up as a server option in the output of `twistd --help`, and running `twistd echo --port=1235` will start an echo server on port 1235.

Twisted comes with a pluggable authentication system for servers called `twisted.cred`, and a common use of the plugin system is to add an authentication pattern to an application. One can use `twisted.cred AuthOptionMixin` to add command-line support for various kinds of authentication off the shelf, or to add a new kind. For example, one could add authentication via a local Unix password database or an LDAP server using the plugin system.

`twistd` comes with plugins for many of Twisted's supported protocols, which turns the work of spinning up a server into a single command. Here are some examples of `twistd` servers that ship with Twisted:

`twistd web --port 8080 --path .`
> Run an HTTP server on port 8080, serving both static and dynamic content out of the current working directory.

`twistd dns -p 5553 --hosts-file=hosts`
> Run a DNS server on port 5553, resolving domains out of a file called `hosts` in the format of /etc/hosts.

`sudo twistd conch -p tcp:2222`
> Run an ssh server on port 2222. ssh keys must be set up independently.

`twistd mail -E -H localhost -d localhost=emails`
> Run an ESMTP POP3 server, accepting email for localhost and saving it to the `emails` directory.

`twistd` makes it easy to spin up a server for testing clients, but it is also pluggable, production-grade code.

In that respect, Twisted's application deployment mechanisms via TAC files, plugins, and `twistd` have been a success. However, anecdotally, most large Twisted deployments end up having to rewrite some of these management and monitoring facilities; the architecture does not quite expose what system administrators need. This is a reflection of the fact that Twisted has not historically had much architectural input from system administrators—the people who are experts at deploying and maintaining applications.

Twisted would be well-served to more aggressively solicit feedback from expert end users when making future architectural decisions in this space.

21.3 Retrospective and Lessons Learned

Twisted recently celebrated its 10th anniversary. Since its inception, inspired by the networked game landscape of the early 2000s, it has largely achieved its goal of being an extensible, cross-platform, event-driven networking engine. Twisted is used in production environments at companies from Google and Lucasfilm to Justin.TV and the Launchpad software collaboration platform. Server implementations in Twisted are the core of numerous other open source applications, including BuildBot, BitTorrent, and Tahoe-LAFS.

Twisted has had few major architectural changes since its initial development. The one crucial addition was `Deferred`, as discussed above, for managing pending results and their callback chains.

There was one important removal, which has almost no footprint in the current implementation: Twisted Application Persistence.

Twisted Application Persistence

Twisted Application Persistence (TAP) was a way of keeping an application's configuration and state in a pickle. Running an application using this scheme was a two-step process:

1. Create the pickle that represents an Application, using the now defunct `mktap` utility.
2. Use `twistd` to unpickle and run the Application.

This process was inspired by Smalltalk images, an aversion to the proliferation of seemingly ad hoc configuration languages that were hard to script, and a desire to express configuration details in Python.

TAP files immediately introduced unwanted complexity. Classes would change in Twisted without instances of those classes getting changed in the pickle. Trying to use class methods or attributes from a newer version of Twisted on the pickled object would crash the application. The notion of "upgraders" that would upgrade pickles to new API versions was introduced, but then a matrix of upgraders, pickle versions, and unit tests had to be maintained to cover all possible upgrade paths, and comprehensively accounting for all interface changes was still hard and error-prone.

TAPs and their associated utilities were abandoned and then eventually removed from Twisted and replaced with TAC files and plugins. TAP was backronymed to Twisted Application Plugin, and few traces of the failed pickling system exist in Twisted today.

The lesson learned from the TAP fiasco was that to have reasonable maintainability, persistent data needs an explicit schema. More generally, it was a lesson about adding complexity to a project: when considering introducing a novel system for solving a problem, make sure the complexity of that solution is well understood and tested and that the benefits are clearly worth the added complexity before committing the project to it.

web2: a lesson on rewrites

While not primarily an architectural decision, a project management decision about rewriting the Twisted Web implementation has had long-term ramifications for Twisted's image and the maintainers' ability to make architectural improvements to other parts of the code base, and it deserves a short discussion.

In the mid-2000s, the Twisted developers decided to do a full rewrite of the `twisted.web` APIs as a separate project in the Twisted code base called web2. web2 would contain numerous improvements over `twisted.web`, including full HTTP 1.1 support and a streaming data API.

web2 was labelled as experimental, but ended up getting used by major projects anyway and was even accidentally released and packaged by Debian. Development on web and web2 continued concurrently for years, and new users were perennially frustrated by the side-by-side existence of both projects and a lack of clear messaging about which project to use. The switchover to web2 never happened, and in 2011 web2 was finally removed from the code base and the website. Some of the improvements from web2 are slowly getting ported back to web.

Partially because of web2, Twisted developed a reputation for being hard to navigate and structurally confusing to newcomers. Years later, the Twisted community still works hard to combat this image.

The lesson learned from web2 was that rewriting a project from scratch is often a bad idea, but if it has to happen make sure that the developer community understands the long-term plan, and that the user community has one clear choice of implementation to use during the rewrite.

If Twisted could go back and do web2 again, the developers would have done a series of backwards-compatible changes and deprecations to `twisted.web` instead of a rewrite.

Keeping Up with the Internet

The way that we use the Internet continues to evolve. The decision to implement many protocols as part of the core software burdens Twisted with maintaining code for all of those protocols. Implementations have to evolve with changing standards and the adoption of new protocols while maintaining a strict backwards-compatibility policy.

Twisted is primarily a volunteer-driven project, and the limiting factor for development is not community enthusiasm, but rather volunteer time. For example, RFC 2616 defining HTTP 1.1 was released in 1999, work began on adding HTTP 1.1 support to Twisted's HTTP protocol implementations in 2005, and the work was completed in 2009. Support for IPv6, defined in RFC 2460 in 1998, is in progress but unmerged as of 2011.

Implementations also have to evolve as the interfaces exposed by supported operating systems change. For example, the `epoll` event notification facility was added to Linux 2.5.44 in 2002, and Twisted grew an epoll-based reactor to take advantage of this new API. In 2007, Apple released OS 10.5 Leopard with a `poll` implementation that didn't support devices, which was buggy enough behavior for Apple to not expose `select.poll` in its build of Python[5]. Twisted has had to work around this issue and document it for users ever since.

Sometimes, Twisted development doesn't keep up with the changing networking landscape, and enhancements are moved to libraries outside of the core software. For example, the Wokkel project[6], a collection of enhancements to Twisted's Jabber/XMPP support, has lived as a to-be-merged independent project for years without a champion to oversee the merge. An attempt was

---

[5]http://twistedmatrix.com/trac/ticket/4173
[6]http://wokkel.ik.nu/

made to add WebSockets to Twisted as browsers began to adopt support for the new protocol in 2009, but development moved to external projects after a decision not to include the protocol until it moved from an IETF draft to a standard.

All of this being said, the proliferation of libraries and add-ons is a testament to Twisted's flexibility and extensibility. A strict test-driven development policy and accompanying documentation and coding standards help the project avoid regressions and preserve backwards compatibility while maintaining a large matrix of supported protocols and platforms. It is a mature, stable project that continues to have very active development and adoption.

Twisted looks forward to being the engine of your Internet for another ten years.

Yesod
Michael Snoyman

Yesod is a web framework written in the Haskell programming language. While many popular web frameworks exploit the dynamic nature of their host languages, Yesod exploits the static nature of Haskell to produce safer, faster code.

Development began about two years ago and has been going strong ever since. Yesod cut its teeth on real life projects, with all of its initial features born out of an actual, real-life need. At first, development was almost entirely a one-man show. After about a year of development the community efforts kicked in, and Yesod has since blossomed into a thriving open source project.

During the embryonic phase, when Yesod was incredibly ephemeral and ill-defined, it would have been counter-productive to try and get a team to work on it. By the time it stabilized enough to be useful to others, it was the right time to find out the downsides to some of the decisions that had been made. Since then, we have made major changes to the user-facing API to make it more useful, and are quickly solidifying a 1.0 release.

The question you may ask is: Why another web framework? Let's instead redirect to a different question: Why use Haskell? It seems that most of the world is happy with one of two styles of language:

- Statically typed languages, like Java, C# and C++. These languages provide speed and type safety, but are more cumbersome to program with.
- Dynamically typed languages, like Ruby and Python. These languages greatly increase productivity (at least in the short run), but run slowly and have very little support from the compiler to ensure correctness. (The solution to this last point is unit testing. We'll get to that later.)

This is a false dichotomy. There's no reason why statically typed languages need to be so clumsy. Haskell is able to capture a huge amount of the expressivity of Ruby and Python, while remaining a strongly typed language. In fact, Haskell's type system catches many more bugs than Java and its ilk. Null pointer exceptions are completely eliminated; immutable data structures simplify reasoning about your code and simplify parallel and concurrent programming.

So why Haskell? It is an efficient, developer-friendly language which provides many compile-time checks of program correctness.

The goal of Yesod is to extend Haskell's strengths into web development. Yesod strives to make your code as concise as possible. As much as possible, every line of your code is checked for correctness at compile time. Instead of requiring large libraries of unit tests to test basic properties, the compiler does it all for you. Under the surface, Yesod uses as many advanced performance techniques as we can muster to make your high-level code fly.

22.1 Compared to Other Frameworks

In general terms, Yesod is more similar to than different than the leading frameworks such as Rails and Django. It generally follows the Model-View-Controller (MVC) paradigm, has a templating system that separates view from logic, provides an Object-Relational Mapping (ORM) system, and has a front controller approach to routing.

The devil is in the details. Yesod strives to push as much error catching to the compile phase instead of runtime, and to automatically catch both bugs and security flaws through the type system. While Yesod tries to maintain a user-friendly, high-level API, it uses a number of newer techniques from the functional programming world to achieve high performance, and is not afraid to expose these internals to developers.

The main architectural challenge in Yesod is balancing these two seemingly conflicting goals. For example, there is nothing revolutionary about Yesod's approach to routing (called *type-safe URLs*[1]. Historically, implementing such a solution was a tedious, error-prone process. Yesod's innovation is to use Template Haskell (a form of code generation) to automate the boilerplate required to bootstrap the process. Similarly, type-safe HTML has been around for a long while; Yesod tries to keep the developer-friendly aspect of common template languages while keeping the power of type safety.

22.2 Web Application Interface

A web application needs some way to communicate with a server. One possible approach is to bake the server directly into the framework, but doing so necessarily limits your options for deployment and leads to poor interfaces. Many languages have created standard interfaces to address this issue: Python has WSGI and Ruby has Rack. In Haskell, we have WAI: Web Application Interface.

WAI is not intended to be a high-level interface. It has two specific goals: generality and performance. By staying general, WAI has been able to support backends for everything from standalone servers to old school CGI and even works directly with Webkit to produce faux desktop applications. The performance side will introduce us to a number of the cool features of Haskell.

Datatypes

One of the biggest advantages of Haskell—and one of the things we make the most use of in Yesod—is strong static typing. Before we begin to write the code for how to solve something, we need to think about what the data will look like. WAI is a perfect example of this paradigm. The core concept we want to express is that of an application. An application's most basic expression is a function that takes a request and returns a response. In Haskell lingo:

```
type Application = Request -> Response
```

This just raises the question: what do `Request` and `Response` look like? A request has a number of pieces of information, but the most basic are the requested path, query string, request headers, and request body. And a response has just three components: a status code, response headers and response body.

How do we represent something like a query string? Haskell keeps a strict separation between binary and textual data. The former is represented by `ByteString`, the latter by `Text`. Both are

---
[1] http://www.yesodweb.com/blog/2012/01/aosa-chapter#file1414-routes

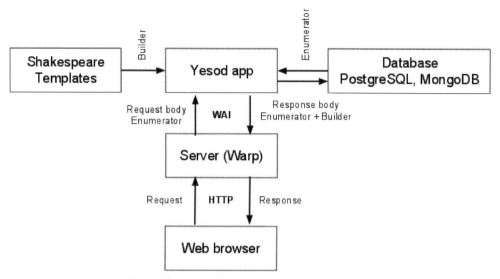

Figure 22.1: Overall structure of a Yesod application

highly optimized datatypes that provide a high-level, safe API. In the case of a query string we store the raw bytes transferred over the wire as a ByteString and the parsed, decoded values as Text.

Streaming

A ByteString represents a single memory buffer. If we were to naively use a plain ByteString for holding the entire request or response bodies, our applications could never scale to large requests or responses. Instead, we use a technique called enumerators, very similar in concept to generators in Python. Our Application becomes a consumer of a stream of ByteStrings representing the incoming request body, and a producer of a separate stream for the response.

We now need to slightly revise our definition of an Application. An Application will take a Request value, containing headers, query string, etc., and will consume a stream of ByteStrings, producing a Response. So the revised definition of an Application is:

```
type Application = Request -> Iteratee ByteString IO Response
```

The IO simply explains what types of side effects an application can perform. In the case of IO, it can perform any kind of interaction with the outside world, an obvious necessity for the vast majority of web applications.

Builder

The trick in our arsenal is how we produce our response buffers. We have two competing desires here: minimizing system calls, and minimizing buffer copies. On the one hand, we want to minimize system calls for sending data over the socket. To do this we need to store outgoing data in a buffer. However, if we make this buffer too large, we will exhaust our memory and slow down the application's response time. On the other hand, we want to minimize the number of times data is copied between buffers, preferably copying just once from the source to destination buffer.

Haskell's solution is the *builder*. A builder is an instruction for how to fill a memory buffer, such as: place the five bytes "hello" in the next open position. Instead of passing a stream of memory buffers to the server, a WAI application passes a stream of these instructions. The server takes the stream and uses it to fill up optimally sized memory buffers. As each buffer is filled, the server makes a system call to send the data over over the wire and then starts filling up the next buffer.

(The optimal size for a buffer will depend on many factors such as cache size. The underlying blaze-builder library underwent significant performance testing to determine the best trade-off.)

In theory, this kind of optimization could be performed in the application itself. However, by encoding this approach in the interface, we are able to simply prepend the response headers to the response body. The result is that, for small to medium-sized responses, the entire response can be sent with a single system call and memory is copied only once.

Handlers

Now that we have an application, we need some way to run it. In WAI parlance, this is a *handler*. WAI has some basic, standard handlers, such as the standalone server Warp (discussed below), FastCGI, SCGI and CGI. This spectrum allows WAI applications to be run on anything from dedicated servers to shared hosting. But in addition to these, WAI has some more interesting backends:

Webkit: This backend embeds a Warp server and calls out to QtWebkit. By launching a server, then launching a new standalone browser window, we have faux desktop applications.

Launch: This is a slight variant on Webkit. Having to deploy the Qt and Webkit libraries can be a bit burdensome, so instead we just launch the user's default browser.

Test: Even testing counts as a handler. After all, testing is simply the act of running an application and inspecting the responses.

Most developers will likely use Warp. It is lightweight enough to be used for testing. It requires no config files, no folder hierarchy and no long-running, administrator-owned process. It's a simple library that gets compiled into your application or run via the Haskell interpreter. Warp is an incredibly fast server, with protection from all kinds of attack vectors, such as Slowloris and infinite headers. Warp can be the only web server you need, though it is also quite happy to sit behind a reverse HTTP proxy.

The PONG benchmark measures the requests per second of various servers for the 4-byte response body "PONG". In the graph shown in Figure 22.2, Yesod is measured as a framework on top of Warp. As can be seen, the Haskell servers (Warp, Happstack and Snap) lead the pack.

Most of the reasons for Warp's speed have already been spelled out in the overall description of WAI: enumerators, builders and packed datatypes. The last piece in the puzzle is from the Glasgow Haskell Compiler's (GHC's) multithreaded runtime. GHC, Haskell's flagship compiler, has lightweight green threads. Unlike system threads, it is possible to spin up thousands of these without serious performance hits. Therefore, in Warp each connection is handled by its own green thread.

The next trick is asynchronous I/O. Any web server hoping to scale to tens of thousands of requests per second will need some type of asynchronous communication. In most languages, this involves complicated programming involving callbacks. GHC lets us cheat: we program as if we're using a synchronous API, and GHC automatically switches between different green threads waiting for activity.

Under the surface, GHC uses whatever system is provided by the host operating system, such as `kqueue`, `epoll` and `select`. This gives us all the performance of an event-based I/O system, without worrying about cross-platform issues or writing in a callback-oriented way.

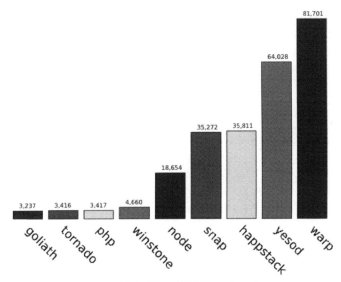

Figure 22.2: Warp PONG benchmark

Middleware

In between handlers and applications, we have `middleware`. Technically, middleware is an *application transformer*: it takes one Application, and returns a new one. This is defined as:

```
type Middleware = Application -> Application
```

The best way to understand the purpose of middleware is to look at some common examples:

- gzip automatically compresses the response from an application.
- jsonp automatically converts JSON responses to JSON-P responses when the client provided a callback parameter.
- autohead will generate appropriate HEAD responses based on the GET response of an application.
- debug will print debug information to the console or a log on each request.

The idea here is to factor out common code from applications and let it be shared easily. Note that, based on the definition of middleware, we can easily stack these things up. The general workflow of middleware is:

1. Take the request value and apply some modifications.
2. Pass the modified request to the application and receive a response.
3. Modify the response and return it to the handler.

In the case of stacked middleware, instead of passing to the application or handler, the in-between middleware will actually be passing to the inner and outer middleware, respectively.

Wai-test

No amount of static typing will obviate the need for testing. We all know that automated testing is a necessity for any serious applications. `wai-test` is the recommended approach to testing a WAI application. Since requests and responses are simple datatypes, it is easy to mock up a fake request, pass it to an application, and test properties about the response. `wai-test` simply provides some convenience functions for testing common properties like the presence of a header or a status code.

22.3 Templates

In the typical Model-View-Controller (MVC) paradigm, one of the goals is to separate logic from the view. Part of this separation is achieved through the use of a template language. However, there are many different ways to approach this issue. At one end of the spectrum, for example, PHP/ASP/JSP will allow you to embed any arbitrary code within your template. At the other end, you have systems like StringTemplate and QuickSilver, which are passed some arguments and have no other way of interacting with the rest of the program.

Each system has its pros and cons. Having a more powerful template system can be a huge convenience. Need to show the contents of a database table? No problem, pull it in with the template. However, such an approach can quickly lead to convoluted code, interspersing database cursor updates with HTML generation. This can be commonly seen in a poorly written ASP project.

While weak template systems make for simple code, they also tend towards a lot of redundant work. You will often need to not only keep your original values in datatypes, but also create dictionaries of values to pass to the template. Maintaining such code is not easy, and usually there is no way for a compiler to help you out.

Yesod's family of template languages, the Shakespearean languages, strive for a middle ground. By leveraging Haskell's standard referential transparency, we can be assured that our templates produce no side effects. However, they still have full access to all the variables and functions available in your Haskell code. Also, since they are fully checked for both well-formedness, variable resolution and type safety at compile time, typos are much less likely to have you searching through your code trying to pin down a bug.

Why the Name Shakespeare?
The HTML language, Hamlet, was the first language written, and originally based its syntax on Haml. Since it was at the time a "reduced" Haml, Hamlet seemed appropriate. As we added CSS and Javascript options, we decided to keep the naming theme with Cassius and Julius. At this point, Hamlet looks nothing like Haml, but the name stuck anyway.

Types

One of the overarching themes in Yesod is proper use of types to make developers' lives easier. In Yesod templates, we have two main examples:

1. All content embedded into a Hamlet template must have a type of `Html`. As we'll see later, this forces us to properly escape dangerous HTML when necessary, while avoiding accidental double-escaping as well.
2. Instead of concatenating URLs directly in our template, we have datatypes—known as type-safe URLs—which represent the routes in our application.

As a real-life example, suppose that a user submits his/her name to an application via a form. This data would be represented with the `Text` datatype. Now we would like to display this variable, called name, in a page. The type system—at compile time—prevents it from being simply stuck into a Hamlet template, since it's not of type Html. Instead we must convert it somehow. For this, there are two conversion functions:

1. toHtml will automatically escape any entities. So if a user submits the string <script src="http://example.com/evil.js"></script>, the less-than signs will automatically be converted to &<.
2. preEscapedText, on the other hand, will leave the content precisely as it is now.

So in the case of untrusted input from a possibly nefarious user, toHtml would be our recommended approach. On the other hand, let us say we have some static HTML stored on our server that we would like to insert into some pages verbatim. In that case, we could load it into a Text value and then apply preEscapedText, thereby avoiding any double-escaping.

By default, Hamlet will use the toHtml function on any content you try to interpolate. Therefore, you only need to explicitly perform a conversion if you want to avoid escaping. This follows the dictum of erring on the side of caution.

```
name <- runInputPost $ ireq textField "name"
snippet <- readFile "mysnippet.html"
return [hamlet|
    <p>Welcome #{name}, you are on my site!
    <div .copyright>#{preEscapedText snippet}
|]
```

The first step in type-safe URLs is creating a datatype that represents all the routes in your site. Let us say you have a site for displaying Fibonacci numbers. The site will have a separate page for each number in the sequence, plus the homepage. This could be modeled with the Haskell datatype:

```
data FibRoute = Home | Fib Int
```

We could then create a page like so:

```
<p>You are currently viewing number #{show index} in the sequence. Its value is #{fib index}.
<p>
    <a href=@{Fib (index + 1)}>Next number
<p>
    <a href=@{Home}>Homepage
```

Then all we need is some function to convert a type-safe URL into a string representation. In our case, that could look something like this:

```
render :: FibRoute -> Text
render Home = "/home"
render (Fib i) = "/fib/" ++ show i
```

Fortunately, all of the boilerplate of defining and rendering type-safe URL datatypes is handled for the developer automatically by Yesod. We will cover that in more depth later.

The Other Languages

In addition to Hamlet, there are three other languages: Julius, Cassius and Lucius. Julius is used for Javascript; however, it's a simple pass-through language, just allowing for interpolation. In other words, barring accidental use of the interpolation syntax, any piece of Javascript could be dropped into Julius and be valid. For example, to test the performance of Julius, jQuery was run through the language without an issue.

The other two languages are alternate CSS syntaxes. Those familiar with the difference between Sass and Less will recognize this immediately: Cassius is whitespace delimited, while Lucius uses braces. Lucius is in fact a superset of CSS, meaning all valid CSS files are valid Lucius files. In addition to allowing text interpolation, there are some helper datatypes provided to model unit sizes and colors. Also, type-safe URLs work in these languages, making it convenient for specifying background images.

Aside from the type safety and compile-time checks mentioned above, having specialized languages for CSS and Javascript give us a few other advantages:

- For production, all the CSS and Javascript is compiled into the final executable, increasing performance (by avoiding file I/O) and simplifying deployment.
- By being based around the efficient builder construct described earlier, the templates can be rendered very quickly.
- There is built-in support for automatically including these in final webpages. We will get into this in more detail when describing widgets below.

22.4 Persistent

Most web applications will want to store information in a database. Traditionally, this has meant some kind of SQL database. In that regard, Yesod continues a long tradition, with PostgreSQL as our most commonly used backend. But as we have been seeing in recent years, SQL isn't always the answer to the persistence question. Therefore, Yesod was designed to work well with NoSQL databases as well, and ships with a MongoDB backend as a first-class citizen.

The result of this design decision is Persistent, Yesod's preferred storage option. There are really two guiding lights for Persistent: make it as back-end-agnostic as possible, and let user code be completely type-checked.

At the same time, we fully recognize that it is impossible to completely shield the user from all details of the backend. Therefore, we provide two types of escape routes:

- Back-end-specific functionality as necessary. For example, Persistent provides features for SQL joins and MongoDB lists and hashes. Proper portability warnings will apply, but if you want this functionality, it's there.
- Easy access to performing raw queries. We don't believe it's possible for any abstraction to cover every use case of the underlying library. If you just have to write a 5-table, correlated subquery in SQL, go right ahead.

Terminology

The most primitive datatype in Persistent is the `PersistValue`. This represents any raw data that can appear within the database, such as a number, a date, or a string. Of course, sometimes you'll have some more user-friendly datatypes you want to store, like HTML. For that, we have the `PersistField` class. Internally, a `PersistField` expresses itself to the database in terms of a `PersistValue`.

All of this is very nice, but we will want to combine different fields together into a larger picture. For this, we have a `PersistEntity`, which is basically a collection of `PersistFields`. And finally, we have a `PersistBackend` that describes how to create, read, update and delete these entities.

As a practical example, consider storing a person in a database. We want to store the person's name, birthday, and a profile image (a PNG file). We create a new entity `Person` with three fields: a `Text`, a `Day` and a `PNG`. Each of those gets stored in the database using a different `PersistValue` constructor: `PersistText`, `PersistDay` and `PersistByteString`, respectively.

There is nothing surprising about the first two mappings, but the last one is interesting. There is no specific constructor for storing PNG content in a database, so instead we use a more generic type (a `ByteString`, which is just a sequence of bytes). We could use the same mechanism to store other types of arbitrary data.

(The commonly held best practice for storing images is to keep the data on the filesystem and just keep a path to the image in the database. We do not advocate against using that approach, but are rather using database-stored images as an illustrative example.)

How is all this represented in the database? Consider SQL as an example: the `Person` entity becomes a table with three columns (name, birthday, and picture). Each field is stored as a different SQL type: `Text` becomes a `VARCHAR`, `Day` becomes a `Date` and `PNG` becomes a `BLOB` (or `BYTEA`).

The story for MongoDB is very similar. `Person` becomes its own *document*, and its three fields each become a MongoDB *field*. There is no need for datatypes or creation of a schema in MongoDB.

Persistent	SQL	MongoDB
PersistEntity	Table	Document
PersistField	Column	Field
PersistValue	Column type	N/A

Type Safety

Persistent handles all of the data marshaling concerns behind the scenes. As a user of Persistent, you get to completely ignore the fact that a `Text` becomes a `VARCHAR`. You are able to simply declare your datatypes and use them.

Every interaction with Persistent is strongly typed. This prevents you from accidentally putting a number in the date fields; the compiler will not accept it. Entire classes of subtle bugs simply disappear at this point.

Nowhere is the power of strong typing more pronounced than in refactoring. Let's say you have been storing users' ages in the database, and you realize that you really wanted to store birthdays instead. You are able to make a single line change to your entities declaration file, hit compile, and automatically find every single line of code that needs to be updated.

In most dynamically-typed languages, and their web frameworks, the recommended approach to solving this issue is writing unit tests. If you have full test coverage, then running your tests will immediately reveal what code needs to be updated. This is all well and good, but it is a weaker solution than true types:

- It is all predicated on having full test coverage. This takes extra time, and worse, is boilerplate code that the compiler should be able to do for you.
- You might be a perfect developer who never forgets to write a test, but can you say the same for every person who will touch your codebase?

- Even 100% test coverage doesn't guarantee that you really have tested every case. All it's done is proven you've tested every line of code.

Cross-Database Syntax

Creating an SQL schema that works for multiple SQL engines can be tricky enough. How do you create a schema that will also work with a non-SQL database like MongoDB?

Persistent allows you to define your entities in a high-level syntax, and will automatically create the SQL schema for you. In the case of MongoDB, we currently use a schema-less approach. This also allows Persistent to ensure that your Haskell datatypes match perfectly with the database's definitions.

Additionally, having all this information gives Persistent the ability to perform more advanced functions, such as migrations, for you automatically.

Migrations

Persistent not only creates schema files as necessary, but will also automatically apply database migrations if possible. Database modification is one of the less-developed pieces of the SQL standard, and thus each engine has a different take on the process. As such, each Persistent backend defines its own set of migration rules. In PostgreSQL, which has a rich set of ALTER TABLE rules, we use those extensively. Since SQLite lacks much of that functionality, we are reduced to creating temporary tables and copying rows. MongoDB's schema-less approach means no migration support is required.

This feature is purposely limited to prevent any kind of data loss. It will not remove any columns automatically; instead, it will give you an error message, telling you the unsafe operations that are necessary in order to continue. You will then have the option of either manually running the SQL it provides you, or changing your data model to avoid the dangerous behavior.

Relations

Persistent is non-relational in nature, meaning it has no requirement for backends to support relations. However, in many use cases, we may want to use relations. In those cases, developers will have full access to them.

Assume we want to now store a list of skills with each user. If we were writing a MongoDB-specific app, we could go ahead and just store that list as a new field in the original Person entity. But that approach would not work in SQL. In SQL, we call this kind of relationship a one-to-many relationship.

The idea is to store a reference to the "one" entity (person) with each "many" entity (skill). Then if we want to find all the skills a person has, we simply find all skills that reference that person. For this reference, every entity has an ID. And as you might expect by now, these IDs are completely type-safe. The datatype for a Person ID is PersonId. So to add our new skill, we would just add the following to our entity definition:

```
Skill
    person PersonId
    name Text
    description Text
    UniqueSkill person name
```

This ID datatype concept comes up throughout Persistent and Yesod. You can dispatch based on an ID. In such a case, Yesod will automatically marshal the textual representation of the ID to the internal one, catching any parse errors along the way. These IDs are used for lookup and deletion with the get and delete functions, and are returned by the insertion and query functions insert and selectList.

22.5 Yesod

If we are looking at the typical Model-View-Controller (MVC) paradigm, Persistent is the model and Shakespeare is the view. This would leave Yesod as the controller.

The most basic feature of Yesod is routing. It features a declarative syntax and type-safe dispatch. Layered on top of this, Yesod provides many other features: streaming content generation, widgets, i18n, static files, forms and authentication. But the core feature added by Yesod is really routing.

This layered approach makes it simpler for users to swap different components of the system. Some people are not interested in using Persistent. For them, nothing in the core system even mentions Persistent. Likewise, while they are commonly used features, not everyone needs authentication or static file serving.

On the other hand, many users *will* want to integrate all of these features. And doing so, while enabling all the optimizations available in Yesod, is not always straightforward. To simplify the process, Yesod also provides a scaffolding tool that sets up a basic site with the most commonly used features.

Routes

Given that routing is really the main function of Yesod, let's start there. The routing syntax is very simple: a *resource pattern*, a name, and request methods. For example, a simple blog site might look like:

```
/ HomepageR GET
/add-entry AddEntryR GET POST
/entry/#EntryId EntryR GET
```

The first line defines the homepage. This says "I respond to the root path of the domain, I'm called HomepageR, and I answer GET requests." (The trailing "R" on the resource names is simply a convention, it doesn't hold any special meaning besides giving a cue to the developer that something is a route.)

The second line defines the add-entry page. This time, we answer both GET and POST requests. You might be wondering why Yesod, as opposed to most frameworks, requires you to explicitly state your request methods. The reason is that Yesod tries to adhere to RESTful principles as much as possible, and GET and POST requests really have very different meanings. Not only do you state these two methods separately, but later you will define their handler functions separately. (This is actually an optional feature in Yesod. If you want, you can leave off the list of methods and your handler function will deal with all methods.)

The third line is a bit more interesting. After the second slash we have #EntryId. This defines a parameter of type EntryId. We already alluded to this feature in the Persistent section: Yesod will now automatically marshal the path component into the relevant ID value. Assuming an SQL backend (Mongo is addressed later), if a user requests /entry/5, the handler function will get called with an argument `EntryId` 5. But if the user requests `/entry/some-blog-post`, Yesod will return a 404.

This is obviously possible in most other web frameworks as well. The approach taken by Django, for instance, would use a regular expression for matching the routes, e.g. `r"/entry/(+)"`. The Yesod approach, however, provides some advantages:

- Typing "EntryId" is much more semantic/developer-friendly than a regular expression.
- Regular expressions cannot express everything (or at least, can't do so succinctly). We can use `/calendar/#Day` in Yesod; do you want to type a regex to match dates in your routes?
- Yesod also automatically marshals the data for us. In our calendar case, our handler function would receive a `Day` value. In the Django equivalent, the function would receive a piece of text which it would then have to marshal itself. This is tedious, repetitive and inefficient.
- So far we've assumed that a database ID is just a string of digits. But what if it's more complicated? MongoDB uses GUIDs, for example. In Yesod, your `#EntryId` will still work, and the type system will instruct Yesod how to parse the route. In a regex system, you would have to go through all of your routes and change the \d+ to whatever monstrosity of regex is needed to match GUIDs.

Type-Safe URLs

This approach to routing gives birth to one of Yesod's most powerful features: type-safe URLs. Instead of just splicing together pieces of text to refer to a route, every route in your application can be represented by a Haskell value. This immediately eliminates a large number of 404 Not Found errors: it is simply not possible to produce an invalid URL. (It is still possible to produce a URL that would lead to a 404 error, such as by referring to a blog post that does not exist. However, all URLs will be formed correctly.)

So how does this magic work? Each site has a route datatype, and each resource pattern gets its own constructor. In our previous example, we would get something that looks like:

```
data MySiteRoute = HomepageR
                 | AddEntryR
                 | EntryR EntryId
```

If you want to link to the homepage, you use `HomepageR`. To link to a specific entry, you would use the `EntryR` constructor with an `EntryId` parameter. For example, to create a new entry and redirect to it, you could write:

```
entryId <- insert (Entry "My Entry" "Some content")
redirect RedirectTemporary (EntryR entryId)
```

Hamlet, Lucius and Julius all include built-in support for these type-safe URLs. Inside a Hamlet template you can easily create a link to the add-entry page:

```
<a href=@{AddEntryR}>Create a new entry.
```

The best part? Just like Persistent entities, the compiler will keep you honest. If you change any of your routes (e.g., you want to include the year and month in your entry routes), Yesod will force you to update every single reference throughout your codebase.

Handlers

Once you define your routes, you need to tell Yesod how you want to respond to requests. This is where *handler functions* come into play. The setup is simple: for each resource (e.g., HomepageR) and request method, create a function named methodResourceR. For our previous example, we would need four functions: getHomepageR, getAddEntryR, postAddEntryR, and getEntryR.

All of the parameters collected from the route are passed in as arguments to the handler function. getEntryR will take a first argument of type EntryId, while all the other functions will take no arguments.

The handler functions live in a Handler monad, which provides a great deal of functionality, such as redirecting, accessing sessions, and running database queries. For the last one, a typical way to start off the getEntryR function would be:

```
getEntryR entryId = do
    entry <- runDB $ get404 entryId
```

This will run a database action that will get the entry associated with the given ID from the database. If there is no such entry, it will return a 404 response.

Each handler function will return some value, which must be an instance of HasReps. This is another RESTful feature at play: instead of just returning some HTML or some JSON, you can return a value that will return either one, depending on the HTTP Accept request header. In other words, in Yesod, a resource is a specific piece of data, and it can be returned in one of many *representations*.

Widgets

Assume you want to include a navbar on a few different pages of your site. This navbar will load up the five most recent blog posts (stored in your database), generate some HTML, and then need some CSS and Javascript to style and enhance.

Without a higher-level interface to tie these components together, this could be a pain to implement. You could add the CSS to the site-wide CSS file, but that's adding extra declarations you don't always need. Likewise with the Javascript, though a bit worse: having that extra Javascript might cause problems on a page it was not intended to live on. You will also be breaking modularity by having to generate the database results from multiple handler functions.

In Yesod, we have a very simple solution: widgets. A widget is a piece of code that ties together HTML, CSS and Javascript, allowing you to add content to both the head and body, and can run any arbitrary code that belongs in a handler. For example, to implement our navbar:

```
-- Get last five blog posts. The "lift" says to run this code like we're in the handler.
entries <- lift $ runDB $ selectList [] [LimitTo 5, Desc EntryPosted]
toWidget [hamlet|
<ul .navbar>
    $forall entry <- entries
        <li>#{entryTitle entry}
|]
toWidget [lucius| .navbar { color: red } |]
toWidget [julius|alert("Some special Javascript to play with my navbar");|]
```

But there is even more power at work here. When you produce a page in Yesod, the standard approach is to combine a number of widgets together into a single widget containing all your page content, and then apply `defaultLayout`. This function is defined per site, and applies the standard site layout.

There are two out-of-the-box approaches to handling where the CSS and Javascript go:

1. Concatenate them and place them into `style` and `script` tags, respectively, within your HTML.
2. Place them in external files and refer to them with `link` and `script` tags, respectively.

In addition, your Javascript can be automatically minified. Option 2 is the preferred approach, since it allows a few extra optimizations:

1. The files are created with names based on a hash of the contents. This means you can place cached values far in the future without worries of users receiving stale content.
2. Your Javascript can be asynchronously loaded.

The second point requires a bit of elaboration. Widgets not only contain raw Javascript, they also contain a list of Javascript dependencies. For example, many sites will refer to the jQuery library and then add some Javascript that uses it. Yesod is able to automatically turn all of that into an asynchronous load via `yepnope.js`.

In other words, widgets allow you to create modular, composable code that will result in incredibly efficient serving of your static resources.

Subsites

Many websites share common areas of functionality. Perhaps the two most common examples of this are serving static files and authentication. In Yesod, you can easily drop in this code using a *subsite*. All you need to do is add an extra line to your routes. For example, to add the static subsite, you would write:

```
/static StaticR Static getStatic
```

The first argument tells where in the site the subsite starts. The static subsite is usually used at `/static`, but you could use whatever you want. `StaticR` is the name of the route; this is also entirely up to you, but convention is to use `StaticR`. `Static` is the name of the static subsite; this is one you do not have control over. `getStatic` is a function that returns the settings for the static site, such as where the static files are located.

Like all of your handlers, the subsite handlers also have access to the `defaultLayout` function. This means that a well-designed subsite will automatically use your site skin without any extra intervention on your part.

22.6 Lessons Learned

Yesod has been a very rewarding project to work on. It has given me an opportunity to work on a large system with a diverse group of developers. One of the things that has truly shocked me is how different the end product has become from what I had originally intended. I started off Yesod by creating a list of goals. Very few of the main features we currently tout in Yesod are in that list, and a good portion of that list is no longer something I plan to implement. The first lesson is:

You will have a better idea of the system you need after you start working on it. Do not tie yourself down to your initial ideas.

As this was my first major piece of Haskell code, I learned a lot about the language during Yesod's development. I'm sure others can relate to the feeling of "How did I ever write code like this?" Even though that initial code was not of the same caliber as the code we have in Yesod at this point, it was solid enough to kick-start the project. The second lesson is:

Don't be deterred by supposed lack of mastery of the tools at hand. Write the best code you can, and keep improving it.

One of the most difficult steps in Yesod's development was moving from a single-person team—me—to collaborating with others. It started off simply, with merging pull requests on GitHub, and eventually moved to having a number of core maintainers. I had established some of my own development patterns, which were nowhere explained or documented. As a result, contributors found it difficult to pull my latest unreleased changes and play around with them. This hindered others both when contributing and testing.

When Greg Weber came aboard as another lead on Yesod, he put in place a lot of the coding standards that were sorely lacking. To compound the problems, there were some inherent difficulties playing with the Haskell development toolchain; specifically in dealing with Yesod's large number of packages. One of the goals of the entire Yesod team has since been to create standard scripts and tools to automate building. Many of these tools are making their way back into the general Haskell community. The final lesson is:

Consider early on how to make your project approachable for others.

[chapter 23]

Yocto
Elizabeth Flanagan

The Yocto Project is an open source project that provides a common starting point for developers of embedded Linux systems to create customized distributions for embedded products in a hardware-agnostic setting. Sponsored by the Linux Foundation, Yocto is more than a build system. It provides tools, processes, templates and methods so developers can rapidly create and deploy products for the embedded market. One of the core components of Yocto is the Poky Build system. As Poky is a large and complex system, we will be focusing on one of its core components, BitBake. BitBake is a Gentoo-Portage-inspired build tool, used by both the Yocto Project and OpenEmbedded communities to utilize metadata to create Linux images from source.

In 2001, Sharp Corporation introduced the SL-5000 PDA, named Zaurus, which ran an embedded Linux distribution, Lineo. Not long after the Zaurus's introduction, Chris Larson founded the OpenZaurus Project, a replacement Linux distribution for the SharpROM, based on a build system called buildroot. With the founding of the project, people began contributing many more software packages, as well as targets for other devices, and it wasn't long before the build system for OpenZaurus began to show fragility. In January 2003, the community began discussing a new build system to incorporate the community usage model of a generic build system for embedded Linux distributions. This would eventually become OpenEmbedded. Chris Larson, Michael Lauer, and Holger Schurig began work on OpenEmbedded by porting hundreds of OpenZaurus packages over to the new build system.

The Yocto Project springs from this work. At the project's core is the Poky build system, created by Richard Purdie. It began as a stabilized branch of OpenEmbedded using a core subset of the thousands of OpenEmbedded recipes, across a limited set of architectures. Over time, it slowly coalesced into more than just an embedded build system, but into a complete software development platform, with an Eclipse plugin, a fakeroot replacement and QEMU based images. Around November 2010, the Linux Foundation announced that this work would all continue under the heading of the Yocto Project as a Linux Foundation-sponsored project. It was then established that Yocto and OpenEmbedded would coordinate on a core set of package metadata called OE-Core, combining the best of both Poky and OpenEmbedded with an increased use of layering for additional components.

23.1 Introduction to the Poky Build System

The Poky build system is the core of the Yocto Project. In Poky's default configuration, it can provide a starting image footprint that ranges from a shell-accessible minimal image all the way up to a Linux Standard Base-compliant image with a GNOME Mobile and Embedded (GMAE) based reference user interface called Sato. From these base image types, metadata layers can be added to extend functionality; layers can provide an additional software stack for an image type, add a board support package (BSP) for additional hardware or even represent a new image type. Using the 1.1 release of Poky, named "edison", we will show how BitBake uses these recipes and configuration files to generate an embedded image.

From a very high level, the build process starts out by setting up the shell environment for the build run. This is done by sourcing a file, oe-init-build-env, that exists in the root of the Poky source tree. This sets up the shell environment, creates an initial customizable set of configuration files and wraps the BitBake runtime with a shell script that Poky uses to determine if the minimal system requirements have been met.

For example, one of the things it will look for is the existence of Pseudo, a fakeroot replacement contributed to the Yocto Project by Wind River Systems. At this point, bitbake core-image-minimal, for example, should be able to create a fully functional cross-compilation environment and then create a Linux image based on the image definition for core-image-minimal from source as defined in the Yocto metadata layer.

Figure 23.1: High-level overview of Poky task execution

During the creation of our image, BitBake will parse its configuration, include any additional layers, classes, tasks or recipes defined, and begin by creating a weighted dependency chain. This process provides an ordered and weighted task priority map. BitBake then uses this map to determine what packages must be built in which order so as to most efficiently fulfill compilation dependencies. Tasks needed by the most other tasks are weighted higher, and thus run earlier during the build process. The task execution queue for our build is created. BitBake also stores the parsed metadata summaries and if, on subsequent runs, it determines that the metadata has changed, it can re-parse only what

BitBake recipe for grep

```
DESCRIPTION = "GNU grep utility"
HOMEPAGE = "http://savannah.gnu.org/projects/grep/"
BUGTRACKER = "http://savannah.gnu.org/bugs/?group=grep"

SECTION = "console/utils"

LICENSE = "GPLv3"
LIC_FILES_CHKSUM = "file://COPYING;md5=8006d9c814277c1bfc4ca22af94b59ee"

PR = "r0"

SRC_URI = "${GNU_MIRROR}/grep/grep-${PV}.tar.gz"
SRC_URI[md5sum] = "03e3451a38b0d615cb113cbeaf252dc0"
SRC_URI[sha256sum]="e9118eac72ecc71191725a7566361ab7643edfd3364869a47b78dc934a357970"

inherit autotools gettext

EXTRA_OECONF = "--disable-perl-regexp"

do_configure_prepend
() {
rm
-f ${S}/m4/init.m4
}

do_install () {
  autotools_do_install
  install -d ${D}${base_bindir}
  mv ${D}${bindir}/grep ${D}${base_bindir}/grep.${PN}
  mv ${D}${bindir}/egrep ${D}${base_bindir}/egrep.${PN}
  mv ${D}${bindir}/fgrep ${D}${base_bindir}/fgrep.${PN}
}

pkg_postinst_${PN}() {
  update-alternatives --install ${base_bindir}/grep grep grep.${PN} 100
  update-alternatives --install ${base_bindir}/egrep egrep egrep.${PN} 100
  update-alternatives --install ${base_bindir}/fgrep fgrep fgrep.${PN} 100
}

pkg_prerm_${PN}() {
  update-alternatives --remove grep grep.${PN}
  update-alternatives --remove egrep egrep.${PN}
  update-alternatives --remove fgrep fgrep.${PN}
}
```

has changed. The BitBake scheduler and parser are some of the more interesting architectural designs of BitBake and some of the decisions surrounding them and their implementation by BitBake contributors will be discussed later.

BitBake then runs through its weighted task queue, spawning threads (up to the number defined by BB_NUMBER_THREADS in conf/local.conf) that begin executing those tasks in the predetermined order. The tasks executed during a package's build may be modified, prepended- or appended-to through its recipe. The basic, default package task order of execution starts by fetching and unpacking package source and then configuring and cross-compiling the unpacked source. The compiled source is then split up into packages and various calculations are made on the compilation result such as the creation of debug package information. The split packages are then packaged into a supported package format; RPM, ipk and deb are supported. BitBake will then use these packages to build the root file system.

Poky Build System Concepts

One of the most powerful properties of the Poky build system is that every aspect of a build is controlled by metadata. Metadata can be loosely grouped into configuration files or package recipes. A recipe is a collection of non-executable metadata used by BitBake to set variables or define additional build-time tasks. A recipe contains fields such as the recipe description, the recipe version, the license of the package and the upstream source repository. It may also indicate that the build process uses autotools, make, distutils or any other build process, in which case the basic functionality can be defined by classes it inherits from the OE-Core layer's class definitions in ./meta/classes. Additional tasks can also be defined, as well as task prerequisites. BitBake also supports both _prepend and _append as a method of extending task functionality by injecting code indicated by using prepend or append suffix into the beginning or end of a task.

Configuration files can be broken down into two types. There are those that configure BitBake and the overall build run, and those that configure the various layers Poky uses to create different configurations of a target image. A layer is any grouping of metadata that provides some sort of additional functionality. These can be BSP for new devices, additional image types or additional software outside of the core layers. In fact, the core Yocto metadata, meta-yocto, is itself a layer applied on top of the OE-Core metadata layer, meta which adds additional software and image types to the OE-Core layer.

An example of how one would use layering is by creating a NAS device for the Intel n660 (Crownbay), using x32, the new 32-bit native ABI for x86-64, with a custom software layer that adds a user interface.

Given the task at hand, we could split this functionality out into layers. At the lowest level we would utilize a BSP layer for Crownbay that would enable Crownbay-specific hardware functionality, such as video drivers. As we want x32, we would use the experimental meta-x32 layer. The NAS functionality would be layered on top of this by adding the Yocto Project's example NAS layer, meta-baryon. And lastly, we'll use an imaginary layer called meta-myproject, to provide the software and configuration to create a graphical user interface for configuration of the NAS.

During the setup of the BitBake environment, some initial configuration files are generated by sourcing oe-build-init-env. These configuration files allow us quite a bit of control over how and what Poky generates. The first of these configuration files is bblayers.conf. This file is what we will use to add additional layers in order to build our example project.

Here's an example of a bblayers.conf file:

```
# LAYER_CONF_VERSION is increased each time build/conf/bblayers.conf
# changes incompatibly
LCONF_VERSION = "4"
BBFILES ?= ""
BBLAYERS = " \
/home/eflanagan/poky/meta \
/home/eflanagan/poky/meta-yocto \
/home/eflanagan/poky/meta-intel/crownbay \
/home/eflanagan/poky/meta-x32 \
/home/eflanagan/poky/meta-baryon\
/home/eflanagan/poky/meta-myproject \
"
```

The BitBake layers file, bblayers, defines a variable BBLAYERS that BitBake uses to look for BitBake layers. In order to fully understand this, we should also look at how our layers are actually constructed. Using meta-baryon [1] as our example layer, we want to examine the layer configuration file. This file, conf/layer.conf, is what BitBake parses after its initial parsing of bblayers.conf. From here it adds additional recipes, classes and configuration to the build.

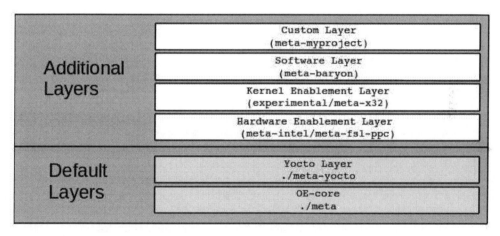

Figure 23.2: Example of BitBake layering

Here's meta-baryon's layer.conf:

```
# Layer configuration for meta-baryon layer
# Copyright 2011 Intel Corporation
# We have a conf directory, prepend to BBPATH to prefer our versions
BBPATH := "${LAYERDIR}:${BBPATH}"

# We have recipes-* directories, add to BBFILES
BBFILES := "${BBFILES} ${LAYERDIR}/recipes-*/*/*.bb ${LAYERDIR}/recipes-*/*/*.bbappend"

BBFILE_COLLECTIONS += "meta-baryon"
BBFILE_PATTERN_meta-baryon := "^${LAYERDIR}/"
BBFILE_PRIORITY_meta-baryon = "7"
```

---

[1] git://git.yoctoproject.org/meta-baryon

All of the BitBake configuration files help generate BitBake's datastore which is used during the creation of the task execution queue. During the beginning of a build, BitBake's BBCooker class is started. The cooker manages the build task execution by *baking* the *recipes*. One of the first things the cooker does is attempt to load and parse configuration data. Remember, though, that BitBake is looking for two types of configuration data. In order to tell the build system where it should find this configuration data (and in turn where to find recipe metadata), the cooker's parseConfigurationFiles method is called. With few exceptions, the first configuration file that the cooker looks for is bblayers.conf. After this file is parsed, BitBake then parses each layer's layer.conf file.

Once layer configuration files are parsed, parseConfigurationFiles then parses bitbake.conf whose main purpose is to set up global build time variables, such as directory structure naming for various rootfs directories and the initial LDFLAGS to be used during compile time. Most end users will never touch this file as most anything needed to be changed here would be within a recipe context, as opposed to build wide or could be overridden in a configuration file such as local.conf.

As this file is parsed, BitBake also includes configuration files that are relative to each layer in BBLAYERS and adds the variables found in those files to its data store.

Here is a portion of a bitbake.conf showing included configuration files:

```
include conf/site.conf
include conf/auto.conf
include conf/local.conf
include conf/build/${BUILD_SYS}.conf
include conf/target/${TARGET_SYS}.conf
include conf/machine/${MACHINE}.conf
```

23.2 BitBake Architecture

Before we delve into some of BitBake's current architectural design, it would help to understand how BitBake once worked. In order to fully appreciate how far BitBake has come, we will consider the initial version, BitBake 1.0. In that first release of BitBake, a build's dependency chain was determined based on recipe dependencies. If something failed during the build of an image, BitBake would move on to the next task and try to build it again later. What this means, obviously, is that builds took a very long time. One of the things BitBake also did is keep each and every variable that a recipe used in one very large dictionary. Given the number of recipes and the number of variables and tasks needed to accomplish a build, BitBake 1.0 was a memory hog. At a time when memory was expensive and systems had much less, builds could be painful affairs. It was not unheard of for a system to run out of memory (writing to swap!) as it slugged through a long running build. In its first incarnation, while it did the job (sometimes), it did it slowly while consuming an enormous amount of resources. Worse, as BitBake 1.0 had no concept of a data persistence cache or shared state, it also had no ability to do incremental builds. If a build failed, one would have to restart it from scratch.

A quick diff between the current BitBake version used in Poky "edison" 1.13.3 and 1.0 shows the implementation of BitBake's client-server architecture, the data persistence cache, its datastore, a copy-on-write improvement for the datastore, shared state implementation and drastic improvements in how it determines task and package dependency chains. This evolution has made it more reliable, more efficient and more dynamic. Much of this functionality came out of necessity for quicker, more reliable builds that used fewer resources. Three improvements to BitBake that we will examine are the implementation of a client-server architecture, optimizations around BitBake's data storage and work done on how BitBake determines its build and task dependency chain.

BitBake IPC

Since we now know a good deal about how the Poky build system uses configurations, recipes and layers to create embedded images, we're prepared to begin to look under the hood of BitBake and examine how this is all combined. Starting with the core BitBake executable, bitbake/bin/bake, we can begin to see the process BitBake follows as it begins to set up the infrastructure needed to begin a build. The first item of interest is BitBake's Interprocess Communications (IPC). Initially, BitBake had no concept of a client-server. This functionality was factored into the BitBake design over a period of time in order to allow BitBake to run multiple processes during a build, as it was initially single-threaded, and to allow different user experiences.

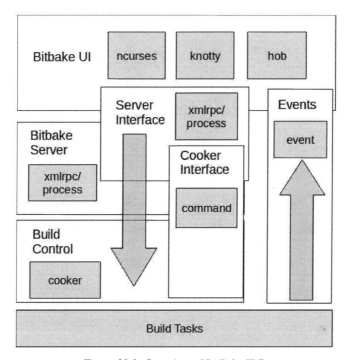

Figure 23.3: Overview of BitBake IPC

All Poky builds are begun by starting a user interface instance. The user interface provides a mechanism for logging of build output, build status and build progress, as well as for receiving events from build tasks through the BitBake event module. The default user interface used is *knotty*, BitBake's command line interface. Called knotty, or "(no) tty", since it handles both ttys and non-ttys, it is one of a few interfaces that are supported. One of these additional user interfaces is Hob. Hob is the graphical interface to BitBake, a kind of "BitBake commander". In addition to the typical functions you would see in the knotty user interface, Hob (written by Joshua Lock) brings the ability to modify configuration files, add additional layers and packages, and fully customize a build.

BitBake user interfaces have the ability to send commands to the next module brought up by the BitBake executable, the BitBake server. Like the user interface, BitBake also supports multiple different server types, such as XMLRPC. The default server that most users use when executing BitBake from the knotty user interface is BitBake's process server. After bringing up the server, the BitBake executable brings up the cooker.

The cooker is a core portion of BitBake and is where most of the particularly interesting things that occur during a Poky build are called from. The cooker is what manages the parsing of metadata, initiates the generation of the dependency and task trees, and manages the build. One of the functions of BitBake's server architecture is allowing multiple ways of exposing the command API, indirectly, to the user interface. The command module is the worker of BitBake, running build commands and triggering events that get passed up to the user interface through BitBake's event handler. Once the cooker is brought up from the BitBake executable, it initializes the BitBake datastore and then begins to parse all of Poky's configuration files. It then creates the runqueue object, and triggers the build.

BitBake DataSmart Copy-on-Write Data Storage

In BitBake 1.0, all BitBake variables were parsed and stored in one very large dictionary during the initialization of that version's data class. As previously mentioned, this was problematic in that very large Python dictionaries are slow on writes and member access, and if the build host runs out of physical memory during the build, we end up using swap. While this is less likely in most systems in late 2011, when OpenEmbedded and BitBake were first starting up, the average computer's specification usually had less than one or two gigabytes of memory.

This was one of the major pain points in early BitBake. Two major issues needed to be worked out in order to help increase performance: one was precomputation of the build dependency chain; the other was to reduce the size of data being stored in memory. Much of the data being stored for a recipe doesn't change from recipe to recipe; for example, with TMPDIR, BB_NUMBER_THREADS and other global BitBake variables, having a copy of the entire data environment per recipe stored in memory was inefficient. The solution was Tom Ansell's copy-on-write dictionary that "abuses classes to be nice and fast". BitBake's COW module is both an especially fearless and clever hack. Running python BitBake/lib/bb/COW.py and examining the module will give you an idea of how this copy-on-write implementation works and how BitBake uses it to store data efficiently

The DataSmart module, which uses the COW dictionary, stores the data from the initial Poky configuration, data from .conf files and .bbclass files, in a dict as a data object. Each of these objects can contain another data object of just the diff of the data. So, if a recipe changes something from the initial data configuration, instead of copying the entire configuration in order to localize it, a diff of the parent data object is stored at the next layer down in the COW stack. When an attempt is made to access a variable, the data module will use DataSmart to look into the top level of the stack. If the variable is not found it will defer to a lower level of the stack until it does find the variable or throws an error.

One of the other interesting things about the DataSmart module centers around variable expansion. As BitBake variables can contain executable Python code, one of the things that needs to be done is run the variable through BitBake's bb.codeparser to ensure that it's valid Python and that it contains no circular references. An example of a variable containing Python code is this example taken from ./meta/conf/distro/include/tclibc-eglibc.inc:

```
LIBCEXTENSION = "${@['', '-gnu'][(d.getVar('ABIEXTENSION', True) or '') != '']}"
```

This variable is included from one of the OE-Core configuration files, ./meta/conf/distro/include/defaultsetup.conf, and is used to provide a set of default options across different distro configurations that one would want to lay on top of Poky or OpenEmbedded. This file imports some eglibc-specific variables that are set dependent on the value of another BitBake variable ABIEXTENSION. During the creation of the datastore, the Python code within this variable needs to be parsed and validated to ensure tasks that use this variable will not fail.

BitBake Scheduler

Once BitBake has parsed the configuration and created its datastore, it needs to parse the recipes required for the image and produce a build chain. This is one of the more substantial improvements to BitBake. Originally, BitBake took its build priorities from a recipe. If a recipe had a DEPENDS, it would try to figure out what to build in order to satisfy that dependency. If a task failed because it lacked a prerequisite needed for its buildout, it was simply put to the side and attempted later. This had obvious drawbacks, both in efficiency and reliability.

As no precomputed dependency chain was established, task execution order was figured out during the build run. This limited BitBake to being single-threaded. To give an idea of how painful single-threaded BitBake builds can be, the smallest image "core-image-minimal" on a standard developer machine in 2011 (Intel Core i7, 16 gigabytes of DDR3 memory) takes about three or four hours to build a complete cross-compilation toolchain and use it to produce packages that are then used to create an image. For reference, a build on the same machine with BB_NUMBER_THREADS at 14 and PARALLEL_MAKE set to "-j 12" takes about 30 to 40 minutes. As one could imagine, running single-threaded with no precomputed order of task execution on slower hardware that had less memory with a large portion wasted by duplicate copies of the entire datastore took much longer.

Dependencies

When we talk of build dependencies, we need to make a distinction between the various types. A build dependency, or DEPENDS, is something we require as a prerequisite so that Poky can build the required package, whereas a runtime dependency, RDEPENDS, requires that the image the package is to be installed on also contains the package listed as an RDEPENDS. Take, for example, the package task-core-boot. If we look at the recipe for it in

meta/recipes-core/tasks/task-core-boot.bb

we will see two BitBake variables set: RDEPENDS and DEPENDS. BitBake uses these two fields during the creation of its dependency chain.

Here is a portion of task-core-boot.bb showing DEPENDS and RDEPENDS:

```
DEPENDS = "virtual/kernel"
 ...

RDEPENDS_task-core-boot = "\
base-files \
base-passwd \
busybox \
initscripts \
 ...
```

Packages aren't the only thing in BitBake with dependencies. Tasks also have their own dependencies. Within the scope of BitBake's runqueue, we recognize four types: internally dependent, DEPENDS dependent, RDEPENDS dependent and inter-task dependent.

Internally dependent tasks are set within a recipe and add a task before and/or after another task. For example, in a recipe, we could add a task called do_deploy by adding the line addtask deploy before do_build after do_compile. This would add a dependency for running the do_deploy task prior to do_build being started, but after do_compile is completed. DEPENDS and RDEPENDS dependent tasks are tasks that run after a denoted task. For example, if we wanted to run do_deploy of a package after the do_install of its DEPENDS or RDEPENDS, our recipe would include do_deploy[deptask] = 'do_install' or do_deploy[rdeptask] = 'do_install'. For inter-task dependencies, if we wanted a task to be dependent on a different package's task we would add, using the above example of do_deploy, do_deploy[depends] = "<target's name>:do_install".

RunQueue

As an image build can have hundreds of recipes, each with multiple packages and task, each with its own dependency, BitBake is now tasked with trying to sort this out into something it can use as an order of execution. After the cooker has gotten the entire list of packages needed to be built from the initialization of the bb.data object, it will begin to create a weighted task map from this data in order to produce an ordered list of tasks it needs to run, called the *runqueue*. Once the runqueue is created, BitBake can begin executing it in order of priority, tasking out each portion to a different thread.

Within the provider module, BitBake will first look to see if there is a PREFERRED_PROVIDER for a given package or image. As more than one recipe can provide a given package and as tasks are defined in recipes, BitBake needs to decide which provider of a package it will use. It will sort all the providers of the package, weighting each provider by various criteria. For example, preferred versions of software will get a higher priority than others. However, BitBake also takes into account package version as well as the dependencies of other packages. Once it has selected the recipe from which it will derive its package, BitBake will iterate over the DEPENDS and RDEPENDS of that recipe and proceed to compute the providers for those packages. This chain reaction will produce a list of packages needed for image generation as well as providers for those packages.

Runqueue now has a full list of all packages that need to be built and a dependency chain. In order to begin execution of the build, the runqueue module now needs to create the TaskData object so it can begin to sort out a weighted task map. It begins by taking each buildable package it has found, splitting the tasks needed to generate that package and weighing each of those tasks based on the number of packages that require it. Tasks with a higher weight have more dependents, and therefore are generally run earlier in the build. Once this is complete, the runqueue module then prepares to convert the TaskData object into a runqueue.

The creation of the runqueue is somewhat complex. BitBake first iterates through the list of task names within the TaskData object in order to determine task dependencies. As it iterates through TaskData, it begins to build a weighted task map. When it is complete, if it has found no circular dependencies, unbuildable tasks or any such problems, it will then order the task map by weight and return a complete runqueue object to the cooker. The cooker will begin to attempt to execute the runqueue, task by task. Depending upon image size and computing resources, Poky may take from a half-hour to hours to generate a cross-compilation toolchain, a package feed and the embedded Linux image specified. It is worth noting that from the time of executing bitbake <image_name> from the command line, the entire process up to right before the execution of the task execution queue has taken less than a few seconds.

23.3 Conclusion

In my discussions with community members and my own personal observations, I've identified a few areas where things should, perhaps, have been done differently, as well as a few valuable lessons. It is important to note that "arm chair quarterbacking" a decade-long development effort is not meant as a criticism of those who've poured their time and effort into a wholly remarkable collection of software. As developers, the most difficult part of our job is predicting what we will need years down the road and how we can set up a framework to enable that work now. Few can achieve that without some road bumps.

The first lesson is to be sure to develop a written, agreed-upon standards document that is well understood by the community. It should be designed for maximum flexibility and growth.

One place where I've personally run into this issue is with my work in OE-Core's license manifest creation class, especially with my experiences working with the LICENSE variable. As no clearly documented standard existed for what LICENSE should contain, a review of the many recipes available showed many variations. The various LICENSE strings contained everything from Python abstract syntax tree-parsable values to values that one would have little hope of gaining meaningful data from. There was a convention that was commonly used within the community; however, the convention had many variations, some less correct than others. This wasn't the problem of the developer who wrote the recipe; it was a community failure to define a standard.

As little prior work was actually done with the LICENSE variable outside of checking for its existence, there was no particular concern about a standard for that variable. Much trouble could have been avoided had a project-wide agreed-upon standard been developed early on.

The next lesson is a bit more general and speaks to an issue seen not only within the Yocto Project but in other large scale projects that are systems-design specific. It is the one of the most important things developers can do to limit the amount of effort duplication, refactoring and churn their project encounters: spend time—lots of time—on front-end planning and architectural design.

If you think you've spent enough time on architectural design, you probably haven't. If you think you haven't spent enough time on architectural design, you definitely haven't. Spending more time on front end planning won't stop you from later having to rip apart code or even do major architectural changes, but it will certainly reduce the amount of duplicated effort in the long run.

Designing your software to be as modular as possible, knowing that you will end up revisiting areas for anything from minor tweaks to major rewrites, will make it so that when you do run into these issues, code rewrites are less hair-raising.

One obvious place where this would have helped in the Yocto Project is identifying the needs of end users with low memory systems. Had more thought been put into BitBake's datastore earlier, perhaps we could have predicted the problems associated with the datastore taking up too much memory and dealt with it earlier.

The lesson here is that while it is nearly impossible to identify every pain point your project will run into during its lifetime, taking the time to do serious front-end planning will help reduce the effort needed later. BitBake, OE-Core and Yocto are all fortunate in this regard as there was a fair amount of architectural planning done early. This enabled us to be able to make major changes to the architecture without too much pain and suffering.

23.4 Acknowledgements

First, thank you to Chris Larson, Michael Lauer, and Holger Schurig and the many, many people who have contributed to BitBake, OpenEmbedded, OE-Core and Yocto over the years. Thank you also goes to Richard Purdie for his letting me pick his brain, both on historical and technical aspects of OE, and for his constant encouragement and guidance, especially with some of the dark magic of BitBake.

[chapter 24]

ZeroMQ

Martin Sústrik

ØMQ is a messaging system, or "message-oriented middleware", if you will. It's used in environments as diverse as financial services, game development, embedded systems, academic research and aerospace.

Messaging systems work basically as instant messaging for applications. An application decides to communicate an event to another application (or multiple applications), it assembles the data to be sent, hits the "send" button and there we go—the messaging system takes care of the rest.

Unlike instant messaging, though, messaging systems have no GUI and assume no human beings at the endpoints capable of intelligent intervention when something goes wrong. Messaging systems thus have to be both fault-tolerant and much faster than common instant messaging.

ØMQ was originally conceived as an ultra-fast messaging system for stock trading and so the focus was on extreme optimization. The first year of the project was spent devising benchmarking methodology and trying to define an architecture that was as efficient as possible.

Later on, approximately in the second year of development, the focus shifted to providing a generic system for building distributed applications and supporting arbitrary messaging patterns, various transport mechanisms, arbitrary language bindings, etc.

During the third year the focus was mainly on improving usability and flattening the learning curve. We've adopted the BSD Sockets API, tried to clean up the semantics of individual messaging patterns, and so on.

Hopefully, this chapter will give an insight into how the three goals above translated into the internal architecture of ØMQ, and provide some tips for those who are struggling with the same problems.

Since its third year ØMQ has outgrown its codebase; there is an initiative to standardise the wire protocols it uses, and an experimental implementation of a ØMQ-like messaging system inside the Linux kernel, etc. These topics are not covered in this book. However, you can check online resources[1][2][3] for further details.

24.1 Application vs. Library

ØMQ is a library, not a messaging server. It took us several years working on AMQP protocol, a financial industry attempt to standardise the wire protocol for business messaging—writing a

---

[1] http://www.250bpm.com/concepts
[2] http://groups.google.com/group/sp-discuss-group
[3] http://www.250bpm.com/hits

reference implementation for it and participating in several large-scale projects heavily based on messaging technology—to realise that there's something wrong with the classic client/server model of smart messaging server (broker) and dumb messaging clients.

Our primary concern at the time was with the performance: If there's a server in the middle, each message has to pass the network twice (from the sender to the broker and from the broker to the receiver) inducing a penalty in terms of both latency and throughput. Moreover, if all the messages are passed through the broker, at some point it's bound to become the bottleneck.

A secondary concern was related to large-scale deployments: when the deployment crosses organisational boundaries the concept of a central authority managing the whole message flow doesn't apply any more. No company is willing to cede control to a server in different company; there are trade secrets and there's legal liability. The result in practice is that there's one messaging server per company, with hand-written bridges to connect it to messaging systems in other companies. The whole ecosystem is thus heavily fragmented, and maintaining a large number of bridges for every company involved doesn't make the situation better. To solve this problem, we need a fully distributed architecture, an architecture where every component can be possibly governed by a different business entity. Given that the unit of management in server-based architecture is the server, we can solve the problem by installing a separate server for each component. In such a case we can further optimize the design by making the server and the component share the same processes. What we end up with is a messaging library.

ØMQ was started when we got an idea about how to make messaging work without a central server. It required turning the whole concept of messaging upside down and replacing the model of an autonomous centralised store of messages in the center of the network with a "smart endpoint, dumb network" architecture based on the end-to-end principle. The technical consequence of that decision was that ØMQ, from the very beginning, was a library, not an application.

In the meantime we've been able to prove that this architecture is both more efficient (lower latency, higher throughput) and more flexible (it's easy to build arbitrary complex topologies instead of being tied to classic hub-and-spoke model).

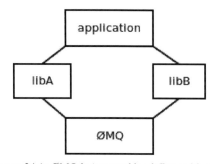

Figure 24.1: ØMQ being used by different libraries

One of the unintended consequences, however, was that opting for the library model improved the usability of the product. Over and over again users express their happiness about the fact that they don't have to install and manage a stand-alone messaging server. It turns out that not having a server is a preferred option as it cuts operational cost (no need to have a messaging server admin) and improves time-to-market (no need to negotiate the need to run the server with the client, the management or the operations team).

The lesson learned is that when starting a new project, you should opt for the library design if at all possible. It's pretty easy to create an application from a library by invoking it from a trivial program; however, it's almost impossible to create a library from an existing executable. A library offers much more flexibility to the users, at the same time sparing them non-trivial administrative effort.

24.2 Global State

Global variables don't play well with libraries. A library may be loaded several times in the process but even then there's only a single set of global variables. Figure 24.1 shows a ØMQ library being used from two different and independent libraries. The application then uses both of those libraries.

When such a situation occurs, both instances of ØMQ access the same variables, resulting in race conditions, strange failures and undefined behaviour.

To prevent this problem, the ØMQ library has no global variables. Instead, a user of the library is responsible for creating the global state explicitly. The object containing the global state is called *context*. While from the user's perspective context looks more or less like a pool of worker threads, from ØMQ's perspective it's just an object to store any global state that we happen to need. In the picture above, libA would have its own context and libB would have its own as well. There would be no way for one of them to break or subvert the other one.

The lesson here is pretty obvious: Don't use global state in libraries. If you do, the library is likely to break when it happens to be instantiated twice in the same process.

24.3 Performance

When ØMQ was started, its primary goal was to optimize performance. Performance of messaging systems is expressed using two metrics: throughput—how many messages can be passed during a given amount of time; and latency—how long it takes for a message to get from one endpoint to the other.

Which metric should we focus on? What's the relationship between the two? Isn't it obvious? Run the test, divide the overall time of the test by number of messages passed and what you get is latency. Divide the number of messages by time and what you get is throughput. In other words, latency is the inverse value of throughput. Trivial, right?

Instead of starting coding straight away we spent some weeks investigating the performance metrics in detail and we found out that the relationship between throughput and latency is much more subtle than that, and often the metrics are quite counter-intuitive.

Imagine A sending messages to B. (See Figure 24.2.) The overall time of the test is 6 seconds. There are 5 messages passed. Therefore the throughput is 0.83 msgs/sec ($\frac{5}{6}$) and the latency is 1.2 sec ($\frac{6}{5}$), right?

Have a look at the diagram again. It takes a different time for each message to get from A to B: 2 sec, 2.5 sec, 3 sec, 3.5 sec, 4 sec. The average is 3 seconds, which is pretty far away from our original calculation of 1.2 second. This example shows the misconceptions people are intuitively inclined to make about performance metrics.

Now have a look at the throughput. The overall time of the test is 6 seconds. However, at A it takes just 2 seconds to send all the messages. From A's perspective the throughput is 2.5 msgs/sec ($\frac{5}{2}$). At B it takes 4 seconds to receive all messages. So from B's perspective the throughput is 1.25 msgs/sec ($\frac{5}{4}$). Neither of these numbers matches our original calculation of 1.2 msgs/sec.

To make a long story short, latency and throughput are two different metrics; that much is obvious. The important thing is to understand the difference between the two and their mutual relationship.

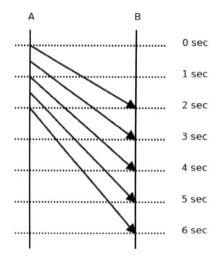

Figure 24.2: Sending messages from A to B

Latency can be measured only between two different points in the system; There's no such thing as latency at point A. Each message has its own latency. You can average the latencies of multiple messages; however, there's no such thing as latency of a stream of messages.

Throughput, on the other hand, can be measured only at a single point of the system. There's a throughput at the sender, there's a throughput at the receiver, there's a throughput at any intermediate point between the two, but there's no such thing as overall throughput of the whole system. And throughput make sense only for a set of messages; there's no such thing as throughput of a single message.

As for the relationship between throughput and latency, it turns out there really is a relationship; however, the formula involves integrals and we won't discuss it here. For more information, read the literature on queueing theory.

There are many more pitfalls in benchmarking the messaging systems that we won't go further into. The stress should rather be placed on the lesson learned: Make sure you understand the problem you are solving. Even a problem as simple as "make it fast" can take lot of work to understand properly. What's more, if you don't understand the problem, you are likely to build implicit assumptions and popular myths into your code, making the solution either flawed or at least much more complex or much less useful than it could possibly be.

24.4 Critical Path

We discovered during the optimization process that three factors have a crucial impact on performance:
- Number of memory allocations
- Number of system calls
- Concurrency model

However, not every memory allocation or every system call has the same effect on performance. The performance we are interested in in messaging systems is the number of messages we can transfer between two endpoints during a given amount of time. Alternatively, we may be interested in how long it takes for a message to get from one endpoint to another.

However, given that ØMQ is designed for scenarios with long-lived connections, the time it takes to establish a connection or the time needed to handle a connection error is basically irrelevant. These events happen very rarely and so their impact on overall performance is negligible.

The part of a codebase that gets used very frequently, over and over again, is called the *critical path*; optimization should focus on the critical path.

Let's have a look at an example: ØMQ is not extremely optimized with respect to memory allocations. For example, when manipulating strings, it often allocates a new string for each intermediate phase of the transformation. However, if we look strictly at the critical path—the actual message passing—we'll find out that it uses almost no memory allocations. If messages are small, it's just one memory allocation per 256 messages (these messages are held in a single large allocated memory chunk). If, in addition, the stream of messages is steady, without huge traffic peaks, the number of memory allocations on the critical path drops to zero (the allocated memory chunks are not returned to the system, but re-used over and over again).

Lesson learned: optimize where it makes difference. Optimizing pieces of code that are not on the critical path is wasted effort.

24.5 Allocating Memory

Assuming that all the infrastructure was initialised and a connection between two endpoints has been established, there's only one thing to allocate when sending a message: the message itself. Thus, to optimize the critical path we had to look into how messages are allocated and passed up and down the stack.

It's common knowledge in the high-performance networking field that the best performance is achieved by carefully balancing the cost of message allocation and the cost of message copying[4]. For small messages, copying is much cheaper than allocating memory. It makes sense to allocate no new memory chunks at all and instead to copy the message to preallocated memory whenever needed. For large messages, on the other hand, copying is much more expensive than memory allocation. It makes sense to allocate the message once and pass a pointer to the allocated block, instead of copying the data. This approach is called "zero-copy".

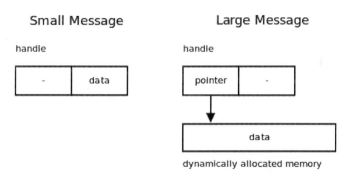

Figure 24.3: Message copying (or not)

ØMQ handles both cases in a transparent manner. A ØMQ message is represented by an opaque handle. The content of very small messages is encoded directly in the handle. So making a copy of

---

[4]For example, http://hal.inria.fr/docs/00/29/28/31/PDF/Open-MX-IOAT.pdf. See different handling of "small", "medium" and "large" messages.

the handle actually copies the message data. When the message is larger, it's allocated in a separate buffer and the handle contains just a pointer to the buffer. Making a copy of the handle doesn't result in copying the message data, which makes sense when the message is megabytes long (Figure 24.3). It should be noted that in the latter case the buffer is reference-counted so that it can be referenced by multiple handles without the need to copy the data.

Lesson learned: When thinking about performance, don't assume there's a single best solution. It may happen that there are several subclasses of the problem (e.g., small messages vs. large messages), each having its own optimal algorithm.

24.6 Batching

It has already been mentioned that the sheer number of system calls in a messaging system can result in a performance bottleneck. Actually, the problem is much more generic than that. There's a non-trivial performance penalty associated with traversing the call stack and thus, when creating high-performance applications, it's wise to avoid as much stack traversing as possible.

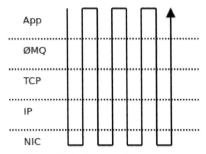

Figure 24.4: Sending four messages

Consider Figure 24.4. To send four messages, you have to traverse the entire network stack four times (i.e., ØMQ, glibc, user/kernel space boundary, TCP implementation, IP implementation, Ethernet layer, the NIC itself and back up the stack again).

However, if you decide to join those messages into a single batch, there would be only one traversal of the stack (Figure 24.5). The impact on message throughput can be overwhelming: up to two orders of magnitude, especially if the messages are small and hundreds of them can be packed into a single batch.

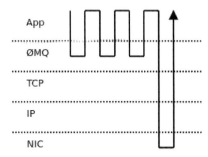

Figure 24.5: Batching messages

On the other hand, batching can have negative impact on latency. Let's take, for example, the well-known Nagle's algorithm, as implemented in TCP. It delays the outbound messages for a certain amount of time and merges all the accumulated data into a single packet. Obviously, the end-to-end latency of the first message in the packet is much worse than the latency of the last one. Thus, it's common for applications that need consistently low latency to switch Nagle's algorithm off. It's even common to switch off batching on all levels of the stack (e.g., NIC's interrupt coalescing feature).

But again, no batching means extensive traversing of the stack and results in low message throughput. We seem to be caught in a throughput versus latency dilemma.

ØMQ tries to deliver consistently low latencies combined with high throughput using the following strategy: when message flow is sparse and doesn't exceed the network stack's bandwidth, ØMQ turns all the batching off to improve latency. The trade-off here is somewhat higher CPU usage—we still have to traverse the stack frequently. However, that isn't considered to be a problem in most cases.

When the message rate exceeds the bandwidth of the network stack, the messages have to be queued—stored in memory till the stack is ready to accept them. Queueing means the latency is going to grow. If the message spends one second in the queue, end-to-end latency will be at least one second. What's even worse, as the size of the queue grows, latencies will increase gradually. If the size of the queue is not bound, the latency can exceed any limit.

It has been observed that even though the network stack is tuned for lowest possible latency (Nagle's algorithm switched off, NIC interrupt coalescing turned off, etc.) latencies can still be dismal because of the queueing effect, as described above.

In such situations it makes sense to start batching aggressively. There's nothing to lose as the latencies are already high anyway. On the other hand, aggressive batching improves throughput and can empty the queue of pending messages—which in turn means the latency will gradually drop as the queueing delay decreases. Once there are no outstanding messages in the queue, the batching can be turned off to improve the latency even further.

One additional observation is that the batching should only be done on the topmost level. If the messages are batched there, the lower layers have nothing to batch anyway, and so all the batching algorithms underneath do nothing except introduce additional latency.

Lesson learned: To get optimal throughput combined with optimal response time in an asynchronous system, turn off all the batching algorithms on the low layers of the stack and batch on the topmost level. Batch only when new data are arriving faster than they can be processed.

24.7 Architecture Overview

Up to this point we have focused on generic principles that make ØMQ fast. From now on we'll have a look at the actual architecture of the system (Figure 24.6).

The user interacts with ØMQ using so-called "sockets". They are pretty similar to TCP sockets, the main difference being that each socket can handle communication with multiple peers, a bit like unbound UDP sockets do.

The socket object lives in the user's thread (see the discussion of threading models in the next section). Aside from that, ØMQ is running multiple worker threads that handle the asynchronous part of the communication: reading data from the network, enqueueing messages, accepting incoming connections, etc.

There are various objects living in the worker threads. Each of these objects is owned by exactly one parent object (ownership is denoted by a simple full line in the diagram). The parent can live in a different thread than the child. Most objects are owned directly by sockets; however, there are couple of cases where an object is owned by an object which is owned by the socket. What we get is a tree of objects, with one such tree per socket. The tree is used during shut down; no object can

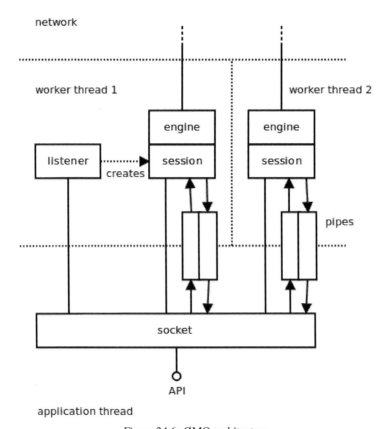

Figure 24.6: ØMQ architecture

shut itself down until it closes all its children. This way we can ensure that the shut down process works as expected; for example, that pending outbound messages are pushed to the network prior to terminating the sending process.

Roughly speaking, there are two kinds of asynchronous objects; there are objects that are not involved in message passing and there are objects that are. The former have to do mainly with connection management. For example, a TCP listener object listens for incoming TCP connections and creates an engine/session object for each new connection. Similarly, a TCP connector object tries to connect to the TCP peer and when it succeeds it creates an engine/session object to manage the connection. When such connection fails, the connector object tries to re-establish it.

The latter are objects that are handling data transfer itself. These objects are composed of two parts: the *session object* is responsible for interacting with the ØMQ socket, and the *engine object* is responsible for communication with the network. There's only one kind of the session object, but there's a different engine type for each underlying protocol ØMQ supports. Thus, we have TCP engines, IPC (inter-process communication) engines, PGM[5] engines, etc. The set of engines is extensible—in the future we may choose to implement, say, a WebSocket engine or an SCTP engine.

The sessions are exchanging messages with the sockets. There are two directions to pass messages in and each direction is handled by a pipe object. Each pipe is basically a lock-free queue optimized for fast passing of messages between threads.

---

[5]Reliable multicast protocol, see RFC 3208.

Finally, there's a context object (discussed in the previous sections but not shown on the diagram) that holds the global state and is accessible by all the sockets and all the asynchronous objects.

24.8 Concurrency Model

One of the requirements for ØMQ was to take advantage of multi-core boxes; in other words, to scale the throughput linearly with the number of available CPU cores.

Our previous experience with messaging systems showed that using multiple threads in a classic way (critical sections, semaphores, etc.) doesn't yield much performance improvement. In fact, a multi-threaded version of a messaging system can be slower than a single-threaded one, even if measured on a multi-core box. Individual threads are simply spending too much time waiting for each other while, at the same time, eliciting a lot of context switching that slows the system down.

Given these problems, we've decided to go for a different model. The goal was to avoid locking entirely and let each thread run at full speed. The communication between threads was to be provided via asynchronous messages (events) passed between the threads. This, as insiders know, is the classic *actor model*.

The idea was to launch one worker thread per CPU core—having two threads sharing the same core would only mean a lot of context switching for no particular advantage. Each internal ØMQ object, such as say, a TCP engine, would be tightly bound to a particular worker thread. That, in turn, means that there's no need for critical sections, mutexes, semaphores and the like. Additionally, these ØMQ objects won't be migrated between CPU cores so would thus avoid the negative performance impact of cache pollution (Figure 24.7).

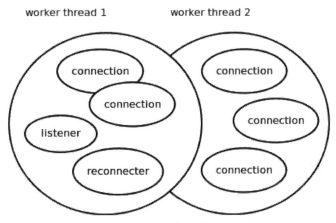

Figure 24.7: Multiple worker threads

This design makes a lot of traditional multi-threading problems disappear. Nevertheless, there's a need to share the worker thread among many objects, which in turn means there has to be some kind of cooperative multitasking. This means we need a scheduler; objects need to be event-driven rather than being in control of the entire event loop; we have to take care of arbitrary sequences of events, even very rare ones; we have to make sure that no object holds the CPU for too long; etc.

In short, the whole system has to become fully asynchronous. No object can afford to do a blocking operation, because it would not only block itself but also all the other objects sharing the same worker thread. All objects have to become, whether explicitly or implicitly, state machines.

With hundreds or thousands of state machines running in parallel you have to take care of all the possible interactions between them and—most importantly—of the shutdown process.

It turns out that shutting down a fully asynchronous system in a clean way is a dauntingly complex task. Trying to shut down a thousand moving parts, some of them working, some idle, some in the process of being initiated, some of them already shutting down by themselves, is prone to all kinds of race conditions, resource leaks and similar. The shutdown subsystem is definitely the most complex part of ØMQ. A quick check of the bug tracker indicates that some 30–50% of reported bugs are related to shutdown in one way or another.

Lesson learned: When striving for extreme performance and scalability, consider the actor model; it's almost the only game in town in such cases. However, if you are not using a specialised system like Erlang or ØMQ itself, you'll have to write and debug a lot of infrastructure by hand. Additionally, think, from the very beginning, about the procedure to shut down the system. It's going to be the most complex part of the codebase and if you have no clear idea how to implement it, you should probably reconsider using the actor model in the first place.

24.9 Lock-Free Algorithms

Lock-free algorithms have been in vogue lately. They are simple mechanisms for inter-thread communication that don't rely on the kernel-provided synchronisation primitives, such as mutexes or semaphores; rather, they do the synchronisation using atomic CPU operations, such as atomic compare-and-swap (CAS). It should be understood that they are not literally lock-free—instead, locking is done behind the scenes on the hardware level.

ØMQ uses a lock-free queue in pipe objects to pass messages between the user's threads and ØMQ's worker threads. There are two interesting aspects to how ØMQ uses the lock-free queue.

First, each queue has exactly one writer thread and exactly one reader thread. If there's a need for 1-to-N communication, multiple queues are created (Figure 24.8). Given that this way the queue doesn't have to take care of synchronising the writers (there's only one writer) or readers (there's only one reader) it can be implemented in an extra-efficient way.

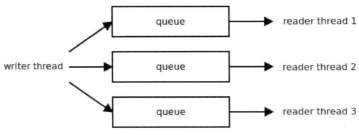

Figure 24.8: Queues

Second, we realised that while lock-free algorithms were more efficient than classic mutex-based algorithms, atomic CPU operations are still rather expensive (especially when there's contention between CPU cores) and doing an atomic operation for each message written and/or each message read was slower than we were willing to accept.

The way to speed it up—once again—was batching. Imagine you had 10 messages to be written to the queue. It can happen, for example, when you received a network packet containing 10 small messages. Receiving a packet is an atomic event; you cannot get half of it. This atomic event results in the need to write 10 messages to the lock-free queue. There's not much point in doing an atomic operation for each message. Instead, you can accumulate the messages in a "pre-write" portion of the queue that's accessed solely by the writer thread, and then flush it using a single atomic operation.

The same applies to reading from the queue. Imagine the 10 messages above were already flushed to the queue. The reader thread can extract each message from the queue using an atomic operation. However, it's overkill; instead, it can move all the pending messages to a "pre-read" portion of the queue using a single atomic operation. Afterwards, it can retrieve the messages from the "pre-read" buffer one by one. "Pre-read" is owned and accessed solely by the reader thread and thus no synchronisation whatsoever is needed in that phase.

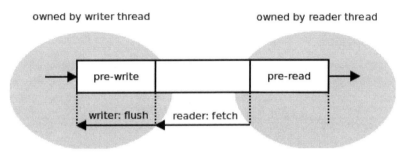

Figure 24.9: Lock-free queue

The arrow on the left of Figure 24.9 shows how the pre-write buffer can be flushed to the queue simply by modifying a single pointer. The arrow on the right shows how the whole content of the queue can be shifted to the pre-read by doing nothing but modifying another pointer.

Lesson learned: Lock-free algorithms are hard to invent, troublesome to implement and almost impossible to debug. If at all possible, use an existing proven algorithm rather than inventing your own. When extreme performance is required, don't rely solely on lock-free algorithms. While they are fast, the performance can be significantly improved by doing smart batching on top of them.

24.10 API

The user interface is the most important part of any product. It's the only part of your program visible to the outside world and if you get it wrong the world will hate you. In end-user products it's either the GUI or the command line interface. In libraries it's the API.

In early versions of ØMQ the API was based on AMQP's model of exchanges and queues[6]. I spent the end of 2009 rewriting it almost from scratch to use the BSD Socket API instead. That was the turning point; ØMQ adoption soared from that point on. While before it was a niche product used by a bunch of messaging experts, afterwards it became a handy commonplace tool for anybody. In a year or so the size of the community increased tenfold, some 20 bindings to different languages were implemented, etc.

The user interface defines the perception of a product. With basically no change to the functionality—just by changing the API—ØMQ changed from an "enterprise messaging" product to a "networking" product. In other words, the perception changed from "a complex piece of infrastructure for big banks" to "hey, this helps me to send my 10-byte-long message from application A to application B".

---

[6]See the AMQP specification at https://www.amqp.org/confluence/download/attachments/720900/amqp0-9-1.pdf. From a historical perspective it's interesting to have a look at the white paper from 2007 that tries to reconcile AMQP with a brokerless model of messaging. The white paper is at http://www.zeromq.org/whitepapers:messaging-enabled-network.

Lesson learned: Understand what you want your project to be and design the user interface accordingly. Having a user interface that doesn't align with the vision of the project is a 100% guaranteed way to fail.

One of the important aspects of the move to the BSD Sockets API was that it wasn't a revolutionary freshly invented API, but an existing and well-known one. Actually, the BSD Sockets API is one of the oldest APIs still in active use today; it dates back to 1983 and 4.2BSD Unix. It's been widely used and stable for literally decades.

The above fact brings a lot of advantages. Firstly, it's an API that everybody knows, so the learning curve is ludicrously flat. Even if you've never heard of ØMQ, you can build your first application in couple of minutes thanks to the fact that you are able to reuse your BSD Sockets knowledge.

Secondly, using a widely implemented API enables integration of ØMQ with existing technologies. For example, exposing ØMQ objects as "sockets" or "file descriptors" allows for processing TCP, UDP, pipe, file and ØMQ events in the same event loop. Another example: the experimental project to bring ØMQ-like functionality to the Linux kernel[7] turned out to be pretty simple to implement. By sharing the same conceptual framework it can re-use a lot of infrastructure already in place.

Thirdly and probably most importantly, the fact that the BSD Sockets API survived almost three decades despite numerous attempts to replace it means that there is something inherently right in the design. BSD Sockets API designers have—whether deliberately or by chance—made the right design decisions. By adopting the API we can automatically share those design decisions without even knowing what they were and what problem they were solving.

Lesson learned: While code reuse has been promoted from time immemorial and pattern reuse joined in later on, it's important to think of reuse in an even more generic way. When designing a product, have a look at similar products. Check which have failed and which have succeeded; learn from the successful projects. Don't succumb to Not Invented Here syndrome. Reuse the ideas, the APIs, the conceptual frameworks, whatever you find appropriate. By doing so you are allowing users to reuse their existing knowledge. At the same time you may be avoiding technical pitfalls you are not even aware of at the moment.

24.11 Messaging Patterns

In any messaging system, the most important design problem is that of how to provide a way for the user to specify which messages are routed to which destinations. There are two main approaches, and I believe this dichotomy is quite generic and applicable to basically any problem encountered in the domain of software.

One approach is to adopt the Unix philosophy of "do one thing and do it well". What this means is that the problem domain should be artificially restricted to a small and well-understood area. The program should then solve this restricted problem in a correct and exhaustive way. An example of such approach in the messaging area is MQTT[8]. It's a protocol for distributing messages to a set of consumers. It can't be used for anything else (say for RPC) but it is easy to use and does message distribution well.

The other approach is to focus on generality and provide a powerful and highly configurable system. AMQP is an example of such a system. Its model of queues and exchanges provides the

---
[7]https://github.com/250bpm/linux-2.6
[8]http://mqtt.org/

user with the means to programmatically define almost any routing algorithm they can think of. The trade-off, of course, is a lot of options to take care of.

ØMQ opts for the former model because it allows the resulting product to be used by basically anyone, while the generic model requires messaging experts to use it. To demonstrate the point, let's have a look how the model affects the complexity of the API. What follows is implementation of RPC client on top of a generic system (AMQP):

```
connect ("192.168.0.111")
exchange.declare (exchange="requests", type="direct", passive=false,
    durable=true, no-wait=true, arguments={})
exchange.declare (exchange="replies", type="direct", passive=false,
    durable=true, no-wait=true, arguments={})
reply-queue = queue.declare (queue="", passive=false, durable=false,
    exclusive=true, auto-delete=true, no-wait=false, arguments={})
queue.bind (queue=reply-queue, exchange="replies",
    routing-key=reply-queue)
queue.consume (queue=reply-queue, consumer-tag="", no-local=false,
    no-ack=false, exclusive=true, no-wait=true, arguments={})
request = new-message ("Hello World!")
request.reply-to = reply-queue
request.correlation-id = generate-unique-id ()
basic.publish (exchange="requests", routing-key="my-service",
    mandatory=true, immediate=false)
reply = get-message ()
```

On the other hand, ØMQ splits the messaging landscape into so-called "messaging patterns". Examples of the patterns are "publish/subscribe", "request/reply" or "parallelised pipeline". Each messaging pattern is completely orthogonal to other patterns and can be thought of as a separate tool.

What follows is the re-implementation of the above application using ØMQ's request/reply pattern. Note how all the option tweaking is reduced to the single step of choosing the right messaging pattern ("REQ"):

```
s = socket (REQ)
s.connect ("tcp://192.168.0.111:5555")
s.send ("Hello World!")
reply = s.recv ()
```

Up to this point we've argued that specific solutions are better than generic solutions. We want our solution to be as specific as possible. However, at the same time we want to provide our customers with as wide a range of functionality as possible. How can we solve this apparent contradiction?

The answer consists of two steps:

1. Define a layer of the stack to deal with a particular problem area (e.g. transport, routing, presentation, etc.).
2. Provide multiple implementations of the layer. There should be a separate non-intersecting implementation for each use case.

Let's have a look at the example of the transport layer in the Internet stack. It's meant to provide services such as transferring data streams, applying flow control, providing reliability, etc., on the top of the network layer (IP). It does so by defining multiple non-intersecting solutions: TCP for connection-oriented reliable stream transfer, UDP for connectionless unreliable packet transfer, SCTP for transfer of multiple streams, DCCP for unreliable connections and so on.

Note that each implementation is completely orthogonal: a UDP endpoint cannot speak to a TCP endpoint. Neither can a SCTP endpoint speak to a DCCP endpoint. It means that new implementations can be added to the stack at any moment without affecting the existing portions of the stack. Conversely, failed implementations can be forgotten and discarded without compromising the viability of the transport layer as a whole.

The same principle applies to messaging patterns as defined by ØMQ. Messaging patterns form a layer (the so-called "scalability layer") on top of the transport layer (TCP and friends). Individual messaging patterns are implementations of this layer. They are strictly orthogonal—the publish/subscribe endpoint can't speak to the request/reply endpoint, etc. Strict separation between the patterns in turn means that new patterns can be added as needed and that failed experiments with new patterns won't hurt the existing patterns.

Lesson learned: When solving a complex and multi-faceted problem it may turn out that a monolithic general-purpose solution may not be the best way to go. Instead, we can think of the problem area as an abstract layer and provide multiple implementations of this layer, each focused on a specific well-defined use case. When doing so, delineate the use case carefully. Be sure about what is in the scope and what is not. By restricting the use case too aggressively the application of your software may be limited. If you define the problem too broadly, however, the product may become too complex, blurry and confusing for the users.

24.12 Conclusion

As our world becomes populated with lots of small computers connected via the Internet—mobile phones, RFID readers, tablets and laptops, GPS devices, etc.—the problem of distributed computing ceases to be the domain of academic science and becomes a common everyday problem for every developer to tackle. The solutions, unfortunately, are mostly domain-specific hacks. This article summarises our experience with building a large-scale distributed system in a systematic manner. It focuses on problems that are interesting from a software architecture point of view, and we hope that designers and programmers in the open source community will find it useful.

Bibliography

[aut12] Autoconf, 2012.

[CKP05] Manuel M. T. Chakravarty, Gabriele Keller, and Simon Peyton Jones. Associated type synonyms. In *Proceedings of the Tenth ACM SIGPLAN International Conference on Functional Programming*, ICFP '05, pages 241–253. ACM, 2005.

[ecl12] Eclipse home page, 2012.

[Ent11a] Enthought. Kiva source code, 2011.

[Ent11b] Enthought. PDF reference and Adobe extensions to the PDF specification, 2011.

[For09] Message Passing Interface Forum. *MPI: A Message-Passing Interface Standard, Version 2.2*, September 2009.

[GFB+04] Edgar Gabriel, Graham E. Fagg, George Bosilca, Thara Angskun, Jack J. Dongarra, Jeffrey M. Squyres, Vishal Sahay, Prabhanjan Kambadur, Brian Barrett, Andrew Lumsdaine, Ralph H. Castain, David J. Daniel, Richard L. Graham, and Timothy S. Woodall. Open MPI: Goals, concept, and design of a next generation MPI implementation. In *Proc. 11th European PVM/MPI Users' Group Meeting*, pages 97–104, September 2004.

[GGHL+96] Al Geist, William Gropp, Steve Huss-Lederman, Andrew Lumsdaine, Ewin Lusk, William Saphir, Tony Skjellum, and Mark Snir. MPI-2: Extending the Message-Passing Interface. In *Euro-Par '96 Parallel Processing*, pages 128–135. Springer Verlag, 1996.

[GLP93] A. Gill, J. Launchbury, and S. L. Peyton Jones. A Short Cut to Deforestation. In *ACM Conference on Functional Programming and Computer Architecture (FPCA'93)*. ACM, 1993.

[HHPW07] Paul Hudak, John Hughes, Simon Peyton Jones, and Philip Wadler. A History of Haskell: being lazy with class. In *Proceedings of the Third ACM SIGPLAN Conference on the History of Programming Languages*, pages 12-1–12-55. ACM, 2007.

[Knu86] Donald E. Knuth. *Computers & Typesetting B: TeX: The Program*. Addison Wesley, 1986.

[Mar10] The Haskell 2010 Report, 2010. http://www.haskell.org/haskellwiki/Language_and_library_specification#The_Haskell_2010_report.

[McG07]   Paul McGuire. *Getting Started with Pyparsing*. O'Reilly Media, 2007.

[Mes93]   Message Passing Interface Forum. MPI: A Message Passing Interface. In *Proc. Supercomputing '93*, pages 878–883. IEEE Computer Society Press, November 1993.

[MHJP08] Simon Marlow, Tim Harris, Roshan P. James, and Simon Peyton Jones. Parallel generational-copying garbage collection with a block-structured heap. In *Proceedings of the 7th International Symposium on Memory Management*, ISMM '08, pages 11–20. ACM, 2008.

[MPT04]   Simon Marlow, Simon Peyton Jones, and Wolfgang Thaller. Extending the Haskell Foreign Function Interface with Concurrency. In *Proceedings of the ACM SIGPLAN Workshop on Haskell*, pages 57–68, September 2004.

[PM02]   Simon Peyton Jones and Simon Marlow. Secrets of the Glasgow Haskell Compiler inliner. *Journal of Functional Programming*, 12:393–434, July 2002.

[PTH01]   Simon L. Peyton Jones, Andrew Tolmach, and Tony Hoare. Playing by the rules: rewriting as a practical optimisation technique in GHC. In Ralf Hinze, editor, *2001 Haskell Workshop*. ACM SIGPLAN, September 2001.

[PVWW06] Simon Peyton Jones, Dimitrios Vytiniotis, Stephanie Weirich, and Geoffrey Washburn. Simple unification-based type inference for GADTs. In *Proceedings of the Eleventh ACM SIGPLAN International Conference on Functional Programming*, pages 50–61. ACM, 2006.

[Ray]   Why GPSes suck, and what to do about it. http://esr.ibiblio.org/?p=801.

[SCPD07] Martin Sulzmann, Manuel Chakravarty, Simon Peyton Jones, and Kevin Donnelly. System F with type equality coercions. In *ACM SIGPLAN International Workshop on Types in Language Design and Implementation (TLDI'07)*. ACM, 2007.

[She06]   Maxim Shemanarev. Anti-Grain Geometry: A high quality rendering engine for C++, 2002-2006.

[SPS+00] Richard M. Stallman, Roland Pesch, Stan Shebs, et al. *Debugging with GDB: The GNU Source-Level Debugger*. Free Software Foundation, 2000.

Colophon

The image on the cover is of New York's Equitable Building, photographed and modified by James Howe (`http://www.jameshowephotography.com`).

The cover font is Junction by Caroline Hadilaksono. The text font is TeXGyre Termes and the heading font is TeXGyre Heros, both by Bogusław Jackowski and Janusz M. Nowacki. The code font is Inconsolata by Raph Levien.

Tenet

* When someone says go do something, ask which parts you want me to focus on.

* Also be proactive, instead of reactive in estimates of work to be done